With cuts in school budgets, class trips and outings that ~~diverse learning experiences are more important than ever.~~

From nature walks to museum adventures, class trips provide unique educational opportunities. An important part of learning is exploring new environments and learning about other cultures, helping to foster tolerance and understanding. People learn in different ways—through hearing, seeing, touching, talking, or doing. Class trips provide this multi-dimensional learning environment that helps reinforce classroom curriculum.

The Directory is divided into 5 sections. The first is Transportation Services & Charter Buses. The second is Attractions, which is divided into Regional Highlights (new this year) and by States. The third is Overnights & Retreats. The fourth is Destinations, which has featured cities and regions. The fifth is a quick reference of State Learning Standards and Scout Merit Badge categories to assist you when planning trips. For your convenience we have a Table of Contents and an Alphabetical Index to help you access all the information in the Directory.

In trying to improve the usefulness of the Class Trip Directory, for the 2009-2010 edition we have included a brief description for each listing as well as information that facilitates trip planning for you. The following information is included in all the detailed listings: Registration Information, Food Selection, Recommended Length of Visit, Recommended Ratio of Student to Staff, Admission Procedure, Ticket/Voucher Return Policy.

Each school, scout council, home school association in Connecticut, Delaware, New Jersey, New York and Pennsylvania should have received their own complimentary copy of the 2009-2010 Class Trip Directory. If you are interested in obtaining your own personal copy, you can purchase it at bookstores and online for $9.95, or call us directly at 212-947-2177.

We invite you to visit our website **ClassTrips.com**, where we update information on a daily basis. This year we have included a section on Group Savings and Special Offers. We are also pleased to inform you about a new website that we launched in May 2009, **EducatorsResources.com**, which contains Fundraising Resources, Information on School Assembly and Outreach Programs, and a Teacher Mall with a directory of supplies for Teachers.

We welcome any suggestions on how to make the Directory more effective. Please let us know by emailing us at **info@familypublications.com**.

The staff at Family Publications wishes you an exciting and fulfilling school year!

Family Publications

TABLE OF CONTENTS

TRANSPORTATION SERVICES & CHARTER BUSES

TRANSPORTATION SERVICES & CHARTER BUSES

ACADEMY BUS TOURS, 111 Paterson Ave., Hoboken, New Jersey 07030. Telephone: 800-442-7272. Fax: 201-420-8087. Email: sales@academybus.com. Website: www.academybus.com. GEOGRAPHIC AREAS SERVED: NY, NJ, PA. GROUP SIZE: 55 per vehicle.

Academy Bus Tours is the largest privately owned and operated bus company in the USA providing the finest in chartered motor coach transportation for student groups. We specialize in group transportation for one day and overnight educational and recreational trips to destinations such as Washington DC, Boston MA, Philadelphia PA, Great Adventure, Hershey Park and Dorney Park. Ask about our special low, low rates for local trips during school hours in the NYC area. New this year: The Mercedes Mini-Bus, a 15 passenger vehicle with comfortable seating, video, and plenty of room for luggage. Call toll free 800-442-7272, or visit us online at www.academybus.com.

CITYSIGHTS NY, 49 West 45th St., New York, New York 10036. Telephone: 718-560-3988. Fax: 718-560-3968. Email: Bdelgado@citysightsny.com. Website: www.citysightsny.com. Contact: Blanca Espinosa. GEOGRAPHIC AREAS SERVED: NYC, Tri-State Area. GROUP SIZE: Any size group.

We operate a large fleet of modern, deluxe equipment to accommodate any size group. Our fleet consists of 10-seat vans, 21-seat minibuses, 49-seat and 56-seat coaches and new double decker buses, uniquely-designed with seating on the top deck only to provide our guests with the best possible views of Manhattan's attractions, neighborhoods and places of interest. Special amenities include climate control, radio cassette players, PA systems, VCR, lavatories, reclining seats and panoramic windows. Airport Transfers, City Sightseeing Tours, Local Transfers, One Day Charters, and Multi-Day Charters. We arrange complete group services including city sightseeing in any language, dining, theater, cultural and arts venues, attraction visits or any other activity.

EXCELLENT BUS SERVICE INC., 55 Bartlett St., Brooklyn, NY, 11206. Tel: 718-963-1495. Email: coachbus@gmail.com. Hrs: 9AM-6PM. GEOGRAPHIC AREAS SERVED: US and Canada. GROUP SIZE: 49 and 55 passenger vehicles.

We proudly present the Bus and Motor coach industry's most creative and inspired charter and tour solutions for your local and long distance trips, convention, tour, sightseeing and transfers. Excellent Bus Service owns and operates its own fleet of late model luxury coach bus rentals. Every motor coach is maintained with our client's safety, security and comfort in mind. If your School or College has an upcoming trip just contact us, and we will be glad to help you with your trip, and you will be glad that you have contacted us. When you're looking for the perfect charter bus service, look no further than Excellent Bus Service's safe and reliable fleet of charter commercial passenger vehicles.

GRAY LINE NEW YORK SIGHTSEEING, 49 W. 45th St., New York, NY 10036. Tel: 212-397-2600, ext. 4. Website: www.NewYorkSightseeing.com GEOGRAPHIC AREAS SERVED: NYC, Tri-State Area. GROUP SIZE: Any size group.

Groups and Charters. 82-seat open-top double decker bus—climate controlled lower level, accompanied by NY Licensed Tour Guide. 49-seat and 55-seat deluxe motor coach—comfortable seating with lavatory facility and audio-visual equipped. 30-seat mini-coach vehicles are climate controlled. We proudly serve New York City and other areas upon request. More than 83 years of trusted sightseeing services, Gray Line New York Sightseeing is the source for NYC's best double decker and deluxe motorcoach. We are home of New York City's first and only amphibious NYC Ducks! Easy, convenient, reliable services. The most well-known sightseeing brand in the world! (See New York City Featured City Page on page 230.)

For more additional information on class trips, please visit us at

ClassTrips.com

On Metro-North, groups of 10 or more pay the lowest possible fares.

The Metro-North Group Travel Program.

You may already know that Metro-North provides fast, frequent, and reliable service throughout New York and Connecticut. But did you know about our Group Travel Program?

Parties of 10 or more enjoy the **lowest available fares** when traveling together. It doesn't matter if you're going to New York City or to stations in New York or Connecticut. Our Group Travel Office can plan it all for you.

Whether you're planning a class trip, or a birthday party, corporate event, or other excursion, we'll help you organize train travel that's comfortable, convenient, and memorable.

For more information, call 212-499-4398. Or visit **www.mta.info**; under Metro-North Railroad, select Travel.

And start getting your group together.

MTA Metro-North Railroad *Going your way*

www.mta.info

MONSEY TOURS, 870 Dean St., Brooklyn, NY 11238. Tel: 800-232-8687 or 718-623-9000. Fax: 718-623-1850. Website: www.monseybus.com. GEOGRAPHIC AREAS SERVED: U.S. & Canada. GROUP SIZE: 49 & 55 passenger vehicles.

In 2005, Monsey Tours was the only NYC Board of Education certified coach bus vendor and we are still a contracted vendor for the Board. Our company is very familiar with all school trips and specializes in overnight college tours. School Groups are our #1 priority! We operate coach transportation for all occasions throughout the US and Canada. Our coaches are luxurious and renowned for their excellence in maintenance and cleanliness. Relax in the comfort of our plush, reclining seats and enjoy our other amenities such as A/C, cassette, PA system, VCR, DVD and lavatory. Our motorcoach drivers are friendly, courteous and professional with a comprehensive knowledge of all aspects of travel. With a proven track throughout our many years of outstanding service, safety has been #1 with us. Monsey Tours is certified by NYC Board of Education. So when you need to arrange for your next trip, call us at Monsey Tours and you'll join the multitude of satisfied school customers. Let the good times roll!

MTA METRO-NORTH RAILROAD, Group Travel Department, Graybar Building, 420 Lexington Avenue, 9th Floor, New York, NY 10017. Telephone: 212-499-4398. Email: groupsales@mnr.org.

MTA Metro-North Group Travel offers substantial savings for groups of ten or more. And since free parking is available on weekends at most Metro-North Railroad stations, you'll save even more. Relax in comfort while enjoying scenic views, historic landmarks, and the excitement of rail travel. Whether it's a class trip, family outing, or a company picnic, Metro-North's friendly Group Travel staff can suggest fun trips to New York City, upstate New York, and Connecticut, and even help you create one of your own. It all starts with a safe, easy, memorable train ride. Call Metro-North Group Travel today at 212-499-4398. (See ad on page 9.)

ROHRER TOUR & CHARTER CO. AND CAPITOL TRAILWAYS, 1061 South Cameron St., Harrisburg, Pennsylvania 17104. Telephone: 1-800-735-2400 ext. 23. Fax: 717-233-7716. Website: www.rohrertravel.com. Geographic Areas Served: The surrounding counties of Dauphin, Perry, Cumberland, York, Lancaster, Lebanon, Berks and Schuylkill in PA. GROUP SIZE: Feature up to 55 passenger, lift equipment buses with video and on-board audio capabilities.

Rohrer Tour & Charter Co. and Capitol Trailways represent the top two bus companies in the south central Pennsylvania region. In business since the 1930's, both companies specialize in youth and student transportation packages. Owned by Bieber Transportation. Both companies work for WorldStrides, Inc., the nation's largest student tour operator and have traditionally ranked high in service and driver evaluation by the school groups they served. Safety and security are uppermost in service to student groups. More information is available at Rohrertravel.com and Capitoltrailways.com.

TROLLEY TOURS, INC., 216 Route 9 / PO Box 418, Forked River, New Jersey 08731. TEL: 800-468-0446. EMAIL: trolleytours@verizon.net. WEBSITE: www.trolleytoursinc.net.

We offer a wide variety of services to youth groups including group day trip packages, multi-day group and excursions to all US and Canadian destinations. Deluxe Van Hool and MCI Motorcoach touring buses with seating for 56 and 57passengers, wheelchair accessible. Motorcoachs are equipped with Video, Stereo, Lavatory, Panoramic view and many other features. In addition to state of the art tour buses, Trolley Tours provides groups with highly trained and experienced drivers and a dedicated and friendly sales staff. With over 35 years experience in the group tour industry our quality service is unsurpassed.

ATTRACTIONS

- **Regional Highlights**

- **By State**

AMUSEMENT & THEME PARKS

ADVENTURELAND AMUSEMENT PARK. For the past 45 plus years the Adventureland Family has been creating miles of smiles for so many families across Long Island, Queens and N.Y. City. From Roller Coasters to Ferris Wheels, From the Big Kid "Adventure Falls" Log Flume Ride to the Lil' Kid "Lil Dipper" Log Flume Ride. Farmingdale, NY. 631-694-6868. www.Adventureland.us. REGION: Suffolk County, LI. (See main listing and ad on page 160.)

BLACKBEARD'S CAVE. Entertainment and physical education for school groups of all ages, sizes and budgets. Attractions include Go-Karts, Bumper Boats, jousting, arcade, batting cages, rock climbing and more. Bayville, NJ. 732-914-1896. www.blackbeardscave.com. REGION: Ocean County, Southern NJ. (See main listing on page 44.)

COCO KEY INDOOR WATER RESORT. Come experience 65,000 sq. ft. of wet and wild adventures under one roof and 84 degrees all year at our indoor water resorts. Come for the day or overnight. Locations: CT: Waterbury 203-706-1000. (See main listing on page 240.); MA: Danvers/Boston 978-777-2500 and Fitchburg 978-342-7100; NJ: Mt Laurel 856-234-7300. (See main listing on page 57.) (For all locations see ad on page 24.) www.cocokeywaterresort.com/boston.

THE FUN SPOT. Entertainment for all ages! Gold Rush Adventure Golf featuring cascading waterfalls, streams and caves. Participate in our mining experience and feed our fish. Race on our Lemans Go-Kart Track with hairpin turns, bridge and underpass. Queensbury, NY. 518-792-8989. www.thefunspot.net. REGION: Warren County, Adirondacks Region NY. (See main listing on page 142.)

HERSHEYPARK. Hersheypark, located in Central Pennsylvania, is home to more than 65 rides and attractions including 11 roller coasters, The Boardwalk at Hersheypark, award-winning live entertainment, and our newest water feature - The SEAquel. Ask about our Educational Days and free Educational guides. Hershey, PA. 800-242-4236. www.hersheypark.com/groups. REGION: Dauphin County, Central PA. (See main listing on page 173.)

LAKE COMPOUNCE THEME PARK. Offers your students an opportunity to enhance their skills in a fun environment. We have more than 50 thrilling rides and attractions along with self-guided programs in math, science, physics, and geology. Bristol, CT. 860-583-3300. www.lakecompounce.com. REGION: Hartford County, North Central CT. (See main listing on page 18.)

MOUNTAIN CREEK WATERPARK is home to 2 dozen water attractions including the new "Alpine Pipeline," "High Anxiety," "Colorado River" and our mammoth "High Tide Wave pool." Located in beautiful Sussex County, NJ. Only 47 miles outside of Manhattan. Vernon, NJ. 973-864-8400. mountaincreekwaterpark.com. REGION: Sussex County, Northern NJ.

QUASSY AMUSEMENT PARK. Traditional family amusement park with more than two-dozen rides and attractions including the "Saturation Station" interactive water play: home of the gigantic "Tunnel Twister" waterslides! Group rates to fit any budget with economical food plans available. MIddlebury, CT. 800-FOR-PARK (800-367-7275). www.quassy.com. REGION: New Haven County, South Central CT.

PLAYLAND PARK has over 50 major and Kiddyland rides and attractions for children of all ages to enjoy! From the famous and historic Dragon Coaster, and other original treasures, to the latest in high-speed, thrill and water rides, Playland has it all! Rye, NY. 914-813-7016. www.ryeplayland.org. REGION: Westchester County, Hudson Valley Region NY. (See main listing on page 134.)

SESAME PLACE. Share in the spirit of imagination with your students and experience whirling rides, colorful shows and furry friends at the nation's only theme park based entirely on the award-winning television show, Sesame Street. Education programs are also available. Langhorn, PA. 866-GO-4-ELMO. www.sesameplace.com. REGION: Bucks County, South East PA. (See main listing and ad on page 174.)

SUPERSONIC SPEEDWAY FUN PARK. Play mini golf, arcade games, ride the go-carts, use the batting cages, enjoy numerous rides, have a picnic, use the shooting gallery, and much more! And come and visit the restaurant & ice cream shop for a meal and a snack. Your group will have a blast! 518-634-7200. (See main listing on page 134.)

VICTORIAN GARDENS AMUSEMENT PARK. Located in the heart of New York City at Wollman Rink in Central Park. Victorian Gardens returns to town from Late May-Mid Sept. 2010, featuring: handcrafted rides for children ages 2-12, interactive games and activities, face painting, balloon sculptors and live entertainment. Manhattan. 212-982-2229. www.victoriangardensnyc.com. REGION: New York County, NYC. (See main listing and ad on page 73.)

FAUNA

ADVENTURE AQUARIUM. Features over 60 exhibits filled with exotic and amazing creatures including hippos, sharks, penguins and African birds in a free-flight aviary. Also, experience and touch sharks, jellyfish, lobsters, stingrays and more. Camden, NJ. 800-616-JAWS. www.adventureaquarium.com. REGION: Camden County, Southern NJ. (See main listing and ad on page 45)

ATLANTIS MARINE WORLD AQUARIUM. Features more than 100 exhibits and interactive experiences, including the Lost City of Atlantis Shark Exhibit, Coral Reef display, Penguin Pavilion, Shark Reef Lagoon, Sea Lion Shows and Interactive Salt Marsh. Riverhead. NY. 631-208-9200, ext. 105. www.atlantismarineworld.com. REGION: Suffolk County, LI. (See main listing and ad on page 161.)

CONNECTICUT'S BEARDSLEY ZOO. 52 acres dedicated to animals of North and South America including wolves, bison, otters, alligators and over 120 other species. The zoo also has a rustic New England Farmyard, home to goats, pigs, cows, sheep, and more. Bridgeport, CT. 203-394-6565. www.beardsleyzoo.org. REGION: Fairfield County, South West CT. (See main listing and ad on page 18.)

LAKE TOBIAS WILDLIFE PARK. Over 100 acres of rolling hills are scattered with herds of buffalo, deer, yak, watusi and more. Also features interesting animals like monkeys, tigers and ostriches along with a Petting Zoo and Reptile Building. Halifax, PA. 717-362-9126. www.laketobias.com. REGION: Dauphin County, Central PA. (See main listing on page 175.)

THE MARITIME AQUARIUM AT NORWALK. Offers fun and educational experiences for students. Come close to sharks, seals, river otters, frogs and sea turtles and even closer at two interactive touch tanks. Interactive exhibits, classroom and field programs and hands-on study cruises are also available. Norwalk, CT. 203-852-0700. www.maritimeaquarium.org. REGION: Fairfield County, South West CT. (See main listing and ad on page 19.)

WILDLIFE CONSERVATION SOCIETY. Manages the world's largest system of urban wildlife parks including the Bronx Zoo, Central Park Zoo, New York Aquarium, Prospect Park Zoo and Queens Zoo. Exhibits are themed natural habitats for the animals. 718-220-5100. www.wcs.org. REGION: Bronx County, NYC.

FLORA

AGROFORESTRY RESOURCE CENTER, Cornell Cooperative Extension of Greene County Tree Farm. Educational center and model forest offering programs in wildlife, forest stewardship, gardening and agriculture. 518-622-9820. www.agroforestrycenter.org. REGION: Greene County, Catskills Region NY.

BROOKLYN BOTANIC GARDEN offers a variety of opportunities to develop students' appreciation of nature. Programs include: a guided tour to learn more about the Garden; the Garden Exploration Tour, which includes a planting activity; or school workshops, covering a wide range of topics designed to support national and local science standards. 718-623-7200. www.bbg.org. REGION: Kings County, NYC. (See main listing on page 83.)

CAMDEN CHILDREN'S GARDEN. Enjoy the various themed gardens, learn about butterflies, ride some of our amusements & enjoy a day at the Garden. On-site Garden Lessons are available, offered on the grounds and designed for students K–8th grades. 856-365-8733. www.CamdenChildrensGarden.org. REGION: Camden County, Southern NJ. (See main listing on page 49.)

LONGWOOD GARDENS is a place of unparalleled beauty, offering a new experience every day of the year with one-of-a kind events, wonderful concerts, and delicious fine and casual cuisine. Our exciting School & Youth Programs nurture student curiosity while focusing on learning. 610-388-1000. www.longwoodgardens.org. REGION: Chester County, South East PA. (See main listing and ad on page 180.)

THE NEW YORK BOTANICAL GARDEN. With 250 acres of plants from around the world, your students can discover the wonders of nature up close. Students participate in hands-on activities from sowing seeds and harvesting crops, examining wetlands, dissecting plant parts to investigating plants as food. 718-817-8181. www.nybg.org/edu. REGION: Bronx County, NYC. (See main listing on page 83.)

OLD WESTBURY GARDENS. Enjoy nature walks on trails throughout 200 acres. Explore scenic woodlands, gardens, an enchanting Thatched Cottage, ponds, lakes, and wide open spaces. Special events, April through December. Picnic or enjoy refreshments in the Gardens' outdoor café. 516-333-0048. www.oldwestburygardens.org. REGION: Nassau County, LI. (See main listing on page 163.)

INTERACTIVE LIVING HISTORY

FORT DELAWARE MUSEUM OF COLONIAL HISTORY. Living history depiction of the colonial settlers of the Upper Delaware River Valley during the French & Indian War through the start of the American Revolution. A tour of the facilities includes demonstrations of early settlers' lifestyles and craft-making such as a blacksmith, spinners, weavers, candle makers and barn loomers. Narrowsburg, NY. 845-252-6660. www.co.sullivan.ny.us. REGION: Sullivan County, Catskills Region NY.

HISTORIC PHILADELPHIA, INC.. Offers tours & performances that make history exciting and fun, including the Lights of Liberty sound & light show, Colonial Kids Quest, The Condensed American Revolution - a comedic journey through our nation's birth and more. Philadelphia, PA. 215-629-5801, ext. 209. www.historicphiladelphia.org. REGION: Philadelphia County, South East PA. (See main listing on page 189.)

HISTORIC RICHMOND TOWN is a living history village and museum complex on 25 acres of a 100-acre site with 15 restored buildings. Staten Island, NY. 718-351-1611, ext. 280. REGION: Richmond County, NYC.

LIVING THE EXPERIENCE. Reenactment of the Underground Railroad. Our guests go back into the 1800's, hearing inspiring stories and participating as an enslaved African being brought over on a slave ship, then to auction, then to bondage, then to their freedom. ChurchTowne of Lancaster, PA. 800-510-5899 ext. 113. www.bethelamelancaster.org. REGION: Lancaster County, South East PA. (See main listing on page 189.)

MASHANTUCKET PEQUOT MUSEUM & RESEARCH CENTER. Offers interactive experiences such as descending a glacial crevasse and walking through a 16th century Native American village. These eye-opening, life-size exhibits are complimented by an array of experiential education programs. Mashantucket, CT. 860-396-6839. www.pequotmuseum.org. REGION: New London County, South East CT. (See main listing on page 25 and ad on page 34.)

MEDIEVAL TIMES DINNER & TOURNAMENT. Step back in time and experience spectacular horsemanship, amazing swordplay, medieval games of skill and an authentic jousting tournament. As the tournament takes place your students are served a feast fit for a king. Lyndhurst. 201-933-2220 ext. 213. www.medievaltimes.com. REGION: Bergen County, Northern NJ. (See main listing and ad on page 60.)

MUSEUM VILLAGE. See, touch, hear, and understand life in 19th century America on a 17 acre site, which includes a Weave Shop, Dress Emporium, Blacksmith, Broom Maker, Pharmacy, General Store, Barber Shop, School House, and more. Monroe, NY. 845-782-8248. REGION: Orange County, Hudson Valley Region NY.

MYSTIC SEAPORT – THE MUSEUM OF AMERICA AND THE SEA. The village and ship's area is an active living history museum with 17 acres of exhibits portraying coastal life in New England in the 19th century. Mystic, CT. 860-572-5315. REGION: New London County, South East CT. (See main listing and ad on page 35.)

NYC DUCKS offers a multi-media experience, simulating Henry Hudson's journey. Entertaining and informative tour guides point out some of New York City's world-famous sites as the NYC Ducks travel from Times Square to the Hudson River. New York, NY. 888-838-2570. www.NYCDucks.com. REGION: New York County, NYC. (See main listing and ad on page 98.)

OLD BARRACKS MUSEUM. Experience another dimension to history as you and your students interact with living history interpreters in our exciting "Meet the Past" programs. Enter the world of 1777 and share the trials, tribulations and joys of ordinary people living in extraordinary times. 609-396-1776. www.barracks.org. REGION: Mercer County, Central NJ. (See main listing on page 69.)

OLD BETHPAGE VILLAGE RESTORATION. Experience life in a recreated mid-19th-century American village. The 209-acre village includes an assortment of homes, farms and businesses. Old Bethpage, NY. 516-572-8408. REGION: Nassau County, LI.

QUIET VALLEY LIVING HISTORICAL FARM. Experience different aspects of 19th century farm life through activities and tours. Stroudsburg, PA. 570-992-6161. REGION: Monroe County, North East PA.

SOUTH STREET SEAPORT. A slice of old New York with its historic pier, ships and cobblestone streets provide a picturesque legacy of the past. The Maritime Museum, tours of historic ships, and walking tours makes learning fun. The food court offers student groups an array to select from with its special Food Court Dining vouchers. 212-732-9287. www.southstreetseaport.com. REGION: New York County, NYC. (See main listing and ad on page 116.)

WATER FUN

BUCKS COUNTY RIVER COUNTRY. Family oriented river adventures on the Historic Delaware River. Since 1969 we've been offering 2 hour to full day Tubing, Rafting, Canoeing, Kayaking trips. Point Pleasant, Pennsylvania. 215-297-5000. www.rivercountry.net. REGION: Bucks County, South East PA. (See main listing on page 172.)

HUDSON RIVER RAFTING COMPANY. Hudson River Rafting Company (since 1979) offers world class rafting on the Hudson River Gorge (17 miles), one of America's 10 best rafting trips. Raft the Sacandaga River's large dam release; rafting/tubing; excellent for youth groups, 6 trips per day. North Creek, NY. 800-888-7238. www.hudsonriverrafting.com. REGION: Warren County, Adirondacks Region NY. (See main listing and ad on page 131.)

JERRY'S 3 RIVER CAMPGROUND. Your students will have a fun-filled adventure while learning to work as a team. Enjoy white water rafting, canoeing, and camping on the Delaware River, one of the most scenic and historic areas in the East. Pond Eddy, NY. 845-557-6078. www.jerrys3rivercampground.com. REGION: Washington County, Capital Region NY. (See main listing on page 132.)

JUNIATA RIVER ADVENTURES. 2 hour to overnight river trips available on a scenic, leisurely flowing river. Trips offer students a variety of outdoor river activities including wildlife, fishing and swimming. Beach volley court and picnic tables on site. 717-320-1102. www.juniatariveradventures.com. REGION: Juniata County, Central PA. (See main listing on page 172.)

KITTATINNY CANOE. Award winning, family owned and operated, offering 69 years of outdoor fun and excitement for all ages and abilities. Kittatinny operates on the Scenic Delaware River, running through two National Parks. Enjoy an abundance of wildlife from a new perspective. 800-FLOAT-KC (356-2852). www.kittatinny.com. REGIONS: NY, PA, NJ. (See main listing on page 132.)

MOXIE OUTDOOR ADVENTURES offers daily white-water rafting trips. Combine your rafting trip with another of our youth adventures for an exciting two day adventure. We offer discounted rates and packages that make it affordable and most of all fun! Your group will experience the adventure of a lifetime. 2 locations: Charlemont, MA and The Forks, ME. 800-866-6943. www.moxierafting.com. REGIONS: Franklin County, Western MA & Somerset County, Central ME.

NORTH COUNTRY RIVERS offers daily whitewater rafting trips in Maine (Apr-Oct). Camping, cabin and meals packages available. No experience needed, all equipment & guides provided. 25 Years Experience as Maine's Premier Rafting Outfitter. Bingham, Maine. 800-348-8871. www.northcountryrivers.com. REGION: Somerset County, Central ME.

PEMI-BAKER RIVER ADVENTURES. Since 1995 Pemi-Baker River Adventures has been providing canoe, kayak, raft and tube trips for individuals, families and groups. River tubing is very popular with camps and family groups. We can accommodate up to 64 people at a time for tubing. Plymouth, NH. 603-536-5652. www.pbriveradventures.com. REGION: Grafton County, NH. (See main listing on page 43.)

POCONO WHITEWATER ADVENTURES. This year take your classroom outdoors! Join us for an exciting rafting, biking, or paintball adventure. We're Fun, Healthy, Close, & Affordable! PoconoWhitewater.com. Open Daily! 1-800-WHITEWATER (944-8392). REGION: Carbon County, North East PA. (See main listing on page 173.)

SACANDAGA OUTDOOR CENTER. The Adirondacks premier adventure & fun location. Just minutes from Lake George and Saratoga with spectacular location at the confluence of two rivers. Offering Whitewater Rafting, Tubing, Kayaking, Canoeing, Hiking, Fishing and Mt Biking. 518-696-RAFT. www.4soc.com. REGIONS: Saratoga County, Capital Region NY & Warren County, Adirondacks Region NY. (See main listing on page 132-133.)

TUBBY TUBES COMPANY - OUTDOOR FUN PARK. Enjoy Lazy River Tubing, Rafting and kayaking on the Lower Hudson River Gorge. Cool off, swim, relax and explore nature in the wonderful Adirondacks. All ages welcome. 518-696-5454. Warren County, Adirondacks Region NY. (See main listing on page 133.)

ZOAR OUTDOOR offers whitewater rafting, canoeing, kayaking, zip line canopy tours, fly fishing, biking and rock climbing in western Massachusetts. Onsite lodging and camping for multi-day stays. Charlemont, MA. 800-532-7483. www.zoaroutdoor.com. REGION: Franklin County, Western MA. (See main listing on page 206.)

CONNECTICUT

AMUSEMENT & THEME PARKS

LAKE COMPOUNCE THEME PARK, 822 Lake Ave., Bristol, CT 06010. Tel: 860-583-3300. Fax: 860-585-9987. Email: Info@lakecompounce.com. Website: www.lakecompounce.com. Hrs: Mid-May - Oct. 31; See website for hours of operation. Contact: Group Sales. GRADE LEVEL: All grades. GROUP TYPE: All youth groups & homeschoolers. PROGRAM TYPE: Day Trips, Self-guided Activities. REGISTRATION: Mail, Online. TICKET/VOUCHER RETURN POLICY: Tickets can be returned by the contact person on the day of their event. FOOD: Variety of menu selections, Place to eat on site, Beverages available, Meal vouchers. ARRIVAL TIPS: Bus parking. COST: Varies. One chaperone is free with every 10 paid students.

New England's Family Theme Park offers your students an opportunity to enhance their skills in a fun environment. Twelve dates in May and June are available for our Outdoor Educational Programs with special pricing and hours. Programs meet the needs of students in grades K-12. Self-guided programs in math, science, physics, and geology. We have more than 50 thrilling rides and attractions, including Thunder N' Lightning - a screaming swing ride, and Zoomers Gas N' Go – a family ride that takes you on a journey through the 1950's in a 1956 corvette replica. To reserve your date or to receive an information package call or visit the website. SUPPORTS CT STATE & NATIONAL LEARNING STANDARDS IN: Science. SUPPORTS SCOUT MERIT BADGE ACHIEVEMENT IN: Science. (See Regional Highlights on page 10.) REGION: Hartford County, North Central CT.

ANIMALS • AQUARIUMS • ZOOS

ACTION WILDLIFE FOUNDATION, 337 Torrington Rd., Goshen, CT 06756. Tel: 860-482-4465. Hrs: Daily 10AM-5PM (petting zoo, safari are seasonal). K-8th grade. Self-guided tours, Guided tours. Wildlife sanctuary located on more than 100 acres, featuring over 350 exotic animals. COST: Fee. REGION: Lichfield County, North West CT.

CONNECTICUT'S BEARDSLEY ZOO, 1875 Noble Ave., Bridgeport, CT 06610-1646. Tel: 203-394-6565. Website: www.beardsleyzoo.org. Hrs: Daily 9AM-4PM. GRADE LEVEL: All grades. GROUP TYPE: All youth groups & homeschoolers. PROGRAM TYPE: Day Trips, Self-guided Tours, Guided Tours, Workshops, Performances. COST: Varies.

52 acres dedicated to wild and wonderful animals of North and South America with a few surprises. A stroll through the Zoo will introduce visitors to wolves, bison, otters, alligators, and over 120 other species. For those who like their animals a little less wild, Connecticut's Beardsley Zoo has a rustic New England Farmyard, home to goats, pigs, cows, sheep, and many other barnyard favorites. The Zoo's historic Carousel, Picnic Grove, Greenhouse, Gift and Snack shops make a trip to the Zoo fun for everyone. SUPPORTS CT STATE & NATIONAL LEARNING STANDARDS IN: Science. SUPPORTS SCOUT MERIT BADGE ACHIEVEMENT IN: Animal Science. (See Regional Highlights on page 12.) REGION: Fairfield County, South West CT.

THE MARITIME AQUARIUM AT NORWALK, 10 N. Water St., Norwalk, Connecticut 06854. Tel: 203-852-0700. Fax: 203-838-5416. Hrs: Daily 10AM-5PM (until 6 PM July & August). Contact: 203-852-0700 ext. 2206 (for reserv.). GRADE LEVEL: All grades. GROUP TYPE: All youth groups & homeschoolers. PROGRAM TYPE: Day trips, Self-guided tours, Guided Tours, Workshops, Outreach Programs. Multiple programs can be booked for large groups. MAX. GROUP SIZE: 1,200. Most programs for groups of 28. Email: reservations@maritimeaquarium.org. Website: www.maritimeaquarium.org. REGISTRA-TION: Mail, Phone. Tickets mailed prior to visit. TICKET/VOUCHER RETURN POLICY: Varies. FOOD: Variety of menu selections, Vegetarian, Can bring own food, Place to eat on site, Beverages available. RECOMM. LENGTH OF VISIT: 1 hour min. IMAX movies run 40 minutes. RECOMM. RATIO OF STUDENT TO STAFF: 7:1 required. ARRIVAL TIPS: Expedite check in, Bus parking, Bus drop off and pick up at designated entrance. COST: Varies.

The Maritime Aquarium engages students with fun and educational adventures into the underwater world of Long Island Sound and beyond. Come close to sharks, seals, river otters, frogs and sea turtles and even closer at two interactive touch tanks. Interactive exhibits, classroom and field programs and hands-on study cruises. New for 2009-10: Penguins! African penguins with views above and below water. "African Underwater Safari" exhibit with fish, snakes, geckos and more. IMAX movies include "Deep Sea." See web site for latest movie listings. You can also download Educational Resources Guides. SUPPORTS CT STATE, NY STATE & NATIONAL STANDARDS IN: Science, Social Studies. SUPPORTS SCOUT MERIT BADGE ACHIEVEMENT IN: Animal Science. (See Regional Highlights on page 12.) REGION: Fairfield County, South West CT.

MYSTIC AQUARIUM & INSTITUTE FOR EXPLORATION, 55 Coogan Blvd., Mystic, CT 06355. Tel: 860-572-5955, ext. 520. Hrs: Daily 9AM-5PM. Summer 9AM-6PM (last entry at 5) Self-guided Tours, Guided Tours. There are 70 exhibits with over 12,000 fishes, invertebrates, and marine mammals, representing 425 species from around the world. COST: Fee. REGION: New London County, South East CT.

QUINEBAUG VALLEY TROUT HATCHERY, 141 Trout Hatchery Rd., Central Village, CT 06332. Tel: 860-564-7542. Hrs: Daily 8AM-3:30PM. Guided Tours. One of the largest hatcheries in the east, producing brook, brown and rainbow trout annually. COST: Free. REGION: Windham County, North East CT.

UNITED TECHNOLOGIES WILDLIFE SANCTUARY, 950 Trout Brook Dr., West Hartford, CT 06119. Tel: 860-231-2830 ext. 50. Hrs: Varies. Self-guided Tours, Guided Tours. Indoor/outdoor facility housing over 100 animals from 71 species. COST: Fee. REGION: Hartford County, North Central CT.

ART • ARCHITECTURE • SCULPTURE

ALDRICH CONTEMPORARY ART MUSEUM, 258 Main St., Ridgefield, CT 06877. Tel: 203-438-4519. Hrs: Tues.-Sun. 12-5PM. Self-guided Tours, Guided Tours. Features work by emerging and mid-career artists. COST: Fee; Free on Tues. REGION: Fairfield County, South West CT.

FLORENCE GRISWOLD MUSEUM, 96 Lyme St., Old Lyme, CT 06371. Tel: 860-434-5542. Hrs: Tues.-Sat. 10AM-5PM, Sun. 1-5PM. Self-guided Tours, Workshops. Home of American Impressionism. COST: Fee. REGION: New London County, South East CT.

NEW BRITAIN MUSEUM OF AMERICAN ART, 56 Lexington St., New Britain, CT 06052. Tel: 860-229-0257. Hrs: Tues., Wed., Fri. 11AM-5PM, Thurs. 11AM-8PM, Sat. 10AM-5PM, Sun. 12-5PM. Self-guided Tours, Guided Tours. 5,000 works of American art from drawings to sculptures. COST: Fee. REGION: Hartford County, South East CT.

WADSWORTH ATHENEUM MUSEUM OF ART, 600 Main St., Hartford, CT 06103. Tel: 860-278-2670. Hrs: Wed.-Fri. 11AM-5PM, First Thursdays 11AM-8PM, Sat. & Sun. 10AM-5PM. Self-guided Tours, Guided Tours. Features a vast collection of European & American art. COST: Fee. REGION: Hartford County, North Central CT.

BOTANICAL GARDENS & NATURE CENTERS

THE BARTLETT ARBORETUM & GARDENS, 151 Brookdale Rd., Stamford, CT. Tel: 203-322-6971. Hrs: Daily dawn-dusk. Visitors center: Mon.-Fri. 8:30AM-4:30PM. Self-guided Tours, Guided Tours, Workshops. Living museum of majestic trees, rare plant collections, gardens, varied natural habitats and landscapes. COST: Fee; Free on Wednesdays and for children under 12. REGION: Fairfield County, South West CT.

THE CONNECTICUT COLLEGE ARBORETUM, 270 Mohegan Ave., New London, CT 06320. Tel: 860-439-5020. Hrs: Daily dawn-dusk. Self-guided Tours, Guided Tours, Workshops. 750 acres of forests, meadows and wetlands. COST: Free. REGION: New London County, South East CT.

NEW CANAAN NATURE CENTER, 144 Oenoke Ridge, New Canaan, CT 06840. Tel: 203-966-9577. Hrs: Mon.-Sat. 9AM-4PM. Self-guided Tours, Guided Tours. Environmental education center offering a variety of horticultural experiences. COST: Fee. REGION: Fairfield County, South West CT.

ROARING BROOK NATURE CENTER, 70 Gracey Rd., Canton, CT 06019. Tel: 860-693-0263. Hrs: Tues.-Sat. 10AM-5PM, Sun. 1-5PM, Mon. 10AM-5PM (summer only). Self-guided Tours, Guided Tours. Features 5 miles of hiking trails on about 100 acres of a state owned wildlife preserve. COST: Fee. REGION: Hartford County, North Central CT.

CHILDREN'S MUSEUMS

THE CHILDREN'S MUSEUM, 950 Trout Brook Dr., West Hartford, CT 06119. Tel: 860-231-2824. Hrs: Tues.-Sat. 10AM-5PM, Sun 12-5PM. Pre K-7th grade. Self-guided Tours, Workshops. Provides learning experiences in science and nature. COST: Fee. REGION: Hartford County, North Central CT.

STEPPING STONES MUSEUM FOR CHILDREN, Mathews Park, 303 W. Ave., Norwalk, CT 06851. Tel: 203-899-0606. Fax: 203-899-0530. Email: info@steppingstonesmuseum.org. Website: www.steppingstonesmuseum.org. Hrs: School year: Tues. 1-5PM, Wed.-Sun. 10AM-5PM; Summer Jul. 1 - Labor Day: Daily 10AM-5PM. GRADE LEVEL: Pre K-6th. GROUP TYPE: All youth groups & homeschoolers. PROGRAM TYPE: Day Trips, Overnight Trips, Self-guided Tours, Guided Tours, Performances, Workshops. COST: $9 general admission, program prices vary.

Stepping Stones Museum for Children, an award-winning children's museum, provides hands-on exhibits and programs designed to promote children's understanding of their world through interactive experiences. Children can climb a kapok tree in a tropical rainforest, learn how to protect endangered species, report "live" from inside the human body and role-play as doctors and dentists in the Healthyville Community Center. Choose from: Discovery Tour: 90-minute guided tours available Monday 9:20AM–3PM, Tuesday 9:20AM–11AM. $145 per class, Preschool up to 20 students, 4 adults. $155 per class, Grades K–4 up to 25 students, 5 adults. Self-Guided Group Visit: Bring a group of children to the museum to enjoy our unique exhibits on your own. Two-hour visits available Thursday and Friday 10AM–3PM. $105 per class, up to 20 students, 4 adults/$5 per additional person. SUPPORTS CT STATE & NATIONAL LEARNING STANDARDS IN: Health, the Arts, Science and Mathematics. SUPPORTS SCOUT MERIT BADGE ACHIEVEMENT IN: Animal Science, Environmental Science, Health and Safety. REGION: Fairfield County, South West CT.

TIMEXPO® THE TIMEX MUSEUM, 175 Union St., Brass Mill Commons, Waterbury, CT 06706. Tel: 800-225-7742. Email: cconti@timexpo.com. Website: www.timexpo.com. Hrs: Tues.-Sat. 10AM-5PM. Contact: Cathy Conti. GRADE LEVEL: All grades. GROUP TYPE: All youth groups & homeschoolers. PROGRAM TYPE: Day Trips, Self-guided Tours, Guided Tours, Workshops. COST: Varies.

The Timexpo® The Timex Museum is an educational tool with many opportunities for your students to learn in a fun hands-on environment. Our many programs encourage students' participation and small group activities. We begin our tours by telling the history of Waterbury's Clock Industry and how we have progressed from the "Shadow Stick" to the latest Timex technology. Continue your journey through a time tunnel exploring the voyages of Thor Heyerdahl and the possibilities of "Coincidence or Connections" between ancient civilizations. Located in the easy-to-access Brass Mill Commons in one of Waterbury's old brass mill buildings, enjoy three floors of exhibits that allow students to wind their way through the history of time, past, present and future. SUPPORTS CT STATE & NATIONAL LEARNING STANDARDS IN: History/Social Studies. SUPPORTS SCOUT MERIT BADGE ACHIEVEMENT IN: Social Studies. REGION: New Haven County, South Central CT.

CIDERING

NEW CANAAN NATURE CENTER, 144 Oenoke Ridge, New Canaan, CT 06840. Tel: 203-966-9577. Cidering Hrs: Last week of Sept.-first week November. Observe the apple cidering process with an old-fashioned press. Help with picking apples, using the hand press and have a taste of pasteurized cider. COST: Fee. REGION: Fairfield County, South West CT.

STAMFORD MUSEUM AND NATURE CENTER, 39 Scofieldtown Rd., Stamford, CT 06903. Tel: 203-322-1646. Cidering Hrs: Last week Sept.-first week November 9:30, 10:30, 11:30. Take part in the process of apple cidering. Help pick apples and grind them into cider. Learn the life cycle of the apple tree and the difference between apple cider and apple juice. COST: Varies. REGION: Fairfield County, South West CT.

FARMS & PICK-YOUR-OWN

BISHOP'S ORCHARDS, 1355 Boston Post Road, Guilford, CT 06437-2399. Tel: 203-453-2338. Fax: 203-458-7125. Email: farminfo@bishopsorchards.com. Website: www.bishopsorchards.com. Hrs: Pick Your Own, Open most days, determined by crop availability and weather. Check Daily by calling 203-458-PICK (7425). GRADE LEVEL: All grades. GROUP TYPE: All youth groups & homeschoolers. PROGRAM TYPE: Day Trips, Guided Activities. COST: Apple Harvest Tour $3 per person or $90 minimum. Apple Wagonride Tour - $100 per wagon, 30-35 people per wagon. Pick Your Own Groups: Call for details and prices. Additional Packages available.

The Bishop family represents the fine tradition of growing the finest quality native fruits and vegetables since 1871. Our pick-your-own season starts in June with strawberries and goes through October with apples and pumpkins. Our "big red apple" is a landmark known to many from near and far. Learn about agriculture and food, such as apple cidering. Also visit our llamas and goats. We look forward to having your group enjoy the fun at Bishop's Orchards! Bishop's SUPPORTS CT STATE & NATIONAL LEARNING STANDARDS IN: Science. SUPPORTS SCOUT MERIT BADGE ACHIEVEMENT IN: Science. REGION: New Haven County, South Central CT.

EASY PICKIN'S ORCHARD, 46 Bailey Rd., Enfield, CT 06082. Tel: 860-763-3276. Hrs: Mon.-Thurs. 9AM-12PM, Fri.-Sun. 9AM-5PM. PYO: Apples, Peaches, Plums, Pears, Berries, Vegetables and Herbs. COST: Fee. REGION: Hartford County, North Central CT.

FAIRVUE FARMS, 199 Rte. 171, Woodstock, CT 06281. Tel: 860-928-9483. Hrs: Tours by appointment. Offers guided tours where groups can watch the milking process. Students learn about modern agriculture, including the milking process, where cows are housed, feeding, milk storage and nutrition. Your tour guide is a farm employee who will be happy to answer your questions. COST: Fee. REGION: Windham County, North East CT.

FISH FAMILY FARM CREAMERY & DAIRY FARM, 20 Dimock Lane, Bolton, CT 06043. Tel: 860-646-9745. Hrs: Mon.-Sat. 8AM-6PM. Self-Guided Activities. One of the state's few remaining dairy farms that milk cows and pasteurize and bottle their own milk. COST: Free. REGION: Tolland County, North East CT.

FREUND'S FARM MARKET, 324 Norfolk Rd., E. Canaan, CT 06024. Tel: 860-824-0650. Hrs: Daily, 9AM-6PM. PYO: Pumpkins and Popcorn. See first hand how cows live, what they eat, how they are cared for and how they produce milk. COST: Fee. REGION: Litchfield County, North West CT.

GOTTAS FARM, 661 Glastonbury Turnpike, Portland, CT 06480. Tel: 860-342-1844. Hrs: Mon.-Fri. 8AM-7PM, Sat.-Sun. 8AM-6:30PM. PYO: Apples, strawberries and peaches. COST: Fee. REGION: Middlesex County, South Central CT.

LYMAN ORCHARDS, Junction of Rtes. 147 & 157, Middlefield, Connecticut 06455. Tel: 860-349-1793. Hrs: Open 7 days a week. Sept./Oct. 9AM-7PM. Remainder of year 9AM-6PM. PYO: Apples, Peaches, Nectarines, Pears, Berries and Pumpkins. There is also a corn maze. COST: Fee. REGION: Middlesex County, South Central CT.

MAPLE LANE FARM, 57 N.W. Corner Rd., Preston, CT 06365. Tel: 860-889-3766. Hrs: Vary. PYO: Apples, Pumpkins and Berries. COST: Fee. REGION: New London County, South East CT.

WRIGHT'S ORCHARD AND DRIED FLOWER FARM, 271 S. River Rd., Tolland, CT 06084. Tel: 860-872-1665. Hrs: Nov.-Dec.: Daily 1-5PM, Closed Wed. PYO: Apples, Peaches and Pumpkins. Large selection of dried flowers and fresh fruits and vegetables. COST: Fee. REGION: Tolland County, North East CT.

HEALTH & NUTRITION

FIELD TRIP FACTORY, Telelphone: 800-987-6409. Fax: 773-342-9513. Email: info@fieldtripfactory.com. Hrs: Mon.-Fri. 8AM-6PM. GRADE LEVEL: Pre K-6th. GROUP TYPE: All youth groups & homeschoolers. PROGRAM TYPE: Day Trips, Guided Tours. COST: Free.

Field Trip Factory offers free community-based field trips. Our learning adventures teach valuable life-skills including health and nutrition, science, responsibility and more. All field trips are grade and age appropriate, meet learning standards, enrich classroom curriculum for teachers and fulfill badge requirements for scouts. See what is available in your area at www.fieldtripfactory.com or call 1-800-987-6409. SUPPORTS STATE LEARNING STANDARDS IN: Health & Safety, Math, Physical Education, Science. SUPPORTS SCOUT BADGE ACTIVITIES IN: Health & Safety, Life Skills, Personal Fitness. (See ad on page 56.) REGION: Throughout all 50 states.

HISTORIC RAILROAD EXCURSIONS

ESSEX STEAM TRAIN & RIVERBOAT, The Valley Railroad Company, 1 Railroad Ave., P.O. Box 452, Essex, CT 06426. Tel: 860-767-0103, 800-377-3987. Hrs: Vary. Guided Tours. Operating live steam trains in the Connecticut River Valley since 1971. COST: Fee. REGION: Middlesex County, South Central CT.

RAILROAD MUSEUM OF NEW ENGLAND/NAUGATUCK RAILROAD COMPANY, 242 E. Main St., Thomaston, CT 06787. Tel: 860-283-RAIL. Hrs: May-Dec.: Sat.-Sun. 12 & 2PM, Tues. 10AM-6PM. Self-guided Tours, Guided Tours. Learn about the region's rich railroad heritage and take a scenic train ride. COST: Free/Fee. REGION: Litchfield County, North West CT.

**For additional information on trips and
group savings and special offers for youth groups please visit**

ClassTrips.com

INDOOR AMUSEMENT CENTERS

COCO KEY WATER RESORT AT HOLIDAY INN, 3580 East Main Street, Waterbury, CT 06705. Tel: 203-706-1000. Email: ruby.meng@hiwaterbury.com. Website: cocokeywaterresort.com. Hrs: 11AM-8PM. Contact: Ruby Meng. GRADE LEVEL: PreK-12th. GROUP TYPE: All youth groups & homeschoolers. PROGRAM TYPE: Day Trips, Overnight Trips. REGISTRATION: Mail, Online, Phone, Prepay. TICKET/VOUCHER RETURN POLICY: Subject to contract terms. FOOD: Variety, Kosher, Vegetarian, Place to eat on site, Beverages available, Meal vouchers. RECOMMENDED LENGTH OF VISIT: 2-3 hours. RECOMMENDED RATIO OF CAMPER TO STAFF: 10:1. ADMISSION: Expedite check in, Bus parking, Bus drop off and pick up at designated entrance. COST: Call for Seasonal Rates & Discounts.

CoCo Key Water Resort is Connecticut' newest indoor water resort! Open all year, come experience 65,000 sq. ft. of wet and wild adventures inspired by the Florida Keys.   SUPPORTS CT STATE & NATIONAL LEARNING STANDARDS IN: Physical Education. SUPPORTS SCOUT MERIT BADGE ACHIEVEMENT IN: Physical Ed/Recreation. (See other listing in NJ on page 57 and under Regional Highlights on page 10.) REGION: New Haven County, South Central CT.

FUSION ZONE, 380 New Hartford Rd # 5, Barkhamsted, CT 06063. Tel: 860-379-9663. Fax: 860-379-9606. Email: info@fusionzonect2.com. Website: www.fusionzonect2.com. Hrs: Vary. Contact: Armando Maestre. GRADE LEVEL: All grades. GROUP TYPE: All youth groups & homeschoolers. PROGRAM TYPE: Self-guided Activities, Guided Activities. MIN. GROUP SIZE: 20. REGISTRATION: Online, Phone. FOOD: Can bring own food, Place to eat on site, Beverages available. RECOMM. LENGTH OF VISIT: Varies. RECOMM. RATIO OF STUDENT TO STAFF: 10:1. ARRIVAL TIPS: Bus parking, Bus drop off and pick up at designated entrance. COST: Varies.

Fusion Zone is a group-friendly entertainment center featuring laser tag and a variety of arcade games. Come in and play laser tag in our 3,300 square foot arena filled with heart pumping, adrenaline kicking music, lights and action. We also offer racing cars, motorcycle games, shooting hoops, temporary airbrush tattoos, and try our dance machine! Group packages are available, and designed to accommodate every budget. Fusion Zone is your ultimate party headquarters - come see what all the action is about! SUPPORTS CT STATE & NATIONAL LEARNING STANDARDS IN: Physical Education. SUPPORTS SCOUT MERIT BADGE ACHIEVEMENT IN: Physical Ed/Recreation. REGION: Litchfield County, North West CT.

INTERACTIVE LIVING HISTORY

MASHANTUCKET PEQUOT MUSEUM & RESEARCH CENTER, 110 Pequot Dr., P.O. Box 3180, Mashantucket, CT 06338. Tel: 860-396-6839. Email: kdavis@mptn-nsn.gov. Website: www.pequotmuseum.org. Hrs: Wed.-Sat. 10AM-4PM, last admission at 3PM. Contact: Kathy Davis. GRADE LEVEL: All grades. GROUP TYPE: All youth groups & home-schoolers. PROGRAM TYPE: Day Trips, Self-guided Tours, Guided Tours, Performances, Workshops. REGISTRATION: Mail, Phone, Email. TICKET/VOUCHER RETURN POLICY: Pay upon arrival for those in group. FOOD: Variety of menu selections, Vegetarian, Can bring own food, Place to eat on site, Beverages available. RECOMM. LENGTH OF VISIT: 1-3 hours. RECOMM. RATIO OF STUDENT TO STAFF: Grades K-3, 5:1; Grades 4-12, 10:1. ARRIVAL TIPS: Expedite check in, Bus parking, Bus drop off and pick up at designated entrance. COST: Varies.

A visit to the Pequot Museum is not just a class trip, its an adventure! Students journey back in time to see and feel history come alive as never before. Exploring new worlds, they descend a glacial crevasse, walk through a 16th century Native American village, and stand next to life-size figures of the first people of New England as they hunt a herd of caribou. These eye-opening, life-size exhibits are complimented by an array of experiential education programs relevant to your curriculum. Dramatic films, computer interactive programs on archaeology, glaciers, and more make this an experience of a lifetime. SUPPORTS CT STATE & NATIONAL LEARNING STANDARDS IN: History, Science. SUPPORTS SCOUT MERIT BADGE ACHIEVEMENT IN: Native Lore. (See ad under Social Studies on page 34, New London Featured City Page on page 225 and Regional Highlights on page 14.) REGION: New London County, South East CT.

MAPLE SUGARING

Follow the maple sugaring process from sap to syrup. Season runs February-March; confirm times with venue. Reserve in the Fall.

4H CENTER AT AUER FARM, 158 Auer Farm Rd., Bloomfield, CT 06002. Tel: 860-242-7144. Hrs: Vary. Observe the entire maple sugaring process, from how the sap drains out of maple trees to what happens in the sugar house. COST: Fee. REGION: Hartford County, North Central CT.

BUSHY HILL FIELD SCHOOL INCARNATION CENTER, 253 Bushy Hill Road, Ivoryton, CT 06442. Tel: 860-767-2148. Hrs: Vary. Features naturalism, history and math skills to enliven the experience of making syrup. Cost: Varies. (See main listing on page 26.) REGION: Middlesex County, South Central CT.

FLANDERS NATURE CENTER & LAND TRUST, 5 Churchill Rd., Woodbury, CT 06798. Tel: 203-263-3711. Hrs: Vary. Learn the history of maple sugaring starting with Native Americans to the Colonial Period. Learn how to identify maple trees and what tools are used in the process. COST: Fee. REGION: Fairfield County, South West CT.

NORTHWEST PARK SUGARHOUSE, 145 Lang Rd., Windsor, CT 06095. Tel: 860-285-1886. Hrs: Mon.-Sat. 8:30AM-4:30PM, Sun. 1-4PM. Help tap the maple tree, collect sap from it, observe how sap cooks into maple syrup and have a taste. COST: Free. REGION: Hartford County, North Central CT.

SHARON AUDUBON CENTER, 325 Cornwall Bridge Rd., Sharon, CT 06069. Tel: 860-364-0520. Hrs: Vary. Learn what sugaring is, how sap comes out of the tree and help collect the sap and filter it. Experience a recreation of colonial and Native American maple sugaring practices such as using hot rocks to make maple sugar. COST: Fee. REGION: Litchfield County, North West CT.

PLANETARIUMS

Please call for planetarium show times. Experience a realistic and scientifically accurate simulation of the night sky in a domed theater.

THE CHILDREN'S MUSEUM, 950 Trout Brook Dr., West Hartford, CT 06119. Tel: 860-231-2824. Hrs: Vary. Pre K-7th grade. Program topics include astronauts, the solar system, atoms & molecules, and a holiday program. COST: Fee. REGION: Hartford County, North Central CT.

THE DISCOVERY MUSEUM & PLANETARIUM, 4450 Park Ave., Bridgeport, CT 06604. Tel: 203-372-3521. Hrs: Vary. Current planetarium shows educate students on topics which include stars, planets, space travel and comets. (See ad and main listing on page 27.) COST: Fee/Free. REGION: Fairfield County, South West CT.

MYSTIC SEAPORT - THE MUSEUM OF AMERICA AND THE SEA, P.O. Box 6000, 75 Greenmanville Avenue, Mystic, CT 06355. Tel: 860-572-5309. Discover stars under the planetarium dome. COST: Varies. (See ad and main listing under Social Studies on page 34, New London Featured City Page on page 225 and Regional Highlights on page 15.) REGION: New London County, South East CT.

SCIENCE & ENVIRONMENTAL EDUCATION

BUSHY HILL FIELD SCHOOL INCARNATION CENTER, 253 Bushy Hill Road (mailing address: PO Box 577), Ivoryton, CT 06442. Tel: 860-767-2148. Fax: 860-767-8432. Website: www.bushyhill.org. Contact: Erik Becker, Director. GRADE LEVEL: All grades. GROUP TYPE: All youth groups & homeschoolers. PROGRAM TYPE: Day Trips, Guided Activities, Guided Tours, Overnights/ Retreats, Workshops. MAX. GROUP SIZE: 80. COST: Varies.

Our goal at Bushy Hill is to help people of all ages develop a strong connection with, and reverence for, our natural world. We believe that through this connection we come to better understand our selves, each other, and the world we live in. We provide natural history and primitive studies programs for schools, scouts, pre-schools and teachers. Our Native American studies program is very popular. With stations showcasing pre-history, contact period, and plains culture. Maple Sugaring is a late winter-spring program that features naturalism, history and math skills to enliven the experience of making syrup. Our wetland program features a pond probe, exploration of our beautiful cedar swamp and a look at microscopic pond life. SUPPORTS CT STATE CURRICULUM IN: Science, Nature Study, Social Studies. REGION: Middlesex County, South Central CT.

4H CENTER AT AUER FARM, 158 Auer Farm Rd., Bloomfield, CT 06002. Tel: 860-242-7144. Hrs: Vary. Self-guided Activities, Guided Activities. 120-acre farm provides hands-on experiences in the Center's animal barn, gardens, farmland and orchards. This 120-acre farm provides valuable hands-on experiences in the Center's animal barn, gardens, farmland and orchards. In this setting, students see cows, chickens, pigs and goats. They plant seeds, harvest apples, pick pumpkins, observe milking and make ice cream. Students learn how agricultural science affects everyday life. Lessons on biology, biotechnology, horticulture and math address content standards and expected performances in science.COST: Fee. REGION: Hartford County, North Central CT.

BRUCE MUSEUM OF ARTS & SCIENCE, 1 Museum Dr., Greenwich, CT 06830. Tel: 203-869-6786. Hrs: Tues.-Sat. 10AM-5PM, Sun. 1-5PM. Self-guided Tours, Guided Tours, Workshops. Collections in fine and decorative arts, natural science and anthropology. COST: Fee. REGION: Fairfield County, South West CT.

CONNECTICUT AUDUBON SOCIETY: Center in Fairfield, Tel: 203-259-0416; Center in Glastonbury, Tel: 860-633-8402; Center in Pomfret, Tel: 860-928-4948 & Center in Trail Wood, Tel: 860-928-4948; Birdcraft Museum: Tel: 203-259-0416; Coastal Center at Milford Point, Tel: 203-878-7440; Ragged Hill Woods Program, Telephone: 860-377-3477. Self-guided Tours, Guided Tours, Workshops. Venues offer science-based educational programs, focusing on state's bird populations and habitats. COST: Fee. REGION: Statewide CT.

CRRA TRASH MUSEUM, 211 Murphy Road, Hartford, CT 06114. Tel: 860-757-7765. Hrs: Wed.-Fri. 12-4PM. Self-guided Tours, Guided Tours. Tour the 6,500 square feet of educational exhibits that trace the history of recycling. COST: Free. REGION: Hartford County, North Central CT.

DINOSAUR STATE PARK, 400 West St., Rocky Hill, CT 06067. Tel: 860-529-5816. Hrs: Tues.-Sun. 9AM-4:30PM. Self-guided Tours, Guided Tours, Workshops. Features more than 500 Early Jurassic dinosaur footprints preserved in place within the museum, alongside interactive exhibits. COST: Fee. REGION: Hartford County, Central CT.

DISCOVERY MUSEUM AND PLANETARIUM, 4450 Park Avenue, Bridgeport, Connecticut 06604. Tel: 203-372-3521, ext. 121. Fax: 203-374-1929. Email: Hawkins@discoverymuseum.org Website: www.discoverymuseum.org. Hrs: Tues.-Sat. 10AM-5PM, Sun. 12-5PM, Open Mon. for groups & in the summer. Contact: David Hawkins ext. 121. GRADE LEVEL: Pre K-9th. GROUP TYPE: All youth groups & homeschoolers. PROGRAM TYPE: Day Trips, Self-guided Tours, Self-guided Activities, Workshops. MAX. GROUP SIZE: 30 per classroom, 25 for Pre K. MIN. GROUP SIZE: 12. COST: Varies by topic & group size.

Hands-on Brains-On Learning! Experience the wonder of science discovery through interactive permanent and traveling exhibits, first class lessons aligned with CT science standards, planetarium shows and CT's only Challenger Learning Center. Memorable lessons and demos cover a wide range of engaging topics and can be customized. Check out our website for a full list of programs and for info on our current traveling exhibit. The Discovery Museum is located at 4450 Park Avenue, Bridgeport, CT 06604 just 1 mile south of Merritt Parkway Exit 47 South. SUPPORTS CT STATE & NATIONAL LEARNING STANDARDS IN: Math, Science, Technology. SUPPORTS SCOUT MERIT BADGE ACHIEVEMENT IN: Science/Technology. REGION: Fairfield County, South West CT.

EARTHPLACE THE NATURE DISCOVERY CENTER, 10 Woodside Lane, Westport, CT 06880. Tel: 203-227-7253. Hrs: Mon.-Sat. 9AM-5PM, Sun. 1-4PM. Self-guided Tours, Guided Tours, Workshops. Maintains a 62-acre wildlife sanctuary with trails, contains an interactive natural history museum and houses live wildlife. COST: Fee. REGION: Fairfield County, South West CT.

THE ELI WHITNEY MUSEUM, 915 Whitney Ave., Hamden, CT 06517. Tel: 203-777-1833. Hrs: Winter: Wed., Thurs., Fri., Sun. 12-5PM, Sat. 10AM-3PM; Summer: Daily 11AM-4PM. Self-guided Tours, Guided Tours, Workshops. Exhibits on Whitney and his most famous invention, the cotton gin along with hands-on projects. COST: Free/Fee. REGION: New Haven County, South Central CT.

ENVIRONMENTAL LEARNING CENTERS OF CONNECTICUT, Tel: 860-589-8200. Indian Rock Nature Preserve, 501 Wolcott Rd., Bristol, CT 06010. Tel: 860-583-1234. Harry C. Barnes Memorial Nature Center, 175 Shrub Rd., Bristol, CT 06010. Tel: 860-589-6082. Hrs: Vary. Self-guided Tours, Workshops. Offers a variety of hands-on experiential programs that encourage the conservation and enjoyment of the natural world. COST: Fee. REGION: Hartford County, North Central CT.

FLANDERS NATURE CENTER & LAND TRUST, 5 Churchill Rd. Woodbury, CT. 06798. Tel: 203-263-3711. Hrs: Mon.-Fri. 9AM-5PM, trails open daily. Self-guided Tours, Guided Tours, Workshops. Consists of 6 nature preserves, a 200-acre farm and nature center. Educational programs focus on Nature or The Farm. COST: Free/Fee. REGION: Fairfield County, South West CT.

THE GARBAGE MUSEUM, 1410 Honeyspot Rd. Extension, Stratford, CT 06615. Tel: 203-381-9571. Hrs: Wed.-Fri. 12-4PM. Summer Hrs: Tues.-Fri. 10AM-4PM. Self-guided Tours, Guided Tours. Focuses on the challenges and solutions of waste management through interactive exhibits such as the Trash-o-saurus, a dinosaur made from a ton of trash, which is how much trash the average person throws away in a year. COST: Fee. REGION: Fairfield County, South West CT.

KELLOGG ENVIRONMENTAL CENTER/OSBORNE HOMESTEAD MUSEUM, 500 Hawthorne Ave., Derby, CT 06418. Tel: 203-734-2513. Hrs: Tues.-Sat. 9AM-4:30PM. 4th-12th grades. Self-guided Tours, Workshops. The Osborne Homestead Museum celebrates the life of Frances Osborne Kellogg, an accomplished businesswoman and conservationist. The Kellogg Environmental Center's nature inquiry-based field studies cover many topics for school groups as well as programs designed for scout groups. COST: Free. REGION: New Haven County, South Central CT.

MASHANTUCKET PEQUOT MUSEUM & RESEARCH CENTER, 110 Pequot Dr., P.O. Box 3180, Mashantucket, CT 06338. Tel: 860-396-6839. Email: kdavis@mptn-nsn.gov. Website: www.pequotmuseum.org. Hrs: Wed.-Sat. 10AM-4PM, last admission at 3PM. Contact: Kathy Davis. GRADE LEVEL: All grades. GROUP TYPE: All youth groups & homeschoolers. PROGRAM TYPE: Day Trips, Self-guided Tours, Guided Tours, Performances, Workshops. REGISTRATION: Mail, Phone, Email. TICKET/VOUCHER RETURN POLICY: Pay upon arrival for those in group. FOOD: Variety of menu selections, Vegetarian, Can bring own food, Place to eat on site, Beverages available. RECOMM. LENGTH OF VISIT: 1-3 hours. RECOMM. RATIO OF STUDENT TO STAFF: Grades K-3, 5:1; Grades 4-12, 10:1. ARRIVAL TIPS: Expedite check in, Bus parking, Bus drop off and pick up at designated entrance. COST: Varies. (See main listing under Interactive Living History on page 25, ad under Social Studies on page 34 and see Regional Highlights on page 14.) REGION: New London County, South East CT.

NEW CANAAN NATURE CENTER, 144 Oenoke Ridge, New Canaan, CT 06840. Tel: 203-966-9577. Hrs: Mon.-Sat. 9AM-4PM. Self-guided Tours, Guided Tours. A 40-acre site which features unusual habitat diversity, including wet and dry meadows, two ponds, wet and dry woodlands, dense thickets, an old orchard, wildflower garden and a cattail marsh. In addition there is a greenhouse, an animal care center, an apple cider house and a Discovery Center with hands-on exhibits. COST: Fee. REGION: Fairfield County, South West CT.

NEW POND FARM, 101 Marchant Rd., West Redding, CT 06896. Tel: 203-938-2117. Hrs: Vary. Provides learning opportunities in natural science, Native American heritage, farming traditions, astronomy and the arts. COST: Fee. REGION: Fairfield County, South West CT.

NORTHWEST PARK, 145 Lang Rd., Windsor, CT 06095. Tel: 860-285-1886. Hrs: Mon.-Sat. 8:30AM-4:30PM, Sun. 1-4PM. Self-guided activities, Guided Activities. Offers hands-on discovery activities, Nature Center and Animal Barn scavenger hunts and nature hikes that explore a variety of Northwest Park habitats. COST: Free. REGION: Hartford County, North Central CT.

PROJECT OCEANOLOGY, Avery Point off Eastern Point Rd., 1084 Shenncossett Rd., Groton, CT 06340. Tel: 860-445-9007. Fax: 860-449-8008. Email: oceanology@aol.com. Website: www.oceanology.org. GRADE LEVEL: 5th-College. GROUP TYPE: All youth groups & homeschoolers. PROGRAM TYPE: Day Trips, Overnight Trips, Guided Tours, Workshops. REGISTRATION: Phone. FOOD: Variety of menu selections, Vegetarian, Can bring own food, Place to eat on site, Beverages available. RECOMM. LENGTH OF VISIT: Varies. ARRIVAL TIPS: Bus parking, Bus drop off and pick up at designated entrance. COST: Varies.

A one-of-a-kind, hands-on, minds-on science immersion experience. Project O has fully-equipped research vessels, marine laboratories, computer labs, and a hostel complete with bunk beds, shower facilities, dining facilities. Typical student activities include a 2 1/2 hour oceanographic cruise aboard our fully-equipped, U.S. Coast Guard certified research vessel using scientific instruments such as otter trawls, plankton nets, sediment corers and salinity meters. Back on shore, students can explore tidal marshes, rocky intertidal zones, sandy beaches and near shore fishes. In our waterfront marine laboratories, students can identify plankton, conduct a chemical analysis of seawater, study the behavior of marine animals or design their own experiments. SUPPORTS CT STATE & NATIONAL LEARNING STANDARDS IN: Science. SUPPORTS SCOUT MERIT BADGE ACHIEVEMENT IN: Ecology, Health & Safety, Oceanography, Recreation, Technology, Science. (See New London Featured City Page on page 225.) REGION: New London County, South East CT.

SCHOONER INC., 60 South Water St., New Haven, CT 06519. Tel: 203-865-1737. Fax: 203-624-8816. Email: manager@schoonerinc.org. Website: www.schoonerinc.org. Hrs: 9-5PM. Contact: Karen DeForge. GRADE LEVEL: All grades. GROUP TYPE: All youth Groups. PROGRAM TYPE: Day Trips, Guided Activities. MAX. GROUP SIZE: 40. MIN. GROUP SIZE: 10. REGISTRATION: Phone, Prepay. RECOMM. LENGTH OF VISIT: 3 hours. RECOMM. RATIO OF STUDENT TO STAFF: 15:1. ARRIVAL TIPS: Bus Parking. COST: Fee.

Keep science exciting, relevant, and close to home for your students... Coastal Encounters-On the shores of Long Island Sound, students are able to connect concepts that they have learned in the classroom to the world around them with hands-on exploration and inquiry based activities. Harbor Discover Cruise-For 4th-12th grade students, a trip on board the schooner Quinnipiack provides an unparalleled experience from our floating classroom. Students take part in a hands-on environmental, marine science, and sailing program on a tall ship. For more information visit www.schoonerinc.org. SUPPORTS CT STATE & NATIONAL LEARNING STANDARDS IN: Science. REGION: New Haven County, South Central CT.

STEWART B. MCKINNEY NATIONAL WILDLIFE REFUGE, 733 Old Clinton Rd., Westbrook, CT 06498. Tel: 860-399-2513. Hrs: Vary. Self-guided Tours, Guided Tours. Includes a variety of habitats and native wildlife. COST: Free. REGION: Middlesex County, South Central CT.

TALCOTT MOUNTAIN SCIENCE CENTER, 324 Montevideo Rd., Avon, CT 06001. Tel: 860-677-8571. Hrs: Daily 8AM-4:30PM. Workshops. The Center occupies more than 20 acres atop Talcott Mountain. Laboratory and field workshops focuses on increasing students' understanding and appreciation for their physical world. COST: Fee. REGION: Hartford County, North Central CT.

WEST ROCK NATURE CENTER, 1080 Wintergreen Ave., Hamden, CT 06514. Tel: 203-946-8016. Hrs: Mon.-Fri. 10AM-4PM. Self-guided Tours, Guided Tours. 43 acres of upland woods containing over 300 different plant species. COST: Free. REGION: New Haven County, South Central CT.

WOODCOCK NATURE CENTER, 56 Deer Run Rd., Wilton, CT 06897. Tel: 203-762-7280. Hrs: Mon.-Fri. 9:30AM-4:30PM. Pre K-5th grade. Self-guided Tours, Guided Tours, Workshops. 149 acres of state-protected land, includes a pond, wetlands, and 3 miles of accessible woodland trails. The Center is home to a variety of living local and exotic creatures including snakes, frogs, and lizards. COST: Fee. REGION: Fairfield County, South West CT.

YALE PEABODY MUSEUM OF NATURAL HISTORY, Yale University, 170 Whitney Ave., New Haven, CT 06520. Tel: 203-432-5050. Hrs: Mon.-Sat. 10AM-5PM, Sun. 12-5PM. Self-guided Tours, Guided Tours. The Museum's collections provide a record of the history of the earth, its life and its cultures. COST: Fee; Free Thursdays 2-5PM & under 3 yrs old. REGION: New Haven County, South Central CT.

SEAPORTS & LIGHTHOUSES

MYSTIC SEAPORT – THE MUSEUM OF AMERICA AND THE SEA, 75 Greenmanville Ave., Mystic, CT 06355. Tel: 860-572-5309. Hrs: Mon.-Fri. 10AM-5PM, Sat.-Sun. 9AM-5PM. The village and ship's area is an active living history museum with 17 acres of exhibits portraying coastal life in New England in the 19th century. COST: Fee/Free for members & under age 5. (See main listing and ad under Social Studies on page 34-35.) REGION: New London County, South East CT.

NORWALK SEAPORT ASSOCIATION & SHEFFIELD ISLAND LIGHTHOUSE, 132 Water St., S. Norwalk, CT 06854. Tel: 203-838-9444. Hrs: Mon.-Fri. 9AM-5PM. Guided Tours. Obtain a greater understanding of local sea creatures with the help of Seaport educators and hands-on observations and learn about local maritime history at the 140-year-old lighthouse. COST: Fee. REGION: Fairfield County, South West CT.

SKIING & SNOWBOARDING

MOHAWK MTN SKI AREA, 46 Great Hollow Rd., Cornwall, CT 06753. Tel: 860-672-6100. Fax: 860-672-0117. Email: office@mohawkmtn.com. Website: www.mohawkmtn.com. Hrs: Thanksgiving-Easter. Contact: Jennifer Wolinski. GRADE LEVEL: All grades. GROUP TYPE: All youth groups & homeschoolers. PROGRAM TYPE: Day Trips. MAX. GROUP SIZE: 800. MIN. GROUP SIZE: 15. COST: Group size determines price. Please contact for details.

Welcome to Mohawk Mountain, Connecticut's premier snow resort, serving southern New England since 1947 with an exciting winter sport environment featuring skiing and snowboarding. Mohawk features 24 trails for skiing and snowboarding, using state of the art snow making equipment, five chairlifts, two "wonder carpet" for beginners and amenities for all snow sport enthusiasts. Join us for the best skiing and snowboarding in Connecticut. Celebrating our 61th year of snowmaking and the home to the invention of the snowmaking we are looking forward to making you a winter enthusiast. Groups Wanted! SUPPORTS CT STATE & NATIONAL LEARNING STANDARDS IN: Physical Education. SUPPORTS SCOUT MERIT BADGE ACHIEVEMENT IN: Skiing, Sports. REGION: Litchfield County, North West CT.

SKI SUNDOWN SKI AREA, 126 Ratlum Rd. (Mailing Address: P.O. Box 208), New Hartford, CT 06057. Tel: 860-379-7669. Fax: 860-379-1853. Email: groupservices@skisundown.com. Website: www.skisundown.com. Hrs: Late Nov.-Early Apr., open 7 days and 7 nights in season. Contact: Group Services. GRADE LEVEL: All grades. GROUP TYPE: All youth groups. PROGRAM TYPE: Day Trips, Guided Tours, Self-guided Activities. MIN. GROUP SIZE: 10. REGISTRATION: Mail, Phone. FOOD: Variety, Place to eat on site, Beverages available. RECOMM. RATIO OF STUDENT TO STAFF: 10:1. ARRIVAL TIPS: Expedite check in, Bus Parking. COST: Contact Group Services for rates.

Ski Sundown offers skiing & snowboarding fun on 15 trails (beginner to advanced terrain) with 100% snowmaking. Group Programs - 4, 5 or 6 week programs, one day or night per week, Mon-Fri for groups of 10 or more, ages 8+. Leaders and chaperones receive complimentary skiing benefits. Group Day Trips - Discounted lift tickets, equipment rentals, group lessons and lift/lesson/rental packages apply to every member of your group of 10 or more. Snowmaking Tours - Learn about the science and history of snowmaking from the early days of the ski industry to today's cutting edge, energy efficient technology. SUPPORTS CT STATE & NATIONAL LEARNING STANDARDS IN: Physical Education, Science. SUPPORTS SCOUT MERIT BADGE ACHIEVEMENT IN: Physical Ed/Recreation. REGION: Litchfield County, North West CT.

SOCIAL STUDIES

AMERICAN CLOCK & WATCH MUSEUM, 100 Maple St., Bristol, CT 06010 Tel: 860-583-6070. Hrs: Daily 10AM-5PM. Self-Guided Tours, Guided Tours, Workshops. Features a collection of American manufactured clocks and watches. COST: Fee. REGION: Hartford County, North Central CT.

THE BARNUM MUSEUM, 820 Main St., Bridgeport, CT 06604. Tel: 203-331-1104. Hrs: Tues.-Sat. 10AM-4:30PM, Sun. 12-4:30PM. Self-guided Tours, Guided Tours. Features collections relating to P.T. Barnum & the history of Bridgeport. COST: Fee. REGION: Fairfield County, South West CT.

BUSH-HOLLEY HISTORIC SITE, 39 Strickland Rd., Cos Cob, CT 06807. Tel: 203-869-6899. Hrs: Vary. Self-guided Tours, Guided Tours, Workshops. The site was the home and business headquarters of colonial merchant and mill owner David Bush. Visitors learn about the life of the Bush family and exhibits focus on the art and artists of the Cos Cob art colony and aspects of Greenwich history. COST: Fee. REGION: Fairfield County, South West CT.

COLEY HOUSE AND FARM, 104 Weston Rd., Weston, CT 06883. Tel: 203-226-1804. Hrs: Sat. 9:30AM-12:30PM & By appt. Guided Tours, Workshops. Historical estate from the 13th century. COST: Free. REGION: Fairfield County, South West CT.

CONNECTICUT ANTIQUE MACHINERY ASSOCIATION MUSEUM, Rte. 7, Kent, CT 06757. Tel: 860-927-0050. Hrs: May-Oct., Wed.-Sun. 10AM-4PM. Self-guided Tours, Guided Tours, Workshops. Learn about early industrial and agricultural methods. COST: Fee. REGION: Litchfield County, North West CT.

CONNECTICUT'S OLD STATE HOUSE, 800 Main St., Hartford, CT 06103. Tel: 860-522-6766. Hrs: Mon.-Fri. 9AM-5PM, Tues.-Fri. 11AM-5PM, Sat. 10AM-5PM. Guided Tours. Tour the Senate Chamber, City Council room, and the Supreme Courtroom; an interactive exhibit tells the story of Hartford and the Old State House. COST: Fee. REGION: Hartford County, North Central CT.

CONNECTICUT TROLLEY MUSEUM, 58 North Rd., East Windsor, CT 06088. Tel: 860-627-6540. Hrs: Vary, closed Tues. Day Trips, Self-guided Tours, Guided Tours. Focuses on the trolley era through the preservation and operation of an electric railway. Trolley Rides available. COST: Fee. REGION: Hartford County, North Central CT.

DANBURY RAILWAY MUSEUM, 120 White St., Danbury, CT 06810. Tel: 203-778-8337. Hrs: Wed.-Sat. 10AM-4PM, Sun. 12-4PM. Self-guided Tours, Guided Tours. Offers railroad history, tours, train rides, a collection of original and restored rolling stock, and opportunities for hands-on railroad work. COST: Fee. REGION: Fairfield County, South West CT.

ESSEX STEAM TRAIN & RIVERBOAT RIDE, 1 Railroad Ave., Essex, CT 06426. Tel: 860-767-0103. Hrs: Vary. Guided Tours. Experience the natural wonder of the Connecticut River on a steam train ride and/ or a riverboat ride. COST: Fee. REGION: Middlesex County, South Central CT.

FIRE MUSEUM, 230 Pine St., Manchester, CT 06040. Tel: 860-649-9436. Hrs: Mid Apr.-Mid Nov.: Sat. 12-4PM & by appt. Self-guided Tours. Displays of historic, antique fire fighting apparatus and equipment. COST: Sugg. Donation. REGION: Hartford County, North Central CT.

FREEDOM SCHOONER AMISTAD, Long Wharf Pier, New Haven, CT 06510. Tel: 203-498-9000. Hrs: Vary. Guided Tours. Connecticut Flagship & Tall Ship Ambassador, the Freedom Schooner Amistad visits ports around the Atlantic Ocean as a monument of freedom, justice and human cooperation among all races and religions. The message is founded on the telling of the Amistad Story where kidnapped Africans were set free by a pro-slavery U.S. Supreme Court because black and white abolitionists work tirelessly to win their freedom. The Amistad is one of a very few monuments that can be actually invited to your neighborhood. Call to see if there is a visit scheduled near your school. COST: Fee. REGION: New Haven County, South Central CT.

THE GOLDEN AGE OF TRUCKING MUSEUM, 1101 Southford Rd., Middlebury, CT 06762. Tel: 203-577-2181. Hrs: Thurs.-Sat. 10AM-4PM, Sun. 12-4PM, Self-guided Tours. Display of antique trucks ranging from the early 1900s until 1974. Exhibits focuses on the history of American truck transportation. COST: Fee. REGION: Litchfield County, North West CT.

HARRIET BEECHER STOWE CENTER, 77 Forest St., Hartford, CT 06105. Tel: 860-522-9258. Hrs: Wed.-Sat. 9:30AM-4:30PM, Sun. 12-4:30PM, call for Summer Hrs. Guided Tours. Learn about Stowe's life and her famous anti-slavery novel, Uncle Tom's Cabin, through a guided tour of the Stowe House. Also visit the extensive library. COST: Fee. REGION: Hartford County, North Central CT.

HISTORIC SHIP NAUTILUS/SUBMARINE FORCE MUSEUM, 1 Crystal Lake Road, Groton, CT 06349-5501. Tel: 800-343-0079. Fax: 860-405-0568. Email: director@submarinemuseum.org. Website: www.submarinemuseum.org. Hrs: Call for hours and special events. Contact: Mike Riegel. GRADE LEVEL: All grades. GROUP TYPE: All youth groups & homeschoolers. PROGRAM TYPE: Day Trips, Self-guided Tours. COST: Free.

Tour the world's first nuclear-powered submarine, Historic Ship NAUTILUS and visit the Navy's official submarine museum. Experience the rich heritage of the US Submarine Force from the Revolutionary War to the present. Free admission. Open year round, closed Tuesdays from November through April, the next to the last week of April and the first week of November. Call for hours and special events. RVs & Buses welcome. 1.5 miles north off I-95 Exit 86. Toll free 800-343-0079. SUPPORTS STATE & NATIONAL LEARNING STANDARDS IN: History/Social Studies. SUPPORTS SCOUT MERIT BADGE ACHIEVEMENT IN: Social Studies. (See New London Featured City Page on page 225.) REGION: New London County, South East CT.

HOYT BARNUM HOUSE, 713 Bedford St., Stamford, CT 06902. Tel: 203-329-1183. Hrs: By appointment. K-6th grade. Guided Tours. Representative of the second American building period, post 1675. COST: Fee. REGION: Fairfield County, South West CT.

HUNT HILL FARM, 44 Upland Rd., New Milford, CT 06776. Tel: 860-355-0300. Hrs: Wed.-Sat. 10AM-5PM, Sun. 12PM-5PM. Guided Tours. Historic farm from the 18th century. COST: Free. REGION: Litchfield County, North West CT.

INSTITUTE FOR AMERICAN INDIAN STUDIES, 38 Curtis Rd., Washington, CT 06793. Tel: 860-868-0518. Hrs: Mon.-Sat. 10AM-5PM, Sun. 12-5PM. Self-guided Tours, Guided Tours. Museum & Research Center dedicated to furthering interest in the indigenous peoples of the Americas. COST: Fee. REGION: Litchfield County, North West CT.

LITCHFIELD HISTORY MUSEUM, Corner of East & South St., Litchfield, CT 06759. Tel: 860-567-4501. Hrs: Mid April-Nov. Tues.-Sat. 11AM-5PM, Sun. 1-5PM, and all year by appt. Self-guided Tours, Guided Tours by appt. Explore the evolution of a small New England town from its earliest European settlement to the present day. COST: Fee. REGION: Litchfield County, North West CT.

LOCKWOOD-MATHEWS MANSION MUSEUM, Mathews Park, 295 West Ave., Norwalk, CT 06850. Tel: 203-838-9799. Hrs: Wed.-Sun. 12-4PM, or by appt. Self-guided Tours, Guided Tours. One of the earliest surviving Second Empire Style country houses in the U.S. COST: Fee. REGION: Fairfield County, South West CT.

MARION ANDERSON STUDIO, DANBURY MUSEUM & HISTORICAL SOCIETY, 43 Main St., Danbury, CT 06810. Tel: 203-743-5200. Hrs: Mon.-Fri. 8AM-4PM & by appt. Guided Tours, Workshops. Visit Marian Anderson's rehearsal studio. She was the first African American woman opera singer who performed at the Metropolitan Opera House. The site features some of her clothing, scripts and other artifacts. COST: Fee. REGION: Fairfield County, South West CT.

THE MARK TWAIN HOUSE & MUSEUM, 351 Farmington Ave., Hartford, CT 06105. Tel: 860-247-0998. Hrs: Mon.-Sat. 9:30AM-5:30PM, Sun. 12-5:30PM; Jan.-Mar.: closed Tues. Guided Tours, Workshops. Experience Mark Twain's life in 19th century America during a visit to The Mark Twain House and Museum and learn about his literary achievements. COST: Fee. REGION: Hartford County, North Central CT.

MUSEUM OF CONNECTICUT HISTORY, Connecticut State Library, 231 Capitol Ave., Hartford, Connecticut 06106. Tel: 860-757-6535. Hrs: Mon.-Fri. 9AM-4PM, Sat. 9AM-3PM. 4th-12th grade. Self-guided Tours, Guided Tours. Connecticut's history from the Colonial era to the present. COST: Free. REGION: Hartford County, North Central CT.

MYSTIC SEAPORT – THE MUSEUM OF AMERICA AND THE SEA, P.O. Box 6000, 75 Greenmanville Avenue, Mystic, CT 06355. Tel: 860-572-5309. Fax: 860-572-5326. Email: sarah.spencer@mysticseaport.org. Website: www.mysticseaport.org. Hrs: Apr.-Oct.: Daily 9AM-5PM; Nov.-Mar.: Daily 10AM-4PM. Contact: Sarah Spencer. Reservations: 860-572-5322. GRADE LEVEL: All grades. GROUP TYPE: All youth groups & homeschoolers. PROGRAM TYPE: Day Trips, Overnight Trips, Self-guided Tours, Guided Tours, Workshops, Performances. REGISTRATION: Mail, Phone. FOOD: Variety of menu selections, Can bring own food, Place to eat on site, Beverages available. RECOMM. LENGTH OF VISIT: 3-4 hours. RECOMM. RATIO OF STUDENT TO STAFF: 5:1. ARRIVAL TIPS: Expedite check in, Bus parking, Bus drop off and pick up at designated entrance. COST: Varies.

Immerse yourself in American maritime history at Mystic Seaport The Museum of America and the Sea. Explore a re-created 19th-century maritime village, discover stars under the planetarium dome, see a working shipyard in action, and climb aboard authentic tall ships, including the Charles W. Morgan, the last wooden whaleship in the world. Discover the crafts and industries of a thriving coastal community while getting involved in hands-on demonstrations. Mystic Seaport is located off I-95, Exit 90 in Mystic, Connecticut. For information and reservations, call 860-572-5322. Or visit www.mysticseaport.org. SUPPORTS CT STATE & NATIONAL LEARNING STANDARDS IN: Science, Social Studies. SUPPORTS SCOUT MERIT BADGE ACHIEVEMENT IN: Citizenship, American Heritage. (See New London Featured City Page on page 225 and Regional Highlights on page 15.) REGION: New London County, South East CT.

NATHAN HALE HOMESTEAD, 2299 South St., Coventry, Connectiuct 06238. Tel: 860-742-6917. Hrs: Mid-May - Mid-Oct.: Wed.-Sun. 1-4PM. Guided Tours, Workshops. Through objects and documents, such as diaries and inventories, learn about the life of Nathan Hale. Special Programs: Mystery Tour: How do we know what we know? Students utilize objects and documents, such as diaries and inventories, to learn about the Hale Homestead. Tour and Hands-On History Activities: Complement your house or landscape tour with one of the following activities. Hearth and Health; Swifts and Spindles; Spy for a Day; Reading, Writing and Whirligigs and more.COST: Fee. REGION: Hartford County, North Central CT.

NEW ENGLAND AIR MUSEUM, Bradley International Airport, 36 Perimeter Rd., Windsor Locks, CT 06096. Tel: 860-623-3305. Hrs: Daily 10AM-5PM. Self-guided Tours. Aviation history and technology, particularly in regard to Connecticut's contributions. COST: Fee. REGION: Hartford County, North Central CT.

NORWALK MUSEUM, 41 N. Main St., Norwalk, CT 06854. Tel: 203-866-0202. Hrs: Wed.-Sun. 1-5PM. Self-guided Tours, Guided Tours, Workshops. Variety of exhibits relating the art and history of the area. COST: Free. REGION: Fairfield County, South West CT.

OLD LIGHTHOUSE MUSEUM, 7 Water St., Stonington, CT 06378. Tel: 860-535-1440. Hrs: May 1-Oct. 31: Daily 10AM-5PM. Self-guided Tours, Guided Tours. Exhibits depict the rich and varied history of Stonington's harbor. COST: Fee. REGION: New London County, South East CT.

PUTNAM COTTAGE, 243 E. Putnam Avenue, Greenwich, CT 06830. Tel: 203-869-9697. Hrs: Apr.-Nov.: Sun. 1-4PM, or by appt. Guided Tours. Historic tavern from the American Revolution. COST: Fee. REGION: Fairfield County, South West CT.

STATE CAPITOL, 210 Capitol Ave., Hartford, CT 06106. Tel: 860-240-0222. Hrs: Mon.-Fri. 9:15AM-1:15PM, tours every quarter past the hour. Group reservations may be made by calling 860-240-0222 weekdays 9AM-3PM. To arrange a meeting with your local representative or his/her staff, call your representative's office 4-8 weeks in advance. 3rd-12th grade for Guided Tours. Self-guided Tours (Self-guided tour booklets about the State Capitol are available), Guided Tours. Learn the history of the Capitol, a National Historic Landmark, or take a free one hour guided tour. COST: Free. REGION: Hartford County, North Central CT.

STATE SUPREME COURT, 231 Capitol Ave., Hartford, CT 06106. Tel: 860-757-2270. Hrs: Mon.-Fri. 9AM-4PM. Guided Tours. Students may take a tour of the courtroom, and view historical murals and portraits. COST: Free. REGION: Hartford County, North Central CT.

WEIR FARM NATIONAL HISTORIC SITE, 735 Nod Hill Rd., Wilton, CT 06897. Tel: 203-834-1896. Hrs: May-Oct.: Wed.-Sun. 9AM-5PM; Nov.-Apr.: Thurs.-Sun. 10AM-4PM. Self-guided Tours, Guided Tours. Have you ever wished that you could walk right into a painting? At Weir Farm National Historic Site, you can. At the farm, artwork becomes an interactive experience. By melding art, history, and nature, Weir Farm National Historic Site enables students to step back into a landscape that inspired three generations of artists and inspired countless works of art. You and your students can become part of this artistic tradition by learning, exploring, and creating in a place where the "landscape and air are full of promise." COST: Free. REGION: Fairfield County, South West CT.

THEATER · DANCE · MUSIC

THE PAPER BAG PLAYERS, 225 West 99th St., NY, NY 10025. Performance locations: Bridgeport, Hartford, Stamford. Tel: 800-777-2247/212-663-0390. Fax: 212-663-1076. Email: pbagp@verizon.net. Website: thepaperbagplayers.org. Hrs: Vary. GRADE LEVEL: K–3rd grade. GROUP TYPE: All youth groups and homeschoolers. PROGRAM TYPE: Performances. COST: Varies. (See ad and main listing in NYC on page 125.) REGION: Fairfield County, South West CT & Hartford County, North Central CT.

WARNER THEATRE, 68 Main Street, PO Box 1012, Torrington, CT 06790. Tel: 860-489-7180. Fax: 860-482-4076. Email: marilyn@wildwoodassoc.com. Website: www.warnertheatre.org. Hrs: Mon.-Fri 10AM-6PM, Sat. 10AM-2PM. Contact: Marilyn Plaskiewicz. GRADE LEVEL: Pre K -9th. GROUP TYPE: School Group. PRO-GRAM TYPE: Performances. MAX. GROUP SIZE: 1700. REGISTRATION: Phone. RECOMM. LENGTH OF VISIT: 2 hours. RECOMM. RATIO OF STUDENT TO STAFF: 10:1. ARRIVAL TIPS: Expedite check in, Bus drop off and pick up at designated entrance. COST: $7 per student; chaperones free.

The Warner Theatre's, Daytime Performances for Young Audiences Series. Series of live performances: The Midnight Ride of Paul Revere - grades 3-9, Click, Clack, Moo - grades PreK-4, From the Mixed Up Files of Mrs. Basil Frankweiler - grades 3-6, Jigsaw Jones - grades 1-4, Charlotte's Web - grades K-5. Each performance is approximately 90 minutes. Study guides can be downloaded prior to the show at www.warnertheatre.org. SUPPORTS CT STATE & NATIONAL LEARNING STANDARDS IN: The Arts. SUPPORTS SCOUT MERIT BADGE ACHIEVEMENT IN: The Arts, Performing Arts. REGION: Litchfield County, North West CT.

TRIP SERVICES

MTA METRO-NORTH RAILROAD, Group Travel Department, Graybar Building, 420 Lexington Ave., 9th Floor, New York, NY 10017. Tel: 212-499-4398. Email: groupsales@mnr.org.

MTA Metro-North Group Travel offers substantial savings for groups of ten or more. And since free parking is available on weekends at most Metro-North Railroad stations, you'll save even more. Relax in comfort while enjoying scenic views, historic landmarks, and the excitement of rail travel. Whether it's a class trip, family outing, or a company picnic, Metro-North's friendly Group Travel staff can suggest fun trips to New York City, upstate New York, and Connecticut, and even help you create one of your own. It all starts with a safe, easy, memorable train ride. Call Metro-North Group Travel today at 212-499-4398. (See ad under Transportation on page 7.)

DELAWARE

ANIMALS · AQUARIUMS · ZOOS

BOMBAY HOOK NATIONAL WILDLIFE REFUGE, 2591 Whitehall Neck Rd., Smyrna, DE 19977. Tel: 302-653-6872. Hrs: Daily Sunrise-Sunset. Self-guided Tours, Guided Tours. One of the largest expanses of nearly unaltered tidal salt marsh in the mid-Atlantic region. COST: Fee. REGION: Kent County, Central DE.

BRANDYWINE ZOO, 1001 North Park Dr., Wilmington, DE 19802. Tel: 302-571-7747. Hrs: Daily 10AM-4PM. Self-guided Tours, Guided Tours by appt. Home to 120 animals, representing 56 species on 12 acres. COST: Fee. REGION: New Castle County, Northern DE.

ART · ARCHITECTURE · SCULPTURE

BIGGS MUSEUM OF AMERICAN ART, 406 Federal St., Dover, DE 19904. Tel: 302-674-2111. Hrs: Tues.-Sat. 9AM-4:30PM, Sun. 1:30-4:30PM. Self-guided Tours. Includes fourteen galleries of American paintings and Delaware Valley silver and furniture from the 18th through mid-20th centuries. COST: Free. REGION: Kent County, Central DE.

DELAWARE ART MUSEUM, 2301 Kentmere Parkway, Wilmington, DE 19806. Tel: 302-571-9590. Hrs: Tues.-Sat. 10AM-4PM, Sun 12-4PM. Guided Tours. Focuses on American art and illustrations from the 19th century to present, Copeland Sculpture Garden and the largest collection of British Pre-Raphaelites Art in the USA. COST: Fee. REGION: New Castle County, Northern DE.

DELAWARE CENTER FOR THE CONTEMPORARY ARTS, 200 S. Madison St., Wilmington, DE 19801. Tel: 302-656-6466. Hrs: Tues., Thurs.-Sat. 10AM-5PM, Wed. & Sun. 12-5PM. Self-guided Tours, Guided Tours. A non-collecting museum, currently presents nearly 30 exhibitions annually of regionally, nationally, and internationally recognized artists. COST: Fee. REGION: New Castle County, Northern DE.

FARMS & PICK-YOUR-OWN

FILASKY'S PRODUCE, 1343 Bunker Hill Rd., Middletown DE 19709. Tel: 302-378-2754. Hrs: Vary. PYO: Pumpkins, Peppers, Tomatoes, Strawberries. COST: Fee. Pre K-3rd grade. REGION: New Castle County, Northern DE.

JOHNSON'S COUNTRY MARKET, 37049 Johnson Rd., Selbyville, DE 19975. Tel: 302-436-7171. Hrs: Daily 9AM-6PM. PYO: Pumpkins. COST: Fee. REGION: Sussex County, Southern DE.

LOBLOLLY ACRES, 3893 Turkey Point Rd., Woodside, DE 19980. Tel: 302-284-9255. Hrs: May-Dec.: Daily 9AM-5PM. PYO: Pumpkins, Strawberries. Christmas trees. COST: Fee. REGION: Kent County, Central DE.

RAMSEY'S FARM, P.O. Box 7560, Wilmington, DE 19803. Tel: 302-477-1499. Hrs: Vary seasonally. PYO: Pumpkins. COST: Fee. REGION: New Castle County, Northern DE.

GARDENS & NATURE CENTERS

ASHLAND NATURE CENTER, 3511 Barley Mill Rd., Hockessin, DE 19707. Tel: 302-239-2334. Hrs: Mon.-Fri. 8:30AM-4:30PM. Self-guided Tours, Guided Activities. Offers educational programs as well as four self-guiding nature trails through meadows, woodlands and marshes. COST: Fee. REGION: New Castle County, Northern DE.

BRANDYWINE PARK, 1021 W. 18th Street, Wilmington, DE 19802. Tel: 302-577-7020. Hrs: 8AM-Sunset. Self-guided Tours, Guided Tours. Picturesque park that runs along either side of the Brandywine River. COST: Free. REGION: New Castle County, Northern DE.

CORKS POINT OUTDOORS, McQuail Rd. 508 S. Chapel St., Smyrna, DE 19977. Tel: 302-738-1374. Hrs: Vary. Guided Tours. Provides nature tours throughout the scenic Delaware Bayshore region. COST: Fee. REGION: New Castle County, Northern DE.

EDWARD H. MCCABE NATURE PRESERVE, on Rt. 257, Milton, DE 19968. Tel: 302-654-4707. Hrs: Dawn-Dusk. Self-guided Tours, Guided Tours. Observe a wide range of Delaware's ecosystems, including tidal marshes, upland forests and Atlantic white cedar swamp. COST: Fee. REGION: Sussex County, Southern DE.

GOODSTAY GARDENS, University of Delaware Wilmington Campus, 2600 Pennsylvania Ave., Wilmington, DE 19805. Tel: 302-573-4450. Hrs: Call for hours. Guided Tours. Houses a mansion that is surrounded by Tutor gardens. COST: Fee. REGION: New Castle County, Northern DE.

NEMOURS MANSION & GARDENS, 1600 Rockland Rd, Wilmington, DE 19603. Tel: 800-651-6912. Hrs: Vary. Guided Tours. 6th-12th grade. Set among spectacular French formal gardens, the Louis XVI-style chateau was built for Alfred I. DuPont and contains 102 rooms furnished with fine examples of antique furniture, rare rugs, tapestries and outstanding works of art. COST: Fee. REGION: New Castle County, Northern DE.

HEALTH & NUTRITION

FIELD TRIP FACTORY, Telephone: 800-987-6409. Fax: 773-342-9513. Email: info@fieldtripfactory.com. Website: www.fieldtripfactory.com. Hrs: Mon.-Fri. 8AM-6PM. GRADE LEVEL: Pre K-6th. GROUP TYPE: All youth groups & homeschoolers. PROGRAM TYPE: Day Trips, Guided Tours. COST: Free.

Field Trip Factory offers free community-based field trips. Our learning adventures teach valuable life-skills including health and nutrition, science, responsibility and more. All field trips are grade and age appropriate, meet learning standards, enrich classroom curriculum for teachers and fulfill badge requirements for scouts. See what is available in your area at www.fieldtripfactory.com or call 1-800-987-6409. SUPPORTS STATE LEARNING STANDARDS IN: Health & Safety, Math, Physical Education, Science. SUPPORTS SCOUT BADGE ACTIVITIES IN: Health & Safety, Life Skills, Personal Fitness. (See ad on page 56.) REGION: Throughout all 50 states.

HISTORIC RAILROAD EXCURSIONS

WILMINGTON & WESTERN RAILROAD, 2201 Newport Gap Pike (Rt. 41N), Wilmington, DE 19808. Tel: 302-998-1930. Email: schedule@wwrr.com. Website: www.wwrr.com. Hrs: Vary. Contact: Carole Wells. GRADE LEVEL: Pre K-5th. GROUP TYPE: All youth groups & homeschoolers. PROGRAM TYPE: Day Trips. REGISTRATION: Online, Phone, Prepay. FOOD: Can bring own food, Place to eat on site, Beverages available. RECOMM. LENGTH OF VISIT: 2 hours. RECOMM. RATIO OF STUDENT TO STAFF: 10:1. ARRIVAL TIPS: Bus parking. COST: Please call for prices. (See main listing on page 42 and Wilmington Featured City Page on page 245.) REGION: New Castle County, Northern DE.

INDOOR AMUSEMENT CENTERS

AMF PRICE LANES, 3215 Kirkwood Hwy., Wilmington, DE 19808. Tel: 302-998-8806. Fax: 302-998-7435. Website: www.amf.com. Hrs: Mon. 11AM-12AM, Tues.-Thurs. 9AM-10PM, Fri. 9AM-1AM, Sat. 12PM-1AM, Sun. 12-10PM. GRADE LEVEL: All grades. GROUP TYPE: All youth groups & homeschoolers. PROGRAM TYPE: Self-guided Activities. COST: Varies.

If you need some fun, come bowling with us at Price Lanes. You can give a bowling party to celebrate a milestone in life, generate friendly competition, or just bring together a group for pure entertainment. We can accommodate any group event, provide just the right food and beverages, and take care of any special needs. AMF staff will help you plan an unforgettably enjoyable event at a strikingly different place. You can choose one of our standard packages or customize a party package that suits your group's individual needs. We'll do all the work while you have all the fun! SUPPORTS DE STATE & NATIONAL LEARNING STANDARDS IN: Physical Education. SUPPORTS SCOUT MERIT BADGE ACHIEVEMENT IN: Physical Ed/Recreation. (See Wilmington Featured City Page on page 245.) REGION: New Castle County, Northern DE.

INTERACTIVE LIVING HISTORY

THE DELAWARE AGRICULTURAL MUSEUM & VILLAGE, 866 N. DuPont Highway, Dover, DE 19901. Tel: 302-734-1618. Hrs: Tues.-Sat. 10AM-3PM. Guided Tours by appt. 4,000 artifacts displayed in the main exhibit building and fifteen historic structures associated with the 19th century farming community. COST: Fee. REGION: Kent County, Central DE.

FORT DELAWARE STATE PARK, 108 Old Reedy Point Bridge Rd., Delaware City, DE 19706. Tel: 302-834-7941. Hrs: Mon.-Fri. 8AM-4PM. Self-guided Tours, Guided Tours by appt. Experience hands-on history at the Union fortress dating back to 1859. COST: Fee. REGION: New Castle County, Northern DE.

GREENBANK MILLS & PHILIPS FARM, 500 Greenbank Rd., Wilmington, DE 19808. Tel: 302-999-9001. Hrs: Sat. 10AM-4PM & by appt. Guided Tours. Focuses on a variety of aspects of the Early Republic (1790-1830): the gristmill, the textile factory, and daily life at the 1794 Philips House and 19th century farm with heritage livestock. COST: Fee. REGION: New Castle County, Northern DE.

HISTORICAL SOCIETY OF DELAWARE, 505 North Market St., Wilmington, DE 19801. Tel: 302-655-7161. Hrs: Mon. 1-5PM, Tues.-Fri. 9AM-5PM. Self-guided Tours, Guided Tours, Workshops. Focus on Delaware's history and culture heritage. Museums and historic sites include Delaware History Center, Delaware History Museum, Old Town Hall, Willingtown Square, The Read House & Gardens and Historic New Castle. COST: Varies. REGION: New Castle County, Northern DE.

JOHN DICKINSON PLANTATION, 340 Kitts Hummock Rd., Dover, DE 19901. Tel: 302-739-3277. Hrs: Tues.-Sat. 10AM-3:30PM; Sun. 1:30-4:30PM. Guided Tours, Group Tours by appt. Historic home of one of the founding fathers of the U.S. COST: Free. REGION: Kent County, Central DE.

KALMAR NYCKEL FOUNDATION MUSEUM & SHIPYARD, 1124 E. 7th St., Wilmington, DE 19801. Tel: 302-429-7447. Hrs: By appt. Sails and Guided Tours. Recreation of the ship that brought the first settlers to the Delaware Valley in 1638 as well as a historic shipyard and museum. COST: Fee. REGION: New Castle County, Northern DE.

MAPLE SUGARING

Follow the maple sugaring process from sap to syrup. Season runs February-March; confirm times with venue. Reserve in the Fall.

ABBOTT'S MILL NATURE CENTER, 15411 Abbott's Pond Rd., Milford, DE. 19963. Tel: 302-422-0847. Hrs: Mon.-Fri. 9AM-4PM. Guided Tours, Guided Activities. Year-round natural, cultural, and agricultural history programs available. COST: Fee. REGION: Sussex County, Southern DE.

ASHLAND NATURE CENTER, Brackenville & Barley Mill Rds., Hockessin, DE 19707. Tel: 302-239-2334. Hrs: Mon.-Fri. 8:30AM-4:30PM. Self-guided Tours, Guided Activities. Offers educational programs as well as four self-guiding nature trails through meadows, woodlands and marshes. COST: Fee. REGION: New Castle County, Northern DE.

SCIENCE & ENVIRONMENTAL EDUCATION

DELAWARE ARCHAEOLOGY MUSEUM, 316 S. Governor's Ave., Dover, DE 19901. Tel: 302-739-4266. Hrs: Tues.-Sat. 9AM-4:30PM, Sun. 1:30-4:30PM. Self-guided Tours, Guided Tours. Exhibits artifacts from the 17th-20th centuries, highlighting more than 11,000 years of human habitation in the state of Delaware. COST: Free. REGION: Kent County, Central DE.

DELAWARE MUSEUM OF NATURAL HISTORY, 4840 Kennett Pike, Wilmington, DE 19807. Tel: 302-658-9111. Hrs: Mon.-Sat. 9:30AM-4:30PM, Sun. 12-4:30PM. Self-guided Tours, Guided Tours, Workshops. Exhibits focus on the natural world. Highlights: Dinosaur Gallery; Hall of Birds; Hall of Mammals; Animal Adaptations; Discovery Room; a simulated coral reef; a Science in Action paleontology lab. COST: Fee. REGION: New Castle County, Northern DE.

IRON HILL MUSEUM, 1355 Old Baltimore Pike, Newark, DE 19702. Tel: 302-368-5703. Hrs: By appt. Guided Tours. Focuses on the natural and cultural history of the Iron Hill area. COST: Fee. REGION: New Castle County, Northern DE.

SOCIAL STUDIES

ABBOTT'S MILL NATURE CENTER, 15411 Abbott's Pond Rd., Milford, DE. 19963. Tel: 302-422-0847. Hrs: Mon.-Fri. 9AM-4PM. Guided Tours, Guided Activities. Year-round natural, cultural and agricultural history programs available. COST: Fee. REGION: Sussex County, Southern DE.

AMSTEL HOUSE, 2 E. 4th St., New Castle, DE 19720. Tel: 302-322-2794. Hrs: Apr. 1-Dec. 31: Wed.-Sat. 11AM-4PM, Sun. 1-4PM. 2nd-12th grade. Guided Tours. One of New Castle's few surviving colonial buildings. COST: Fee. REGION: New Castle County, Northern DE.

DELAWARE HISTORY MUSEUM, 504 Market St., Wilmington, DE 19801. Tel: 302-656-0637. Hrs: Wed.-Fri. 11AM-4PM, Sat. 10AM-4PM. Self-guided Tours, Guided Tours. Features interactive exhibits on Delaware history, including displays of costumes, children's toys and paintings. COST: Fee. REGION: New Castle County, Northern DE.

DELAWARE SPORTS MUSEUM & HALL OF FAME, 801 Shipyard Drive, Wilmington, DE 19801. Tel: 302-425-3263. Hrs: Apr.-Oct.: Tues.-Sat. 12-5PM. Group tours by appt. Self-Guided Tours, Guided Tours. Displays memorabilia, artifacts, uniforms and photographs of Delaware's sports history. COST: Fee. REGION: New Castle County, Northern DE.

DELAWARE STATE POLICE MUSEUM, 1425 N. DuPont Hwy., Dover, DE 19901. Tel: 302-739-7700. Hrs: Mon.-Fri. 9AM-3PM. Self-guided Tours, Guided Tours. Focuses on the history of the State Police in Delaware from its inception in 1923 to the present. COST: Free. REGION: Kent County, Central DE.

DISCOVERSEA SHIPWRECK MUSEUM, 708 Ocean Hwy., 2nd Fl., Fenwick Island, DE 19944. Tel: 302-539-9366. Hrs: Jun.-Aug.: Daily 11AM-8PM; Sept.-May: Sat. & Sun. 11AM-4PM. Weekday tours for school groups available by appt. Self-guided Tours, Guided Tours. Home of one of the largest collections of shipwrecked and recovered artifacts in the Mid-Atlantic. COST: Free. REGION: Sussex County, Southern DE.

GOVERNOR ROSS MANSION & PLANTATION, 1101 North Pine St. Ext., Seaford, DE 19973. Tel: 302-628-9500. Hrs: Sat. & Sun. 1-4PM & by appt. Self-guided Tours, Guided Tours. Explore a complete Victorian Italianate mansion with slave quarters, barns, sheds and spacious grounds. COST: Fee. REGION: Sussex County, Southern DE.

LEGISLATIVE HALL (State Capital), Court St. & Legislative Ave., Dover, DE 19901. To book a tour call 302-739-9194. Hrs: By appt. Guided Tours. Created in 1931, today Legislative Hall provides formal chambers for the Senate and House of Representatives. COST: Free. REGION: Kent County, Central DE.

LEWES HISTORICAL SOCIETY, 110 Shipcarpenter St., Lewes, DE 19958. Tel: 302-645-7670. Hrs: By appt. Guided Tours. Features 12 restored historic properties in one of America's most historic towns. COST: Fee. REGION: Sussex County, Southern DE.

LIGHTSHIP OVERFALLS (LV118), adjacent to Canal Front Park in downtown Lewes, on the Canal, DE 19958. Tel: 302-644-8050. Hrs: By appt. Guided Tours. Decommissioned U.S. Coast Guard vessel that served as a floating lighthouse off the North Atlantic coast from 1938 to 1971. COST: Fee/Free for members. REGION: Sussex County, Southern DE.

NANTICOKE INDIAN MUSEUM, John Williams Hwy. (Rt. 24), Millsboro, DE 19966. Tel: 302-945-7022. Hrs: Tues.-Sat. 10AM-4PM, Sun. 12-4PM. Self-guided Tours, Guided Tours. Exhibits and artifacts give a glimpse into the history of the Nanticoke Indians. COST: Fee. REGION: Sussex County, Southern DE.

OLD STATE HOUSE, 25 The Green, Dover, DE 19901. Tel: 302-739-4266. Hrs: Tues.-Sat. 9AM-4:30PM, Sun. 1:30-4:30PM; Open State Holiday Mondays. Guided Tours. The original home to both state and Kent County governments. Includes information about past legislative and judicial actions that impacted the lives of men, women, children, slaves, and free African-Americans. COST: Free. REGION: Kent County, Central DE.

ROCKWOOD PARK, 610 Shiley Rd., Wilmington, DE 19809. Tel: 302-761-4342. Hrs: Gardens & Park: Daily 6AM-10PM. Guided Tours: Wed.-Sun. on the hour, 10AM-3PM; closed on Mon. & Tues. Guided Tours, Workshops. A 19th century Victorian mansion surrounded by two miles of walking trails, beautiful gardens, forests and streams. Tours and programs focus on nature and Victorian times. COST: $2/child. REGION: New Castle County, Northern DE.

WILMINGTON & WESTERN RAILROAD, 2201 Newport Gap Pike (Rt. 41N), Wilmington, DE 19808. Tel: 302-998-1930. Email: schedule@wwrr.com. Website: www.wwrr.com. Hrs: Vary. Contact: Carole Wells. GRADE LEVEL: Pre K-5th. GROUP TYPE: All youth groups & homeschoolers. PROGRAM TYPE: Day Trips. REGISTRATION: Online, Phone, Prepay. FOOD: Can bring own food, Place to eat on site, Beverages available. RECOMM. LENGTH OF VISIT: 2 hours. RECOMM. RATIO OF STUDENT TO STAFF: 10:1. ARRIVAL TIPS: Bus parking. COST: Please call for prices.

All Aboard Delaware's Museum in Motion! Wilmington & Western Railroad offers trips back in time where you can ride on vintage trains. Create childhood memories - Steam and diesel powered locomotives dating to the early 1900's. School and Day Camp trains are part of a school-railroad curriculum cooperative. These trips offer a scenic trip with narration especially for young railroaders. Your students will come away from this visit with a new appreciation of the men and machines that built this country and for the history of the Red Clay Valley. www.wwrr.com. 302-998-1930. SUPPORTS DE STATE & NATIONAL LEARNING STANDARDS IN: History/Social Studies. SUPPORTS SCOUT MERIT BADGE ACHIEVEMENT IN: Social Studies. (See Wilmington Featured City Page on page 245.) REGION: New Castle County, Northern DE.

WINTERTHUR MUSEUM & COUNTRY ESTATE, Route 52 (5105 Kennett Pike, Winterthur, DE 19735. Tel: 302-888-4792. Hrs: Tues.-Sun. 10AM-5PM. Self-guided Tours, Guided Tours. Museum's collections of antiques and Americana with a hands-on learning room. Learn about country estate life by exploring the farmland, the 60-acre naturalistic Garden and the fairy-tale children's garden, Enchanted Woods. COST: Fee. REGION: New Castle County, Northern DE.

THEATER · DANCE · MUSIC

DELAWARE SYMPHONY ORCHESTRA, 818 North Market Street, Wilmington, DE 19801. Tel: 302-656-7442. Hrs: Vary. K-8th grade. Presents more than 40 classical, chamber and special concerts per season, plus numerous educational programs and activities. COST: Fee. REGION: New Castle County, Northern DE.

DELAWARE THEATRE COMPANY, 200 Water St., Wilmington, DE 19801. Tel: 302-594-1100. Hrs: Vary. 6th-12th grade. Programming includes a mix of the classics as well as contemporary plays and musicals. COST: Fee. REGION: New Castle, Northern DE.

DUPONT THEATRE, DuPont Building, 1007 N. Market St & West 11th St., Wilmington, DE 19801. Tel: 1-800-338-0881. Hrs: Vary. Pre K-9th grade. Presents a Children's Series which includes performances such as The Legend of Sleepy Hollow and The Velveteen Rabbit. COST: Fee. REGION: New Caste County, Northern DE.

THE NEW CANDLELIGHT THEATRE, 2208 Millers Rd., Ardentown, DE 19810. Tel: 302-475-2313. Fax: 302-475-2320. Email: nctboxoffice@gmail.com. Website: www.newcandlelighttheatre.com. Hrs: 10AM-5PM. Contact: Maureen T. Cotellese, Box Office Manager; AJ Garcia, Group Sales Manager. GRADE LEVEL: All grades. GROUP TYPE: All youth groups & homeschoolers. PROGRAM TYPE: Day Trips, Performances, Workshops. MAX. GROUP SIZE: 150. MIN. GROUP SIZE: 2. REGISTRA-TION: Mail, Phone, Prepay. TICKET/VOUCHER RETURN POLICY: Tickets are non-refundable, non-exchangeable. FOOD: Buffet dinner included. RECOMM. LENGTH OF VISIT: 4-4.5 hours. RECOMM. RATIO OF STUDENT TO STAFF: 10:1. ARRIVAL TIPS: Expedite check in, Bus parking, Bus drop off and pick up at designated entrance. COST: $32-55.

The New Candlelight Theatre, nestled in the heart of Arden, DE, located just 10 minutes from downtown Wilmington and 30 minutes from Center City, Philadelphia, is a theatrical experience that will thrill and excite the most seasoned of theatergoers! As our guests, you will enjoy a unique dining experience featuring a gourmet buffet, salad bar and desserts, Broadway caliber productions starring actors from around the country who have starred on Broadway, national tours, regional theatre, television, and film. Upcoming performances include "Oklahoma" and "Joseph and the Amazing Technicolor Dreamcoat." Call now to reserve. SUPPORTS DE STATE & NATIONAL LEARNING STANDARDS IN: The Arts. SUPPORTS SCOUT MERIT BADGE ACHIEVEMENT IN: The Arts, Performing Arts. (See Wilmington Featured City Page on page 245.) REGION: New Castle, Northern DE.

THE PAPER BAG PLAYERS, 225 West 99th St., NY, NY 10025. Performance location: Nov. 14 & 15, 2009 at Mitchell Hall, University of Delaware in Newark, DE. Tel: 800-777-2247/212-663-0390. Fax: 212-663-1076. Email: pbagp@verizon.net. Website: www.thepaperbagplayers.org. Hrs: Vary. GRADE LEVEL: K–3rd grade. GROUP TYPE: All youth groups and homeschoolers. PROGRAM TYPE: Performances. COST: Varies. (See ad and main listing in NYC on page 125.) REGION: New Castle, Northern DE.

NEW JERSEY

ADVENTURE SPORTS & OUTDOOR LEARNING

COMBAT SPORTS, La Valley Dr., Manalapan, NJ 07726. Tel: 866-926-6228. Email: info@combatsportsusa.com. Website: www.combatsportsusa.com. Hrs: Daily 9AM-8PM in season. Contacts: Robert & Sue. GRADE LEVEL: 4th-adults. GROUP TYPE: All youth groups. PROGRAM TYPE: Day Trips, Self-guided Activities. REGISTRATION: Mail, Phone, Submit waiver forms prior to visit, Prepay. FOOD: Can bring own food, Place to eat on site, Beverages available. RECOMM. LENGTH OF VISIT: 2 hours. RECOMM. RATIO OF STUDENT TO STAFF: 10:1 to 15:1. ARRIVAL TIPS: Expedite check in, Bus parking. COST: Inquire about special group rates.

New Jersey's ultimate outdoor laser tag game that's a fun, high-energy, adrenaline-pumping activity suitable for ages 9 and up. Experience the excitement at our 20 acre park, conveniently located off Route 33 in Manalapan (Central NJ). We can also travel to your location to hold events with our inflatable obstacle field. We utilize safe, high tech infrared units with a range of 900+ feet. We accommodate up to 150 children an hour. Special school pricing makes it affordable. Worked with over 120 schools and summer programs in 2008; references available. SUPPORTS NJ STATE & NATIONAL LEARNING STANDARDS IN: Physical Education, Team Building. REGION: Monmouth County, Central NJ.

AMUSEMENT & THEME PARKS

BLACKBEARD'S CAVE, 136 Rte. 9, Bayville, NJ 08721. Tel: 732-914-1896. Fax: 732-286-1564. Website: www.blackbeardscave.com. Hrs: Memorial Day-Oct. 31, Daily 9AM-12AM. Off Season: Golf driving range and arcade open year round. Contact: Rich Kopka. GRADE LEVEL: All grades. GROUP TYPE: All youth groups & homeschoolers. PROGRAM TYPE: Day Trips, Self-guided Activities. MAX. GROUP SIZE: 1000. COST: Group rates: $14 per person for groups 100+.

Blackbeard's Cave, located at the Jersey Shore, is a fun filled entertainment center suitable for groups of all ages, sizes and budgets. The attractions at the park include an amazing 1/4 mile Go-Kart track with bridges and tunnels, Bumper Boats with a cave & real waterfalls, a Eurobungee, jousting, an arcade, an award-winning 20-hole Miniature Golf Course, Driving Range, Batting Cages, Rock Climbing, Water Wars, and the exciting Splatter Zone Paintball Arena. We also have a special area just for the little ones, Adventure Station at Blackbeard's Cave offers over a dozen children's amusement rides. We also feature a Snack Bar and a Family Restaurant, with running HO train layouts, available to host outdoor Pizza or BBQ Parties in our Picnic Area. Our park is dedicated to Safety, Cleanliness and Fun. SUPPORTS NJ STATE & NATIONAL LEARNING STANDARDS IN: Physical Education. SUPPORTS SCOUT MERIT BADGE ACHIEVEMENT IN: Physical Ed/Recreation. (See Regional Highlights on page 10.) REGION: Ocean County, Southern NJ.

JENKINSON'S BOARDWALK, 300 Ocean Avenue, Point Pleasant Beach, NJ 08742. Tel: 732-892-3274. Fax: 732-892-3069. Email: groupsales.jenkinsons@comcast.net. Website: www.jenkinsons.com. Hrs: Year round. Call for seasonal schedules. Contact: Deanne Heckel. GRADE LEVEL: All grades. GROUP TYPE: All youth groups & homeschoolers. PROGRAM TYPE: Day Trips, Self-guided Tours, Guided Tours, Workshops. Amusement park rides, beach, miniature golf, funhouse, and an aquarium. COST: Varies. (See ad and main listing under Animals-Aquariums-Zoos on page 46.) REGION: Ocean County, Southern NJ.

ANIMALS • AQUARIUMS • ZOOS

ADVENTURE AQUARIUM, Delaware River Waterfront, 1 Aquarium Dr., Camden, NJ 08103. Tel: 800-616-JAWS. Email: groups@adventureaquarium.com. Website: www.adventureaquarium.com. Hrs: Daily 9:30AM-5PM and holidays. Contact: Mike Perez. GRADE LEVEL: All grades. GROUP TYPE: All youth groups & homeschoolers. PROGRAM TYPE: Day Trips, Self-guided Tours, Guided Tours, Workshops. REGISTRATION: Mail, Online, Phone, Prepay, Tickets mailed prior to visit. TICKET/VOUCHER RETURN POLICY: No refunds/returns; a credit in the amount can be used for a future visit. FOOD: Variety of menu selections, Vegetarian, Can bring own food, Place to eat on site, Beverages available, Meal vouchers. RECOMM. LENGTH OF VISIT: 2-2.5 hours. RECOMM. RATIO OF STUDENT TO STAFF: 5:1. ARRIVAL TIPS: Expedite check in, Bus parking, Bus drop off and pick up at designated entrance. COST: School Groups: $10 students, complimentary chaperones 1:10 ratio, $10 additional chaperones. Youth Groups: $9.50 child (2-12), $13 adult.

Adventure Aquarium on the Camden Waterfront features nearly 200,000 square feet of exhibit space, over 2 million gallons of water, and over 60 exhibits filled with exotic and amazing creatures! Visitors are in for adventure as they visit the West African River Experience featuring hippopotamuses and over 20 species of African birds in a free-flight aviary. Surround yourself with nearly 30 sharks in a suspended 40-foot walk-through tunnel of the Shark Realm; observe the mystery of the Shark Rays and the rare Great Hammerhead in Ocean Realm; dive into one of the immersive movies showing in the 4D Theater; catch a penguin, seal or hippo show; or attend one of the various scheduled animal feedings. Our motto is "Don't Just Look…Touch!" Now experience and touch sharks, jellyfish, lobsters, stingrays and so much more in an all-new way with five interactive attractions! Advanced reservations required, call 800-616-JAWS. For more information and updates, visit www.AdventureAquarium.com. SUPPORTS NJ STATE & NATIONAL LEARNING STANDARDS IN: Science, Math. SUPPORTS SCOUT MERIT BADGE ACHIEVEMENT IN: Animal Science. (See Regional Highlights on page 12.) REGION: Camden County, Southern NJ.

BERGEN COUNTY ZOOLOGICAL PARK, 216 Forest Ave., Paramus, NJ 07652. Tel: 201-262-3771. Hrs: Daily 10AM-4:30PM. Self-guided Tours, Workshops. Animals from North and South America. Exhibit areas include: The North American Great Plains exhibit; The Farmyard; The Central and South American animals; The North American Wetlands Aviary. There is a nearby playground.COST: Fee. REGION: Bergen County, Northern NJ.

CAPE MAY COUNTY PARK AND ZOO, Rte. 9 & Crest Haven Rd., Cape May Court House, NJ 08210. Tel: 609-465-5271. Hrs: Fall/Winter: Daily 10AM-3:45PM, Spring/Summer: Daily 10AM-4:45PM. Self-guided Tours, Guided Tours by appt. Nearly 80 acres of exhibits including over 175 different species of mammals, birds, amphibians and reptiles totaling nearly 550 animals. COST: Free/Fee. REGION: Cape May County, Southern NJ.

JENKINSON'S AQUARIUM & BOARDWALK, 300 Ocean Ave., Point Pleasant Beach, NJ 08742. Tel: 732-892-3274. Fax: 732-892-3069. Email: groupsales.jenkinsons@comcast.net. Website: www.jenkinsons.com. Hrs: Year round. Call for seasonal schedules. Contact: Deanne Heckel. GRADE LEVEL: All grades. GROUP TYPE: All youth groups & homeschoolers. PROGRAM TYPE: Day Trips, Self-Guided Tours, Guided Tours, Workshops. COST: Varies.

You can combine fun and learning at Jenkinson's Aquarium & Boardwalk. Jenkinson's offers many group packages and rates for all its facilities. Our Aquarium is a place for discovery. Sharks, seals, penguins, and tropical birds are all found in their own habitats. Knowledgeable staff members provide guided tours and hands-on learning experiences. Groups over 20 people can enjoy fun-filled packages including: the aquarium, miniature golf, funhouse, and amusement park rides. All groups and all ages have fun at Jenkinson's! SUPPORTS NJ STATE & NATIONAL LEARNING STANDARDS IN: Science, Health & Safety. SUPPORTS SCOUT MERIT BADGE ACHIEVEMENT IN: Science & Environment. REGION: Ocean County, Southern NJ.

JOHNSON'S CORNER FARM, 133 Church Rd, Medford, New Jersey 08055. Tel: 609-654-8643. Fax: 609-953-3554. Email: reservation@johnsonsfarm.com. Hrs: 8AM-7PM. Website: www.johnsonsfarm.com. Contact: Bonnie. GRADE LEVEL: Children ages 2-12. GROUP TYPE: School, Scout, Homeschoolers, After-school groups. PROGRAM TYPE: Day Trips, Self-guided Tours, Guided Tours, Guided Activities, Self-guided Activities. MAX. GROUP SIZE: 300. COST: Varies, check our website. (See ad and main listing under Farms-Pick Your Own on page 53.) REGION: Burlington County, Southern NJ.

LAKOTA WOLF PRESERVE, 89 Mt. Pleasant Rd., Columbia, NJ 07832. Tel: 877-733-9653. Hrs: Tues.-Sun., call for hrs. Guided Tours. Tundra, Timber, and Arctic wolves viewed in a natural surrounding. COST: Fee. REGION: Warren County, Northern NJ.

MARINE MAMMAL STRANDING CENTER, 3625 Brigantine Blvd., Brigantine, NJ 08203. Tel: 609-266-0538. Hrs: Winter: Sat. 10AM-4PM; May 2-June 12: Sat. 10AM-4PM & Sun. 11AM-2PM; Jun.13-Sept. 7 daily 10AM-4PM. Guided Tours. Dedicated to the rescue and rehabilitation of stranded or otherwise stressed marine mammals and sea turtles. COST: Sugg. donation/Fee. REGION: Atlantic County, Southern NJ.

PEQUEST TROUT HATCHERY, 605 Pequest Rd., Oxford, NJ 07863. Tel: 908-637-4125. Hrs: Mon-Fri, 10AM-4PM. Self-guided Tours, Guided Tours by app't. Offers visitors a look at how more than 600,000 brook, brown and rainbow trout are raised each year for stocking the public waters of New Jersey. COST: Free. REGION: Warren County, Northern NJ.

POPCORN PARK ZOO, Humane Way, Forked River, NJ 08731. Tel: 609-693-1900. Hrs: Mon.-Fri. 11AM-4:30PM, Sat. & Sun. 11AM-4:15PM. Self-guided Tours. Sanctuary and refuge established to provide a refuge for sick wildlife. COST: Fee. REGION: Ocean County, Southern NJ.

THE RAPTOR TRUST, 1390 White Bridge Rd., Millington, NJ 07946. Tel: 908-647-1091. Hrs: Daily during daylight hours. Self-guided Tours, Workshops. One of the premier wild bird rehabilitation centers in the United States. COST: Fee. REGION: Morris County, Northern NJ.

SPACE FARMS ZOO AND MUSEUM, 218 Rte. 519, Sussex, NJ 07461. Tel: 973-875-5800. Website: www.spacefarms.com. Hrs: May 1-Oct. 31, Daily 9AM-5PM. GRADE LEVEL: All grades. GROUP TYPE: All youth groups & homeschoolers. PROGRAM TYPE: Day Trips, Self-guided Tours. COST: Varies.

Tour and explore nature and history. Visit hundreds of wild animals & tour unique displays of rural American history. Space Farms Zoo and Museum has provided fun and educational insights into the animal world since 1927. The Zoo is the largest privately owned collection of North American wildlife in the world and includes over 100 different species. The Museum houses over 100,000 items of "America," including antique cars, wagons, Indian artifacts, farm equipment, dolls, and more. Recreation areas include miniature golf, playground, and picnic tables. Family atmosphere restaurant. Open 7 days a week through October 31. Call for info and directions. Visit our website: www.spacefarms.com for further information. SUPPORTS NJ STATE & NATIONAL LEARNING STANDARDS IN: Science, Social Studies. SUPPORTS SCOUT MERIT BADGE ACHIEVEMENT IN: Animal Science, American Heritage. REGION: Sussex County, Northern NJ.

TURTLE BACK ZOO, 560 Northfield Ave., West Orange, NJ 07052. Tel: 973-731-5800. Hrs: Mon.-Sat. 10AM-4:30PM, Sun. 11AM-5:30PM. Self-guided Tours, Guided Tours. Naturalistic exhibits. Highlights: The American Alligator; Black Bear; Essex Farm; Great Plains; Prairie Dogs; Reptile Center; River Otter; Wolf Woods; Penguin Coast; South America. COST: Fee. REGION: Essex County, Northern NJ.

ART • ARCHITECTURE • SCULPTURE

GROUNDS FOR SCULPTURE, 18 Fairgrounds Rd., Hamilton, NJ 08619. Tel: 609-586-0616. Hrs: Tues.-Sun., 10AM-6PM. Self-guided Tours, Guided Tours, Workshops. Sculpture garden that displays works by American and international sculptors in a variety of styles and media. COST: Fee. REGION: Mercer County, Central NJ.

HIRAM BLAUVELT ART MUSEUM, 705 Kinderkamack Rd., Oradell, NJ 07649. Tel: 201-261-0012. Hrs: Wed.-Fri. 10AM-4PM, Sat. & Sun. 2-5PM. Self-Guided Tours, Guided Tours. Wildlife art and big game collections of the late Hiram Blauvelt, philanthropist, conservationist and collector. COST: Free/Sugg Donation. REGION: Bergen County, Northern NJ.

HUNTERDON MUSEUM OF ART, 7 Lower Center St., Clinton, NJ 08809. Tel: 908-735-8415. Hrs: Tues.-Sun. 11AM-5PM. Self-guided Tours, Guided Tours, Workshops. Presents changing exhibitions of contemporary art in a 19th century stone mill. COST: Fee. REGION: Hunterdon County, Central NJ.

THE JANE VOORHEES ZIMMERLI ART MUSEUM, 71 Hamilton St., New Brunswick, NJ 08901. Tel: 732-932-7237. Fax: 732-932-8201. Hrs: Tues.-Fri. 10AM-4:30PM, Sat.-Sun. 12-5PM. (Closed Aug., Closed Tues. in July). Guided Tours. Collection includes 50,000 works of art. Highlights: Russian and Soviet art, French nineteenth-century art and American 19th and 20th century art with a concentration on early 20th century and contemporary prints. COST: Fee. REGION: Middlesex County, Central NJ.

MONTCLAIR ART MUSEUM, 3 S. Mountain Ave., Montclair, NJ 07042. Tel: 973-746-5555. Hrs: Wed.-Sun. 12AM-5PM. 2nd-12th grade. Self-guided Tours, Guided Tours, Workshops. Collects, preserves and presents American and Native American art, presentations of under recognized artists and a commitment to the artist and culture of New Jersey. COST: Varies. REGION: Essex County, Northern NJ.

THE NOYES MUSEUM OF ART, 733 Lily Lake Rd., Oceanville, NJ 08231. Tel: 609-652-8848. Hrs: Tues.-Sat. 10AM-4:30PM, Sun. 12-5PM. Self-guided Tours, Guided Tours, Workshops. Fine arts museum that features American art, especially folk art & crafts. COST: Fee. REGION: Atlantic County, Southern NJ.

PRINCETON UNIVERSITY ART MUSEUM, McCormick Hall, Princeton, NJ 08544. Tel: 609-258-3788. Hrs: Tues.-Sat. 10AM–5PM, Sun. 1–5PM. Self-guided Tours, Guided Tours. Over 60,000 works of art covering the globe and stretching from the past to today. COST: Free. REGION: Mercer County, Central NJ.

THE VISUAL ART CENTER OF NEW JERSEY, 68 Elm St., Summit, NJ 07901. Tel: 908-273-9121. Fax: 908-273-1457. Email: jayres@artcenternj.org. Website: www.artcenternj.org. Hrs: Program Dates: Sept. 2009–Jun. 2010, Tours available Mon.–Fri., Times - 10–11:30AM, 12:30–2PM, 3:30–5PM. Contact: Jennifer Ayres. GRADE LEVEL: All grades. GROUP TYPE: All youth groups & homeschoolers. PROGRAM TYPE: Day Trips, Exhibits, Guided Activities, Guided Tours. MAX. GROUP SIZE: 50. MIN. GROUP SIZE: 5. COST: $5 per student.

The Visual Art Center of New Jersey offers an exciting art education program for teachers and their students with our Gallery Education Tour Program. The Gallery Education Tour program gives students (Preschool – High School) a unique opportunity to learn about contemporary art through Main Gallery exhibitions and create art with professional teaching artists in the Art Center's state of the art studios. The program consists of 3 age specific programs: The Amazing Artbox (Preschool Program), Artful Adventures (Elementary/Middle School Program) and Art Tech (High School Program). SUPPORTS NJ STATE & NATIONAL LEARNING STANDARDS IN: Visual Arts. SUPPORTS SCOUT MERIT BADGE ACHIEVEMENT IN: Visual Arts. REGION: Union County, Northern NJ.

WHEATON ARTS AND CULTURAL CENTER, 1501 Glasstown Rd. (Exit 26, Rte. 55), Millville, NJ 08332. Tel: 800-998-4552. Fax: 856-825-2410. Email: mail@wheatonarts.org. Website: www.wheatonarts.org. Hrs: Jan.-Mar.: Fri., Sat. & Sun. 10AM-5PM; Apr.-Dec., Tues.-Sun. 10AM-5PM. GRADE LEVEL: All grades. GROUP TYPE: All youth groups and homeschoolers. PROGRAM TYPE: Day Trips, Self-guided Tours, Guided Tours, Workshops. COST: Minimum: $6.00 per student.

One of southern New Jersey's best arts destinations. The Museum of American Glass has the most comprehensive collection of American glass in the country including the world's largest bottle. Watch hot molten glass transformed into works of art during the Glass Studio demonstration. Visit the artists in the Pottery, Woodworking and Flameworking Studios. The Down Jersey Folklife Center showcases southern New Jersey's rich cultural traditions. Open year round. Playground and picnic area. Gallery of Fine Craft and museum stores. Full service restaurant located adjacent to the grounds. Call for group rates and information. SUPPORTS NJ STATE & NATIONAL LEARNING STANDARDS IN: Core Curriculum Standards. SUPPORTS SCOUT MERIT BADGE ACHIEVEMENT IN: The Arts. REGION: Cumberland County, Southern NJ.

ARTS & CRAFTS

GLASSWORKS STUDIO INC., 151 South St., Ste 103B, Morristown, NJ 07960. Telephone: 973-656-0800. Fax: 973-656-0881. Email: umakeglass@verizon.net. Website: www.umakeglass.com. Hrs: Weekday mornings until Noon by reservation only; walk-ins welcome during regular studio hours. Check website for times. Contact: Stacey Schlosser. GRADE LEVEL: Pre K & up. GROUP TYPE: All youth groups & homeschoolers. PROGRAM TYPE: Day Trips, Workshops. MAX. GROUP SIZE: 60. REGISTRATION: Mail, Online, Phone. FOOD: Place to eat not within site. RECOMM. LENGTH OF VISIT: 1.5 hours. COST: Varies.

A glassworks creative experience is like no other! Your students will be entertained, educated and enthralled with their ability to create an original piece of glass art. Each piece is kiln fired and possibly kiln formed to the student's choice. They are further processed and packaged for pick up and distribution in approximately one week. Groups are welcome by appointment Tuesday through Friday 9AM-12PM for 20 – 60 students. Smaller groups and individuals are welcome during public studio hours. Note: Schools returning to Glassworks get 2 staff projects for free. SUPPORTS NJ STATE & NATIONAL LEARNING STANDARDS IN: The Arts. SUPPORTS SCOUT MERIT BADGE ACHIEVEMENT IN: The Arts. REGION: Morris County, Northern NJ.

BOTANICAL GARDENS & NATURE CENTERS

CAMDEN CHILDREN'S GARDEN, 3 Riverside Dr., Camden, New Jersey 08103. Tel: 856-365-8733. Fax: 856-365-9750. Email: info@camdenchildrensgarden.org. Website: www.CamdenChildrensGarden.org. Hrs: 10AM-4 PM. Contact: Cate Rigoulot. GRADE LEVEL: Pre K-8th. GROUP TYPE: All youth groups. PROGRAM TYPE: Day Trips, Self-guided Tours, Guided Activities, Workshops. MAX. GROUP SIZE: 500. MIN. GROUP SIZE: 10. REGISTRATION: Mail, Phone, Prepay. FOOD: Can bring own food, Beverages available. RECOMM. LENGTH OF VISIT: 2 hours. RECOMM. RATIO OF STU-DENT TO STAFF: 5:1. ARRIVAL TIPS: Bus Parking, Bus drop off and pick up at desig-nated entrance. COST: $6.00 Child - Group Rate $5.50 for additional chaperones.

Visit the Camden Children's Garden and enjoy the various themed gardens, learn about butterflies, ride some of our amusements & enjoy a day at the Garden. On-site Garden Lessons are available, offered on the grounds and designed for students K–8th. All of our lessons are aligned with the NJ Core Curriculum Content Standards and are between 30-45 minutes. Costs range from $55.00 to $80.00 per lesson. Group admission price is $6.00 per student, which includes admission and two tokens to ride the Spring Butterfly, Train, or Carousel. One adult is required for every five (5) students/children and receives free admission. Other adults in the group are $5.50. SUPPORTS NJ STATE & NATIONAL LEARNING STANDARDS IN: Science. SUPPORTS SCOUT MERIT BADGE ACHIEVEMENT IN: Science. (See Regional Highlights on page 13.) REGION: Camden County, Southern NJ.

CORA HARTSHORN ARBORETUM AND BIRD SANCTUARY, 324 Forest Dr. S., Short Hills, NJ 07078. Tel: 973-376-3587. Hrs: Mon.-Fri. 9AM–4:30PM, Sat. 10AM-3PM. Self-guided Tours, Guided Tours. Students experience the natural world through creative, interactive indoor and outdoor activities. COST: Free/Fee. REGION: Essex County, Northern NJ.

FRELINGHUYSEN ARBORETUM, 53 E. Hanover Ave., Morristown, NJ 07962. Tel: 973-326-7600. Hrs: Grounds open daily from 8AM-Sunset. Information Center Daily 9AM-4:30PM. Self-guided Tours, Guided Tours. 127-acres of woodlands, meadows, gardens with horticultural activities. COST: Free/Fee. REGION: Morris County, Northern NJ.

LEAMING'S RUN GARDENS, 1845 Rte. 9 N., Swainton, NJ 08210. Tel: 609-465-5871. Hrs: Mid-May-Mid-Oct.: Daily 9:30AM-5PM. Self-guided Tours, Guided Tours. 25 themed gardens, fernery and shady bamboo grove. COST: Fee. REGION: Cape May County, Southern NJ.

LEONARD J. BUCK GARDEN, Somerset County Park Commission, 11 Layton Rd., Far Hills, NJ 07931. Tel: 908-234-2677. Hrs: Mon.-Fri. 10AM-4PM, Sat. 10AM-5PM, Sun. 12-5PM (No weekend hours Dec.-Mar.). Self-guided, Guided Tours. Alpine and woodland gardens situated in a 33-acre wooded stream valley. COST: Free/Fee/Sugg. Donation. REGION: Somerset County, Central NJ.

NEW JERSEY BOTANICAL GARDEN, Ringwood State Park, Morris Rd., Ringwood, NJ 07456. Tel: 973-962-9534. Self-guided Tours, Guided Tours, Workshops. Contains formal gardens, winding paths and a safe haven for unusual plant species from around the world. COST: Free/Fee. REGION: Passaic County, Northern NJ.

REEVES-REED ARBORETUM, 165 Hobart Ave., Summit, NJ 07901. Tel: 908-273-8787. Hrs: Daily dawn-to-dusk. Self-guided Tours, Guided Tours, Workshops. Trees, shrubs and herbaceous plants are identified in their natural settings for study and appreciation. Native flora, new plant introductions and unusual specimens that can be grown in this region are also on display. COST: Free/Fee. REGION: Union County, Northern NJ.

CAVES & MINES

FRANKLIN MINERAL MUSEUM, 32 Evans St., Franklin, New Jersey 07416. Tel: 973-827-3481. Fax: 973-827-0149. Email: mineralinfo@earthlink.net. Website: www.franklinmineralmuseum.com. Hrs: Mar.-Dec., Mon.-Fri. 10AM-4PM, Sat. 10AM-5PM, Sun. 11AM-5PM. Contact: Doreen Longo. GRADE LEVEL: All grades. GROUP TYPE: All youth groups. PROGRAM TYPE: Day Trips, Self-guided Tours, Guided Tours, Workshops. COST: Varies. (See ad and main listing under Science & Environmental Ed. on page 63.) REGION: Sussex County, Northern NJ.

CHILDREN'S MUSEUMS

COMMUNITY CHILDREN'S MUSEUM, 77 E. Blackwell St., Dover, NJ 07801. Tel: 973-366-9060. Hrs: Thurs.-Sat. 10AM-5PM. Hrs: By appt. for groups of 10+. Self-guided Tours. Contextual interactive exhibits focusing on art, science and world cultures. COST: Fee. REGION: Morris County, Northern NJ.

GARDEN STATE DISCOVERY MUSEUM, 2040 Springdale Rd., Ste. 100, Cherry Hill, NJ 08003. Tel: 856-424-1233. Hrs: Daily 9:30AM-5:30PM. Infant-10 yrs. Self-guided Tours, Guided Tours, Workshops. 15 large interactive areas that focus on science, art and world cultures. COST: Fee. REGION: Camden County, Southern NJ.

IMAGINE THAT CHILDREN'S MUSEUM, 4 Vreeland Rd., Florham Park, NJ 07932. Tel: 973-966-8000. Fax: 973-966-8990. Hrs: 10AM-5:30PM Contact: Maria or Deborah for field trip reservations. E-mail: imaginethatmuseum@aol.com. Website: www.imaginethatmuseum.com. GRADE LEVEL: Pre K-2nd. GROUP TYPE: All youth groups. PROGRAM TYPE: Day Trips, Self-guided Tours, Self-guided Activities, Guided Activities, Performances. MAX. GROUP SIZE: 250. MIN. GROUP SIZE: 10. REGISTRATION: Phone. FOOD: Variety, Can bring own food, Place to eat on site, Beverages available. RECOMM. LENGTH OF VISIT: 2-2.5 hours. RECOMM. RATIO OF STUDENT TO STAFF: 4:1 ARRIVAL TIPS: Bus Parking. COST: $8 per student.

Imagine That Discovery Museum for Children features more than 50 exhibits with hands-on learning opportunities for kids Pre-K to Grade 2. We have a Pirate Ship, real Fire Truck, Car and Airplane, as well as Space Shuttle, Dance Studio, Grocery Store, Arts & Crafts area and much more! Safe, clean indoor environment perfect for all seasons and weather. Private lunch rooms, on-site cafe, Gift Shop and live performance puppet shows make Imagine That a terrific place to bring your little ones. Birthday Parties and special occasion packages available. Ample Free Parking! www.imaginethatmuseum.com. SUPPORTS NJ STATE & NATIONAL LEARNING STANDARDS IN: The Arts, English, History/Social Studies, Science. SUPPORTS NJ SCOUT MERIT BADGE ACHIEVEMENT IN: The Arts, Family Life, Health & Safety, Life Skills, Performing Arts, Safety, Social Studies, Science/Technology. REGION: Morris County, Northern NJ.

NEW JERSEY CHILDREN'S MUSEUM, 599 Valley Health Plaza, Paramus, NJ 07652. Tel: 201-262-5151. Hrs: Groups: Mon.-Fri. 10AM-6PM. Pre K-1st grades. Self-guided Tours, Performances. Over thirty different hands-on exhibits. COST: Fee. REGION: Bergen County, Northern NJ.

FARMS • PICK-YOUR-OWN • MAZES

ABMA'S FARM, 700 Lawlins Rd., Wyckoff, NJ 07481. Tel: 201-891-0278. Fax: 201-848-9721. Website: www.abmasfarm.com. Hrs: Open all year. Farm Tours in Spring and Summer by appt only; Hayride/pumpkin picking in Fall by appt only. GRADE LEVEL: Spring and summer, K-5th; Hayride/Pumpkin picking, Pre K-up. GROUP TYPE: School & youth groups. PROGRAM TYPE: Day Trips, Self-guided Activities, Guided Tours. MAX GROUP SIZE: 30. MIN.GROUP SIZE: 20. REGISTRATION: Phone. FOOD: Beverages available. RECOMM. LENGTH OF VISIT: 1-2 hours. RECOMM. RATIO OF STUDENT TO STAFF: 10:1. COST: Varies.

Abma's, a 28 acre working farm, still produces fresh poultry, eggs, and 80 varieties of vegetables each year to sell in their quaint 200-year-old Dutch barn. The farm promotes agriculture by offering prearranged farm tours weekdays in the spring and summer for school (K-5th) during the growing season. Fall Season: Mon.-Fri. prearranged hayrides and pumpkin picking, Pre K-8th and youth groups. Abma's also rents incubators to witness the egg-hatching process. They sell fertilized eggs and provide information to teachers. This unique classroom experience brings animal nature first hand to your students! Abma's Farm takes back the chicks. (See ad under Science on page 62.) REGION: Bergen County, Northern NJ.

DEMAREST FARMS, 244 Werimus Rd., Hillsdale, NJ 07642. Tel: 201-666-0350. Website: www.demarestfarms.com. Hrs: Daily from 8AM-7PM during season; weekday pick-your-own reservation slots from 10AM-4PM; weekend pick-your-own 10AM-4:30PM. Recreational farm tours start 1st week of Sept. with hayride and apple picking. Pumpkin picking starts Sept. 22. Call for details. GRADE LEVEL: Pre K-8th. GROUP TYPE: All youth groups & homeschoolers. PROGRAM TYPE: Day Trips, Self-guided Tours. COST: Call for details.

Demarest Farms, located in a lovely country setting, only 20 minutes from the GW Bridge. Bergen County's only pick-your-own Apples, Pumpkins and Peaches!!! Educational farm tours, where children get a real feel of farm life. Apple picking begins the first week in September. Many varieties of apples. Many trees have apples close to the ground so little pickers have the experience of picking their own apples. Pumpkin picking begins the last week of September through October. Hayrides to the orchard. Halloween Corn Maze, where children learn to work together to reach their goal. Picnics allowed. And don't forget to stop by our country store to bring back fall and Halloween decorations for the classroom. Bakery, salad bar, deli, fruits & vegetables, and gourmet food and ice-cream. SUPPORTS NJ STATE & NATIONAL LEARNING STANDARDS IN: Science, Social Studies. SUPPORTS SCOUT MERIT BADGE ACHIEVEMENT IN: Science. REGION: Bergen County, Northern NJ.

HILLVIEW FARMS, 223 Meyersville Rd., Gillette, NJ 07933. Tel: 908-647-0957. Fax: 908-647-6819. Website: www.hillviewfarmsnj.com. Hrs: Guided tours - Mid-Sept.-Oct., Mon.-Fri. 9AM-3PM; Regular hrs. - Sun.-Sat. 10AM-6PM. Contact: Erin Haley. GRADE LEVEL: All grades. GROUP TYPE: All youth groups & homeschoolers. PROGRAM TYPE: Day Trips, Guided Tours, Guided Activities. MIN. GROUP SIZE: 10. COST: $9.50 per person, $3 per chaperone.

Set in the beautiful hills of the Watchung Mountain range, Hillview farms is a quaint, old fashioned, and up to date working farm with a family tradition of 5 generations. With more than 2,000 apple trees and 500 peach trees on 57 acres and numerous farm animals, there is so much to see and do on a guided tour. Meet Farmer Skeeter, learn to press cider and wash potatoes, walk through the fields, collect items for stone soup, hunt for animal burrows and footprints, dig for potatoes, say hello to nubian goats, guinea hens, peahens, peacocks, Indian runner ducks, observe active bee hives, feel the warm down feathers of a new baby chick and taste fresh apple cider! Come visit us! You won't forget it! SUPPORTS NJ STATE & NATIONAL LEARNING STANDARDS IN: Science, Technology. SUPPORTS SCOUT MERIT BADGE ACHIEVEMENT IN: Science/Technology. REGION: Morris County, Northern NJ.

JOHNSON'S CORNER FARM, 133 Church Rd, Medford, NJ 08055. Tel: 609-654-8643. Fax: 609-953-3554. Email: reservation@johnsonsfarm.com. Website: www.johnsonsfarm.com. Hrs: 8AM-7PM. Contact: Bonnie. GRADE LEVEL: Ages 2-12. GROUP TYPE: School, Scout, Homeschoolers, After-school groups. PROGRAM TYPE: Day Trips, Self-guided Tours, Guided Tours, Self-guided Activities, Guided Activities. MAX. GROUP SIZE: 300. COST: Varies, check our website.

Johnson's Farm is a great place to learn. In the Fall, we offer hayrides to pick Apples and Pumpkins. November brings Sweet potatoes, Popcorn and Cotton picking as well as demonstrations of Cider Pressing and Corn shelling. Spring tours start with Egg Hunt Hayrides and continue with Greenhouse Planting and Strawberry Picking tours. Summer tours include picking Blueberries, Peaches or Corn. In 2007 we built a New restroom facility, handicap accessible bus drop off for your safety and convenience. All of our trips include a Hayride, use of our picnic area and animal feeding in our 3 acre animal farm. SUPPORTS NJ STATE & NATIONAL LEARNING STANDARDS IN: Science, Social Studies. SUPPORTS SCOUT MERIT BADGE ACHIEVEMENT IN: Science & Social Studies. REGION: Burlington County, Southern NJ.

SCARECROW HOLLOW CORN MAZE, 335 Quinton-Hancocks Bridge Rd., Salem, NJ 08079. Tel: 856-935-3469. Fax: 856-935-2624. Email: flowood@hughes.net. Website: www.scarecrowhollow.org. Hrs: Open daily for school tours beginning 9/14/09-10/30/09. Contact: Florence Wood. GRADE LEVEL: Pre K-8th. GROUP TYPE: All youth groups & homeschoolers. PROGRAM TYPE: Day Trips, Self-guided Activities, Guided Activities. MIN. GROUP SIZE: 20. REGISTRATION: Mail, Online, Phone. FOOD: Variety of menu selections, Can bring own food, Place to eat on site, Beverages available. RECOMM. LENGTH OF VISIT: 2 hours. RECOMM. RATIO OF STUDENT TO STAFF: 5:1. ARRIVAL TIPS: Bus parking. COST: Please call or visit website for fee information ($50.00 minimum fee per group).

Explore Salem County's rich heritage of the family farm as you get lost in our maze. Bring your class to Scarecrow Hollow this fall for an educational and entertaining field trip. The day will combine the natural beauty of the countryside with a challenging program of problem-solving events and activities. Our programs are designed to increase children's awareness of the natural world through observation and hands on activities. We will be welcoming school parties Monday to Friday September 14th through October 30th. We limit the number of school parties at any one time, so please book early to avoid disappointment. SUPPORTS NJ STATE & NATIONAL LEARNING STANDARDS IN: Science, Social Studies, Team Building. SUPPORTS SCOUT MERIT BADGE ACHIEVEMENT IN: Science, Social Studies, Team Building. REGION: Salem County, Southern NJ.

FIELD DAYS · RECREATION

SPACE ODYSSEY USA - THE HOTTEST ENTERTAINMENT VENUE, 491 South Dean St., Englewood, NJ 07631. Tel: 877-772-2340. Fax: 201-567-3825. Website: www.spaceodysseyusa.com. Hrs: 10AM/7 days a week. Contact: Kathiya Zelasco ext.13. GRADE LEVEL: All grades. GROUP TYPE: All youth groups & homeschoolers. PROGRAM TYPE: Day Trips, Self-guided Activities. COST: Varies, Super Special Saving $ Packages Available.

Space Odyssey USA - The Hottest Entertainment Venue in Bergen County!!! 26,000 sq. ft. Galaxy of fun, Pure Energy & Excitement!!! 3,000 sq. ft. glow-in-the-dark arena for Lasertag and our exclusive Paint-less Paintball, Glow-in-the-Dark Bowling Alleys, 3-level indoor playground, Train ride, Galaxy Court - Multi purpose sports court, Intergalactic night club, Large Arcade - featuring the best video/redemption games available on this planet! Cafe/Snack Bar, Sweet Treats - a wall assortment of candy. Open 365 days a year and will accommodate all of your group needs and last minute rainy day bookings! Fully air-conditioned, organized check-in and free bus parking in our private parking lot. We specialize in school class trips, camp groups, D.A.R.E. and project graduations, as well as Bar/BatMitzvahs & Super Sweet 16's!! SUPPORT NJ STATE & NATIONAL LEARNING STANDARDS IN: Health & Safety. SUPPORTS SCOUT MERIT BADGE ACHIEVEMENT IN: Sports & Games. (See ad under Indoor Amusement Centers on page 58.) REGION: Bergen County, Northern NJ.

VACAMAS PROGRAMS FOR YOUTH, 256 Macopin Rd., W. Milford, NJ 07480. Tel: 973-838-2568. Fax: 973-838-7534. Email: conference@vacamas.org. Website: www.vacamas.org. Hrs: Year Round, 24 hrs/day depending on residential or day trips. Contact: Conference Center Coordinator. GRADE LEVEL: All grades. GROUP TYPE: All youth groups & homeschoolers. PROGRAM TYPE: Day Trips, Overnight Trips, Workshops. MAX. GROUP SIZE: 400. COST: Fee.

Vacamas offers class trips, field days, overnights, and weekend retreats. We special-ize in environmental education, leadership development, teambuilding, challenge course, and high ropes course. With 500 wooded acres in Northern NJ, we are only 45 minutes from NYC. Vacamas can accommodate any number of participants on day trips all year long. We offer counselors for activities or run your own program. In addition to our specialties, we offer: arts and crafts, sports, creative arts, night hikes, healthy lifestyle programs, campfires, and more! Meals can be provided or self-pre-pared. Vacamas will work with your group to create the perfect trip. References fur-nished upon request. SUPPORTS NJ STATE & NATIONAL LEARNING STANDARDS IN: The Arts, Camping, Health Education, Physical Education/Recreation, Science, Social Studies. SUPPORTS SCOUT MERIT BADGE ACHIEVEMENT IN: The Arts, Life Styles, Science, Skiing, Skating, Sports & Games, Technology. REGION: Passaic County, Northern NJ.

XANADU MEADOWLANDS, 1 Meadowlands Plaza, Suite 1010, E. Rutherford, NJ 07073. Tel: 201-528-2150. Fax: 201-528-2151. Email: tourism@meadowlandsxanadu.com. Website: www.meadowlandsxanadu.com. Hrs: 365 days, Mon-Sat 10AM-10PM, Sun 10AM-6PM. Contact: Tourism & Group Sales Dept. GRADE LEVEL: All grades. GROUP TYPE: All youth groups & homeschoolers. PROGRAM TYPE: Day Trips, Overnight Trips, Self-guided Tours, Guided Tours, Self-guided Activities, Guided Activities, Performances, Workshops. MAX. GROUP SIZE: 1000. MIN. GROUP SIZE: 10. REGISTRATION: Mail, Online, Phone, Submit waiver forms prior to visit, Prepay, Tickets mailed prior to visit. FOOD: Variety of menu selections, Kosher, Vegetarian, Place to eat on site, Beverages available, Meal vouchers. RECOMM. LENGTH OF VISIT: 4 hours. RECOMM. RATIO OF STUDENT TO STAFF: 10:1 (K-8th); 20:1 (9th-12th). ARRIVAL TIPS: Expedite check in, Bus parking, Bus drop off and pick up at designated entrance. COST: Entrance free, cost for individual paid attractions.

Xanadu Meadowlands is the newest, most exciting experiential entertainment and shopping destination in North America. This awe-inspiring venue features America's tallest Ferris wheel with breathtaking views of Manhattan, year-round indoor skiing and snowboarding, restaurants for all tastes, indoor skydiving, movie theaters, live concerts, shopping and much more. Xanadu Meadowlands is located in East Rutherford, New Jersey just minutes from Times Square, New York. Coming Soon. Discover Xanadu at meadowlandsxanadu.com. SUPPORTS NJ STATE & NATIONAL LEARNING STANDARDS IN: The Arts, English, Math, Health & Safety, History/Social Studies, Language Arts, Physical Education, Science, Technology. SUPPORTS SCOUT MERIT BADGE ACHIEVEMENT IN: The Arts, Camping, Citizenship, Family Life, Health & Safety, Life Skills, Performing Arts, Personal Fitness, Physical Ed/Recreation, Safety, Social Studies, Science/Technology. REGION: Bergen County, Northern NJ.

HEALTH & NUTRITION

FIELD TRIP FACTORY, Telephone: 800-987-6409. Fax: 773-342-9513. Email: info@fieldtripfactory.com. Website: www.fieldtripfactory.com. Hrs: Mon.-Fri. 8AM-6PM. GRADE LEVEL: Pre K-6th. GROUP TYPE: All youth groups & homeschoolers. PROGRAM TYPE: Day Trips, Guided Tours. COST: Free.

Field Trip Factory offers free community-based field trips. Our learning adventures teach valuable life-skills including health and nutrition, science, responsibility and more. All field trips are grade and age appropriate, meet learning standards, enrich classroom curriculum for teachers and fulfill badge requirements for scouts. See what is available in your area at www.fieldtripfactory.com or call 1-800-987-6409. SUPPORTS STATE LEARNING STANDARDS IN: Health & Safety, Math, Physical Education, Science. SUPPORTS SCOUT BADGE ACTIVITIES IN: Health & Safety, Life Skills, Personal Fitness. REGION: Throughout all 50 states.

HISTORIC RAILROAD EXCURSIONS

BLACK RIVER & WESTERN RAILROAD, PO Box 232, Ringoes, NJ 08551. Tel: 908-782-6622. Email: info@brrht.org. Website: www.brrht.org. Hrs: Seasonal, Sat.-Sun. Weekday trips by appointment. Contact: Michael Shea. GRADE LEVEL: All grades. GROUP TYPE: All youth groups. PROGRAM TYPE: Day Trips, Self-guided Tours, Self-guided Activities. MAX. GROUP SIZE: 180. MIN. GROUP SIZE: 20. REGISTRATION: Phone, Prepay. TICKET/VOUCHER RETURN POLICY: All ticket sales are final; tickets may be used on all trains except certain special events. FOOD: Can bring own food. RECOMM. LENGTH OF VISIT: 2 hours. RECOMM. RATIO OF STUDENT TO STAFF: 20:1. ARRIVAL TIPS: Bus Parking, Bus drop off and pick up at designated entrance. COST: Adults $14, children $7, discounts available for groups of 20 or more.

Come experience small town short-line railroading in beautiful Hunterdon County, NJ. Enjoy a 75 minute train ride in our antique passenger coaches on the Black River & Western Railroad. Trains on our railroad, built in 1854, are powered by diesel-electric and steam locomotives. Guided tours of our yard facilities are available upon request. Special events include the Santa Express, North Pole Express, Crazy Train Maize, Great Train Robbery, Railroad Days, Saturday Night Special, and more! SUPPORTS NJ STATE & NATIONAL LEARNING STANDARDS IN: Science, Technology. SUPPORTS SCOUT MERIT BADGE ACHIEVEMENT IN: Science/Technology. REGION: Hunterdon County, Central NJ.

ICE SKATING

BRIDGEWATER SPORTS ARENA, 1425 Frontier Rd., Bridgewater, NJ 08807. Tel: 732-627-0006. Fax: 732-627-0973. Email: info@bsaarena.com. Website: www.BSAarena.com. Hrs: Daily 6AM-12AM. Contact: Lynn Wilson. GRADE LEVEL: All grades. GROUP TYPE: All youth groups & homeschoolers. PROGRAM TYPE: Day Trips, Self-guided Activities, Guided Activities. REGISTRATION: Mail, Phone, Prepay. FOOD: Variety of menu selections, Can bring own food, Place to eat on site, Beverages available. RECOMM. LENGTH OF VISIT: 1.5-4 hours. ARRIVAL TIPS: Bus parking. COST: Varies.

Bridgewater Sports Arena is conveniently located at the intersection of routes 22 and 287 in Bridgewater, New Jersey. BSA offers an unforgettable day of activities in our stimulating sports and entertainment center. Choose from ice skating in one of our 3 ice rinks; play laser tag in our black-light lit, fog filled, arena equipped with high-tech lasers or visit BSA's Arcade which is stocked with more then 60 games, skeeball, pinball, and various sports and video simulators. For kids age 10 and under our Softplay Gym is a blast. Softplay is a three story jungle-gym playmazium complete with tunnels, bridges, ball-pit, slides, and moonwalk. Combine any of our great activities with each other and food and you have a guaranteed good time for you and your group. SUPPORTS NJ STATE & NATIONAL LEARNING STANDARDS IN: Health Education. SUPPORTS SCOUT MERIT BADGE ACHIEVEMENT IN: Skating, Sports & Games. (See ad under Field Days & Recreation on page 54.) REGION: Somerset County, Central NJ.

INDOOR AMUSEMENT CENTERS

COCO KEY WATER RESORT AT MOUNT LAUREL MARRIOTT, 915 Route 73, Mount Laurel, NJ 08054. Tel: 877-494-COCO/856-234-7300. Email: coco@mtlaurelmarriot.com. Website: cocokeywaterresort.com. Hrs: 11AM-8PM. Contact: Kate Bromley. GRADE LEVEL: Pre K-12th. GROUP TYPE: All youth groups & homeschoolers. PROGRAM TYPE: Day Trips, Overnight Trips. REGISTRATION: Mail, Online, Phone, Prepay. TICK-ET/VOUCHER RETURN POLICY: Subject to contract terms. FOOD: Variety, Kosher, Vegetarian, Place to eat on site, Beverages available, Meal vouchers. RECOMM. LENGTH OF VISIT: 2-3 hours. RECOMM. RATIO OF STUDENT TO STAFF: 10:1. ADMIS-SION: Expedite check in, Bus parking, Bus drop off and pick up at designated entrance. COST: Call for Seasonal Rates & Discounts.

CoCo Key Water Resort is New Jersey' newest indoor water resort! Open all year, come experience 65,000 sq. ft. of wet and wild adventures inspired by the Florida Keys. Outrageous water slides, body flumes, an Adventure River, the Parrot Perch interactive play area, Dip-In Movie theatre, Palm Grotto Spa and Key Quest Arcade. Special overnight getaways with 2-day water park access as low as $35 per person. SUPPORTS NJ STATE & NATIONAL LEARNING STANDARDS IN: Physical Education. SUPPORTS SCOUT MERIT BADGE ACHIEVEMENT IN: Physical Ed/Recreation. (See ad and other listing in CT on page 24 and under Regional Highlights on page 10.) REGION: Burlington County, Southern NJ.

KID JUNCTION, Branchburg: 3322 Route 22 West, Building 12, Branchburg Commons, Branchburg, NJ 08876. Mount Laurel: 16000 Commerce Parkway, Suite A, Mount Laurel, NJ 08054. Tel: (Branchburg) 908-252-0055 (Mount Laurel) 856-273-9500. Fax: (Branchburg) 908-252-0066 (Mount Laurel) 856-273-9550. Email: info@kidjunction.com. Website: www.kidjunction.com. Hrs: Sun.-Thurs. 10AM-6PM, Fri.-Sat. 10AM-8PM. Contact: David Burkhardt. GRADE LEVEL: Pre K-2nd. GROUP TYPE: All youth groups & homeschoolers. PROGRAM TYPE: Guided Activities, Self-guided Activities, Programs. MAX. GROUP SIZE: 170 (including chaperones). MIN. GROUP SIZE: 20. REGISTRATION: Mail, Online, Phone. FOOD: Variety of menu selections, Place to eat on site, Beverages available. RECOMM. LENGTH OF VISIT: 2.5-3 hours. RECOMM. RATIO OF STUDENT TO STAFF: 8-1. ARRIVAL TIPS: Expedite check in, Bus parking. COST: Varies by package, reservations are required.

Kid Junction is the perfect place to host your school's next field trip. Our field trip programs have been designed to foster learning, emotional confidence, and social interaction all through the guise of play! We offer an Award Winning 9200 square foot clean and secure, stand-alone facility that was designed as an open-play space for children from crawling age to 9 years. Enjoy interactive areas that vary in theme, a huge indoor playground/maze with numerous tubes and slides, a sports-themed game arcade with carefully chosen games that foster self-confidence and motor skill coordination, and a 100% Peanut/Tree Nut free café! Group packages available. SUPPORTS NJ STATE & NATIONAL LEARNING STANDARDS IN: Physical Education. SUPPORTS SCOUT MERIT BADGE ACHIEVEMENT IN: Life Skills, Physical Ed/Recreation. REGION: Burlington and Somerset Counties, Southern and Central NJ.

KID-NETIC, 2 Changebridge Rd., Montville, NJ 07045. Tel: 973-331-9001. Fax: 973-331-9002. Email: kidnetic@aol.com. Website: www.kidneticnj.com. Hrs: Seasonal/please call. Contact: Danielle Paul. GRADE LEVEL: Pre K-3rd. GROUP TYPE: All youth groups. PROGRAM TYPE: Day Trips, Guided Activities, Workshops. MAX. GROUP SIZE: 100. MIN. GROUP SIZE: 20. COST: Basic open play: $9.50 per child; Open play + 1 option (options include art/music & movement or lunch) -$11.50 per child or Open play with two options: $13.00 per child.

Kid-netic invites your organization to come play with us. We have a 4,000 square foot indoor play area, with a 3-level play structure, a mat filled floor of all shapes and sizes and a rock climbing wall. We offer different programs to fit your budget. Your organization can choose open play only which provides 2 hours of open play for $9.50 per child. Or you can choose to add options to open play; art, music & movement or lunch. Add one option-$11.50 per child, add two options-$13.00 per child. We will close the facility to the public if your organization can guarantee more than 50 children. SUPPORTS NJ STATE & NATIONAL LEARNING STANDARDS IN: The Arts, Health & Safety, Physical Education. SUPPORTS SCOUT MERIT BADGE ACHIEVEMENT IN: The Arts, Health & Safety, Personal Fitness, Physical Ed/Recreation. REGION: Morris County, Northern NJ.

INTERACTIVE LIVING HISTORY

BARCLAY FARMSTEAD, 209 Barclay Lane, Cherry Hill, NJ 08034. Tel: 856-795-6225. Hrs: Tues.-Fri. 12-4PM; 1st Sun. each month 1-4PM. Guided Tours. 32-acre farmstead built in 1816, with a farmhouse, gardens and trails, offers visitors an opportunity to observe and participate in the agrarian lifestyle that once dominated the South Jersey landscape. COST: Fee. REGION: Camden County, Southern NJ.

BATSTO VILLAGE, Wharton State Forest, 4110 Nesco Rd., Hammonton, NJ 08037. Tel: 609-561-0024. Hrs: Daily 9AM-4PM. Self-guided Tours, Guided Tours. Historic village that is centered around the iron and glass-making industries around 1766. COST: Fee. REGION: Burlington County, Southern NJ.

COOPER GRISTMILL, 66 County Rte. 513 (formerly 24), Chester, NJ 07930. Tel: 908-879-5463. Hrs: May-Oct.: Sat. 10AM-3:30PM & Sun. 12-3:30PM; Jul.-Aug.: Wed.-Fri. 10AM-3:30PM. Self-guided Tours, Guided Tours. Learn about the history of the water-powered mill and the vibrant community once called Milltown. COST: Free/Suggested Donation. REGION: Morris County, Northern NJ.

FOSTERFIELDS LIVING HISTORICAL FARM, 73 Kahdena Rd., Morristown, NJ 07960. Tel: 973-326-7645. Hrs: Apr.-Oct.: Sat. 10AM-5PM, Sun. 12-5PM. Apr.-Jun. & Oct. Wed.-Fri. 1-5PM. July-Sept. Wed.-Fri. 10AM-5PM. Self-guided Tours, Guided Tours, Workshops. 200-acre working farm since 1760. See activities and demonstrations of farming methods and life during the 19th and early 20th centuries. COST: Fee. REGION: Morris County, Northern NJ.

THE HERMITAGE, 335 N. Franklin Tnpk., Ho-Ho-Kus, NJ 07423. Tel: 201-445-8311. Hrs: Wed.-Sun. 1-4PM. Guided Tours. A historic house museum that incorporates a stone house visited by Washington during the Revolutionary War. COST: Fee. REGION: Bergen County, Northern NJ.

HISTORIC COLD SPRING VILLAGE, 720 Rte. 9, Cold Spring, Cape May, NJ 08204. Tel: 609-898-2300, ext. 17. Hrs: Vary. Self-guided Tours, Guided Tours, Workshops. Brings to life the day-to-day activities of villagers in South Jersey from 1790-1840. COST: Fee. REGION: Cape May County, Southern NJ.

HOWELL LIVING HISTORY FARM, 70 Wooden's La., Lambertville, NJ 08530. Tel: 609-737-3299. Hrs: Feb.-Nov.: Tues.-Sat. 10AM-4PM; Apr.-Nov.: Sun. 12-4PM. Self-guided Tours, Guided Tours. Experience turn-of-the-century farming. COST: Free/Fee. REGION: Mercer County, Central NJ.

LONG STREET FARM, Holmdel Park on Long Street Road, Holmdel, NJ 07733. Tel: 732-946-3758. Hrs: Memorial Day-Labor Day, Daily 9AM-5PM; 10AM-4PM thereafter. Self-guided Tours, Guided Tours. Recreates rural life on a general farm in the 1890s. COST: Fee for group tours. REGION: Monmouth County, Central NJ.

For additional information on trips and group savings and special offers for youth groups please visit

ClassTrips.com

MEDIEVAL TIMES DINNER & TOURNAMENT, 149 Polito Ave. (1 mile west of Giants Stadium), Lyndhurst, New Jersey 07071. Telephone: 201-933-2220 ext. 2319 / 1-888-WE-JOUST. Fax: 201-438-2062. Email: Ryan.Acosta@medievaltimes.com. Website: www.medievaltimes.com/njhomepage.htm. Hrs: 11AM and/or 1:30PM. Call for show dates and evening performances. GRADE LEVEL: 1st-12th. GROUP TYPE: All youth groups & homeschoolers. PROGRAM TYPE: Day Trips, Performances. COST: Varies.

Have your students experience the Middle Ages. Imagine a history lesson presented by a King and his Noble Court, set within the walls of an 11th century-style castle. Every detail is painstakingly re-created as your students take a personal journey back to the Middle Ages. Step back in time and experience spectacular horsemanship, amazing swordplay, medieval games of skill and an authentic jousting tournament between six brave knights of the realm. As the tournament takes place your students are served a feast fit for a king. Medieval Times Education in Action program provides an experience that your students will never forget, while reinforcing classroom learning. SUPPORTS NJ STATE & NATIONAL LEARNING STANDARDS IN: History, Social Studies. SUPPORTS SCOUT MERIT BADGE ACHIEVEMENT IN: Social Studies. (See Regional Highlights on page 14.) REGION: Bergen County, Northern NJ.

MILLBROOK VILLAGE, Delaware Water Gap National Recreation Area, Old Mine Rd., 12 mi. N I-80, Millbrook, NJ 07832. Tel: 908-841-9531. Hrs: Sat.-Sun. 10AM-4PM, By app't only. Self-guided Tours, Guided Tours, Demonstrations. Re-creation of a late 19th century rural community. COST: Free. REGION: Warren County, Northern NJ.

RED MILL MUSEUM VILLAGE, 56 Main St., Clinton, NJ 08809. Tel: 908-735-4101. Hrs: Tues.-Sat. 10AM-4PM, Sun. 12-5PM. Self-guided Tours, Guided Tours, Workshops. Visit the historic 1810 Red Mill and the other exhibit-filled restored buildings from the 18th and 19th centuries. COST: Fee. REGION: Hunterdon County, Central NJ.

MAPLE SUGARING

Follow the maple sugaring process from sap to syrup. Season runs February-March; confirm times with venue. Reserve in the Fall.

FOREST RESOURCE EDUCATION CENTER, NJDEP, Visiting: Don Connor Blvd., Jackson, NJ 08527. Mailing: 370 E. Veterans Highway, Jackson, NJ 08527. Tel: 732-928-2360. COST: Free. REGION: Ocean County, Southern NJ.

GREAT SWAMP OUTDOOR EDUCATION CENTER, 247 Southern Blvd., Chatham, NJ 07928. Tel: 973-635-6629. COST: Free/Fee for groups. REGION: Morris County, Northern NJ

HISTORIC COLD SPRING VILLAGE, 720 Rte. 9, Cold Spring, Cape May, NJ 08204. Tel: 609-898-2300, ext. 17. COST: Fee. REGION: Cape May County, Southern NJ.

JAMES A. MCFAUL ENVIRONMENTAL CENTER, 150 Crescent Ave., Wyckoff, NJ 07481. Tel: 201-891-5571. COST: Fee. REGION: Bergen County, Northern NJ.

NEW JERSEY MUSEUM OF AGRICULTURE, 103 College Farm Rd., North Brunswick, NJ 08902. Tel: 732-249-2077. COST: Fee. REGION: Middlesex County, Central NJ.

SCHIFF NATURE PRESERVE, 339 Pleasant Valley Rd., Mendham, NJ 07945. Tel: 973-543-6004. COST: Fee. REGION: Morris County, Northern NJ.

TENAFLY NATURE CENTER, 313 Hudson Ave., Tenafly, NJ 07670. Tel: 201-568-6093. COST: Fee. REGION: Bergen County, Northern NJ.

WEIS ECOLOGY CENTER, 150 Snake Den Rd., Ringwood, NJ 07456. Tel: 973-835-2160. COST: Fee. REGION:: Passaic County, Northern NJ.

MULTIDIMENSIONAL

THE FOLLOWING LISTINGS HAVE MULTIPLE FOCUSES IN THEIR EXHIBIT HALLS COVERING ANTHROPOLOGY, ART, SCIENCE, CULTURE, OR HISTORY.

MONMOUTH MUSEUM, Brookdale Community College Campus, P.O. Box 359, 765 Newman Springs Rd., Lincroft, NJ 07738. Tel: 732-747-2266. Art Galleries: Hrs: Tues.-Sat. 10AM-4:30PM, Sun. 1-5PM. Children's Galleries: Call for hours. Pre K-8th grade. Self-guided Tours, Guided Tours, Workshops. A wide variety of exhibits in all media of art, science & history. Interactive exhibits for children. COST: Fee. REGION: Monmouth County, Central NJ.

MORRIS MUSEUM, 6 Normandy Heights Rd., Morristown, NJ 07960. Tel: 973-971-3700. Hrs: Wed.-Sat. 11AM-5PM (Thurs. until 8PM), Sun. 1-5PM. Self-guided Tours, Guided Tours, Workshops, Performances. Focuses on the visual and performing arts, natural and physical sciences, and humanities. COST: Fee. REGION: Morris County, Northern NJ.

THE NEWARK MUSEUM, 49 Washington St., Newark, NJ 07102. Tel: 973-596-6550. Hrs: Public: Wed.-Fri. 12-5PM, Sat.-Sun. 10AM-5PM; Groups: Tues.-Fri. 9:30AM-12:30PM. Self-guided Tours, Guided Tours, Workshops. Exhibits focus on art and the natural sciences. COST: Fee. REGION: Essex County, Northern NJ.

PLANETARIUMS

Please call for planetarium show times. Experience a realistic and scientifically accurate simulation of the night sky in a domed theater.

COUNTY COLLEGE OF MORRIS PLANETARIUM, 214 Center Grove Rd., Randolph, NJ. Tel: 973-328-5076. Hrs: Vary. COST: Fee. REGION: Morris County, Northern NJ.

GLENFIELD PLANETARIUM, 25 Maple Avenue, Montclair, NJ 7042. Tel: 973-509-4174. Hrs: Vary. COST: Fee. REGION: Essex County, Northern NJ.

MORRIS MUSEUM, 6 Normandy Heights Rd., Morristown, NJ 07960. Tel: 973-971-3700. Hrs: Vary. COST: Fee. REGION: Morris County, Northern NJ.

THE NEWARK MUSEUM, 49 Washington St., Newark, NJ 07102. Tel: 973-596-6550. Hrs: Vary. COST: Fee. REGION: Essex County, Northern NJ.

RARITAN VALLEY COMMUNITY COLLEGE PLANETARIUM, Rte. 28 & Lamington Rd., North Branch, NJ 08876. Tel: 908-231-8805. Hrs: Vary. COST: Fee. REGION: Somerset/Hunterton County, Central NJ.

ROBERT J. NOVINS PLANETARIUM, Ocean County College, Rte. 549, Toms River, NJ. Tel: 732-255-0342/732-255-0343. Hrs: Vary. COST: Fee. REGION: Ocean County, Southern NJ.

SCIENCE & ENVIRONMENTAL EDUCATION

ABMA'S FARM, 700 Lawlins Rd., Wyckoff, NJ 07481. Tel: 201-891-0278. Fax: 201-848-9721. Website: www.abmasfarm.com. Hrs: Open all year. Farm Tours in Spring and Summer by appt only; Hayride/pumpkin picking in Fall by appt only. GRADE LEVEL: Spring and summer, K-5th; Hayride/Pumpkin picking, Pre K-up. GROUP TYPE: School & youth groups. PROGRAM TYPE: Day Trips, Self-guided Activities, Guided Tours. MAX GROUP SIZE: 30. MIN.GROUP SIZE: 20. REGISTRATION: Phone. FOOD: Beverages available. RECOMM. LENGTH OF VISIT: 1-2 hours. RECOMM. RATIO OF STUDENT TO STAFF: 10:1. COST: Varies.

Abma's, a 28 acre working farm, still produces fresh poultry, eggs, and 80 varieties of vegetables each year to sell in their quaint 200-year-old Dutch barn. The farm promotes agriculture by offering prearranged farm tours weekdays in the spring and summer for school (K-5th) during the growing season. Fall Season: Mon.-Fri. prearranged hayrides and pumpkin picking, Pre K-8th and youth groups. Abma's also rents incubators to witness the egg-hatching process. They sell fertilized eggs and provide information to teachers. This unique classroom experience brings animal nature first hand to your students! Abma's Farm takes back the chicks. REGION: Bergen County, Northern NJ.

CIDERING, Call for dates and times. FOSTERFIELDS LIVING HISTORICAL FARM, 73 Kahdena Rd., Morristown, NJ. Tel: 973-326-7645. COST: Fee. Morris County, Northern NJ. JAMES A. MCFAUL ENVIRONMENTAL CENTER, 150 Crescent Ave., Wyckoff, NJ 07481. Tel: 201-891-5571. COST: Fee. REGION: Bergen County, Northern NJ. LORRIMER SANCTUARY, 790 Ewing Ave., Franklin Lakes, NJ 07417. Tel: 201-891-2185. COST: Free/Fee. REGION: Bergen County, Northern NJ. SCHIFF NATURE PRESERVE, 339 Pleasant Valley Rd., Mendham, NJ 07945. Tel: 973-543-6004. COST: Fee. REGION: Morris County, Northern NJ. TENAFLY NATURE CENTER, 313 Hudson Ave., Tenafly, NJ 07670. Tel: 201-568-6093. COST: Fee. REGION: Bergen County, Northern NJ. YMCA CAMP RALPH S. MASON, 23 Birch Ridge Rd., Hardwick, NJ. Tel: 908-362-8217. COST: Fee. (See main listing on page xx.) REGION: Warren County, Northern NJ.

EDWIN B. FORSYTHE NATIONAL WILDLIFE REFUGE, Great Creek Rd., Oceanville, NJ 08231. Tel: 609-652-1665. Hrs: Daily 8AM-4PM. Self-guided Tours, Guided Tours, Workshops. Part of the U.S. Fish & Wildlife Service. 46,000 acres is primarily a tidal salt meadow and marsh, interspersed with shallow coves and bays. The remainder is woodlands. The Refuge is a stop for water birds during their long migrations, an important wintering habitat for waterfowl and critical nesting habitat for beach nesting species. COST: Fee. REGION: Atlantic, Burlington & Ocean Counties, Southern NJ.

ENVIRONMENTAL EDUCATION CENTER, 190 Lord Stirling Rd., Basking Ridge, NJ 07920. Tel: 908-766-2489. Hrs: Daily: Building 9AM-5PM. Grounds: Dawn-Dusk. Self-guided Tours, Guided Tours. 425 acres of a variety of habitats that provide homes for diverse plant and animal populations, includes 8 miles of trails, wildflower, native plant sensory and touch gardens. The Center houses a swamp tank, and a library with mounted animal displays. The Great Swamp Exhibit is under renovation. COST: Free/Fee. REGION: Morris County, Northern NJ.

FAIRVIEW LAKE YMCA CAMPS, 1035 Fairview Lake Road, Newton, NJ 07860. Tel: 800-686-1166. Fax: 973-383-6386. Email: fairviewlake@metroymcas.org. Website: www.fairviewlakeymca.org. Hrs: Daily. Contact: Fairview Lake. GRADE LEVEL: All grades. GROUP TYPE: School, Scout, Weekend. PROGRAM TYPE: Day Trips, Guided Activities, Overnights/Retreats, Workshops. MAX. GROUP SIZE: 325. COST: Varies. (See listing under Overnights & Retreats on page 203.) REGION: Sussex County, Northern NJ.

FLAT ROCK BROOK NATURE CENTER, 443 Van Nostrand Ave., Englewood, NJ 07631. Tel: 201-567-1265. Hrs: Mon-Fri. 9AM-5PM. Sat.-Sun. 1-5PM. Grounds open dawn-dusk. Self-guided Tours, Guided Tours, Workshops. A 150-acre natural woodland preserve and environmental education center situated on the western slope of the Palisades is one of the last remnants of the magnificent Palisades Forest. COST: Free/Fee. REGION: Bergen County, Northern NJ.

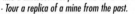
FRANKLIN MINERAL MUSEUM, 32 Evans St., Franklin, NJ 07416. Tel: 973-827-3481. Fax: 973-827-0149. Email: mineralinfo@earthlink.net. Website: www.franklinmineralmuseum.com. Hrs: Museum is open Mar.-Dec., Mon.-Fri. 10AM-4PM, Sat. 10AM-5PM, Sun. 11AM-5PM. Contact: Doreen Longo. GRADE LEVEL: All grades. GROUP TYPE: All youth groups & homeschoolers. PROGRAM TYPE: Day Trips, Self-guided Tours, Guided Tours, Workshops. COST: Varies.

Educational and hands-on fun! Great for kids of all ages! Discover all about fluorescent rocks and minerals found in NJ's "Fluorescent Mineral Capital of the World," view thousands of worldwide minerals and put your hand into a dinosaur's footprint. Tour through a two-story mine replica and travel back in history to experience mining as it once was. Do your own rock collecting on a mine tailings dump dating back to the 1800's then view your collected rocks under a special mineral light to see them in all of their magnificent brilliance. You may also take home the rocks you collect! Groups require an appointment. SUPPORTS NJ STATE & NATIONAL LEARNING STANDARDS IN: Science. SUPPORTS SCOUT MERIT BADGE ACHIEVEMENT IN: Science. REGION: Sussex County, Northern NJ.

GREAT SWAMP OUTDOOR EDUCATION CENTER, 247 Southern Blvd., Chatham, NJ 07928. Tel: 973-635-6629. Hrs: Daily 9AM-4:30PM. Trails open sunrise-sunset. Pre K-College. Self-guided Tours, Guided Tours, Workshops. A mixture of marshes, meadows, dry woods and brush-covered swamps gives this area a unique character, allowing the swamp to support a wide variety of plant and animal life. COST: Free/Fee/Sugg. Donation. REGION: Morris County, Northern NJ.

Greater Newark Conservancy
Inspiring Students, Cultivating Minds
Prudential Outdoor Learning Center
973-642-4646 · www.citybloom.org

GREATER NEWARK CONSERVANCY, Prudential Outdoor Learning Center, 32 Prince St., Newark, NJ 07103. Mailing: 972 Broad St., 8th Floor, Newark, NJ 07021. Tel: 973-642-4646. Email: rsikora@citybloom.org. Website: www.citybloom.org. Hrs: Daily 9AM-5PM. Contact: Robert Sikora, ext.21. GRADE LEVEL: K-12th. GROUP TYPE: All youth groups. PROGRAM TYPE: Day Trips, Self-guided Tours, Guided Tours, Workshops. COST: 25/$200 or special arrangements can be made for larger groups.

From our vibrant Sensory Garden, immersing students in the sights, sounds and scents of nature, to our Urban Wildlife Refuge with a dynamic wetland and pond, the Conservancy's Prudential Outdoor Learning Center is the ideal living classroom to educate your students about the natural world. Conservancy programs are interdisciplinary, hands-on, correlated to NJ CCCS, and designed to inspire young minds. Programs include Urban Habitats, where students discover first hand the diversity of wildlife in cities, What's the Buzz, examining fascinating insects, and Gardening with Nelson Mandela, exploring apartheid and Mandela's inspirational Robbins Island Prison garden in a unique "Living Exhibit" setting. SUPPORTS NJ STATE & NATIONAL LEARNING STANDARDS IN: Science and NJ Core Curriculum. SUPPORTS SCOUT MERIT BADGE ACHIEVEMENT IN: Environmental science, Plant Science, and Gardening. REGION: Essex County, Northern NJ.

HACKENSACK MEADOWLANDS ENVIRONMENT CENTER, 2 DeKorte Park Plaza, Lyndhurst, NJ 07071. Tel: 201-460-8300. Hrs: Mon.-Fri. 9AM-5PM, Sat.-Sun. 10AM-3PM. Self-guided Tours, Guided Tours, Workshops. Focuses on the New Jersey Meadowlands marsh ecosystem. COST: Free/Fee for Tours. REGION: Bergen County, Northern NJ.

HUBER WOODS ENVIRONMENTAL CENTER, 25 Brown's Dock Rd., Locust, NJ 07760. Tel: 732-872-2670. Hrs: Mon.-Fri. 10AM-4PM. Sat. & Sun. 10AM-5PM. Self-guided Tours, Group Guided Tours. 366 acres of forests and meadows, over 8 miles of multi-use trails and an Environmental Center that features hands-on science and Native American activities. COST: Free/Fee. REGION: Monmouth County, Central NJ.

JAMES A. MCFAUL ENVIRONMENTAL CENTER, 150 Crescent Ave., Wyckoff, NJ 07481. Tel: 201-891-5571. Hrs: Grounds are open daily, sunup-sundown. Museum building open weekdays 8AM-4:45PM; weekends & holidays 1-4:45PM. Guided Activities, Guided Tours. 81-acre woodland gardens, animal shelters. waterfowl pond, flowering trees, glassy slopes and an exhibit hall. COST: Fee. REGION: Bergen County, Northern NJ.

For more additional information on class trips, please visit us at
ClassTrips.com

LIBERTY SCIENCE CENTER, 222 Jersey City Blvd., Jersey City, NJ 07305. Tel: 201-253-1302. Email: MMcDonald@lsc.org. Website: www.lsc.org. Hrs: Sept.-Mar., Tues.–Fri. 9AM–4PM, Sat. & Sun. 9AM-5PM, Closed Mondays. Check website for hrs. from March–Aug. Contact: Mary McDonald. GRADE LEVEL: All grades. GROUP TYPE: All youth groups. PROGRAM TYPE: Day Trips, Self-guided Tours, Self-Guided Activities, Workshops, Performances. REGISTRATION: Phone, Submit waiver forms prior to visit, Prepay. FOOD: Variety, Kosher, Vegetarian, Can bring own food, Place to eat on site, Beverages available. RECOMMENDED LENGTH OF VISIT: Varies. ADMISSION: Expedite check-in, Bus parking available. COST: Discounted student group rates.

Give your class the Best Field Trip Ever - with 100's of unique interactive exhibits, real science labs & presentations, hands on experiments and the nation's largest IMAX Dome Theater- a full day of excitement, learning and fun. They will be climbing rocks, creating digital graffiti, walking an I-beam 18 feet in the air, holding tight in a hurricane simulator, greeting creatures in a mini–zoo and so much more. Even better, each exhibition is aligned to Core Curriculum Content Standards – bring your classroom teaching to life! Call today for your free Field Trip Self-Selection Guide. Plan a customized field trip in minutes, ideally suited to your students' grade level, interests and curriculum! The Guide makes organizing your trip a breeze! Call today for your Free Field Trip Self-Selection Guide, or to book your field trip: 201-253-1302. SUPPORTS NJ STATE & NATIONAL LEARNING STANDARDS IN: Science. SUPPORTS SCOUT MERIT BADGE ACHIEVEMENT IN: Science/Technology. REGION: Hudson County, Northern NJ.

LORRIMER NATURE CENTER, 790 Ewing Ave., Franklin Lakes, NJ 07417. Tel: 201-891-2185. Hrs: Wed.-Fri. 9AM-5PM, Sat. 10AM-5PM, Sun. 1-5PM. Trails open dawn-dusk. Self-guided Tours, Guided Tours, Workshops. Part of the New Jersey Audubon Society. The center has a winter bird feeding station, interpretive displays and hands-on exhibits. There is a self-guiding trail system that winds through the 14 acres of land. COST: Fee. REGION: Bergen County, Northern NJ.

MERRILL CREEK RESERVOIR, 34 Merrill Creek Rd., Harmony Township, Washington, NJ 07882. Tel: 908-454-1213. Hrs: Mon.-Fri. 8:30AM-4:30PM, Sat.-Sun. 10AM-4PM. Self-guided Tours. A 650-acre reservoir surrounded by a 290 acre Environmental Preserve and 2,000 additional acres of woods and fields. Naturalist-led environmental education activities. COST: Free. REGION: Warren County, Southern NJ.

NEW JERSEY MARINE SCIENCES CONSORTIUM, Building #22, Fort Hancock, NJ 07732. Tel: 732-872-1300. Hrs: Mon.-Fri. 9AM-5PM. Guided Tours, Workshops. The study of marine and environmental science. COST: Fee. REGION: Monmouth County, Central NJ.

SANDY HOOK BIRD OBSERVATORY, 20 Hartshorne Dr., Fort Hancock, NJ 07732. Tel: 732-872-2500. Hrs: Sep.-Jun.: Tues.-Sat. 10AM-5PM, Sun. 10AM-3PM; Jul.-Aug.: Tues.-Fri. 10AM-5PM, Sat. 10AM-3PM. Guided Tours, Workshops. Part of the New Jersey Audubon Society, it is one of New Jersey's best year-around birding locations, having attracted approximately 340 bird species to its varying habitats as well as over 50 species of butterflies. COST: Fee. REGION: Monmouth County, Central NJ.

SCHIFF NATURE PRESERVE, 339 Pleasant Valley Rd., Mendham, NJ 07945. Tel: 973-543-6004. Hrs: Vary. Self-guided Tours, Guided Tours, Guided Activities. Includes wildlife-habitat improvements, a self-guided nature trail, butterfly and wildflower gardens and exhibits. COST: Fee. REGION: Morris County, Northern NJ.

STONY BROOK - MILLSTONE WATERSHED ASSOCIATION, 31 Titus Mill Rd., Pennington, NJ 08534. Tel: 609-737-3735; Buttinger Nature Center, 609-737-7592. Hrs: Tues.-Fri. 9AM-5PM, Sat. by app't. Pre K-9th grade. Self-guided Tours, Guided Tours, Workshops. Dedicated to enhancing the quality of the natural environment in the 265-square mile region drained by Stony Brook and the Millstone River. Programs focus on the wonders of nature: The oldest trees in central NJ; diverse wildlife; nature trails; a wildflower area; a four-acre research pond; an arboretum; butterfly house; nature center with hands-on exhibits. COST: Free/Fee. REGION: Mercer County, Central NJ.

TENAFLY NATURE CENTER, 313 Hudson Ave., Tenafly, NJ 07670. Tel: 201-568-6093. Hrs: Daily 9AM-5PM. Guided Tours, Guided Activities. 400-acre preserve, which includes more than seven miles of trails, streams, and a 3-acre Pfister's Pond, abundant with wildlife. When trails are open, visitors can hike, bird-watch, observe wildlife, cross-country ski, snowshoe and ice skate on Pfister's Pond. Inside the visitors center, students can browse natural history exhibits and see live animals. Our professional educators can plan a hands-on natural history trip for your group. COST: Fee. REGION: Bergen County, Northern NJ.

TRAILSIDE NATURE & SCIENCE CENTER, 452 New Providence Rd., Mountainside, NJ 07092. Tel: 908-789-3670. Hrs: Daily 12-5PM. Self-guided Tours, Guided Tours. A visitor's center and a natural history museum whose purpose is to interpret the natural and human history of the Watchung Reservation. COST: Sugg. Donation/Fee. REGION: Union County, Northern NJ.

WARREN E. FOX NATURE CENTER, 109 State Highway 50, Mays Landing, NJ 08330. Tel: 609-645-5960. Hrs: Weekdays 8AM-4:30PM, Weekends 8AM-4PM. Self-guided Tours, Workshops. Highlights: Display of trees and their leaves; stuffed animals; Native American artifacts; live animals. Is the headquarters for environmental education in Atlantic County. The center has a display of trees and their leaves, stuffed animals, so you can see what a certain animal really looks like. We have artifacts from Native Americans and the Glassworks factory. Their biggest attraction is their live animals. They keep animals that are indigenous to this area; animals that you just might see on a walk through the woods. They have frogs, turtles, snakes, and lizards. We also keep carnivorous plants- "meat eaters"! COST: Free. REGION: Atlantic County, Southern NJ.

WEIS ECOLOGY CENTER, 150 Snake Den Rd., Ringwood, NJ 07456. Tel: 973-835-2160. Hrs: Wed.-Sun. 8:30AM-4:30PM. Guided Tours, Guided Activities. Focuses on Northern New Jersey Highlands Region. Use the forests, fields and streams as an outdoor classroom for learning. COST: Fee. REGION: Passaic County, Northern NJ.

WOODFORD CEDAR RUN WILDLIFE REFUGE, 4 Sawmill Rd., Medford, NJ 08055. Tel: 856-983-3329. Hrs: Mon.-Sat. 10AM-4PM and Sun. 12-5PM. Self-Guided Tours, Guided Tours, Programs. 184 wooded acres surrounding Cedar Run Lake, Wildlife Rehabilitation Hospital and outdoor live-animal compound, wooded nature trails that link uplands and wetlands and a center with hands-on exhibits and environmental education. COST: Fee. REGION: Burlington County, Southern NJ.

YMCA CAMP RALPH S. MASON, 23 Birch Ridge Rd., Hardwick, NJ 07825. Tel: 908-362-8217. Fax: 908-362-5767. Email: alisonf@campmason.org. Website: www.campmason.org. Hrs: Sep.-Jun. Contact: Alison Fisk, Outdoor Center Director. GRADE LEVEL: K-12th. GROUP TYPE: All youth groups & homeschoolers. PROGRAM TYPE: Day Trips, Overnight Trips, Retreats, Guided Activities, Workshops. Max. Group Size: 350. REGISTRATION: Phone. FOOD: Variety of menu selections, Vegetarian, Place to eat on site, Beverages available. RECOMM. LENGTH OF VISIT: 1-5 days. RECOMM. RATIO OF STUDENT TO STAFF: 4-5 years old: 5:1, 6-8 years old: 6:1, 9-14 years old 8:1, 15-18 years old 10:1. ARRIVAL TIPS: Bus parking, Bus drop off and pick up at designated entrance. COST: Varies.

Since 1900, Mason has been one of New Jersey's most popular sites for outdoor education and group camping. Mason has 600 acres of beautiful forests, streams and lakes, and miles of trails. We offer more than 50 educational, adventure and recreational programs. Educational objectives include environmental thinking, ecology, history and culture, team building and character development, outdoor skills and earth sciences. Our directors will work with you to develop a program that meets your needs. Meals are served buffet style and our accommodations are comfortable, fully winterized dormitory style cabins with indoor bathrooms, sleeping 10 to 14 people, with a total capacity of 350. SUPPORTS NJ STATE & NATIONAL LEARNING STANDARDS IN: Physical Education, Science, Social Studies. SUPPORTS SCOUT MERIT BADGE ACHIEVEMENT IN: Sports, Science, Social Studies. REGION: Warren County, Northern NJ.

SEAPORTS & LIGHTHOUSES

CAPE MAY LIGHTHOUSE MUSEUM, Mid-Atlantic Center for the Arts, 2 Lighthouse Ave. Cape May Pt., NJ 08212. Tel: 609-884-5405. Hrs: Seasonal. Self-guided Tours. Is the oldest operating lighthouse in the US. COST: Fee. REGION: Cape May County, Southern NJ.

NAVESINK LIGHTHOUSE (TWIN LIGHTS) HISTORIC SITE, Lighthouse Rd., Highlands, NJ 07732. Tel: 732-872-1814. Hrs: Labor Day-Memorial Day: Wed.-Sun. 10AM-4:30PM. Self-guided Tours, Guided Tours. History of the lighthouse and their keepers. COST: Fee. REGION: Monmouth County, Central NJ.

SANDY HOOK LIGHTHOUSE, Gateway Sandy Hook, NRA, Middletown Twnshp. P.O. Box 530, Sandy Hook, NJ 07732. Tel: 732-872-5970. Hrs: Apr.-Oct.: Daily 1-5PM. Self-guided Tours, Guided Tours. Tours and talks are given by the New Jersey Lighthouse Society. COST: Free/Sugg Donation. REGION: Monmouth County, Central NJ.

TUCKERTON SEAPORT, 120 W. Main St., Tuckerton, NJ 08087. Tel: 609-296-8868. Hrs: Vary. Daily 10AM-5PM. Self-guided Tours, Guided Tours, Workshops. A working maritime village located along the Tuckerton Creek. COST: Fee. REGION: Ocean County, Southern NJ.

SOCIAL STUDIES

AFRICAN ART MUSEUM OF THE SOCIETY OF AFRICAN MISSIONS, 23 Bliss Ave., Tenafly, NJ 07670. Tel: 201-894-8611. Hrs: Daily 10AM-6PM. Self-guided Tours, Guided Tours. African art including sculpture, painting, costumes, textiles and decorative arts, religion and folklore. COST: Free/Fee. REGION: Bergen County, Northern NJ.

AMERICAN LABOR MUSEUM/BOTTO HOUSE NATIONAL LANDMARK, 83 Norwood St., Haledon, NJ 07508. Tel: 973-595-7953. Hrs.: Wed.-Sat. 1-4PM & by app't. Self-guided Tours. Guided Tours, Workshops. Focuses on the work, workers and the labor movement throughout the world, with special attention to the ethnicity and immigrant experience of American workers. It is headquartered in the historic Botto House National Landmark, the 1908 home of immigrant silk mill workers. COST: Sugg. Donation/Fee for groups. REGION: Passaic County, Northern NJ.

AVIATION HALL OF FAME, Teterboro Airport, Teterboro, NJ 07608. Tel: 201-288-6344. Hrs: Tues.-Sun. 10AM-4PM. Self-guided Tours, Guided Tours. Focus on the 210 years of the state's aviation heritage. COST: Fee. REGION: Bergen County, Northern NJ.

BATTLESHIP NEW JERSEY MUSEUM, 62 Battleship Place, Camden Waterfront, NJ 08103. Tel: 856-966-1652, ext. 144. Hrs: Vary. 3rd-12th grade. Guided Tours. Tour the largest battleship ever built. COST: Fee. REGION: Camden County, Southern NJ.

DESERTED VILLAGE OF FELTVILLE/GLENSIDE PARK, Glenside Ave., Watchung Reservation, Berkeley Heights, NJ 07922. Tel: 908-527-4900. Hrs: Daily 7AM-Dark. Self-guided Tours. Over the course of three centuries, this area has been a farming community, a quasi-utopian mill town, a deserted village, and a summer resort. COST: Free. REGION: Union County, Northern NJ.

EDISON NATIONAL HISTORIC SITE, Main St. & Lakeside Ave., W. Orange, NJ 07052. Tel: 973-736-0550. Group Tours: 973-324-9973. Glenmont, the estate of Thomas and Mia Edison is open for tours, Fri.-Sun. The Edison Laboratory is currently closed for construction. Call for updates on opening. COST: Free/Fee. REGION: Essex County, Northern NJ.

GEORGE WOODRUFF INDIAN MUSEUM, 150 E. Commerce St., Bridgeton, NJ 08302. Tel: 856-451-2620. Hrs: Mon.-Fri. 1-4PM, Sat. 11AM-2PM. Self-guided Tours, Guided Tours. Displays local Leni Lenape artifacts. COST: Free. REGION: Cumberland County, Southern NJ.

THE GREAT FALLS HISTORIC DISTRICT CULTURAL CENTER, 65 McBride Ave. Ext., Paterson, NJ 07501. Tel: 973-279-9587. Hrs: Mon.-Fri. 8:30AM-4:30PM. 3rd grade & up. Self-guided Tours, Guided Tours. The Falls are 77 ft. high & 280 ft. wide. The Center offers exhibits and videos based on Paterson's industrial history. COST: Fee. REGION: Passaic County, Northern NJ.

INDIAN HERITAGE MUSEUM, P.O. Box 225, 730 Rancocas, NJ 08073. Tel: 609-261-4747. Hrs: Tues.-Thurs. 10AM-3PM by app't. Public Hrs: 1st & 3rd Sat. of each month 10AM-3PM. Self-guided Tours, Guided Tours. A museum of American Indian history and culture, several dioramas depict the life of many tribes. The tour includes the outdoor re-created traditional woodland village. There are also self-guided nature trails to explore. COST: Fee. REGION: Burlington County, Southern NJ.

JOCKEY HOLLOW, MORRISTOWN NATIONAL HISTORIC PARK, off Tempe Wick Rd. Mailing: 30 Washington Place, Morristown, NJ 07960. Tel: 973-543-4030 or 973-539-2016, ext. 210 (headquarters). Hrs: Visitor Center open daily 9AM-5PM, Park open daily until sunset. 3rd grade & up, special program for 4th & 5th grades. Self-Guided, Guided Tours. See where Washington and his troops camped during the winter, along with the headquarters he used then. Visit rebuilt soldier residences and the Wick house from the 1700s. 20 miles of trails available for hiking. Combine with a visit to Washington Headquarters/The Ford Mansion. COST: Fee. REGION: Morris County, Northern NJ.

LAMBERT CASTLE MUSEUM, 3 Valley Rd., Paterson, NJ 07503. Tel: 973-247-0085. Hrs: Wed.-Sun. 1PM-4PM. Tour provides overview of silk and iron industry as well as insight into immigration and labor during this period of the Industrial Revolution. COST: Varies. REGION: Passaic County, Northern NJ.

THE MUSEUM OF EARLY TRADES AND CRAFTS, 9 Main St., Madison, NJ 07940. Tel: 973-377-2982. Hrs: Tues.-Sat. 10AM-4PM, Sun. 12-5PM. Summer: Tues.-Sat. 10-4. Self-guided Tours, Guided Tours. Exploring pre-industrial trades and crafts in New Jersey. COST: Fee. REGION: Morris County, Northern NJ.

THE NEW JERSEY HISTORICAL SOCIETY, 52 Park Place, Newark, NJ 07102. Tel: 973-596-8500. Hrs: Museum Tues.-Sat. 10AM-5PM. Library: Wed., Thurs. & Sat. 12-5PM. Self-guided Tours, Guided Tours, Workshops. Explore New Jersey's past through its people, cultures, and architecture. The library collection contains manuscripts, reference books, photographs, & other material documenting New Jersey's history. COST: Free/Fee. REGION: Essex County, Northern NJ.

NEW JERSEY MUSEUM OF AGRICULTURE, 103 College Farm Rd., North Brunswick, NJ 08902. Tel: 732-249-2077. Hrs: Tues.-Sat. 10AM-5PM. Pre K-6th grade. Group Tours, Workshops. Learn about the history of agriculture in New Jersey and why New Jersey is called the Garden State. COST: Fee. REGION: Middlesex County, Central NJ.

NEW JERSEY STATE HOUSE, 125 W. State St., Trenton, NJ 08625. Tel: 609-633-2709. Hrs: Mon.-Fri. 10AM-3PM, Sat. 12-3PM. Guided Tours on the hour. For information on visiting your local New Jersey state senate or assembly representative, call NJ Legislative Information Service Tel: 800-792-8630. COST: Free. REGION: Mercer County, Central NJ.

NEWARK INTERNATIONAL AIRPORT, Port Authority of New York & New Jersey, Newark International Airport, Newark, NJ 07114. Tel: 973-961-6710, 973-961-6265. Hrs: Thurs. 10AM-12PM. 4th-12th grade. Guided Tours. One tour is given per week. Take a tour of the airport, specifically tailored to your group. Ride on the AirTrain and see the first control tower. COST: Free. REGION: Essex County, Northern NJ.

OLD BARRACKS MUSEUM, 101 Barrack St., Trenton, NJ 08608. Tel: 609-396-1776. Fax: 609-777-4000. Email: barracks@voicenet.com. Website: www.barracks.org. Hrs: Daily 10AM-5PM. Contact: Richard Patterson. GRADE LEVEL: 3rd grade & up. GROUP TYPE: All youth groups. PROGRAM TYPE: Self-guided Tours, Guided Tours, Workshops. COST: $6-$12 depending on type.

Experience another dimension to history as you and your students/scouts/group interact with living history interpreters in our exciting "Meet the Past" programs. Enter the world of 1777 and share the trials, tribulations and joys of ordinary people living in extraordinary times. Be recruited into the Continental Army, learn about a soldier's life, witness a weapons demonstration and take an oath. Visit the infirmary to learn about small pox inoculations. Encounter a witness of the Battles of Trenton recalling battling incidents or a Loyalist trying to persuade you to join the opposition. SUPPORTS NJ STATE & NATIONAL LEARNING STANDARDS IN: History/Social Studies. SUPPORTS SCOUT MERIT BADGE ACHIEVEMENT IN: Social Studies. (See Regional Highlights on page 15). REGION: Mercer County, Central NJ.

THE PATERSON MUSEUM, 2 Market St. Paterson, NJ 07501. Tel: 973-321-1260. Hrs: Tues.-Fri. 10AM-4PM & Sat. & Sun. 12:30- 4:30PM. Guided Tours. Exhibits focus on the cultural, industrial, technological, and geological history of the area. COST: Varies. REGION: Passaic County, Northern NJ.

THOMAS A. EDISON CENTER AT MENLO PARK MUSEUM, 37 Christie St., Edison, NJ 08820. Tel: 732-549-3299. Tour Booking & Info: 732-494-4194. Hrs: Thurs.-Sat. 10AM-4PM, & by app't. midweek. 3rd-12th grade. Self-guided Tours, Guided Tours. The small two-room museum includes both original artifacts and interpretive exhibits relating to Edison's major inventions at Menlo Park. The themes covered include: Establishment of the world's first research and development laboratory; Perfection of the incandescent light bulb; Development of a complete electrical distribution system; Invention and progression of the phonograph. COST: Free/Suggested Donation. REGION: Middlesex County, Central NJ.

WASHINGTON CROSSING STATE PARK, 355 Washington Crossing/ Pennington Rd., Titusville, NJ 08560. Tel: Visitors Center 609-737-9304. Hrs: Seasonal. Self-guided Tours, Guided Tours. See a musket demonstration and video reenactment of historical events, then look at 500 artifacts in the museum and Ferry House commemorating this historic event. COST: Fee. REGION: Mercer County, Central NJ.

WASHINGTON'S HEADQUARTERS/FORD MANSION & MUSEUM, 30 Washington Pl., Morristown, NJ 07960. Tel: 973-539-2016. Hrs: Daily 9AM-5PM. Last tour of the day at 4PM. 3rd-12th grade. Guided Tours. Where Washington and his military family lived at the mansion from December, 1779 to June, 1780, as the guests of Mrs. Theodesia Ford. Combine visit to Jockey Hollow, the winter encampment site for Washington and his troops. COST: Free/Fee for Tour. Fees waived with Tax-exempt ID# for schools. REGION: Morris County, Northern NJ.

TEAM BUILDING & CHARACTER EDUCATION

COMBAT SPORTS, La Valley Dr., Manalapan, NJ 07726. Tel: 866-926-6228. Email: info@combatsportsusa.com. Website: www.combatsportsusa.com. Hrs: Daily 9AM-8PM in season. Contacts: Robert & Sue. GRADE LEVEL: 4th-adults. GROUP TYPE: All youth groups. PROGRAM TYPE: Day Trips, Self-guided Activities. REGISTRATION: Mail, Phone, Submit waiver forms prior to visit, Prepay. FOOD: Can bring own food, Place to eat on site, Beverages available. RECOMM. LENGTH OF VISIT: 2 hours. RECOMM. RATIO OF STUDENT TO STAFF: 10:1 to 15:1. ARRIVAL TIPS: Expedite check in, Bus parking. COST: Inquire about special group rates. (See main listing on page 34.) REGION: Monmouth County, Central NJ.

THE FUNPLEX, 182 Route 10 West, East Hanover, NJ 07936. Tel: 973-428-8772. Fax: 973-428-1775. Email: kim@thefunplex.com. Website: www.thefunplex.com. Hrs: Open daily. Mon.-Thurs. 10AM-9PM year round. Contact: Kim Williams. GRADE LEVEL: K-5th. GROUP TYPE: School. PROGRAM TYPE: Day Trips, Guided Activities, Self-guided Activities. COST: Starting at $6.95 per student.

Introducing a brand new program to encourage teamwork and instill character in your students. EduQuest at the Funplex! This is an exciting new educational program designed by teachers utilizing MagiQuest and promoting the same values as the New Jersey Core Curriculum Content Standards 9.1 and 9.2. Sample EduQuest Schedules Grades K-2: Students are told a story of a Kingdom's treasure being stolen. As the story comes to life, students work together to recover the stolen treasure and create the ending to the story. Grades 3-5: Students focus on character traits while completing a series of Quests in cooperative groups. SUPPORTS NJ STATE & NATIONAL LEARNING STANDARDS IN: The Arts, English, Language Arts, Technology. SUPPORTS SCOUT MERIT BADGE ACHIEVEMENT IN: The Arts, Citizenship, Family Life, Life Skills, Safety, Science/Technology. REGION: Morris County, Northern NJ.

THEATER • DANCE • MUSIC

NEW JERSEY PERFORMING ARTS CENTER (NJPAC), 1 Center St., Newark, NJ 07102. Tel: 1-888-GO-NJPAC / Administrative: 973-642-8989 / General Arts Education information: 973-353-8009 / SchoolTime tickets: 973-642-2002. Website: www.njpac.org. Hrs: Call Center: Mon.-Sat. 10AM-3PM, Sun. 10AM-3PM, Box Office: Mon.-Sat. 12-6PM, Sun. 10AM-3PM. GRADE LEVEL: Pre K-12th. GROUP TYPE: All youth groups & home-schoolers. PROGRAM TYPE: Day Trips, Performances, Workshops. REGISTRATION: Mail, Phone, Submit waiver forms prior to visit, Prepay, Tickets mailed prior to visit. TICKET/VOUCHER RETURN POLICY: Exchanges possible if given advanced notice. RECOMM. LENGTH OF VISIT: Varies. RECOMM. RATIO OF STUDENT TO STAFF: 15:1. ARRIVAL TIPS: Expedite check in, Bus parking, Bus drop off and pick up at designated entrance. COST: Varies.

NJPAC boasts the fourth largest arts education program in the nation, offering SchoolTime (field trips) scheduled weekdays 10AM & 12:30PM, with performances also on weekends. 2009-2010 features Paquito D'Rivera, Nai Ni Chen, Paper Bag Players, The Butterfly Hudson Vagabond Puppets, Alvin Ailey American Dance Theater and more. $8-10 tickets. Arts Academy: Arts instruction at schools in dance, theater, or literature lead by NJPAC teaching artists. Early Learning Through The Arts© NJ Wolf Trap Program uses the arts to teach early childhood curriculum and enliven the classroom. Professional Development Workshops for Educators are offered, accredited by NJ DOE. SUPPORTS NJ STATE & NATIONAL LEARNING STANDARDS IN: Theater, core curriculum content standards for the Performing Arts. SUPPORTS SCOUT MERIT BADGE ACHIEVEMENT IN: Performing Arts. REGION: Essex County, Northern NJ.

PUSHCART PLAYERS, 197 Bloomfield Ave, Verona, NJ 07044. Tel: 973-857-1115. Fax: 973-857-4366. Hrs: Performances throughout NJ, call or visit website for dates and times. Email: information@pushcartplayers.org. Website: www.pushcartplayers.org. Contact: Stephanie Carr. GRADE LEVEL: Pre K-8th. GROUP TYPE: School Groups. PROGRAM TYPE: Performances, Workshops. REGISTRATION: Online, Phone. COST: Fee.

Pushcart Players is an award winning professional touring theatre ensemble that offers a wide array of wonderful, wild and witty programming for kids. This outstanding company has been putting the arts into education with musical productions, workshops and after school programs that are "just right" for students, for the past 35 years! All programs are accompanied by a terrific study guide for teachers and fulfill many core curriculum standards in the arts and other subjects. The New York Times says that Pushcart is "A polished, knowing theatre company and a felicitous event for children!" SUPPORTS NJ STATE & NATIONAL LEARNING STANDARDS IN: The Arts, History/Social Studies, Language Arts. SUPPORTS SCOUT MERIT BADGE ACHIEVEMENT IN: The Arts, Performing Arts. REGIONS: CT, DE, LI, NJ, NY, PA.

NEW YORK CITY

ACCOMMODATIONS

DAYS HOTEL BROADWAY, 215 West 94th Street, New York, New York 10705. Tel: 646-698-0526. Fax: 646-698-0505. Email: mbrookewebster@dayshotelnyc.com. Website: www.daysinn.com. Hrs: 24 hours. Contact: Brooke Webster. GRADE LEVEL: All grade levels. GROUP TYPE: All youth groups. MAX. GROUP SIZE: 100. PROGRAM TYPE: Overnight Trips. REGISTRATION: Prepay. TICKET/VOUCHER RETURN POLICY: Group deposits refundable up to thirty (30) days prior to arrival. FOOD: Place to eat not available within site. RECOMM. LENGTH OF VISIT: 3-4 nights. RECOMM. RATIO OF STUDENT TO STAFF: 10:1. ARRIVAL TIPS: Expedite check in. COST: Varies.

A comfortable and affordable home away from home for student and youth groups, located on the upper west side of Manhattan with easy express subway service to all sites of interest in New York City. With 250 spacious rooms of which one third are double/doubles, this is the perfect environment for school groups. Our comfortable rooms have hair dryer, iron & ironing board, safe, complimentary coffee & WiFi. (See New York City Featured City Page on page 226.) REGION: New York County, NYC.

NEW YORK YMCA GUEST ROOMS, Locations: Upper West Side, Upper East Side, Harlem, Brooklyn, Queens. Reservation Sales Center - 5 West 63rd St, New York, NY 10023. Tel: 212 579-7730. Fax: 212 579-4200. Email: vhenry@ymcanyc.org. Website: www.ymcanyc.org/reservation. Hrs: 9AM-5PM. Contact: Valerie Henry. GRADE LEVEL: All grade levels. GROUP TYPE: All Youth Groups. PROGRAM TYPE: Overnight Trips. MAX. GROUP SIZE: 150. REGISTRATION: Mail, Phone. ARRIVAL TIPS: Bus drop off and pick up at designated entrance. COST: Varies.

The New York YMCA's have been providing affordable lodging facilities for student groups for over thirty years. Student groups staying at the YMCAs have the unique opportunity to meet other students visiting from across the globe. Located in the heart of the city, guests staying at the Manhattan YMCA can walk to most sightseeing attractions. The West Side property is located across the street from Central Park at 63rd St & Central Park West. The Vanderbilt Y is a few blocks to the United Nations as well as Rockefeller Center. Private facilities for group leaders or chaperones are also available. (See New York City Featured City Page on page 226.) REGION: New York County, NYC.

AMUSEMENT & THEME PARKS

VICTORIAN GARDENS
AMUSEMENT PARK
AT WOLLMAN RINK IN CENTRAL PARK
Discounted Group Rates Available!
www.victoriangardensnyc.com • 212.982.2229 • sales@victoriangardensnyc.com

VICTORIAN GARDENS - NYC'S PREMIER AMUSEMENT PARK, located at Wollman Rink in Central Park. Enter at 59th St. & 6th Ave. (Central Park South) and walk north. Tel: 212-982-2229. Email: Sales@victoriangardensnyc.com. Hrs: Late May-Mid-Sept.: Mon.-Thurs. 11AM-7PM, Fri. 11AM-8PM, Sat. 10AM-9PM, Sun. 10AM-PM. Website: www.victoriangardensnyc.com. GRADE LEVEL: Early childhood-7th grade. GROUP TYPE: All youth groups & homeschoolers. PROGRAM TYPE: Day Trips, Self-guided Activities. MAX GROUP SIZE: 20-2000. REGISTRATION: Phone, Submit waiver forms prior to visit, Prepay, Tickets mailed prior to visit. FOOD: Variety of menu selections, Place to eat on site, Beverages available, Meal vouchers. RECOMM. LENGTH OF VISIT: 3 hours. RECOMM. RATIO OF STUDENT TO STAFF: 10:1. COST: Special group rates available with 1 complimentary adult admission for every 10 children.

No need to travel miles away from Manhattan to enjoy the fun and thrills of an amusement park! Victorian Gardens Amusement Park is located in the heart of New York City at Wollman Rink in Central Park. Victorian Gardens returns to town from Late May to Mid-September, featuring: handcrafted rides for children ages 2-12, interactive games and activities, face painting, balloon sculptors, and live entertainment. Our concession offers old-time favorites such as cotton candy and caramel corn, as well as special "meal deals" for groups on a tight budget. Shaded picnic area seating is available, and one low price includes unlimited rides all day long, with 1 complimentary adult admission for every 10 group tickets purchased. Group tickets start as low as $10 per person. Perfect for school & scout field trips, end-of-school year celebrations, and fundraising events. Please call for further information so that we can help you plan your special day. SUPPORTS NY STATE & NATIONAL STANDARDS IN: Physical Education. SUPPORTS SCOUT MERIT BADGE ACHIEVEMENT IN: Sports & Games. (See Regional Highlights on page 11.) REGION: New York County, NYC.

ANIMALS • AQUARIUMS • ZOOS

BRONX ZOO/WILDLIFE CONSERVATION SOCIETY PARK, 2300 Southern Blvd., Bronx, NY 10460. Tel: 718-220-5100. Hrs: Daily 10AM-5PM, Sat.-Sun. & Holidays until 5:30PM. Self-guided Tours, Guided Tours. More than 4,000 animals on its sprawling 265 acres of land—much of which has been transformed into natural habitats for the animals. COST: Fee/Free. REGION: Bronx County, NYC.

CENTRAL PARK ZOO, 830 5th Ave. at 64th St., New York, NY 10021. Tel: 212-439-6583. Hrs: Daily 10AM–5PM, Sat.-Sun. & Holidays until 5:30PM. Day Trips, Self-guided Tours, Guided Tours, Workshops, Performances. Themed natural habitats from Penguins to Sea Lions, rain forests to the polar wilds and the Tisch Children's Zoo. COST: Fee/Free. REGION: New York County, NYC.

NEW YORK AQUARIUM, 610 Surf Ave., Brooklyn, New York 11224. Tel: 718-265-3454. Hrs: Daily. Self-guided Tours, Guided Tours, Workshops. Over 8,000 animals in both indoor and outdoor naturalistic exhibits. COST: Fee. REGION: Kings County, NYC.

PROSPECT PARK ZOO, Prospect Park, 450 Flatbush Avenue, Brooklyn, NY 11225. Tel: 718-399-7321. Hrs: Daily: Winter (Nov. 2-Apr. 3): 10AM-4:30PM, Spring (April 4-Nov. 1): 10AM-5PM. Self-guided Tours, Guided Tours, Workshops. 400 animals of 82 species in natural habitat exhibits and a farm-style petting zoo. COST: Fee. REGION: Kings County, NYC.

QUEENS ZOO, 53-51 111th St. Flushing, NY. Tel: 718-271-7361. Hrs: Daily: Winter (Nov. 2-Apr. 3): 10AM-4:30PM, Spring (April 4-Nov. 1): 10AM-5PM. Guided tours, Workshops. Of the zoo's 55 species, indigenous American wildlife is the main attraction. COST. Fee/Free. REGION. Queens County, NYC.

STATEN ISLAND ZOO, 614 Broadway, Staten Island, NY 10310. Tel: 718-442-3100. Hrs: Daily 10AM-4:45PM. Self-guided Tours, Guided Tours, Workshops. Variety of animals in realistic habitats. Highlights: Serpentarium; African Savannah; The Marchi Aquarium; A farm-style petting zoo. COST: Fee. REGION: Richmond County, NYC.

ART · ARCHITECTURE · SCULPTURE

AMERICAN FOLK ART MUSEUM, 45 W. 53rd St. New York, NY 10019. Tel: 212-265-1040. Hrs: Tues.-Sun. 10:30AM-5:30PM (Fri. until 7:30PM). Guided Tours, Workshops. Features 18th and 19th century paintings, quilts, sculptures, and the work of contemporary self-taught artists. COST: Free/Fee. REGION: New York County, NYC.

BRONX MUSEUM OF THE ARTS, 1040 Grand Concourse, Bronx, NY 10456. Tel: 718-681-6000. Hrs: Thurs. & Weekends 11AM-6PM, Fri. 11AM-8PM. Self-guided Tours, Guided Tours. Focuses on 20th century and contemporary art by artists of African, Asian and Latin American ancestry. COST: Fee/Free. REGION: Bronx County, NYC.

THE BROOKLYN MUSEUM, 200 Eastern Pkwy., Brooklyn, NY 11238. Tel: 718-638-5000. Hrs: Wed.-Fri. 10AM-5PM, Sat.-Sun. 11AM-6PM. Self-guided Tours, Guided Tours. Permanent collections range from ancient Egyptian masterpieces to contemporary art, and represent a wide range of cultures. COST: Fee. REGION: Kings County, NYC.

THE CLOISTERS, 99 Margaret Corbin Drive, Fort Tryon Park, New York, NY 10040. Tel: 212-923-3700. Hrs: Mar.-Oct.: Tues.-Sun. 9:30AM-5PM; Nov.-Feb.: Tues.-Sun. 9:30AM-4:45PM. Guided Tours, Self-guided tours. 1st grade & up. Branch of the Metropolitan Museum devoted to the art and architecture of medieval Europe. COST: Fee. REGION: New York County, NYC.

COOPER-HEWITT NATIONAL DESIGN MUSEUM, 2 E. 91st St., New York, NY 10128. Tel: 212-849-8400. Hrs: Mon.-Fri. 10AM-5PM, Sat. 10AM-6PM, Sun. 12-6PM. Self-guided Tours, Guided Tours. The only museum in the nation devoted exclusively to historic and contemporary design. COST: Fee. REGION: New York County, NYC.

DAHESH MUSEUM OF ART, 580 Madison Ave., New York, NY 10022. Tel: 212-759-0606. Hrs: Tues.-Sun. 11AM-6PM. Self-guided Tours, Guided Tours. Exhibits works by Europe's academically trained artists of the 19th and early 20th centuries. COST: Free/Fee. REGION: New York County, NYC.

THE DRAWING CENTER, 35 Wooster St. (bet. Broome & Grand), New York, NY 10013. Tel: 212-219-2166 x119. Email: agood@drawingcenter.org. Website: www.drawingcenter.org. Hrs: Tour & Workshop times: Tues.-Thurs. 10AM-6PM. Contact: Aimee Good, Director of Education & Community Programs. GRADE LEVEL: K-12th. GROUP TYPE: School, After-school. PROGRAM TYPE: Day Trips, Guided Tours, Workshops. MAX. GROUP SIZE: 30. COST: Free.

The Michael Lovenko School Programs make The Drawing Center's exhibitions accessible to diverse audiences. K-12 school groups can participate in free educator-led discussions of the exhibitions and hands-on drawing workshops in the galleries. Pre-visit teaching guides such as preparatory discussion topics and hands-on exercises, along with exhibition information and travel instructions, are available to help plan your visit. Post-visit art exercises and discussion topics are also available for follow-up in the classroom. The Drawing Center is the only not-for-profit institution in the U.S. to focus solely on the exhibition of drawings, both historical and contemporary. It was established in 1977 to provide opportunities and services for emerging and under-recognized artists, to demonstrate the significance and diversity of drawings throughout history, and to stimulate public dialogue on issues of art and culture. SUPPORTS NY STATE & NATIONAL LEARNING STANDARDS IN: The Arts. SUPPORTS SCOUT MERIT BADGE ACHIEVEMENT IN: The Arts. REGION: New York County, NYC.

EL MUSEO DEL BARRIO, 1230 Fifth Ave. at 104th St., New York, NY 10029. Tel: 212-831-7272. Hrs: Wed.-Sun. 11AM-5PM. Self-guided Tours, Guided Tours, Workshops. Dedicated to Puerto Rican, Caribbean and Latin American art. COST: Fee. REGION: New York County, NYC.

SOLOMON R. GUGGENHEIM MUSEUM, 1071 Fifth Avenue at 89th St., New York, NY 10128. Tel: 212-423-3500. Hrs: Sat.-Wed. 10AM-5:45PM, Fri. 10AM-7:45PM. Self-guided Tours, Guided Tours, Workshops. Collection of Impressionist, Post-Impressionist, early Modern, and contemporary art. COST: Fee. REGION: New York County, NYC.

HISPANIC SOCIETY OF AMERICA, Broadway between 155th St. and 156th St., New York, NY 10032. Tel: 212-926-2234. Hrs: Tues.-Sat. 10AM-4:30PM, Sun. 1-4PM. 2nd-12th grade. Self-guided Tours, Guided Tours, Workshops. Museum and reference library for the study of the arts and cultures of Spain, Portugal and South America. COST: Free. REGION: New York County, NYC.

INTERNATIONAL CENTER OF PHOTOGRAPHY (ICP), 1133 Avenue of the Americas at 43rd St., New York, NY 10036. Tel: 212-857-0005. Hrs: Tues.-Thurs. 10AM-6PM, Fri. 10AM-8PM, Sat.-Sun. 10AM-6PM. Day Trips, Self-guided Tours, Guided Tours, Workshops. Collection contains more than 100,000 historical and contemporary photographs. COST: Fee/Free tours for New York City Public Schools. REGION: New York County, NYC.

METROPOLITAN MUSEUM OF ART, 1000 Fifth Ave. at 81st St., New York, NY 10028. Tel: 212-570-3961. Hrs: Tues.-Thurs. & Sun. 9:30AM-5:30PM, Fri.-Sat. until 9PM. K-12th grade. Self-guided Tours, Guided Tours, Workshops. Houses more than two million works of art from ancient to contemporary. COST: Free/Fee. REGION: New York County, NYC.

MUSEUM FOR AFRICAN ART, 3601 43rd Ave., Long Island City, Queens, NY 11101. Tel: 718-784-7700. Hrs: Mon.-Fri. 10AM-5PM. Workshops. Dedicated to increasing public understanding and appreciation of African art and culture. COST: Fee. REGION: Queens County, NYC.

MUSEUM OF ARTS & DESIGN, 2 Columbus Circle, New York, NY 10019. Tel: 212-299-7777. Hrs: Wed.-Sun. 11AM-6PM (Thurs. until 9PM). Self-guided Tours, Guided Tours, Workshops. Displays crafts by American artists. Exhibits include furnishings, glass, works in wood and metal, jewelry, and quilts. COST: Fee. REGION: New York County, NYC.

THE MUSEUM OF BIBLICAL ART, 1865 Broadway at 61st St., New York, NY, 10023. Tel: 212-408-1500. Fax: 212-408-1292. Email: education@mobia.org. Website: www.mobia.org. Hrs: Tues.-Wed. & Fri.-Sun. 10AM-6PM, Thurs. 10AM-8PM. Contact: Laura McManus. GRADE LEVEL: 1st-college. GROUP TYPE: All youth groups & home-schoolers. PROGRAM TYPE: Guided Tours, Self-guided Tours, Workshops. MAX. GROUP SIZE: 40. COST: Guided tours are free; workshop costs vary by program.

The Museum of Biblical Art is a non-profit educational institution whose mission is to better understand how the narratives and symbols of the Bible have influenced the history of art and visual culture. We tailor our programs to meet the needs of individual groups, including public and private schools, after-school programs, and camps. MOBIA staff works one-on-one with teachers to develop engaging curriculum enhancement programs. Arts workshops can accompany tours. Past workshops have included digital photography, bookmaking, and collage. Additional workshops are created regularly. Groups may bring bag lunches or snacks to eat in MOBIA's Education Center. SUPPORTS NY STATE & NATIONAL LEARNING STANDARDS IN: The Arts, History, Language Arts, Social Studies. REGION: New York County, NYC.

MUSEUM OF MODERN ART, 11 W. 53rd Street, New York, NY 10019. Tel: 212-708-9400. Hrs: Daily 10:30AM-5:30PM (Fri. until 8PM), closed Tues. Self-guided Tours, Guided Tours, Workshops. Modern and contemporary art and an extensive film collection. COST: Free/Fee. REGION: New York County, NYC.

THE NOGUCHI MUSEUM, 9-01 33rd Rd. at Vernon Blvd., Long Island City, NY 11106. Tel: 718-204-7088. Hrs: Wed.-Fri. 10AM-5PM, Sat.-Sun. 11AM-6PM. Guided Tours, Workshops. A comprehensive collection of the Japanese-American sculptor Isamu Noguchi in stone, metal, wood, and clay. COST: Fee/Free for NYC public schools. REGION: Queens County, NYC.

QUEENS MUSEUM OF ART, NYC Building, Flushing Meadows, NY 11368. Tel: 718-592-9700. Hrs: Wed.-Fri. 10AM-5PM, Sat.-Sun. 12-5PM. 1st-12th grade. Self-guided Tours, Guided Tours, Workshops. Exhibitions that relate to the contemporary urban life of its constituents. COST: Fee. REGION: Queens County, NYC.

RUBIN MUSEUM OF ART, 150 West 17th Street, New York, NY 10011. Tel: 212-620-5000, ext 345. Fax: 212-675-0443. Email: reservations@rmanyc.org. Website: www.rmanyc.org. Hrs: School tours begin Wed.-Thurs.10AM and Mon., Fri-Sun. 11AM. Closed Tuesdays. Contact: Elizabeth Cintron. GRADE LEVEL: All grades. GROUP TYPE: All youth groups & homeschoolers. PROGRAM TYPE: Self-guided Tours, Guided Tours, Self-guided Activities, Guided Activities. REGISTRATION: Mail, Phone, Prepay. RECOMM. LENGTH OF VISIT: I hour. RECOMM. RATIO OF STUDENT TO STAFF: 15:1. ARRIVAL TIPS: Bus drop off and pick up at designated entrance. COST: Free for all K-12 public school groups. For all other K-12 school groups and colleges, regular admission fees apply.

A field trip to the Rubin Museum of Art is an exciting way to enhance curriculum and expand student learning. Tours for school groups are designed to introduce and develop knowledge of Himalayan traditions while encouraging meaningful explorations of the art. One guide is assigned to every 15 people. RMA guides can adapt tours to make specific curricular connections. Tours last one hour and you and your students are welcome to continue to explore the museum on your own if your schedule permits. Please make your reservation at least two weeks in advance. SUPPORTS NY STATE & NATIONAL LEARNING STANDARDS IN: The Arts, History/Social Studies. SUPPORTS SCOUT MERIT BADGE ACHIEVEMENT IN: The Arts. (See ad under Multicultural on page 100.) REGION: New York County, NYC.

SKYSCRAPER MUSEUM, 39 Battery Pl., New York, NY 10280. Tel: 212-945-6324. Hrs: Wed.-Sun. 12-6PM, guided tours by appt. Mon. & Tues. 10AM-6PM, Wed.-Sun. 10AM-12PM. 2nd grade-College. Self-guided tours, Guided tours. Celebrates the City's rich architectural heritage and examines the historical forces and individuals that have shaped its successive skylines. COST: Fee. REGION: New York County, NYC.

WHITNEY MUSEUM OF AMERICAN ART, 945 Madison Ave. at 75th St., NY, NY 10021. Tel: 1-800-WHITNEY. Hrs: Wed., Thurs., Sat. & Sun. 11AM-6PM, Fri. 1-9PM. Self-guided Tours, Guided Tours. Collections of 20th century American art. COST: Free/Fee. REGION: New York County, NYC.

BEHIND THE SCENE TOURS

APPLEBEE'S. Check website for a location near you. Tel: 888-244-4022. Email: groupsales@applemetro.com. Website: www.applemetrorestaurants.com. GRADE LEVEL: All grades. GROUP TYPE: All youth groups. PROGRAM TYPE: Day Trip, Guided Tour. REGISTRATION: Mail, Online, Phone, Submit Tax Exempt Forms Prior to Visit, Prepay. FOOD: Lunch offered. RECOMM. LENGTH OF VISIT: 90 minutes. RECOMM. RATIO OF STUDENT TO STAFF: 20:1. ARRIVAL TIPS: Bus drop off and pick up at designated entrance. COST: Varies.

New York's favorite restaurant is now New York's favorite classroom. Ask about our new Mad Science Kitchen Chemistry Field Trip & After School Dinner Clubs. Cooking is all about chemistry! You will be treated to Mad Science's most amazing demonstrations. Each program is followed by lunch. Kids feel like chefs for a day as they step into our one of a kind kitchen to learn the basics of food safety and restaurant operations in kitchen tours that are designed to compliment NYS Learning Standards. After dining, each student receives a junior chef certificate with an added bonus to redeem for a special treat on their next visit. The education program is also approved by the board of education. Be sure to ask about our pre-visit materials that fit the New York State learning standards for grades K-12. Mention this ad for additional discounted rates! SUPPORTS NY STATE & NATIONAL LEARNING STANDARDS IN: Social Studies, Health Education. REGION: New York County, NYC.

CHEVYS FRESH MEX. Telephone: 212-262-4022. Fax: 212-262-4050. Website: www.applemetrorestaurants.com. Email: groupsales@applemetro.com. Hrs: Education programs start at 10AM or 10:30AM. Regular dining starts at 11AM. GRADE LEVEL: All grades. GROUP TYPE: All youth groups. PROGRAM TYPE: Guided Tours, Workshops. REGISTRATION: Mail, Online, Phone, Submit Tax Exempt Forms Prior to Visit, Prepay. FOOD: Lunch offered. RECOMM. LENGTH OF VISIT: 90 minutes. RECOMM. RATIO OF STUDENT TO STAFF: 20:1. ARRIVAL TIPS: Bus drop off and pick up at designated entrance. COST: Varies.

Chevys Fresh Mex Tortilla Classes – Have fun with your food. Voted the best restaurant in the New York Area for families, Chevys now brings the fun to groups. Learn the history of Central America's favorite food – the Tortilla. Students learn about food safety and our time-honored recipe for the best tortillas around. Watch as el Machino turns ordinary dough into the basis for a fabulous taco lunch. Ask about our new Mad Science Kitchen Chemistry Field Trip & After School Dinner Clubs. Cooking is all about chemistry! You will be treated to Mad Science's most amazing demonstrations. Education programs start at 10:00 or 10:30AM. Space is limited and subject to availability. Call for pricing and be sure to ask about our free pit kits. Avocado pits from our fresh guacamole and instruction on how to grow your own plant. For pricing & availability at participating NY area Chevys, please call 212-262-4022. Free Pre-Visit Materials Included. SUPPORTS NY STATE & NATIONAL LEARNING STANDARDS IN: Health & Safety. SUPPORTS SCOUT MERIT BADGE ACHIEVEMENT IN: Health & Safety. REGION: New York County, NYC.

HARLEM HIP-HOP TOURS, 69 W. 106th St., Ste. 5B, New York, NY 10025. Telephone: 212-769-9047. Fax: 646-390-5898. Email: info@h3tours.com. Website: www.h3tours.com. Hrs: 9AM-5PM. Contact: Adrienne Smith. GRADE LEVEL: 1st-12th. GROUP TYPE: All youth groups & homeschoolers. PROGRAM TYPE: Day Trips, Overnight Trips, Guided Tours, Guided Activities, Performances, Workshops. MAX. GROUP SIZE: 350, minimum 2. COST: Starts at $15/person.

Harlem Hip-Hop (H3) Tours provides fun and educational field trips for students. We specialize in tours of Harlem and New York City's hip-hop industry. Whether it's a walking tour of Columbia University's campus, a behind-the-scenes tour of the Apollo Theater or a visit to a hip-hop music studio, H3 Tours provides unique, hands-on field trips that augment a student's education. H3 Tours operates Monday thru Saturday, year-round. Tours start at $15pp and can be customized to suit any school's curricular or financial needs. For more information visit www.h3tours.com or call 800-655-2091. SUPPORTS NY STATE & NATIONAL STANDARDS IN: The Arts, History/Social Studies, Physical Education, Technology. SUPPORTS SCOUT MERIT BADGE ACHIEVEMENT IN: The Arts, Citizenship, Performing Arts, Personal Fitness, Physical Ed/Recreation, Social Studies, Science/Technology. REGION: New York County, NYC.

HUNTS POINT TERMINAL PRODUCE COOPERATIVE ASSOCIATION, Terminal Markets, off Bruckner Blvd., Bronx, NY 10474. Tel: 718-589-4095. Hrs: Mon.-Fri., Tour at 9:45AM. Children under 12 yrs not permitted. Guided Tours. Tour this market that supplies 3.3 billion pounds of fruits and vegetables a year to 10 million consumers. COST: Fee. REGION: Bronx County, NYC.

JOYCE GOLD HISTORY TOURS OF NEW YORK, 141 W. 17th St., New York, New York 10011. Telephone: 212-242-5762. Fax: 212-242-6374. Hrs: 8AM-9PM. Email: Joyce@joycegoldhistorytours.com. Website: www.joycegoldhistorytours.com. Contact: Joyce Gold. GRADE LEVEL: All grades. GROUP TYPE: All youth groups. PROGRAM TYPE: Day Trips, Overnight Trips, Guided Tours. MAX. GROUP SIZE: Any size group. COST: Varies. (See main listing under Social Studies on page 110.) REGION: New York County, NYC.

MACY'S, 151 W. 34th St., New York, NY 10001. Tel: 212-494-3827 or 212-494-4662. Email: john.wiltberger@macys.com. Website: www.macys.com/visitor. Hrs: Mon.-Sat. 10AM-9PM, Sun. 11AM-8PM. Contact: John Wiltberger. GRADE LEVEL: High school & college. Appropriate for student groups studying or interested in marketing, business, economics, art and design. GROUP TYPE: School, After-School. PROGRAM TYPE: Day Trips, Guided Tours. REGISTRATION: Online, Phone. FOOD: Variety of menu selections. ARRIVAL TIPS: Bus drop off and pick up at designated entrance. COST: 10+ students, $10/person includes an 11% savings pass.

Macy's offers, by reservation, tours of the world's largest store. Your group will meet in the Visitors Center on the 34th Street Balcony and learn the history of a world-famous retail operation, from its humble one-room beginnings on 14th Street, where the first day's receipts totaled $11.06, to today's 20-story landmark with over 45 acres of floor space. Plus, in celebration of Macy's 150th Anniversary, you will be treated to anecdotes and interesting facts about how business was conducted in the building over 100 years ago. You will then tour various areas of the selling floor to learn about merchandise placement, marketing techniques, visual statements and more. SUPPORTS NY STATE & NATIONAL LEARNING STANDARDS IN: Social Studies. SUPPORTS SCOUT MERIT BADGE ACHIEVEMENT IN: American Business, Career Exploration. REGION: New York County, NYC.

NBC STUDIO TOUR/NBC EXPERIENCE STORE, 30 Rockefeller Plaza, New York, NY 10112. Tel: 212-664-3700. Fax: 212-664-5960. Website: www.nbcstudiotour.com. GRADE LEVEL: 1st-college. GROUP TYPE: All youth groups. PROGRAM TYPE: Day Trips, Guided Tours. MAX. GROUP SIZE: 30. COST: Varies.

Since 1933, NBC has offered this historic tour that takes you behind-the-scenes of NBC's New York operations. An NBC Page will be your ambassador to the world of the Peacock network. The tour gives you the opportunity to visit some of our most famous studios including (but all subject to availability and production schedules): MSNBC, NBC Nightly News, NBC Sports, Late Night with Jimmy Fallon, and Saturday Night Live. Tours are conducted in a working facility that will give you the opportunity to maybe catch a glimpse of a show in pre-production or cross paths with a famous NBC personality. Tour tickets are available at the NBC Experience Store. Other curriculum subjects covered: American History, Current Events, Multimedia, Social Studies, Weather. SUPPORTS NY STATE & NATIONAL LEARNING STANDARDS IN: Science, Social Studies. SUPPORTS SCOUT MERIT BADGE ACHIEVEMENT IN: American Business. REGION: New York County, NYC.

BIKING TOURS & RENTALS

BIKE AND ROLL NYC, Hudson River Park, Pier 84, 557 12th Ave., New York, NY 10036. Tel: 212-260-0400. Fax: 212-564-2525. Email: rachel@bikeandroll.com. Website: www.bikeandroll.com. Hrs: Mar.-Nov. Contact: Rachel Karr. GRADE LEVEL: Middle school and above. GROUP TYPE: All youth groups & homeschoolers. PRO-GRAM TYPE: Day Trips, Guided Tours. REGISTRATION: Mail, Phone, Submit waiver forms prior to visit, Prepay. TICKET/VOUCHER RETURN POLICY: Varies per group. RECOMM. LENGTH OF VISIT: 3-4 hours. ARRIVAL TIPS: Bus drop off and pick up at designated entrance. COST: Varies.

Bike the Greenway! Bike and Roll NYC allows youth and adults alike to experience New York like never before. Our tours are led by knowledgeable guides who always have safety as their first concern. You'll be awed by views of the city skyline as you ride along the car-free Hudson River Park Greenway to beautiful Central Park or over the famous Brooklyn Bridge. For those schools based in New York City, give your students a view of NYC from a different perspective! For those schools visiting NYC-why spend your time sitting on a tour bus? With Bike and Roll your group's trip to New York will be the highlight of the year; active, safe, educational and fun! SUPPORTS NY STATE & NATIONAL LEARNING STANDARDS IN: Physical Education. SUPPORTS SCOUT MERIT BADGE ACHIEVEMENT IN: Physical Ed/Recreation. REGION: New York County, NYC.

BOAT EXCURSIONS & HARBOR CRUISES

CIRCLE LINE SIGHTSEEING CRUISES, Pier 83, W. 42nd St., New York, NY 10036. Tel: 212-630-8885. Fax: 212-631-0569. Email: groups@circleline42.com. Website: www.circleline42.com. Contact: Andreas Sappok. GRADE LEVEL: K-College. GROUP TYPE: All youth groups & homeschoolers. PROGRAM TYPE: Day Trips, Guided Tours. MAX. GROUP SIZE: Circle Line Boat-525 & The Beast-145. COST: Varies.

Full Island cruise around Manhattan Island (3hrs) or Liberty Cruise (90min.). It's fasci-nating and fun all in one! Guides point out major landmarks in the five boroughs and NJ, detailing the 20 bridges, over 25 historic sites and the majestic Statue of Liberty. Students learn the history, geography and architecture. The Beast, a 30-minute speedboat thrill ride around NY Harbor is perfect for field trips. With speeds building up to 45mph, its like a roller coaster on the water. Ask about combination packages. Reservations are necessary, call for times. SUPPORTS NY STATE & NATIONAL LEARN-ING STANDARDS IN: Social Studies. SUPPORTS SCOUT MERIT BADGE ACHIEVEMENT IN: Environmental Science, Water. (See ad under Proms & School Celebrations on page 102.) REGION: New York County, NYC.

HARBOR EXPERIENCE COMPANIES, Located at Pier 16 and 17, South Street Seaport, New York, NY. Tel: 866-983-2542. Fax: 718-834-6369. Email: info@harborexperience.com. Website: www.harborexperience.com. Hrs: 10AM-7PM. Contact: Natalie Hernandez. GRADE LEVEL: K-12. GROUP TYPE: All youth groups & homeschoolers. PROGRAM TYPE: Day Trips, Guided Tours, Workshops. COST: Varies, $16+.

New York Water Taxi, Circle Line Downtown and Water Taxi Beach have merged to create Harbor Experience Companies, the leading waterborne tour and landside recreation company in New York City. Experience the harbor your way for an educational and fun time. Choose the cutting edge, interactive New York Water Taxi for a real New York experience. Circle Line Downtown's ZEPHYR cruise is onboard a one-of- a-kind yacht. If you're looking for a boat ride with a bite choose SHARK. All cruises depart from South Street Seaport where you will find Water Taxi Beach for lunch and fun with miniature golf, skeeball and ping pong. We have something for every taste and every budget. SUPPORTS NY STATE & NATIONAL LEARNING STANDARDS IN: Science & Social Studies. SUPPORTS SCOUT MERIT BADGE ACHIEVEMENT IN: Science, Social Studies. (See New York City Featured City Page on page 230.) REGION: New York County, NYC.

MARCO POLO CRUISES, 2430 FDR Drive East Service Road, New York, NY 10010. Tel: 212-691-6693. Fax: 718-721-2573. Email: info@marcopolocruises.com. Website: www.marcopolocruises.com. Hrs: Vary. Contact: Alex or Ralf. GRADE LEVEL: All grades. GROUP TYPE: All youth groups & homeschoolers. PROGRAM TYPE: Day Trips, Guided Tours. COST: Fee.

Marco Polo Cruises is New York City's premier charter yacht company. Kids love our fun and educational field trip cruises on our Cruise Ships. Sail alongside the expansive Manhattan skyline, famous bridges (Manhattan, Brooklyn and Williamsburgh) the historic Statue of Liberty, and other New York City landmarks like Battery Park, South Street Seaport, Governors Island, Buttermilk Channel, and Brooklyn Navy Yard. Every one of our New York City field trip cruises is customized to fit the needs of each group, including times, departure points, multilingual narrations and more. SUPPORTS NY STATE & NATIONAL LEARNING STANDARDS IN: History/Social Studies. SUPPORTS SCOUT MERIT BADGE ACHIEVEMENT IN: Social Studies. REGION: New York County, NYC.

NY WATERWAY TOURS AND SIGHTSEEING CRUISES, Pier 78, 455 12th Ave. at 38th St., New York, NY 10018. Tel: 800-533-3779/201-902-8711. Email: scher@nywaterway.com. Hrs: Year round, hrs vary. Contact: Maritza Scher 201-902-8711. GRADE LEVEL: All grades. GROUP TYPE: All youth groups & homeschoolers. PROGRAM TYPE: Day Trips, Guided Tours, Performances. MAX. GROUP SIZE: Boat capacity 299, can charter multiple boats. COST: Varies.

Our 90-Minute Skyline Cruise offers views of more attractions than any other cruise in the harbor. A Certified Tour Guide provides interesting facts for your Student Tour Group about all of the sights that make NYC so special, including the Statue of Liberty, Empire State Building, United Nations, the South Street Seaport and the Brooklyn Bridge. The Skyline Cruise is offered year-round and sails seven days a week. Available as an evening City Lights Cruise, perfect for older Student Travelers. Ask about our two unique History Tours & our Architecture Cruise. Each take a more detailed looked at NYC from distinct angles. SUPPORTS NY STATE, NJ STATE & NATIONAL LEARNING STANDARDS IN: Art, History, Social Studies. SUPPORTS SCOUT MERIT BADGE ACHIEVEMENT IN: Environmental Science, Water. (See New York City Featured City Page on page 230.) REGION: New York County, NYC & Bergen County, Northern NJ.

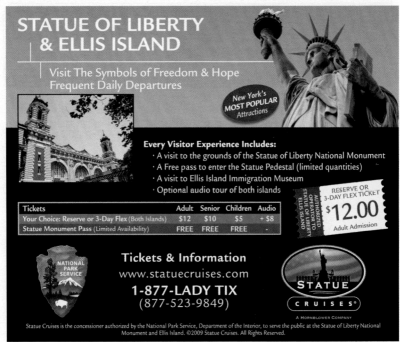

STATUE CRUISES, LLC. Two departure locations: Battery Park in Manhattan or Liberty State Park in Jersey City. Tel: 877-LADY TIX (877-532-9849). Fax: 201-432-1801. Email: info@statuecruises.com. Website www.statuecruises.com. Hrs: Vary, call for schedule. GRADE LEVEL: All grades. GROUP TYPE: All youth groups. PROGRAM TYPE: Day Trips, Self-guided Activities, Guided Tours. REGISTRATION: Mail, Online, Phone, Prepay, Tickets mailed prior to visit. FOOD: Variety of menu selections, Vegetarian, Can bring own food, Place to eat on site, Beverages available, Meal vouchers. RECOMM. LENGTH OF VISIT: One island, 2-3 hours; two islands, 4-5 hours. RECOMM. RATIO OF STUDENT TO STAFF: 10:1. ARRIVAL TIPS: Expedite check in (reserve tickets only), Bus parking (Liberty St. Park only), Bus drop off and pick up at designated entrance (Liberty St. Park only). COST: $12 adults, $10 seniors, $5 children ages 5-12 yrs.

Statue Cruises is the operator of ferry service to the Statue of Liberty National Monument and Ellis Island Immigration Museum. Visit two of the nation's most iconic monuments. Experience history first hand. Multiple daily departures. Great educational and recreational opportunity. Special park programs available; call for details. Group trips can be booked online at www.statuecruises.com or over the phone at 877-LADY TIX (877-523-9849). No booking fees. Two departures locations - Battery Park in Manhattan (convenient for public transportation) or Liberty State Park in Jersey City (plenty of parking available). SUPPORTS NY STATE & NATIONAL LEARNING STANDARDS IN: History/Social Studies. SUPPORTS SCOUT MERIT BADGE ACHIEVEMENT IN: Social Studies, Physical Ed/Recreation. REGION: New York County, NYC.

BOTANICAL GARDENS & NATURE CENTERS

BROOKLYN BOTANIC GARDEN, 1000 Washington Ave., Brooklyn, NY 11225. Tel: 718-623-7200. Fax: 718-857-2430. Website: www.bbg.org. Hrs: Garden: Mid-Mar.-Oct., Tues.-Fri. 8AM-6PM; Nov.-Mid-Mar., Tues.-Fri. 8AM-4:30PM. Closed on Mondays. Contact: Registration Office. GRADE LEVEL: All grades. GROUP TYPE: All youth groups & homeschoolers. PROGRAM TYPE: Day Trips, Self-guided Tours, Guided Tours, Workshops. MAX. GROUP SIZE: 35. COST: Free self-guided visits. Fees vary for guided tours & workshops.

Brooklyn Botanic Garden offers a variety of opportunities to develop students' appreciation of nature. Programs include: a guided tour to learn more about the Garden; the Garden Exploration Tour, which includes a planting activity; or school workshops, covering a wide range of topics designed to support national and local science standards. School groups can preregister to visit the Garden for a self-guided visit, free of charge. Pre-visit materials are available. To pre-register for your self guided visit, go to www.bbg.org/childrensgroups. D.O.E. certified teacher enrichment workshops are offered. Internships and volunteer opportunities for high school and college-age students are available. All school groups must pre-register. SUPPORTS NY STATE & NATIONAL LEARNING STANDARDS IN: Science. SUPPORTS SCOUT MERIT BADGE ACHIEVEMENT IN: Gardening, Nature, Plants. (See Regional Highlights on page 13). REGION: Kings County, NYC.

THE NEW YORK BOTANICAL GARDEN, Bronx River Parkway & Fordham Road, Bronx, NY 10456-5126. Tel: 718-817-8181. Fax: 718-817-8829. Email: school_programs@nybg.org. Website: www.nybg.org/edu. Hrs: Tues.-Sun. Contact: Registration Office. GRADE LEVEL: All grades. GROUP TYPE: All youth groups. PROGRAM TYPE: Day Trips, Self-guided Tours, Guided Tours, Workshops. COST: Varies.

Take an exciting, educational class trip to The New York Botanical Garden, a national leader in informal science education. With 250 acres of plants from around the world, your students can discover the wonders of nature up close. Students participate in hands-on activities from sowing seeds and harvesting crops, examining wetlands, and dissecting plant parts to investigating plants as food. Explore diverse ecosystems from the 50-acre forest to the rain forests and deserts of the Enid A. Haupt Conservatory. Take advantage of the exceptional 12-acre Everett Children's Adventure Garden, the Ruth Rea Howell Family Garden and the Mitsubishi Wild Wetland Trail. Ask about our teacher workshops and open houses. SUPPORTS NY STATE & NATIONAL LEARNING STANDARDS IN: Science. SUPPORTS SCOUT MERIT BADGE ACHIEVEMENT IN: Gardening, Nature, Plants. (See Regional Highlights in page 13). REGION: Bronx County, NYC.

QUEENS BOTANICAL GARDEN, 43-50 Main St., Flushing, NY 11355. Tel: 718-886-3800. Hrs: Apr.-Oct.: Tues.-Fri. 8AM-6PM, Sat.-Sun. 8AM-6PM. Nov.-Mar.: Tues.-Sun. 8AM-4:30PM. Self-guided Tours, Guided Tours. From thematic gardens and historic plantings recalling QBG's World's Fair origins to new gardens showcasing native species and sustainable landscape practices. COST: Fee. REGION: Queens County, NYC.

SNUG HARBOR CULTURAL CENTER & BOTANICAL GARDEN, 1000 Richmond Terrace, Staten Island, NY 10301. Tel: 718-448-2500. Hrs: Tues.-Sun. 10AM-4PM. Pre K-8th grade. Self-guided Tours, Guided Tours. Chinese Scholar's Garden, The Secret Garden, a butterfly, pond, herb, shade, and sensory gardens, barn and farm, and a glasshouse with perennial border. COST: Fee. REGION: Richmond Borough, NYC.

WAVE HILL, 675 West 252nd Street, Bronx, NY 10471. Tel: 718-549-3200. Hrs: Apr. 15-Oct. 14: Tues.-Sun. 9AM-5:30PM; Oct. 15-Apr. 14: Tues.-Sun. 9AM-4:30PM. Self-guided Tours, Guided Tours. A 28-acre public garden, greenhouse and cultural center. COST: Free/Fee. REGION: Bronx County, NYC.

BROADWAY & OFF-BROADWAY

BESTOFBROADWAY.COM'S BROADWAY SCHOOLROOM: Group Sales Box Office, 226 W. 47th St., 10th Floor, New York, NY 10036. Tel: 212-398-8383/ 800-223-7565. Fax: 212-398-8389. Email: info@BestofBroadway.com. Website: www.BestOfBroadway.com & www.BestOfBroadway.com/Schoolroom. Hrs: Mon.-Fri. 9AM-5PM. Contact: Matt Austin. GRADE LEVEL: All grades. GROUP TYPE: All youth groups. PROGRAM TYPE: Day Trips, Performance, Workshops. COST: Varies.

We offer a vast variety of workshops which utilize experienced Broadway professionals who tailor each program for your group(s) by using themes and issues of shows that focus on practical hands-on learning, creating collaborations to dynamically enhance team building both on and off stage, and foster opportunities to obtain and/or fine tune technical, theatrical and life skills. For show tickets, programs, curriculum guides, meals and admission to other attractions that compliment and add value to the students' Broadway and New York City experience "one call does it all!" Proud members of The Student & Youth Travel Association (SYTA). SUPPORTS NY STATE & NATIONAL LEARNING STANDARDS IN: The Arts. SUPPORTS SCOUT MERIT BADGE ACHIEVEMENT IN: Theater. (See ad under Tickets on page 130 and New York City Featured City Page on page 226.) REGION: New York County, NYC.

BILLY ELLIOT THE MUSICAL, Imperial Theatre, 249 West 45th Street, NY, NY 10036. Tel: Call Telecharge at 212-239-6262. Website: www.billyelliotgroups.com. GRADE LEVEL: All grades. GROUP TYPE: All youth groups & homeschoolers. PROGRAM TYPE: Performances. COST: Varies.

"Billy Elliot the Musical" is the new show that has captured Broadway's heart, delighted the critics and swept the awards--winning 10 Tony Awards® including Best Musical! Called "Extraordinarily uplifting" by Time Out New York and "The freshest and most inspiring show in years" by The New York Times, "Billy Elliot" is a joyous, exciting and feel-good celebration of one boy following his heart and making his dreams come true. "Billy Elliot" is brought to life by the original team behind the critically acclaimed movie – director Stephen Daldry, choreographer Peter Darling and writer Lee Hall – along with music legend Elton John. SUPPORTS NY STATE & NATIONAL LEARNING STANDARDS IN: The Arts. SUPPORTS SCOUT MERIT BADGE ACHIEVEMENT IN: Theater. (See ad under Theater-Dance-Music on page 120 and New York City Featured City Page on page 226.) REGION: New York County, NYC.

BLUE MAN GROUP, 434 Lafayette St., New York, NY 10003. Tel: 212-260-8993. Fax: 212-673-8424. Email: groupsnyc@blueman.com. Website: www.blueman.com. Contact: Mary Frembgen. GRADE LEVEL: 6th-college. GROUP TYPE: All youth groups & homeschoolers. PROGRAM TYPE: Performances. MAX. GROUP SIZE: 298. COST: 15 + students is $56-$78 per person.

The critically acclaimed and award-winning Blue Man Group creates theatrical experiences that defy categorization. Three bald and blue characters take the audience on a multimedia journey that is funny, intelligent, and visually stunning. A dynamic live band accompanies them with haunting tribal rhythms, driving the show to its unforgettable climax. "A Sensation!" raves Time Magazine. SUPPORTS NY STATE &

NATIONAL LEARNING STANDARDS IN: The Arts. SUPPORTS SCOUT MERIT BADGE ACHIEVEMENT IN: Theater. (See ad under Theater-Dance-Music on page 120 and New York City Featured City Page on page 227.) REGION: New York County, NYC.

THE GAZILLION BUBBLE SHOW, 340 W. 50th St., New York, NY 10019. Tel: 866-6-GAZTIX.Website: www.gazillionbubbleshow.com. GRADE LEVEL: All grades. GROUP TYPE: All youth groups. PROGRAM TYPE: Performances.

Step into the "unbubblelievable" magical kingdom of Gazillion Bubble Show with 16-time Guinness World Record holder Fan Yang. It is the first and only interactive stage production of its kind complete with fantastic lighting effects, lasers, and jaw-dropping masterpieces of bubble artistry. This show is fun for the whole family and appropriate for all ages. The Gazillion Bubble Show has been featured on "The Oprah Winfrey Show," "The David Letterman Show," "Live with Regis and Kelly," "The Ellen Degeneres Show," "The View," "CBS Sunday Morning," and TV stations around the world. SUPPORTS NY STATE & NATIONAL LEARNING STANDARDS IN: The Arts. SUPPORTS SCOUT MERIT BADGE ACHIEVEMENT IN: Theater. (See ad under Theater-Dance-Music on page 122.) REGION: New York County, NYC.

THE LION KING, The Minskoff Theatre, Broadway & 45th St., NY, NY. Book your Group direct with Disney On Broadway Group Sales: Tel: 212-703-1040 or 1-800-439-9000. Fax: 212-703-1085. Email: groupsales@disneyonbroadway.com. Website: www.disneyonbroadway.com. GRADE LEVEL: All grades. GROUP TYPE: All youth groups & homeschoolers. PROGRAM TYPE: Performances. COST: Varies.

Over 45 million people worldwide have come to discover the wonder, the majesty, and the truly one-of-a-kind experience that is "The Lion King," the world's most spectacular musical. Hailed by Newsweek as "a landmark event in entertainment," "The Lion King" is a breathtaking adventure that stretches the boundaries of Broadway, from the heart of Africa to the plains of your imagination. See it now. Remember it forever. SUPPORTS NY STATE & NATIONAL LEARNING STANDARDS IN: The Arts. SUPPORTS SCOUT MERIT BADGE ACHIEVEMENT IN: Theater. (See ad under Theater-Dance-Music on page 121 and New York City Featured City Page on page 227.) REGION: New York County, NYC.

THE LITTLE MERMAID, Lunt-Fontanne Theatre, Broadway & 46th St, New York, NY 10036. Book your Group direct with Disney On Broadway Group Sales Tel: 212-703-1040 or 1-800-439-9000. Fax: 212-703-1085. Email: groupsales@disneyonbroadway.com. Website: www.disneyonbroadway.com. GRADE LEVEL: All grades. GROUP TYPE: All youth groups & homeschoolers. PROGRAM TYPE: Performances. COST: Varies.

Take a journey to the wonderful world under the sea and beyond your wildest dreams. Disney's "The Little Mermaid" combines a timeless tale, state-of-art stage-craft and irresistible songs (including "Under the Sea," "Kiss the Girl" and "Part of Your World"). It adds up to what Time Magazine calls "one of the most ravishing shows ever seen on a Broadway stage." SUPPORTS NY STATE & NATIONAL LEARNING STANDARDS IN: The Arts. SUPPORTS SCOUT MERIT BADGE ACHIEVEMENT IN: Theater. (See ad under Theater-Dance-Music on page 121 and New York City Featured City Page on page 227.) REGION: New York County, NYC.

MARY POPPINS, New Amsterdam Theatre, 214 West 42nd Street, New York, NY 10036. Book your Group direct with Disney On Broadway Group Sales Tel: 212-703-1040 or 1-800-439-9000. Fax: 212-703-1085. Email: groupsales@disneyonbroadway.com. Website: www.disneyonbroadway.com. GRADE LEVEL: All grades. GROUP TYPE: All youth groups & homeschoolers. PROGRAM TYPE: Performances. COST: Varies.

Believe in the magic of "Mary Poppins," the Broadway musical guaranteed to lift your spirits to new heights. Produced by Disney and Cameron Mackintosh, "Mary Poppins" combines the stories of P.L. Travers and the Academy Award-winning film to create this perfectly magical musical, filled with priceless memories, timeless songs (Chim Chim Cher-ee, Let's Go Fly a Kite, Supercalifragilisticexpialidocious) and more than just a spoonful of spectacular Disney stagecraft. So come, visit the one place on earth where more than just your imagination takes flight, and you too will believe in the magic of "Mary Poppins." SUPPORTS NY STATE & NATIONAL LEARNING STANDARDS IN: The Arts. SUPPORTS SCOUT MERIT BADGE ACHIEVEMENT IN: Theater. (See ad under Theater-Dance-Music on page 121 and New York City Featured City Page on page 228.) REGION: New York County, NYC.

SCHOOL THEATRE TICKET PROGRAM, 1560 Broadway, Suite 1113, New York, NY 10036. Tel: 212-354-4722. Fax: 212-575-4740. Website: www.schooltix.com. Contact: Howard Lev/Suzanne Krebs.

Discounts for all groups and individuals to Broadway, off-Broadway shows, music, dance, opera, sporting events, museums and more. To have your facility added to our mailing list to receive discount coupons, visit our web site and fill out an application. We can arrange groups with a minimum of 15 or more (depending on the show) for all Broadway and off-Broadway shows. Discounts vary per show. Call and speak with one of our representatives. To stay up-to-date about our current offers please visit our web site and join our e-mail club. Don't see the show you want? Contact us. REGION: New York County, NYC.

SHREK THE MUSICAL, Broadway Theater, 1681 Broadway, New York, NY 10019. Tel: 212-239-6262 or 800-432-7780 (outside NY Metro area). Website: www.ShrekTheMusical.com. GRADE LEVEL: All grades, No children under 4. GROUP TYPE: All youth groups & homeschoolers. PROGRAM TYPE: Performances. REGISTRATION: Online, Phone, Prepay. COST: $35.50-120.00.

Time Out New York calls "Shrek The Musical" "The best musical for younger audiences since The Lion King!" Based on the Oscar®-winning DreamWorks film that started it all, this spectacular new production brings the hilarious story of everyone's favorite ogre to life on the Broadway stage. "Shrek The Musical" features a terrific score of 19 all-new songs and a cast of 27 that Newsday calls "extraordinary." Full of big laughs, great dancing and breathtaking scenery, "Shrek The Musical" is part romance, part twisted fairy tale and all irreverent fun for students of all ages. SUPPORTS NY STATE & NATIONAL LEARNING STANDARDS IN: The Arts. SUPPORTS SCOUT MERIT BADGE ACHIEVEMENT IN: Theater. (See ad under Theater-Dance-Music on page 126 and New York City Featured City Page on page 229.) REGION: New York County, NYC.

For more additional information on class trips, please visit us at
ClassTrips.com

STOMP, Orpheum Theater, 2nd Ave. at 8th St., New York, NY. Tel: Groups: 800-Broadway #2. Ticketmaster: 800-982-2787. Websites: www.stomponline.com & Ticketmaster.com. Hrs: Tues.-Fri. 8PM, Sat. 7 & 10:30PM, Sun. 3 & 7PM. GRADE LEVEL: 5th-college. GROUP TYPE: All youth groups & homeschoolers. PROGRAM TYPE: Performances. COST: Varies.

STOMP is explosive, sophisticated, utterly unique and appeals to audiences of all ages. The international percussion sensation has garnered an armful of awards and rave reviews, and has appeared on numerous national television shows. The eight-member troupe uses everything but conventional percussion instruments – matchboxes, wooden poles, brooms, garbage cans, hubcaps – to fill the stage with magnificent rhythms. The New York Times calls it "A sure-fire crowd pleaser with a rock-and-roll heart!" "Wonderful, fabulous, hypnotizing!" raves The Village Voice, and Newsday says, "If you are looking for good entertainment, something that will absolutely amaze you, go to the Orpheum Theatre to have the time of your life!" SUPPORTS NY STATE & NATIONAL STANDARDS IN: The Arts. SUPPORTS SCOUT MERIT BADGE ACHIEVEMENT IN: Theater. (See ad under Theater-Dance-Music on page 126.) REGION: New York County, NYC.

TELECHARGE.COM GROUP SALES, 330 W. 42nd St., 22nd Floor, New York, NY 10036. Tel: 800-432-7780. Fax: 212-302-0997. Email:groupsales@telecharge.com. Website: www.Telecharge.com/groups. Hrs: Mon.–Fri. 9AM–9PM EST, Sat. & Sun. 1–9PM EST. Contact: Dianne Tack. GRADE LEVEL: Late elementary school-college. GROUP TYPE: All youth groups & homeschoolers. PROGRAM TYPE: Performances, Workshops, Day Trips, Overnight Trips, Self-guided Tours, Guided Tours, Self-guided Activities, Guided Activities. MAX. GROUP SIZE: Based on the size of the theatre, minimums start at 10 but vary by show. REGISTRATION: Online, Phone, Prepay, Tickets mailed prior to visit. TICKET/VOUCHER RETURN POLICY: All sales are final. RECOMM. LENGTH OF VISIT: 2-3 Hours is the typical run time on a show. RECOMM. RATIO OF STUDENT TO STAFF: Varies. ARRIVAL TIPS: Bus drop-off and pick-up at designated areas. COST: Prices are determined by each show and venue individually and there is usually a price point that is appropriate for all types of groups. Please contact us for full pricing and schedule options.

For schools, scouts, camps, families, adults - groups of all shapes and sizes, Telecharge.com Group Sales makes planning a trip to Broadway a snap. We sell tickets for all shows in New York, for select venues in Philadelphia, Washington and Las Vegas and can help you make all the arrangements you need. We've got a team of theatre experts who know everything there is to know about life on- or off-stage. Let us help you choose the perfect play or musical, and show you how to make the most of your trip to the theatre. REGION: New York County, NYC.

CHILDREN'S MUSEUMS

BROOKLYN CHILDREN'S MUSEUM, 145 Brooklyn Avenue, Brooklyn, NY 11213. Tel: 718-735-4400. Hrs: Wed.-Fri. 12-5PM, Sat. & Sun. 10AM-5PM. Features hands-on exhibits and activities on science, art and cultures. COST: Fee. REGION: Kings County, NYC.

CHILDREN'S MUSEUM OF MANHATTAN, 212 W. 83rd St., New York, NY 10024. Tel: 212-721-1223. Hrs: Public: Tues.-Sun. 10AM-5PM; School Groups: Mon.-Fri. by appt. only. Pre K-6th grade. Guided Tours, Workshops. Five floors of literature, science, media and art activities and interactive exhibits. COST: Fee. REGION: New York County, NYC.

CHILDREN'S MUSEUM OF THE ARTS, 182 Lafayette St., New York, NY 10013. Tel: 212-274-0986. Hrs: School Groups: Mon.-Tues. 10AM, 12PM & 2PM. Pre K-6th grade. Self-guided Tours, Workshops. Collects, creates and exhibits children's art. COST: Fee. REGION: New York County, NYC.

JEWISH CHILDREN'S MUSEUM, 792 Eastern Parkway, Brooklyn, NY 11213. Tel: 718-907-8888. Hrs: Group Tour Times: Sun. 9:30AM & 10:30AM, Mon.-Thurs. 10AM & 12:30PM. Pre K-8th grade. Self-guided Tours, Guided Tours, Performances. Hands-on exhibits on Jewish life and history. COST: Fee. REGION: Kings County, NYC.

STATEN ISLAND CHILDREN'S MUSEUM, Snug Harbor Cultural Center, 1000 Richmond Terrace., Bldg. M, Staten Island, NY 10301. Tel: 718-273-2060. Hrs: Vary. Pre K-3rd grade. Self-guided Tours, Guided Tours, Workshops, Performances. Interactive exhibits in science, language arts, social studies and the arts. COST: Fee. REGION: Richmond County, NYC.

CIRCUS

ECONOMICS & BUSINESS MARKETS

MUSEUM OF AMERICAN FINANCE, 48 Wall Street, New York, NY 10005. Tel: 212-908-4110. Fax: 212-908-4601. Email: educator@financialhistory.org. Website: www.moaf.org. Hrs: Group tours Mon-Fri 10AM- 2:30PM. Contact: Bill Whitlock. GRADE LEVEL: 5th-College. GROUP TYPE: All Youth Groups. PROGRAM TYPE: Self-guided Tours, Guided Tours. MAX. GROUP SIZE: 30. REGISTRATION: Mail, Online, Phone. TICKET/VOUCHER RETURN POLICY: Cancellation fees of 50% of the total group tour expense will be assessed for last minute cancellations or no-shows. FOOD: Place to eat not available within site. RECOMM. LENGTH OF VISIT: 1.5 hours. RECOMM. RATIO OF STUDENT TO STAFF: 10:1. COST: $100 per group.

The Museum of American Finance, a Smithsonian affiliate, is the nation's only public museum of finance. Located on Wall Street just steps away from the New York Stock Exchange, the Museum offers interactive and engaging exhibits on the subjects of money, finance, entrepreneurship and banking. In 2009, the Museum launched "Tracking the Credit Crisis," a long-term exhibit on the current financial crisis. Educational tours are ideal for students of all ages. Groups work with trained museum educators who use inquiry-based discussion to help build critical thinking skills. SUPPORTS NY STATE & NATIONAL LEARNING STANDARDS IN: The Arts, Math, History/Social Studies. SUPPORTS SCOUT MERIT BADGE ACHIEVEMENT IN: The Arts, Life Skills and Social Studies. REGION: New York County, NYC.

THE FEDERAL RESERVE BANK, 33 Liberty St., New York, New York 10045. Telephone: 212-720-7678. Hrs: Mon.-Fri. 9:30AM, 10:30AM, 11:30AM, 1:30PM, 2:30PM & 3:30PM. 10th-12th grade. Guided Tours, Workshops. Visit one of the 12 federal government banks that make up the Federal Reserve System. COST: Free. REGION: New York County, NYC.

FARMS & PICK-YOUR-OWN

GREEN MEADOWS FARM, 73-50 Little Neck Parkway, Floral Park, NY 11004. Tel: 718-470-0224. Fax: 718-470-1109. Website: www.visitgreenmeadowsfarm.com. Hrs: Vary. Contact: Daniel Keyes. GRADE LEVEL: All grades. GROUP TYPE: All youth groups & homeschoolers. PROGRAM TYPE: Day Trips, Guided Tours, Performances. REGISTRATION: Phone, Prepay, Tickets mailed prior to visit. FOOD: Can bring own food, Place to eat on site. ARRIVAL TIPS: Bus parking. COST: Varies.

Green Meadows Farm offers a guided tour of over 300 farm animals in spring and fall to schools, day care centers and scout groups. The children touch the animals, feed the sheep, milk a cow, ride a pony and everyone takes a hayride. During October and November, all visitors select a pumpkin. During April and May, Green Meadow Farm produces Festival of Cultures. Dancing by Native Americans, Spanish Americans and West Africans. Other activities include Birds of Prey, Barnyard Games, Frogs from Around the World, music, and archery. In July and August, our visitors enjoy our farm activities and a walk through the woods with our birds of prey. SUPPORTS NY STATE & NATIONAL LEARNING STANDARDS IN: Science & Social Studies. SUPPORTS SCOUT MERIT BADGE ACHIEVEMENT IN: Animal Science. REGION: New York County, NYC.

FIELD DAYS & RECREATION

CHELSEA PIERS SPORTS & ENTERTAINMENT COMPLEX, 23rd Street & Hudson River Park, New York, NY 10011. Tel: 212-336-6777. Email: events@chelseapiers.com. Website: www.chelseapiers.com/specialevents. Hrs: Vary. GRADE LEVEL: K-College. GROUP TYPE: All Youth Groups. PROGRAM TYPE: Day Trips, Guided Activities, Workshops. REGISTRATION: Phone. FOOD: Variety. COST: Prices starting at $10 per student.

Chelsea Piers is the perfect location for school field trips and class team building programs. The 28-acre sports complex features indoor ice skating rinks, a gymnastics center, a rock-climbing wall, batting cages, indoor soccer fields, hardwood basketball courts, a 4-level golf driving range and a 40-lane bowling facility. The Chelsea Piers Special Events Team can customize a variety of activities for your group outing to fit your specific needs. Please call or visit our website to reserve a day of fun-filled activities. Chelsea Piers is also a great place for graduation parties and proms! SUPPORTS NY STATE & NATIONAL LEARNING STANDARDS IN: Physical Education. (See ad under Proms & School Celebrations on page 102.) REGION: New York County, NYC.

FISHING AT THE HARLEM MEER. Dana Discovery Center, 110th St. between Fifth & Lenox Avenues, New York, NY. Tel: 212-860-1370. Hrs: Apr.-Oct., Tues.-Sun. 10AM-4PM. K-12th grade. Self-guided Activities. Catch-and-release fishing. Provides bamboo poles and bait with a valid I.D. Reservations required for groups. COST: Fee. REGION: New York County, NYC.

GATEWAY NATIONAL RECREATION AREA, Public Affairs Office, 210 New York Ave., Staten Island, NY 10305. Tel: Jamaica Bay Unit: 718-338-3799; Staten Island Unit: 718-354-4500; Sandy Hook Unit: 732-872-5970. Hrs: Vary by location. Day Trips, Overnight Trips, Self-guided Tours, Guided Tours, Workshops. Programs in environmental education. COST: Free. REGION: Brooklyn, Queens, and Staten Island, NYC.

THE NATIONAL TRACK & FIELD HALL OF FAME (AT THE ARMORY), 216 Ft. Washington Ave. @ W. 168th St. in Upper Manhattan, NY, NY 10032. Tel: 212-923-1803 x11. Email: derrick@ArmoryTrack.com. Website: www.Armoryfoundation.org. Hrs: Daily 10AM-5PM. Contact: Derrick Adkins. GRADE LEVEL: K-12th. GROUP TYPE: All youth groups & homeschoolers. PROGRAM TYPE: Day Trips, Guided Activities. COST: Varies.

The National Track & Field Hall of Fame is a modern tri-level 15,000 Sq. ft. interactive experience designed for elementary through high school students celebrating the history, science and sociology of the sport of Track & Field. The visit concludes in the 75,000 sq. ft. New Balance Track & Field Center with its world class track. Students participate in non-competitive abbreviated mini Track & Field events to end the day, including Track & Field events Races, Relays, Throwing & Jumping! SUPPORTS NY STATE & NATIONAL LEARNING STANDARDS IN: Physical Education, Science, Social Studies. SUPPORTS SCOUT MERIT BADGE ACHIEVEMENT IN: Science, Sports & Games. REGION: New York County, NYC.

RANDALL'S ISLAND GOLF AND RECREATION CENTER, 1 Randall's Island, New York, NY 10035. Tel: 212-427-5689. Fax: 212-427-5681. Email: kelley@randallsislandgolf.com. Website: www.randallsislandgolf.com. Hrs: Daily 7AM-11PM. Contact: Kelley Brooke. GRADE LEVEL: All grades. GROUP TYPE: All youth groups & homeschoolers. PROGRAM TYPE: Day Trips, Self-guided Activities. REGISTRATION: Online, Phone, Prepay. TICKET/VOUCHER RETURN POLICY: Raindate policy. FOOD: Variety, Vegetarian, Place to eat on site, Beverages available. RECOMM. LENGTH OF VISIT: Varies. ARRIVAL TIPS: Expedite check-in, Bus parking, Bus drop off and pick up at designated entrance. COST: Fee, Group rates available.

Randall's Island Golf Center is considered NYC's most beautiful, spacious golf center. The 25 acre facility, overlooking the East River and uptown Manhattan, features 78 hitting stalls on two levels, grass tees, a 320 yard grass landing area, a 36 hole landscaped miniature golf course, a short game area, batting cages, a patio restaurant, a WiFi patio lounge and a special events tent. The facility also has extra activities such as volleyball, badminton, bocce ball, horse shoes, bongo ball and dodge ball. The golf center is the perfect spot within Manhattan to entertain camps and schools for a fraction of the cost that local competitors charge. SUPPORTS NY STATE & NATIONAL LEARNING STANDARDS IN: Physical Education. SUPPORTS SCOUT MERIT BADGE ACHIEVEMENT IN: Physical Ed/Recreation. REGION: New York County, NYC.

WOLLMAN RINK, in Central Park at 59th St., 6th Ave. entrance to the park, New York, New York 10065. Telephone: 212-439-6900 x12. Fax: 212-628-8322. Email: jjohnson@wollmanskatingrink.com. Website: www.wollmanrink.com. Hrs: Oct.-Apr. GRADE LEVEL: All grades. GROUP TYPE: All youth groups & homeschoolers. PROGRAM TYPE: Day Trips, Self-guided Activities, Guided Activities. COST: Varies.

Book your ice skating trip now!!!!! Wollman Rink is New York's most popular class trip destination in Central Park's Winter Wonderland. Also: After School Skating Lesson Programs. Exclusive and non-exclusive facility rentals available for Fundraisers. SUPPORTS NY STATE & NATIONAL LEARNING STANDARDS IN: Physical Education. SUPPORTS SCOUT MERIT BADGE ACHIEVEMENT IN: Skating. (See ad under Ice Skating on page 95.) REGION: New York County, NYC.

GROUP FRIENDLY RESTAURANTS

B.B. KING BLUES CLUB AND GRILL, 237 W. 42nd Street, New York, NY 10036. Tel: 212-997-4511. Fax: 212-997-4545. Email: melanie@bbkingblues.com. Website: www.bbkingblues.com. Hrs: 11AM-12AM. Contact: Melanie Carroll Shammout. GRADE LEVEL: All grades. GROUP TYPE: All Youth Groups. PROGRAM TYPE: Day Trips, Performances. MAX. GROUP SIZE: 650. MIN. GROUP SIZE: 15. REGISTRATION: Mail, Online, Phone, Prepay. FOOD: Variety of menu selections, Vegetarian, Place to eat on site, Beverages available. RECOMM. LENGTH OF VISIT: 1 hour. COST: Menus starting at $15.00.

Located in the heart of Times Square near all major transportation and Broadway shows, B.B. King Blues Club offers a one of a kind music experience that's perfect for groups of all ages & sizes. Your group can dine while enjoying free live music, or check out our weekend brunches with Strawberry Fields Beatles Tribute on Saturdays and the world famous Harlem Gospel Choir on Sundays! We make the entire planning process easy with all inclusive menus, special group rates and events as well as flexible time slots offering availability for Breakfast, Lunch and Dinner. SUPPORTS NY STATE & NATIONAL LEARNING STANDARDS IN: The Arts. SUPPORTS SCOUT MERIT BADGE ACHIEVEMENT IN: The Arts, Performing Arts. (See New York City Featured City Page on page 229.) REGION: New York County, NYC.

DAVE AND BUSTER'S, 234 West 42nd St., New York, NY 10036. Tel: 646-495-2015. Email: Benjamin_Maddy@DaveandBusters.com. Website: www.daveandbusters.com. Hrs: Sales office, 9AM-6PM. Contact: Benjamin Maddy. GRADE LEVEL: K-12th. GROUP TYPE: All youth groups & homeschoolers. PROGRAM TYPE: Self-guided Activities. REGISTRATION: Phone. FOOD: Variety of menu selections, Kosher, Vegetarian, Beverages available. RECOMM. LENGTH OF VISIT: 2-3 hours. RECOMM. RATIO OF STUDENT TO STAFF: 10:1 (before 2:30PM). ARRIVAL TIPS: Expedite check in, Bus parking. COST: Fee.

At Dave & Buster's your group will have a blast! Start out with a delicious meal and then move on to some games in our Million Dollar Midway. Spend an hour with us, or a whole day - at Dave & Buster's it's your call! We have packages for groups of 20 to 2,000; so for your next outing come eat, party & play at Dave & Buster's – your students will thank you! SUPPORTS NY STATE & NATIONAL LEARNING STANDARDS IN: Physical Education. SUPPORTS SCOUT MERIT BADGE ACHIEVEMENT IN: Physical Ed/Recreation. (See ad under Indoor Amusement Centers on page 96 and New York City Featured City Page on page 229.) REGION: New York County, NYC.

ESPN ZONE NYC, 1472 Broadway (42nd & Broadway), New York, NY 10036. Tel: 212-921-3776 (ESPN). Website: Espnzone.com. More than just a meal on the run, ESPN Zone is the hottest stop in the city with great food, high energy and a 10,000 sq. ft. sports arena filled with sports-themed games and interaction. ESPN Zone takes the concept of sports entertainment to a whole new level, and delivers an experience you won't find anywhere else. (See ad under Theme Restaurants on pages 128 and under Field Days and Recreation on page 90 and New York City Featured City Page on page 229.) REGION: New York County, NYC.

MARS 2112 RESTAURANT, 1633 Broadway at 51 St., New York, NY 10019. Tel: 212-582-2112. Fax: 212-245-2112. Email: efeliz@mars2112.com. Website: www.Mars2112.com. Hrs: Daily 11:00AM-9PM. Contact: Ericka Feliz. GRADE LEVEL: K-12th. GROUP TYPE: All youth groups & homeschoolers. MAX. GROUP SIZE: 500. MIN. GROUP SIZE: 15. FOOD: Variety of menu selections. RECOMM. LENGTH OF VISIT: 1.5 - 2 hours. ARRIVAL TIPS: Bus drop off and pick up at designated entrance. COST: From $16.00.

Mars 2112 is a spectacular mingling of reality and fantasy, a 35,000 square foot, bi-level multi-dimensional immersive environment that catapults guests to a whole new universe of escape. Get ready for an intergalactic dining adventure that's totally out-of-this-world! An experience for earthlings of all ages! Space travel, intergalactic shuttle, Arcade Game room (Cyberstreet), Martian food, fantasy and more! Mars 2112 invites your school to participate in our "Etiquette For Earthlings" program (check website for details). (See ad under Theme Restaurants on page 127.) REGION: New York County, NYC.

PLANET HOLLYWOOD, 1540 Broadway, New York, NY 10036. Tel: 212-333-7827. Fax: 212-730-2753. Website: www.planethollywood.com. Hrs: Restaurant: Sun.-Thurs. 11AM to 12AM, Fri. & Sat. 11AM-1AM; Merchandise Shop: Sun.-Thurs. 10AM-1AM, Fri. & Sat. 10AM-2AM. REGISTRATION: Mail, Online, Phone. FOOD: Variety of menu selections, Kosher, Vegetarian, Place to eat on site, Beverages available, Meal vouchers. RECOMM. LENGTH OF VISIT: 1hour, 15 minutes. ARRIVAL TIPS: Bus parking, Bus drop off and pick up at designated entrance. (See ad and main listing under Theme Restaurants on page 130 and New York City Featured City Page on page 230.) REGION: New York County, NYC.

HEALTH & NUTRITION

FIELD TRIP FACTORY, Telephone: 800-987-6409. Fax: 773-342-9513. Email: info@fieldtripfactory.com. Website: www.fieldtripfactory.com. Hrs: Mon.-Fri. 8AM-6PM. GRADE LEVEL: Pre K-6th. GROUP TYPE: All youth groups & homeschoolers. PROGRAM TYPE: Day Trips, Guided Tours. COST: Free.

Field Trip Factory offers free community-based field trips. Our learning adventures teach valuable life-skills including health and nutrition, science, responsibility and more. All field trips are grade and age appropriate, meet learning standards, enrich classroom curriculum for teachers and fulfill badge requirements for scouts. See what is available in your area at www.fieldtripfactory.com or call 1-800-987-6409. SUPPORTS STATE LEARNING STANDARDS IN: Health & Safety, Math, Physical Education, Science. SUPPORTS SCOUT BADGE ACTIVITIES IN: Health & Safety, Life Skills, Personal Fitness. (See ad on page 56.) REGION: Throughout all 50 states.

ICE SKATING

CHELSEA PIERS SPORTS & ENTERTAINMENT COMPLEX, 23rd Street & Hudson River Park, New York, NY 10011. Tel: 212-336-6777. Email:events@chelseapiers.com. Website: www.chelseapiers.com/specialevents. Hrs: Vary. GRADE LEVEL: K - College. GROUP TYPE: All youth groups. PROGRAM TYPE: Day Trips, Guided Activities, Workshops. REGISTRATION: Phone. FOOD: Variety. COST: Prices starting at $10 per student. (See main listing under Field Days & Recreation on page 89 and ad under Proms & School Celebrations on page 102.) REGION: New York County, NYC.

THE POND AT BRYANT PARK, 42nd Street at 6th Avenue, New York, NY 10018. Tel: 212-661-6640. Fax: 212-661-8840. Email: info@upsilonventures.com. Website: www.ThePondatBryantPark.com. Hrs: Nov.-Jan. GRADE LEVEL: All grade levels. GROUP TYPE: All youth groups. PROGRAM TYPE: Day Trips, Self-guided Activities, Guided Activities, Performances. MAX. GROUP SIZE: 700. MIN. GROUP SIZE: 10. FOOD: Variety, Place to eat on site, Beverages available. RECOMM. LENGTH OF VISIT: 2 hours. RECOMM. RATIO OF STUDENT TO STAFF: 15:1. COST: Discounts for schools and non-profits.

Experience a winter wonderland in the heart of Manhattan. The Pond at Bryant Park features NYC's only free admission ice skating rink, and is just steps from Times Square and Grand Central Terminal. Host your group's next winter trip at The Pond, where you can customize your VIP skating package. Rental skates, lockers, bag check services, group skating lessons, private event spaces, and a full-service snack bar are all available, with discounts for schools and non-profit organizations. The Pond at Bryant Park - the coolest ice and the warmest memories. Open November 6, 2009 – January 24, 2010. SUPPORTS NY STATE & NATIONAL LEARNING STANDARDS IN: Physical Education. SUPPORTS SCOUT MERIT BADGE ACHIEVEMENT IN: Personal Fitness, Physical Ed/Recreation. REGION: New York County, NYC.

SEAPORT ICE, South Street Seaport, New York, NY 10038. Tel: 212-661-6640. Fax: 212-661-8840. Email: info@upsilonventures.com. Website: www.SeaportIce.com. Hrs: Winter 2009. GRADE LEVEL: All grades. GROUP TYPE: All youth groups. PROGRAM TYPE: Day Trips, Self-guided Activities, Guided Activities, Performances. MAX. GROUP SIZE: 350. MIN. GROUP SIZE: 10. FOOD: Variety, Place to eat on site, Beverages available. RECOMM. LENGTH OF VISIT: 2 hours. RECOMM. RATIO OF STUDENT TO STAFF: 15:1. COST: Discounts for schools and non-profits.

Seaport Ice is downtown Manhattan's top winter attraction. Amid the visual splendor of tall ships, skyscrapers, and the New York Harbor, this 8,000 sq. ft. ice skating rink offers a unique experience for all ages. An ideal spot for schools and organizations, skating packages can be tailored for each group, with VIP access, skate rentals, bag check services, lessons, and food and beverage options. Call for available dates, and experience downtown Manhattan in a whole new way! SUPPORTS NY STATE & NATIONAL LEARNING STANDARDS IN: Physical Education. SUPPORTS SCOUT MERIT BADGE ACHIEVEMENT IN: Personal Fitness, Physical Ed/Recreation. REGION: New York County, NYC.

WOLLMAN RINK, in Central Park at 59th St., 6th Ave. entrance to the park, New York, New York 10065. Telephone: 212-439-6900 x12. Fax: 212-628-8322. Email: jjohnson@wollmanskatingrink.com. Website: www.wollmanrink.com. Hrs: Oct.-Apr. GRADE LEVEL: All grades. GROUP TYPE: All youth groups & homeschoolers. PROGRAM TYPE: Day Trips, Self-guided Activities, Guided Activities. COST: Varies.

Book your ice skating trip now!!!!! Wollman Rink is New York's most popular class trip destination in Central Park's Winter Wonderland. Also: After School Skating Lesson Programs. Exclusive and non-exclusive facility rentals available for Fundraisers. SUPPORTS NY STATE & NATIONAL LEARNING STANDARDS IN: Physical Education. SUPPORTS SCOUT MERIT BADGE ACHIEVEMENT IN: Skating. REGION: New York County, NYC.

WORLD ICE ARENA, Flushing Meadows Corona Park, Flushing, NY 11355. Tel: 718-760-9001. Website: www.worldice.com. Hrs: Mon.-Fri. after school-5:15PM, Fri. 7-10PM, Sat.-Sun. 12-5PM. GRADE LEVEL: All grades. GROUP TYPE: All youth groups. PROGRAM TYPE: Self-guided Activities, Guided Activities. MAX. GROUP SIZE: 300. COST: Call for details.

Skate where the world skates...at the new World Ice Arena in beautiful Flushing Meadows Corona Park. Situated next to the new CitiField and The United States Tennis Center, this huge ice rink is the perfect place for groups and special events. With over 50 hours of General Skating per week...World Ice is ready when you are. Also visit the City Ice Pavilion, just 2 miles from midtown over the 59th Street Bridge, where the staff is there to help everyone learn. SUPPORTS NY STATE & NATIONAL LEARNING STANDARDS IN: Physical Education. SUPPORTS SCOUT MERIT BADGE ACHIEVEMENT IN: Physical Ed/Recreation. (See New York City Featured City Page on page 227.) REGION: Queens County, NYC.

INDOOR AMUSEMENT CENTERS

KIDS N' ACTION, 1149 McDonald Ave., Brooklyn, NY 11230. Tel: 718-377-1818. Fax: 718-377-6435. www.kidsnaction.com. Hrs: Sun.-Thurs. 10AM-7PM, Fri. 10AM - 2 hrs. before sundown, Sat. Night: 1 hr. after sundown. Website: GRADE LEVEL: Pre K-8th. GROUP TYPE: All youth groups & homeschoolers. PROGRAM TYPE: Day Trips, Self-guided Activities. MAX. GROUP SIZE: 300. MIN. GROUP SIZE: 10. COST: Varies.

Kids N' Action is NY's premier child entertainment center, where we offer a safe, clean, and friendly atmosphere for you and your group! Kids love our four level play-ground that is specifically designed to give younger children their playing field at the lower levels and our older children more advanced fun at the higher levels. We offer a wide range of indoor rides for all ages, including an indoor roller coaster, exhilarat-ing Go-Cart tracks, and a kiddie train ride for the younger ones. Our arcade games are selected to insure the most child friendly entertainment, and include redemption games that allow children to use their skills. SUPPORTS NY STATE & NATIONAL LEARNING STANDARDS IN: Physical Education. SUPPORTS SCOUT MERIT BADGE ACHIEVEMENT IN: Physical Ed/Recreation. REGION: Kings County, NYC.

INTERACTIVE LIVING HISTORY

HISTORIC HOUSE TRUST OF NEW YORK CITY, 830 Fifth Ave., Room 203, New York, NY 10065. Tel: 212-360-8282. 22 historic sites throughout all 5 boroughs with hands-on programs. COST: Fee. REGION: New York County, NYC.

HISTORIC RICHMOND TOWN, 441 Clarke Ave., Staten Island, NY 10306. Tel: 718-351-1611, ext. 280. Hrs: Wed.-Sun. 1-5PM. Self-guided Tours, Guided Tours, Workshops. A living history village that reflects life in Staten Island and its neighbor-ing communities during the colonial period through the early 1900's. COST: Fee. REGION: Richmond County, NYC.

LEFFERTS HISTORIC HOUSE MUSEUM, Prospect Park, Flatbush Ave. at Empire Blvd./Ocean Ave., Brooklyn, NY 11215. Tel: 718-789-2822. Hrs: School and group programs offered year-round, Tues.-Fri. Guided Tours, Workshops. One of a small number of farmhouses surviving from Brooklyn's Dutch settlement period. COST: Free. REGION: Kings County, NYC.

LOWER EAST SIDE TENEMENT MUSEUM, 108 Orchard St., New York, NY 10002. Tel: 212-431-0233. Hrs: Mon.-Fri. 10 AM–5PM, Sat. & Sun. 11AM–4:45PM. Focuses on America's urban immigrant history. COST: Fee. REGION: New York County, NYC.

NYC DUCKS, 49 W. 45th Street, New York, NY 10036. Tel: 1-888-8-DUCKS-0 (1-888-838-2570). Website: www.NYCDucks.com; Captain Henry's Blog at www.NYCDucks.blogspot.com. GRADE LEVEL: All grades. GROUP TYPE: All youth groups. PROGRAM TYPE: Guided Tours. COST: Varies.

NYC's first and only land / water multimedia experience! The NYC Ducks route starts in Times Square, on the east side of Broadway and navigates the streets of Manhattan to the waters of the Hudson River. Along the way, entertaining and informative tour guides point out some of New York City's world-famous sites. At the edge of the Hudson, the Duck will enter the NYC Ducks Theater for an exhilarating multi-media experience, simulating Henry Hudson's journey, complete with the sights and sounds – the rushing wind and other surprises – of an Atlantic sea voyage. Each NYC Duck can accommodate 44 customers or shipmates plus two crewmembers. NYC Ducks will operate March through October, and may extend through November depending on weather conditions. A complimentary Ducks 'quacker' is given to each customer." SUPPORTS NY STATE & NATIONAL LEARNING STANDARDS IN: History/Social Studies. SUPPORTS SCOUT MERIT BADGE ACHIEVEMENT IN: Social Studies. (See Regional Highlights on page 15.) REGION: New York County, NYC.

VAN CORTLAND HOUSE MUSEUM, Broadway at West 246th St., Bronx, NY 10471. Tel: 718-543-3344. Hrs: Tues.-Fri. 10AM-3PM, Sat.-Sun. 11AM-4PM. 4th-12th grade. Guided Tours, Demonstrations. Plantation house from colonial times. COST: Free/Fee. REGION: Bronx County, NYC.

MULTICULTURAL

AFRICAN BURIAL GROUND NATIONAL MONUMENT, 290 Broadway, 1st Fl., New York, NY 10007. Tel: 212-637-2019. Hrs: Visitor Center: Mon.-Fri. 9AM-5PM. Guided Tours, Workshops. During the 17th and 18th centuries, free and enslaved Africans were buried in a 6.6-acre burial ground in lower Manhattan, outside the boundaries of the settlement of New Amsterdam. Today, the site honors the memories of the thousands who were buried. Exhibits, artifacts, a documentary film, and educational programs available at the visitor center. COST: Free. REGION: New York County, NYC.

ASIA SOCIETY IN MIDTOWN, 725 Park Avenue, New York, NY 10021. Tel: 212-288-6400. Hrs: Open to the public Tues.-Sun. 11AM-6PM (Fri. until 9PM). Open to reserved school groups Tues.-Fri. beginning at 10AM. 3rd-12th grade. Guided

Tours. Contains exhibitions from both traditional and contemporary Asian and Asian American art. COST: Fee. REGION: New York County, NYC.

HARLEM, YOUR WAY! TOURS UNLIMITED, INC., 129 W. 130th St., New York, NY 10027. Tel: 212-690-1687. Email: harlemyourway@compuserve.com. Website: www.harlemyourwaytours.com. Contact: Larcelia Kebe. GRADE LEVEL: 3rd-college. GROUP TYPE: All youth groups & homeschoolers. PROGRAM TYPE: Day Trips, Guided Tours, Workshops. COST: Varies.

Since 1983 Harlem, Your Way! Tours has successfully conducted exciting, interactive tours of Harlem, Manhattan, Brooklyn, Bronx and Queens for schools, colleges, tourists, corporations, churches and social organizations. We provide customized planning for individuals and groups. During our tours, which are conducted by knowledgeable, "student friendly" guides, we visit historic districts, cultural institutions, landmarks, churches, museums, memorial sites, restaurants, schools, colleges, concert halls, parks, Rucker playground and jazz clubs. We arrange for professional musicians to provide instruction in Gospel, Jazz, R & B and Hip-Hop Study Programs which culminate in a performance. We can also provide multilingual tours. We arrange People Meeting People Events and programs where groups in the Tri-State Area can meet and engage in activities with groups from abroad. We have walking tours and bus tours, and can provide guided Step-On Service. Two of our tours, the Duke Ellington Interactive Tour and the Harlem Walking Tour, have been cited by the United States Department of Commerce and are included on The American Pathways website. Highlights include a Gospel Tour; Evening Tours of Clubs; Wednesday Nights at The Apollo Theatre. New**Hip Hop Church Tour - Thursdays, 6:00PM-9:00PM. Bilingual Programs: French, Spanish, Portuguese, German and Teacher Workshops. Call for further information. SUPPORTS NY STATE & NATIONAL LEARNING STANDARDS IN: Social Studies. SUPPORTS SCOUT MERIT BADGE ACHIEVEMENT IN: Multicultural, My Community. REGION: New York County, NYC.

ISLAMIC CULTURAL CENTER OF NEW YORK, 1711 Third Ave. at 97th St., New York, NY 10029. Tel: 212-722-5234. Hrs: Tues., Wed., Fri.-Sun. 12-5:30PM. Guided Tours. Take a tour of the first major mosque in NYC. COST: Free. REGION: New York County, NYC.

JACQUES MARCHAIS MUSEUM OF TIBETAN ART, 338 Lighthouse Ave., Staten Island, NY 10306. Tel: 718-987-3500. Hrs: Wed.-Sun. 1-5PM or by appt. Guided Tours, Workshops. Features sculptures, thangka paintings, ritual artifacts, musical instruments and historic photographs of Tibet. COST: Fee. REGION: Richmond County, NYC.

JAPAN SOCIETY, 333 East 47th St., New York, NY 10017. Tel: 212-832-1155. Hrs: Tues.-Thurs. 11AM-6PM, Fri. 11AM-9PM, Sat. & Sun. 11AM-5PM. Guided Tours. Provides exhibits and information on Japan, offering opportunities to experience Japanese culture. COST: Fee. REGION: New York County, NYC.

THE JEWISH MUSEUM, 1109 Fifth Ave., New York, NY 10128. Tel: 212-423-3200. Hrs: Vary. Guided Tours, Workshops. Explores the scope and diversity of Jewish culture. COST: Fee. REGION: New York County, NYC.

MUSEUM OF CHINESE IN AMERICA, 211-215 Centre St., New York, NY 10013. Tel: 212-619-4785. Hrs: Mon.-Sat. 10AM-5PM. Guided Tours. Presents the history, heritage, culture and diverse experiences of people of Chinese descent in the U.S. COST: Fee. REGION: New York County, NYC.

MUSEUM OF JEWISH HERITAGE - A LIVING MEMORIAL TO THE HOLOCAUST, 36 Battery Place, New York, NY 10280. Tel: 646-437-4304. Fax: 646-437-4311. Website: www.mjhnyc.org. GRADE LEVEL: 1st-college. GROUP TYPE: All youth groups & homeschoolers. PROGRAM TYPE: Day Trips, Self-guided Tours, Guided Tours, Workshops, Performances. MAX. GROUP SIZE: 120. COST: Varies.

The Museum of Jewish Heritage A Living Memorial to the Holocaust tells the moving story of 20th century Jewish life from the perspective of those who lived it. Weaving together personal experiences and world events, it paints an evocative portrait of a people, a catastrophe, and an indomitable spirit. It conveys a message of memory and hope that is of universal significance. The Museum is committed to reaching children and adults from a broad spectrum of schools and communities. Guided tours led by highly trained Gallery Educators (themes: heritage; immigration; life during the Holocaust; Israel) available for children and adults. Teacher Workshops and Bilingual Programs available: Spanish, French, Yiddish, German, Hebrew, Japanese, Russian. SUPPORTS NY STATE & NATIONAL LEARNING STANDARDS IN: Social Studies. SUPPORTS SCOUT MERIT BADGE ACHIEVEMENT IN: Museum Discovery, My Heritage. (See ad under Social Studies on page 112.) REGION: New York County, NYC.

THE SHADOW BOX THEATRE, 325 W. End Ave., #12B, New York, NY 10023. Tel: 212-724-0677. Fax: 212-724-0767. Email: shadowboxtheatre@yahoo.com. Website: www.shadowboxtheatre.org. GRADE LEVEL: Pre K-5th. GROUP TYPE: All youth groups & homeschoolers. PROGRAM TYPE: Performances, Workshops, Outreach. MAX. GROUP SIZE: 700. COST: Varies. (See main listing under Theater-Dance-Music on page 125.) REGION: Throughout NYC.

SMITHSONIAN'S NATIONAL MUSEUM OF THE AMERICAN INDIAN, George Gustav Heye Center, 1 Bowling Green, New York, NY 10004. Tel: 212-514-3700 or 212-514-3705. Hrs: Daily 10AM-5PM (Thurs. until 8PM). Self-guided Tours, Guided Tours, Workshops. Dedicated to the preservation, study, and exhibition of the life, languages, literature, history, and arts of Native Americans. COST: Free. REGION: New York County, NYC.

THE STUDIO MUSEUM IN HARLEM, 144 W. 125th St., New York, NY 10027. Tel: 212-864-4500. Hrs: Wed.-Fri. 12-6PM, Sat. 10AM-6PM, Sun. 12-6PM. Self-guided Tours, Guided Tours. Exhibits work by black artists and to promote local art. Collection houses over 1,600 paintings, sculptures, drawings, prints and photographs. COST: Free/Fee. REGION: New York County, NYC.

THE UKRAINIAN MUSEUM, 222 E. 6th St., New York, NY 10003. Tel: 212-228-0110. Hrs: Wed.-Sun. 11:30AM-5PM. Self-guided Tours, Guided Tours, Workshops. Features Ukrainian folk art, fine arts, and documentary material of the past and present. COST: Fee. REGION: New York County, NYC.

WEEKSVILLE HERITAGE CENTER, 1698 Bergen St., Brooklyn, NY 11213. Tel: 718-756-5250. Hrs: School Tours: Tues.-Fri. 1PM, 2PM & 3PM; Sat. 11AM-3PM. Guided Tours. Dedicated to preserving one of the nation's earliest free African American communities. COST: Fee. REGION: Kings County, NYC.

MULTIDIMENSIONAL

THE FOLLOWING LISTINGS HAVE MULTIPLE FOCUSES IN THEIR EXHIBIT HALLS COVERING ANTHROPOLOGY, ART, SCIENCE, CULTURE, OR HISTORY.

AMERICAN MUSEUM OF NATURAL HISTORY, Central Park West at 79th St., New York, NY 10024. Tel: 212-769-5200. Hrs: Daily 10AM-5:45PM. Self-guided Tours, Guided Tours, Workshops. Over 46 permanent exhibition halls on natural history. COST: Free/Fee. REGION: New York County, NYC.

STATEN ISLAND MUSEUM, 75 Stuyvesant Pl., Staten Island, NY 10301. Tel: 718-727-1135. Hrs: Mon.-Fri. 12-5PM, Sat.10AM-5PM, Sun. 12-5PM. Self-guided Tours, Guided Tours. Features collections that offer an interdisciplinary interpretation of the world through art, natural science, and cultural history. COST: Fee. REGION: Richmond County, NYC.

MULTIMEDIA

MUSEUM OF THE MOVING IMAGE, 36-01 35th Ave., Astoria, NY 11106. Tel: 718-784-4520. Hrs: Tues.-Fri.10AM-3PM. Guided Tours, Workshops. Celebrates the history, technology, and art of movies. COST: Fee. REGION: Queens County, NYC.

THE PALEY CENTER FOR MEDIA, 25 West 52nd St., New York, NY 10019. Tel: 212-621-6600. Hrs: Wed.-Sun. 12-6PM (Thurs. until 8PM). Self-guided Tours, Guided Tours, Screenings, Workshops. Contains more than 140,000 television and radio programs and advertisements. COST: Fee. REGION: New York County, NYC.

SONY WONDER TECHNOLOGY LAB, 550 Madison Ave. (at 56th St.), New York, NY 10022. Tel: General Info - 212-833-8100 & Programs and Events - 212-833-7858. Fax: 212-833-4445. Website: www.sonywondertechlab.com. Hrs: Tues.-Sat. 10AM-5PM, Sun. 12-5PM. GRADE LEVEL: 3rd and up. GROUP TYPE: All youth groups & homeschoolers. PROGRAM TYPE: Day Trips, Self-guided Tours, Guided Tours, Self-guided Activities, Guided Activities, Workshops, Films, Outreach Programs, Demonstrations, Exhibits, Performances, Special Events / Festivals. MAX. GROUP SIZE: 35. REGISTRATION: Phone. FOOD: Can bring own food, Place to eat on site. RECOMM. LENGTH OF VISIT: 2 hours. RECOMM. RATIO OF STUDENT TO STAFF: 10:1. ARRIVAL TIPS: Bus drop off and pick up at designated entrance. COST: Free/Fee. (See ad and main listing under Science & Environmental Education on page 106.) REGION: New York County, NYC.

PLANETARIUMS

THE HAYDEN PLANETARIUM AT THE ROSE CENTER FOR EARTH AND SPACE, American Museum of Natural History, Central Park West at 79th St., New York, NY 10024. Tel: 212-769-5200. Hrs: Vary. Day Trips, Self-guided Tours, Guided Tours, Shows. Explore the continuing evolution of the universe. COST: Fee. REGION: New York County, NYC.

PROMS & SCHOOL CELEBRATIONS

SCIENCE & ENVIRONMENTAL EDUCATION

ALLEY POND ENVIRONMENTAL CENTER, 228-06 Northern Blvd., Douglaston, NY, 11363. Tel: 718-229-4000. Hrs: Sept.-June: Sun.-Sat. 9AM-4:30PM. Self-guided Tours, Guided Tours. Wetlands and nature preserve and center. COST: Fee. REGION: Queens County, NYC.

BATTERY PARK CITY PARKS CONSERVANCY, 2 South End Ave., New York, NY. Tel: 212-267-9700 ext. 355. Fax: 212-267-9707. Email: chudon@bpcparks.org. Website: www.bpcparks.org. Hrs: Program offered Apr.-Jun., Sept. & Oct. Contact: Craig Hudon. GRADE LEVEL: 3rd-12th grade. GROUP TYPE: School Groups. PROGRAM TYPE: Workshops. MAX. GROUP SIZE: 30. COST: Free.

BPCPC's Marine Education Program teaches the history, geography and ecology of the Hudson River and its estuary — home to 200 species of fish -- and offers catch-and-release fishing using rod and reel. Students, guided by Marine Education Coordinator Bill Fink and Marine Educators, record the species of fish caught, water and air temperature, wind direction, tide, and salinity. BPCPC operates BPC's 36 acres of parks and gardens. From May 1 through October 31, it offers free events and recreational activities for children and families. In spring and fall, Saturday Go Fish events offer fishing, art projects, and family entertainment. SUPPORTS NY STATE & NATIONAL LEARNING STANDARDS IN: Science, Social Studies. SUPPORTS SCOUT MERIT BADGE ACHIEVEMENT IN: Science. REGION: New York County, NYC.

BELVEDERE CASTLE: THE HENRY LUCE NATURE OBSERVATORY, Mid- Central Park at 79th St., New York, NY 10024. Tel: 212-772-0210. Hrs: Tues.-Sun. 10AM-4:30PM. Self-guided Tours. Learn about nature thru exhibits with telescopes and microscopes. Recorded bird songs can be called up at the push of a button. Visitors can borrow Discovery Kits that contain binoculars, reference material and maps for exploring the many species of fauna or flora in Central Park. COST: Free. REGION: New York County NYC.

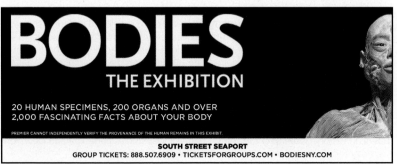

BODIES...THE EXHIBITION, South Street Seaport Exhibition Centre, 11 Fulton St., New York, NY 10038. Tel: 1-888-507-6909. Email: ticketsforgroups@aol.com. Websites: Group Tickets: www.ticketsforgroups.com; Individual Tickets: www.bodiesny.com. Hrs: Mon.-Thurs. 10AM-7PM, Fri.-Sun. 10AM-9PM, last ticket entry is one hour prior to closing. GRADE LEVEL: 1st-12th. GROUP TYPE: All youth groups & homeschoolers. PROGRAM TYPE: Day Trips, Self-guided Tours. COST: Varies, complimentary chaperone tickets.

20 human specimens, 200 organs and 2,000 fascinating facts about the human body. This striking exhibition showcases real human bodies, giving students the opportunity to study human anatomy in a fascinating way like never before. This educational exhibition highlights how amazing the body is and how the intricate systems of the human body carry out extraordinary tasks everyday. Bodies is an excellent teaching opportunity for Science, Anatomy, Health and Biology. We offer special student pricing, complimentary chaperone tickets, downloadable Teacher's Guides, meal vouchers and bus parking info. SUPPORTS NY STATE & NATIONAL LEARNING STANDARDS IN: Science. SUPPORTS SCOUT MERIT BADGE ACHIEVEMENT IN: Science. REGION: New York County, NYC.

BROOKLYN BOTANIC GARDEN, 1000 Washington Ave., Brooklyn, NY 11225. Tel: 718-623-7200. Fax: 718-857-2430. Website: www.bbg.org. Hrs: Garden: Mid-Mar. - Oct., Tues.-Fri. 8AM-6PM; Nov. - Mid-Mar., Tues.-Fri. 8AM-4:30PM. Closed on Mondays. Contact: Registration Office. GRADE LEVEL: All grades. GROUP TYPE: All youth groups & homeschoolers. PROGRAM TYPE: Day Trips, Self-guided Tours, Guided Tours, Workshops. MAX. GROUP SIZE: 35. COST: Free self-guided visits. Fees vary for guided tours & workshops. (See Regional Highlights on page 13 and main listing under Botanical Gardens & Nature Centers on page 83.) REGION: Kings County, NYC.

EMPIRE STATE BUILDING OBSERVATORY, 350 Fifth Ave., New York, NY 10118. Tel: 212-736-3100. Fax: 212-947-1360. Email: sales@esbnyc.com. Website: www.esbnyc.com. Hrs: 8AM-2AM. Contact: Michael Sibrizzi. GRADE LEVEL: K-College. GROUP TYPE: All youth groups & homeschoolers. PROGRAM TYPE: Day Trips, Self-guided Tours, Self-guided Activities. REGISTRATION: Mail, Online, Phone, Prepay, Tickets mailed prior to visit. TICKET/VOUCHER RETURN POLICY: Tickets refundable within 90 days of purchase. RECOMM. LENGTH OF VISIT: Varies. RECOMMENDED RATIO OF STUDENTS TO STAFF: 20:1. COST: Fee.

Introduce your students to the world's most exciting classroom: the legendary Empire State Building Observatory. With customized lesson plans developed in partnership with the Bank Street College of Education that cover everything from social studies, to science, to geography—students of all ages will love learning from the highest point in New York City. In addition, the Empire State Building provides an array of specialized supplemental projects, which focus on areas like the building's historic construction in 1936 and its place in popular culture. With all it has to offer, a class trip to the Empire State Building provides the complete scholastic experience. For more information, go to www.esbnyc.com. Call 212-736-3100 for group sales. SUPPORTS NY STATE & NATIONAL LEARNING STANDARDS IN: Social Studies/Global Studies, Science/Technology, American History/Geography. (See ad on under Social Studies page 109 and New York City Featured City Page on page 227.) REGION: New York County, NYC.

THE GREENBELT ENVIRONMENTAL EDUCATION CENTER, 200 Nevada Avenue, High Rock Park, Staten Island, NY 10306. Tel: 718-667-7475. Hrs: Park: Open daily; education programs by appt. Self-guided Tours, Workshops. Programs foster an appreciation for the natural environment and exploration in natural surroundings. COST: Free/Fee. REGION: Richmond County, NYC.

HUDSON RIVER PARK TRUST, Pier 40, 2nd Floor, W. Houston and West Sts., NY, NY 10014. Tel: 212-627-2020. Fax: 212-627-2021. Email: cfigueroa@hrpt.state.ny.us. Website: www.hudsonriverpark.org. Hrs: Mon.-Fri. Contact: Crist Figueroa, Education Coordinator. GRADE LEVEL: All grades. GROUP TYPE: School, After-school, Scout. PROGRAM TYPE: Day Trips, Guided Tours, Workshops. COST: Free.

Hudson River Park Trust is a joint NY State and City agency whose mission is to design, build and operate a five-mile park along Manhattan's west-side waterfront from Battery Park to 59th Street. HRPT's education programs are free, run approximately 1 1/2 hours and take place outdoors at various locations along the park's waterfront. All programs use hands-on activities that help children explore the biology and ecology of the Hudson River. Three current curricula include: Fishing and Fish Biology: students learn to fish with rods, reels and bait; Plankton and the Food Web: students are given an introduction to plankton (micro-organisms that live in the River) and use plankton nets to gather samples of the organisms. The plankton "catch" is then examined with microscopes and magnifying lenses; Water Quality: at the River, students are introduced to and will use water quality testing equipment including water sampler collector, secchi disk, plankton net, thermometer and a color scale. SUPPORTS NY STATE, & NATIONAL LEARNING STANDARDS IN: Science. SUPPORTS SCOUT MERIT BADGE ACHIEVEMENT IN: Environmental Studies, Nature. REGION: New York County, NYC.

INTREPID SEA, AIR & SPACE MUSEUM, One Intrepid Square, New York, NY 10036. Tel: 212-245-0072. Hrs: Apr. 1-Sept. 30: Mon.-Fri. 10AM-5PM, Sat.-Sun. 10AM-6PM. Oct.1-Mar. 31: Tues.-Sun. 10AM-5PM. Day Trips, Self-guided Tours, Guided Tours, Self-guided Activities, Performances. The Museum is centered on the aircraft carrier Intrepid (CVS-11) and encompasses 30 restored aircraft, a submarine and a range of interactive exhibits. COST: Fee. REGION: New York County, NYC.

THE NEW YORK BOTANICAL GARDEN, Bronx River Parkway & Fordham Road, Bronx, New York 10456-5126. Telephone: 718-817-8181. Fax: 718-817-8829. Email: school_programs@nybg.org. Website: www.nybg.org/edu. Hrs: Tues.-Sun. Contact: Registration Office. GRADE LEVEL: All grades. GROUP TYPE: All youth groups. PROGRAM TYPE: Day Trips, Self-guided Tours, Guided Tours, Workshops. COST: Varies. REGION: Bronx County, NYC.

Take an exciting, educational class trip to The New York Botanical Garden, a national leader in informal science education. With 250 acres of plants from around the world, your students can discover the wonders of nature up close. Students participate in hands-on activities from sowing seeds and harvesting crops, examining wetlands, and dissecting plant parts to investigating plants as food. Explore diverse ecosystems from the 50-acre forest to the rain forests and deserts of the Enid A. Haupt Conservatory. Take advantage of the exceptional 12-acre Everett Children's Adventure Garden, the Ruth Rea Howell Family Garden and the Mitsubishi Wild Wetland Trail. Ask about our teacher workshops and open houses. SUPPORTS NY STATE & NATIONAL LEARNING STANDARDS IN: Science. SUPPORTS SCOUT MERIT BADGE ACHIEVEMENT IN: Gardening, Nature, Plants. (See Regional Highlights in page 13.) REGION: Bronx County, NYC.

NEW YORK CITY CENTER FOR SPACE SCIENCE, 220 Henry Street, New York, NY 10002. Tel: 212-608-6164. Email: info@nyccsse.org. Website: www.nyccsse.org. Hrs: 8AM-4PM. GRADE LEVEL: 5th - 12th. GROUP TYPE: School, Youth. PROGRAM TYPE: Day Trips, Workshops. REGISTRATION: Mail, Online. FOOD: Can bring own food. RECOMM. LENGTH OF VISIT: Half or full day. RECOMM. RATIO OF STUDENT TO STAFF: 12:1. ARRIVAL TIPS: Bus Parking. COST: Call for pricing.

The Center for Space Science Education is a Department of Education facility offering students and teachers opportunities for simulated exploration and excitement. We offer a range of instructional programs aligned to NYC's science scope and sequence for grades 5-12. Our Challenger Learning Center completely engages students in awe-inspiring simulated space mission adventures that include a realistic Mission Control and orbiting Spacecraft. Our Aerospace Education Laboratory is equipped with flight simulators, a wind tunnel and model airplanes providing opportunities to learn aviation skills. SUPPORTS NY STATE & NATIONAL LEARNING STANDARDS IN: Math, Science, Technology. REGION: New York County, NYC.

NEW YORK HALL OF SCIENCE, 47-01 111th St., Queens, NY 11368 (in Flushing Meadows Corona Park). Tel: 718-699-0005. Hrs: Sept.-Jun.: Tues-Thurs 9:30AM-2PM, Fri 9:30AM-5PM, Sat. & Sun. 10AM-6PM. Self-guided Tours, Guided Tours. More than 400 interactive exhibits on sound, light, atoms, microbes, astronomy and more. COST: Fee. REGION: Queens County, NYC.

PROSPECT PARK AUDUBON CENTER AT THE BOATHOUSE, Lincoln Rd. entrance to Prospect Park at Ocean Ave., Brooklyn, NY 11215. Tel: 718-287-3400, ext. 101. Hrs: Thurs.-Sun. 12-6PM, or by appt. K-5th grade. Self-guided Tours, Guided tours. Dedicated to wildlife preservation and natural education. COST: Fee. REGION: Kings County, NYC.

SONY WONDER TECHNOLOGY LAB, 550 Madison Ave. (at 56th St.), New York, NY 10022. Tel: General Info - 212-833-8100 & Programs and Events - 212-833-7858. Fax: 212-833-4445. Website: www.sonywondertechlab.com. Hrs: Tues.-Sat. 10AM-5PM, Sun. 12-5PM. GRADE LEVEL: 3rd and up. GROUP TYPE: All youth groups & homeschoolers. PROGRAM TYPE: Day Trips, Self-guided Tours, Guided Tours, Self-guided Activities, Guided Activities, Workshops, Films, Outreach Programs, Demonstrations, Exhibits, Performances, Special Events / Festivals. MAX. GROUP SIZE: 35. REGISTRATION: Phone. FOOD: Can bring own food, Place to eat on site. RECOMM. LENGTH OF VISIT: 2 hours. RECOMM. RATIO OF STUDENT TO STAFF: 10:1. ARRIVAL TIPS: Bus drop off and pick up at designated entrance. COST: Free/Fee.

Sony Wonder Technology Lab (SWTL) is a four-story, interactive technology and entertainment museum for all ages open free to the public. Explore our exciting new hands on exhibits where you can program a robot, perform virtual surgery, direct an HDTV broadcast, design an animated character and much more! Choose from our guided or self guided tours. Reservations for group visits can be made by calling our General Admission Reservations Line at (212) 833-5414 Tuesday- Friday from 9a.m.-2p.m. Due to the popularity of SWTL, advance reservations are recommended for everyone. Please visit us online to learn more about our exciting new exhibits and for tips on planning your field trip: www.sonywondertechlab.com or call 212/833-8100. SUPPORTS NY STATE & NATIONAL LEARNING STANDARDS IN: Technology, Language Arts, Science, and Career Development/ Occupational Studies. REGION: New York County, NYC.

TOP OF THE ROCK OBSERVATION DECK, 30 Rockefeller Plaza (main entrance is located on 50th St. bet. 5th & 6th Aves), New York, New York 10111. Tel: 212-698-2000. Fax: 212-332-6550. Email: info@topoftherocknyc.com. Website: www.topoftherocknyc.com. Hrs: 8AM-12AM (last elevator goes up at 11:00 PM). Contact: Group Sales. GRADE LEVEL: All grades. GROUP TYPE: All youth groups & homeschoolers. PROGRAM TYPE: Day Trips, Self-guided Tours. REGISTRATION: Phone, Prepay. TICKET/VOUCHER RETURN POLICY: Tickets refundable up to 24 hours prior to the date and time on the ticket; no partial refunds or reissues on group tickets. FOOD: No food offered. RECOMM. LENGTH OF VISIT: 1 hour and 15 minutes. RECOMM. RATIO OF STUDENT TO STAFF: 10:1. ARRIVAL TIPS: Expedite check in, Bus drop off and pick up at designated entrance. COST: Varies.

Discover Top of the Rock Observation Deck, a 3-tiered observation deck atop 30 Rockefeller Plaza, New York City's most amazing attraction! The unforgettable experience includes a multi-media theater exhibit, glass ceiling elevator ride to the top and a panoramic 360-degree, unobstructed view from the 70th floor observatory, 850 feet in the sky! Purchase timed-tickets online at www.topoftherocknyc.com, via telephone 212-698-2000 or at the box office! SUPPORTS NY STATE & NATIONAL LEARNING STANDARDS IN: The Arts, Social Studies. SUPPORTS SCOUT MERIT BADGE ACHIEVEMENT IN: The Arts, Multicultural, Social Studies. (See ad under Social Studies on page 117 and NYC Featured City Page on page 229.) REGION: New York County, NYC.

SEAPORTS

SOUTH STREET SEAPORT, South Street and Fulton, 19 Fulton Street, Suite 201, New York, NY 10038. Tel: 212-732-8257. Fax: 212-964-8056. Website: www.southstreetseaport.com. Email: Carolyn@CJFMarketingInternational.com. Hrs: Vary. Contact: Carolyn Feimster. GRADE LEVEL: All grades. GROUP TYPE: All youth groups & homeschoolers. PRO-GRAM TYPE: Day Trips, Self-guided Tours, Guided Tours, Performances. FOOD: Variety of menu selections, Meal vouchers. COST: Varies. (See ad and main listing under Social Studies on page 116 and Regional Highlights on page 15.) REGION: New York County, NYC.

SOCIAL STUDIES

BARTOW-PELL MANSION MUSEUM, 895 Shore Road, Bronx, NY 10464. Tel: 718-885-1461. Fax: 718-885-9164. Email: info@bpmm.org. Website: www.bpmm.org. Hrs: Mon.-Sun. 9AM-5PM. Contact: Amanda Kraemer. GRADE LEVEL: 2nd-12th. GROUP TYPE: All youth groups. PROGRAM TYPE: Day Trips, Guided Tours, Guided Activities. MAX. GROUP SIZE: 50. REGISTRATION: Phone. FOOD: Can bring own food, Place to eat on site. RECOMM. LENGTH OF VISIT: 1.5 hours. RECOMM. RATIO OF STUDENT TO STAFF: 10:1. COST: Call for rates.

The Bartow-Pell Mansion Museum and Carriage House invites teachers to introduce 17th and 19th-century NYC to students by taking advantage of the Education Program. As the last remaining country house in the Rodman's Neck area of the Bronx, Bartow-Pell with its Greek Revival interiors, is an "away-from-the-classroom laboratory." Students learn about the people and lifestyle of 19th-century in a historic house museum, or about life as a Lenape Indian at our authentic wigwam, guided by caring staff and trained volunteers. SUPPORTS NY STATE & NATIONAL LEARNING STANDARDS IN: The Arts, History/Social Studies, Language Arts, Science, Technology. SUPPORTS SCOUT MERIT BADGE ACHIEVEMENT IN: Citizenship, Family Life, Social Studies, Science/Technology. REGION: Bronx County, NYC.

BIG ONION WALKING TOURS, 476 13th St., Brooklyn, NY 11215. Tel: 212-439-1090. Fax: 718-499-0023. Email: info@bigonion.com. Website: www.bigonion.com. Hrs: Daily Tours. Contact: Seth Kamil. GRADE LEVEL: All grades. GROUP TYPE: All youth groups & homeschoolers. PROGRAM TYPE: Day Trips, Guided Tours. COST: Varies.

Take your students on an unforgettable Big Onion Walking Tour of the ethnic & historic neighborhoods of Manhattan and Brooklyn. Big Onion Walking Tours and the New-York Historical Society, two leaders in interpreting the history of New York City, have joined forces to present the best walking tours of the city. Big Onion has more than 18 years experience conducting educator-led student tours. We offer many ethnic tours, including Harlem, Chinatown, the multi-ethnic Immigrant New York, East Harlem, or the Multi-Ethnic Eating Tour. We also offer over numerous historic district tours, including Central Park, Brooklyn Heights, Greenwich Village, The Financial District, and more! For those students who have lived in NYC all their lives, as well as visitors to the city, Big Onion Walking Tours opens up new neighborhoods to explore. Big Onion was named "New York's Best Walking Tours" by New York Magazine. Approved vendor by NYC Dept. of Ed. SUPPORTS NY STATE & NATIONAL LEARNING STANDARDS IN: Social Studies. SUPPORTS SCOUT MERIT BADGE ACHIEVEMENT IN: American Culture, Multicultural. REGION: All Counties, NYC.

EMPIRE STATE BUILDING OBSERVATORY, 350 Fifth Ave., New York, NY 10118. Tel: 212-736-3100. Fax: 212-947-1360. Email: sales@esbnyc.com. Website: www.esbnyc.com. Hrs: 8AM-2AM. Contact: Michael Sibrizzi. GRADE LEVEL: K-College. GROUP TYPE: All youth groups & homeschoolers. PROGRAM TYPE: Day Trips, Self-guided Tours, Self-guided Activities. REGISTRATION: Mail, Online, Phone, Prepay, Tickets mailed prior to visit. TICKET/VOUCHER RETURN POLICY: Tickets refundable within 90 days of purchase. RECOMM. LENGTH OF VISIT: Varies. RECOMM. RATIO OF STUDENTS TO STAFF: 20:1. COST: Fee.

Introduce your students to the world's most exciting classroom: the legendary Empire State Building Observatory. With customized lesson plans developed in partnership with the Bank Street College of Education that cover everything from social studies, to science, to geography—students of all ages will love learning from the highest point in New York City. In addition, the Empire State Building provides an array of specialized supplemental projects, which focus on areas like the building's historic construction in 1936 and its place in popular culture. With all it has to offer, a class trip to the Empire State Building provides the complete scholastic experience. For more information, go to www.esbnyc.com. Call 212-736-3100 for group sales. SUPPORTS NY STATE & NATIONAL LEARNING STANDARDS IN: Social Studies/Global Studies, Science/Technology, American History/Geography. (See ad on page 109 and New York City Featured City Page on page 227.) REGION: New York County, NYC.

FDNY FIRE ZONE, 34 West 51st St., New York, NY 10020 (in Rockefeller Center). Tel: 212-698-4520. Group reservation call: 212-698-4545. Fax: 212-698-4522. Email: terry@fdnyfirezone.org. Website: www.fdnyfirezone.org. Hrs: Mon.-Sat. 9AM-7PM, Sun. & Holidays 11AM-5PM. Closed New Years, Easter, Thanksgiving and Christmas. Contact: Ada Terry. GRADE LEVEL: K-12th grade. GROUP TYPE: All youth groups & homeschoolers. PROGRAM TYPE: Day Trips, Self-guided Tours. MAX. GROUP SIZE: 30. COST: Varies; group rates available.

Climb on a real fire truck, try on bunker gear, meet a firefighter, feel a "hot" door and learn to crawl through a smoke-filled hallway, even in the dark. The FDNY Fire Zone is state-of-the-art Fire Safety learning center. Through hands-on exhibits and multi-media presentations, including a recreated fire scene, you'll learn how to take action against the power of fire, identify hazards in your home, and develop an escape plan. Visit our store and purchase fully licensed FDNY products. SUPPORTS NY STATE & NATIONAL LEARNING STANDARDS IN: Social Studies. SUPPORTS SECTION 808 OF STATE EDUCATION LAW - Instruction in Fire and Arson Prevention, Injury Prevention, and Life Safety Education. SUPPORTS SCOUT MERIT BADGE ACHIEVEMENT IN: Career Exploration, Fire Safety. REGION: New York County, NYC.

"We rule!"

HARBOR DEFENSE MUSEUM, USAG Fort Hamilton, 230 Sheridan Loop, Brooklyn, NY 11252. Tel: 718-630-4349. Fax: 718-630-4888. Email: richard.j.cox1@us.army.mil. Website: www.hamilton.army.mil. Hrs: Mon-Fri. 10AM-4PM, Sat. 10AM-2PM. Closed Sun.& Federal Holidays. Contact: Richard Cox. GRADE LEVEL: 4th & up. GROUP TYPE: All youth groups & homeschoolers. PROGRAM TYPE: Self-guided Tours, Guided Tours. MAX. GROUP SIZE: 60. REGISTRATION: Phone. FOOD: Can bring own food, Place to eat on site. RECOMM. LENGTH OF VISIT: 1.5 hours. RECOMM. RATIO OF STUDENT TO STAFF: 5:1. ARRIVAL TIPS: Bus parking. COST: Free.

The mission of the Harbor Defense Museum is to preserve the history of Fort Hamilton, and the other fortifications that defended New York City during the nineteenth and twentieth centuries. The museum is located in a free standing bastion located within the old fort's dry moat. In addition to exhibits related to New York City's harbor defenses, the museum also displays objects ranging from a mortar captured at the Battle of Saratoga in 1777, to World War II infantry weapons. The museum is free and group tours are welcome. SUPPORTS NY STATE & NATIONAL LEARNING STANDARDS IN: History. SUPPORTS SCOUT MERIT BADGE ACHIEVEMENT IN: Citizenship, Technology. REGION: Kings County, NYC.

JOYCE GOLD HISTORY TOURS OF NEW YORK, 141 West 17th St., New York, NY 10011. Tel: 212-242-5762. Fax: 212-242-6374. Email: Joyce@joycegoldhistorytours.com. Website: www.joycegoldhistorytours.com. Hrs: 8AM-9PM. Contact: Joyce Gold. GRADE LEVEL: All grades. GROUP TYPE: All youth groups & homeschoolers. PROGRAM TYPE: Day Trips, Overnight Trips, Guided Tours. MAX. GROUP SIZE: Any Size Group. COST: Varies.

Joyce Gold was once a junior high school English teacher and is committed to arranging excellent student tours. Popular tours include Colonial Wall Street, Harlem, Chinatown / Little Italy, Hell's Kitchen, Ellis Island, Gangs of New York—The Bloody Five Points, Jewish Lower East Side, Greenwich Village, Women of Washington Square, Macabre Greenwich Village, Soho and Times Square. Since 1977, Joyce Gold History Tours has been offering fascinating walks and bus rides through time and space in the company of professionals. Our research has unearthed a treasure of fascinating stories—educational and fun—about the city and its people. The New York Times has called Ms. Gold "the doyenne of city tour guides." SUPPORTS NYC, NY STATE, & NATIONAL LEARNING STANDARDS IN: Social Studies. SUPPORTS SCOUT MERIT BADGE ACHIEVEMENT IN: My Community, Multicultural. REGION: New York County, NYC.

LITTLE RED LIGHTHOUSE TOUR, Fort Washington Park, 181st St. & Plaza Lafayette, New York, NY 10033. Tel: 212-304-2365. Hrs: programs begin Mon.-Fri at 10AM and 12PM. Guided Tours. Tour the lighthouse from the famed children's storybook. COST: Fee. REGION: New York County, NYC.

LOUIS ARMSTRONG HOUSE MUSEUM, 34-56 107th St. (at 37th Avenue), Corona, NY, 11368. Tel: 718-478-8274. Hrs: Tues.-Fri. 10AM-5PM, Sat.-Sun. 12-5PM. Guided Tours. Collection of photographs, recordings, documents and artifacts of the jazz legend. COST: Fee. REGION: Queens County, NYC.

LOWER EAST SIDE JEWISH CONSERVANCY, 235 East Broadway, New York, NY 10002. Tel: 212-374-4100. Fax: 212-385-2693. Email: info@nycjewishtours.org. Website: www.NYCJewishtours.org. Hrs: Sun-Fri 10AM-6PM. Contact: Laurie Tobias Cohen, Executive Director. GRADE LEVEL: 2nd-8th. GROUP TYPE: All youth groups. PROGRAM TYPE: Day Trips, Guided Tours. MAX. GROUP SIZE: 70. REGISTRATION: Mail, Online, Phone, Prepay, Tickets mailed prior to visit. FOOD: Variety of menu selections, Kosher, Vegetarian, Can bring own food, Beverages available. RECOMM. RATIO OF STUDENT TO STAFF: 10:1. ARRIVAL TIPS: Expedite check in, Bus parking, Bus drop off and pick up at designated entrance. COST: Free to students/staff.

Lead your students on a journey back in time with our innovative new education program, "A Day in the Life of an Immigrant Child." Through an interactive neighborhood tour, students will appreciate the importance of the Lower East Side in immigrant American history, as well as its vibrancy today. Second to eighth grade students can see what life was like during the peak years of immigration to this country (1880-1924), when Jewish, Irish, and Italian families left Europe for America's shores. Today, the demographics of this ever-changing neighborhood include Chinese and Hispanic residents living side by side. The program meets Learning Standards and aligns with the mandated study of immigration. SUPPORTS NY STATE & NATIONAL LEARNING STANDARDS IN: History/Social Studies. REGION: New York County, NYC.

MADAME TUSSAUDS NEW YORK, 234 West 42nd St., New York, NY 10036. Tel: 888-923-0334 or 212-512-9600 ext. 607. Email: groupsales@madametussaudsny.com. Website: www.madame-tussauds.com. Hrs: Open 365 days a years from 10AM. Last group booked at 8PM. May close early for special events, please call ahead for updated closing times. Contact: Group Sales. GRADE LEVEL: All grades. GROUP TYPE: All youth groups & homeschoolers. PROGRAM TYPE: Day Trips, Self-guided Tours. REGISTRATION: Mail, Online, Phone, Prepay. RECOMM. LENGTH OF VISIT: 1.5-2 hours. RECOMM. RATIO OF STUDENT TO STAFF: 10:1. ARRIVAL TIPS: Expedite check in, Bus drop off and pick up at designated entrance. COST: Group Rates: 15+. For general information, please call 800-246-8872.

Located in the heart of Times Square, there is only one place you can go to see more than 200 world-famous celebrities every day.* Stars of stage and screen, top athletes, and world leaders are already lined up to provide you with the experience of a lifetime. And now, you too can become a star at Madame Tussauds New York! Visit our 85,000 square feet interactive attraction, where you can party in our VIP Room with Carrie Underwood, Fly through Metropolis with Superman, or become an M16 agent with Daniel Craig as James Bond. You can check in with Britney Spears, Bono, Notorious B.I.G., Leonardo DiCaprio, or participate in our newest photo opportunity, Barack Obama in the Presidential Oval Office! Get scared in "Scream"—Madame Tussauds' creepy live-action attraction that transports guests into three iconic horror film settings! An Additional Fee applies for Cinema 4D, a multi-sensory theatre experience. SUPPORTS NYC, NY STATE, & NATIONAL LEARNING STANDARDS IN: Social Studies. SUPPORTS SCOUT MERIT BADGE ACHIEVEMENT IN: Historical Figures. (See New York City Featured City Page on page 228.) REGION: New York County, NYC.

MUSEUM OF THE CITY OF NEW YORK, 1220 5th Ave. (at 103rd St.), New York, NY 10029. Tel: 212-534-1672. Hrs: Tues.-Sun. 10AM-5PM. Self-guided Tours, Guided Tours. Exhibits on New York City history, embracing the past, present, and future of the city and celebrates its cultural diversity. COST: Fee. REGION: New York County, NYC.

NEW YORK CITY FIRE MUSEUM, 278 Spring St., New York, NY 10013. Tel: 212-691-1303. Hrs: Tues.-Sat. 10AM-5PM, Sun. 10AM-4PM. Self-guided Tours, Guided Tours. Houses fire related art and artifacts from the late 18th century to the present. COST: Fee. REGION: New York County, NYC.

NEW YORK CITY POLICE MUSEUM, 100 Old Slip, New York, NY 10005. Tel: 212-480-3100. Hrs: Mon.-Sat. 10AM 5PM. Self guided Tours. Learn about the role of the NYPD and how it has changed over time. COST: Fee. REGION: New York County, NYC.

NEW-YORK HISTORICAL SOCIETY, 170 Central Park West at 77th St., New York, NY 10024. Tel: 212-485-9293. Fax: 212-721-7647. Email: schoolprograms@nyhistory.org. Website: www.nyhistory.org. Hrs: Tues.-Sun. 10AM-6PM. Some school visits possible on Mondays or before 10AM by special arrangement. Contact: School Programs Coordinator. GRADE LEVEL: All grades. GROUP TYPE: All youth groups. PROGRAM TYPE: Day Trips, Self-guided Tours, Guided Tours, Workshops. COST: Varies; class rates available.

Four centuries of artifacts, documents, art and other material make the New-York Historical Society the leading source of information about the history of America and New York's role in the development of the country through changing exhibitions and permanent collections. The Society offers guided learning programs for students in grades K through 12, which allow them to experience history through the expansive and unique collections housed at the institution. Led by highly qualified museum educators, these programs incorporate skills and content outlined in the state curriculum and can be tailored to the specific developmental and curricular needs of your students. SUPPORTS NY STATE & NATIONAL LEARNING STANDARDS IN: Social Studies/History, ELA and Arts. SUPPORTS SCOUT MERIT BADGE ACHIEVEMENT IN: My Community. REGION: New York County, NYC.

NEW YORK TRANSIT MUSEUM, Corner of Boerum Place and Schermerhorn St., Brooklyn, NY 11201. Tel: 718-694-1600, Reservations: 718 694-1873. Hrs: Tues.-Fri. 10AM-4PM, Sat.- Sun. 12-5PM. GRADE LEVEL: All grades. GROUP TYPE: All youth groups & homeschoolers. PROGRAM TYPE: Self-guided Tours, Guided Tours, Workshops, Exhibits. COST: Adults: $5; Ages 3-17: $3; Seniors.: (62 and over): $3 (Seniors. free on Wednesdays).

Housed in an historic 1936 subway station in Brooklyn Heights, this is the nation's largest museum devoted to public transportation history, and one of the premier institutions of its kind in the world. Explore the impact that mass transit has on the development of the New York metropolitan region and its people through exhibitions, tours, and educational programs. Go to www.mta.info for details of current exhibits and programs, or to shop the Museum's online store. (There is also a Gallery Annex & Store located in Grand Central Terminal, in the Shuttle Passage on the Main Concourse: 212-878-1016). SUPPORTS NY STATE & NATIONAL LEARNING STANDARDS IN: History/Social Studies, Science. SUPPORTS SCOUT MERIT BADGE ACHIEVEMENT IN: Social Studies, Science. REGION: Kings County, NYC.

NEW YORK YANKEES, Bronx, NY. Tel: Tour 718-579-4531. Tickets to Yankee games, for groups 718-293-6000. Fax: 718-681-8603. Email: tmorante@yankees.com. Hrs: Daily 10AM-4PM. Contact: Tony Morante. GRADE LEVEL: 1st - college. GROUP TYPE: All youth groups & homeschoolers. PROGRAM TYPE: Day Trips, Guided Tours. REGISTRATION: Online, Phone, Prepay, Tickets mailed prior to visit. TICKET/VOUCHER RETURN POLICY: Non Refundable. FOOD: Kosher, Vegetarian, Place to eat on site, Beverages available, Meal vouchers. RECOMM. LENGTH OF VISIT: 1 hour. RECOMM. RATIO OF STUDENT TO STAFF: 8:1. ARRIVAL TIPS: Expedite check in, Bus parking, Bus drop off and pick up at designated entrance. COST: Varies.

Tour Yankee Stadium and learn about American history from a new and fun perspective, as the evolution of one of the most storied sports teams in the nation comes to life. Philosopher Jacques Barzan said, "Whoever wants to know the hearts and minds of the American People had better understand baseball." In 2009, the Inaugural Season of the Yankees' brand new home, a tour of Yankee Stadium offers a unique and memorable look into the national pastime. Baseball is such an integral part of our shared culture that during the early part of WWII, as the country was focusing on the war effort, President Franklin D. Roosevelt insisted that baseball continue to be played. Did you know that Abraham Lincoln also was an avid baseball fan? As the delegation from Washington, D.C., came to Springfield, Illinois, to inform Lincoln that he had won his party's nomination for president, he stated, "They will have to wait outside until I make this hit!" Baseball, along with mom and apple pie comprise the American trilogy. The tour brings to light the countless other significant events that have taken place at 161st Street and River Ave. since the original Yankee Stadium opened there in 1923. Highlights of the tour include: Yankees Museum, Field and dugout area, batting cage and clubhouse area (when available) and Monument Park.(All sites subject to availability.) Inquire about our school & birthday celebrations. SUPPORTS NY STATE & NATIONAL LEARNING STANDARDS IN: Social Studies. SUPPORTS SCOUT MERIT BADGE ACHIEVEMENT IN: American Heritage, Sports & Games. (See ad under Sports History on page 119 and NYC Featured City Page on page 229.) REGION: Bronx County, NYC.

NY SKYRIDE, 350 Fifth Avenue (entrance for NY SKYRIDE at 33rd St. next to post office), New York, NY 10118. Tel: 888-SKYRIDE. Fax: 212-299-4932. Email: reservations@skyride.com. Website: www.nyskyride.com. Hrs: 8AM-10PM/365 days. Contact: Renee Wilson. GRADE LEVEL: All grades. GROUP TYPE: All youth groups & home-schoolers. PROGRAM TYPE: Day Trips, Films. MAX. GROUP SIZE: 200. REGISTRATION: Mail, Phone, Prepay, Tickets mailed prior to visit. FOOD: Variety of menu selections, Can bring own food, Beverages available. RECOMM. LENGTH OF VISIT: 1/2 hour. RECOMM. RATIO OF STUDENT TO STAFF: 20:1. ARRIVAL TIPS: Expedite check in, Bus drop off and pick up at designated entrance. COST: Group rates 20+.

What flies over the Statue of Liberty, skids across Wall Street, and dives underwater but never leaves the ground? NY SKYRIDE, New York's only aerial virtual tour simu-lator, located on the second floor of the Empire State Building. The NY SKYRIDE expe-rience, narrated by actor Kevin Bacon, is a remarkable adventure combining digital technology, custom designed seats and an 18-foot screen providing you with a unique perspective of NY! Brand new are our curriculums for grades 6-12! We're open 365 days a year, 8am-10pm and we have special pricing for combination tick-ets with the Empire State Building Observatory.   The NY SKYRIDE is safe, fun and entertaining and great for students! SUPPORTS NY STATE & NATIONAL LEARNING STANDARDS IN: Social Studies. SUPPORTS SCOUT MERIT BADGE ACHIEVEMENT IN: American Heritage, History. REGION: New York County, NYC.

RIPLEY'S BELIEVE IT OR NOT! TIMES SQUARE, 234 W. 42nd Street btw. 7th & 8th Aves., New York, NY 10036. Tel: 212-398-3133. Website: www.ripleysnewyork.com. Hrs: Open 365 days a year, from 9AM-1AM (last ticket sold at midnight). Contact: Group Services. GRADE LEVEL: All grades. GROUP TYPE: All youth groups & homeschoolers. PROGRAM TYPE: Day Trips, Self-guided Tours. REGISTRATION: Online, Phone, Prepay, Tickets mailed prior to visit. TICKET/VOUCHER RETURN POLICY: Printed on each order form. FOOD: No food offered. RECOMM. LENGTH OF VISIT: 1.5–2 hours. RECOMM. RATIO OF STUDENT TO STAFF: 10:1. ARRIVAL TIPS: Expedite check in, Bus drop off and pick up at designated entrance. COST: Varies; Group Rates Available for 15+.

The world's most fascinating, exciting and oddly educational attraction has redefined extraordinary with their new location in the heart of Times Square. Amazing by New York standards, Ripley's proudly features more than 500 incredible artifacts that challenge visitors to think differently. With more than 20 thoughtfully themed galleries and an easy reservation process, a visit to Ripley's Believe It or Not! Times Square is the obvious choice for those who want to experience something different, something fun and something that will have guests talking for weeks. Live performances and local oddities entertain and engage visitors of all ages. From fossils and asteroids to mummies and Babe Ruth we invite visitors to conquer the hundreds of weird and unusual artifacts and dozens of outrageous interactive elements housed in our fantastic new location. Photography is welcome and we provide a completely accessible, all-weather adventure 365 days a year. SUPPORTS NY STATE & NATIONAL LEARNING STANDARDS IN: History/Social Studies, Science, The Arts and Tolerance. SUPPORTS SCOUT MERIT BADGE ACHIEVEMENT IN: Social Studies, Science and Art. (See New York City Featured City Page on page 228.) REGION: New York County, NYC.

ROCK & ROLL HALL OF FAME ANNEX NYC, 76 Mercer St., New York, NY 10012. Tel: 1-866-969-2849. Email: sales@ticketsforgroups.com. Website: www.rockannex.com. Hrs: Tues.-Thurs. 11AM-7PM (last entry 6:00PM), Fri. -Sat. 11AM-9PM (last entry 8:00PM), Sun. 11AM-7PM (last entry 6:00PM). GRADE LEVEL: 1st-12th. GROUP TYPE: All youth groups & homeschoolers. PROGRAM TYPE: Day Trips, Self-guided Tours. REGISTRATION: Mail, Online, Phone. RECOMM. LENGTH OF VISIT: Average 1-1.5 hours. RECOMM. RATIO OF STUDENT TO STAFF: 10:1. ARRIVAL TIPS: Bus parking. COST: Varies.

Relive rock's greatest moments! Feel the rush of a live concert as you experience Rock's most electrifying performances. Get lost in the music as you journey through galleries filled with the personal mementos of Rock legends like The Beatles, The Rolling Stones, Madonna and Bruce Springsteen. From guitar heroes like Jimi Hendrix to song poets like Bob Dylan – Connect with the legendary artists that changed our world. SUPPORTS NY STATE & NATIONAL LEARNING STANDARDS IN: The Arts, History/Social Studies. SUPPORTS SCOUT MERIT BADGE ACHIEVEMENT IN: The Arts, Social Studies. REGION: New York County, NYC.

STATUE OF LIBERTY AND ELLIS ISLAND IMMIGRATION MUSEUM, Liberty Island, New York, NY 10004. Tel: 212-363-3206. Hrs: Daily 9AM-5PM. Self-guided Tours, Guided Tours. 1st-12th grade. Visit the pedestal observation levels of the Statue of Liberty and the Ellis Island Immigration Museum. Learn about American immigration and the immigrant experience, and use our free search to find your immigrant ancestors. There is a requirement of 1 adult per 10 students while on the ferry system of in the park. Ticket stating "Monument Acess" are required to enter the monument and are available free from the ferry company with the purchase of a ferry ticket. Call 1-877-LADY-TIX (1-877-523-9849). Ranger-guided tours of the island grounds are given free at scheduled intervals on a first-come, first-served basis. Schedules are posted at the information center on Liberty Island.COST: Free/Fee. REGION: New York County, NYC.

SOUTH STREET SEAPORT, South Street and Fulton, 19 Fulton Street, Suite 201, New York, NY 10038. Telephone: 212-732-8257. Fax: 212-964-8056. Email: Carolyn@CJFMarketingInternational.com. Website: www.southstreetseaport.com. Hrs: Vary. Contact: Carolyn Feimster. GRADE LEVEL: All grades. GROUP TYPE: All youth groups & homeschoolers. PROGRAM TYPE: Day Trips, Self-guided Tours, Guided Tours, Performances. FOOD: Variety of menu selections, Meal vouchers. COST: Varies.

The South Street Seaport is a slice of old New York. Its historic pier and cobblestone streets provide a picturesque legacy of the past, and serves as home to one of the city's most famous shopping, dining and special events destinations. The Maritime Museum, historic ships, the popular Bodies Exhibition and the return of Spiegletent, historic walking tours, the NYC Water Taxi and more makes South Street a must-see venue for students of any age. The food court offers student groups an array to select from with its special Food Court Dining vouchers, VIP Welcome Packets with shopping and dining discounts and student performance space. Visit www.southstreetseaport.com for activities and special events. SUPPORTS NY STATE & NATIONAL LEARNING STANDARDS IN: English, Social Studies, Math. SUPPORTS SCOUT MERIT BADGE ACHIEVEMENT IN: American Heritage. (See Regional Highlights on page 15.) REGION: New York County, NYC.

TOP OF THE ROCK OBSERVATION DECK, 30 Rockefeller Plaza (main entrance is located on 50th St. bet. 5th & 6th Aves), New York, NY 10111. Tel: 212-698-2000. Fax: 212-332-6550. Email: info@topoftherocknyc.com. Website: www.topoftherocknyc.com. Hrs: 8AM-12AM (last elevator goes up at 11:00 PM). Contact: Group Sales. GRADE LEVEL: All grades. GROUP TYPE: All youth groups & homeschoolers. PROGRAM TYPE: Day Trips, Self-guided Tours. REGISTRATION: Phone, Prepay. TICKET/VOUCHER RETURN POLICY: Tickets refundable up to 24 hours prior to the date and time on the ticket; no partial refunds or reissues on group tickets. FOOD: No food offered. RECOMM. LENGTH OF VISIT: 1 hour and 15 minutes. RECOMM. RATIO OF STUDENT TO STAFF: 10:1. ARRIVAL TIPS: Expedite check in, Bus drop off and pick up at designated entrance. COST: Varies.

Discover Top of the Rock Observation Deck, a 3-tiered observation deck atop 30 Rockefeller Plaza, New York City's most amazing attraction! The unforgettable experience includes a multi-media theater exhibit, glass ceiling elevator ride to the top and a panoramic 360-degree, unobstructed view from the 70th floor observatory, 850 feet in the sky! Purchase timed-tickets online at www.topoftherocknyc.com, via telephone 212-698-2000 or at the box office! SUPPORTS NY STATE & NATIONAL LEARNING STANDARDS IN: The Arts, Social Studies. SUPPORTS SCOUT MERIT BADGE ACHIEVEMENT IN: The Arts, Multicultural, Social Studies. (See ad on page 117 and NYC Featured City Page on page 229.) REGION: New York County, NYC.

THEODORE ROOSEVELT BIRTHPLACE NATIONAL HISTORIC SITE, 28 E. 20th St., New York, NY 10003. Tel: 212-260-1616. Hrs: Tues.-Sat. 9AM-5PM. Guided Tours. Visit the birthplace and boyhood home of the 26th president. COST: Free. REGION: New York County, NYC.

UNITED NATIONS, First Avenue at 46th St., New York, NY 10017. Tel: 212-963-TOUR (8687). Hrs: Mon.-Fri. 9:30AM-4:45PM. 1st grade-College. Day Trips, Guided Tours. Visit the meeting rooms where nations gather, see works of art from around the world, and learn about global issues. COST: Fee. REGION: New York County, NYC.

WATERFRONT MUSEUM, Pier 44, 290 Conover Street, Brooklyn, New York 11231. Telephone: 718-624-4719 ext. 11. Email: dsharps@waterfrontmuseum.org. Website: www.waterfrontmuseum.org. Hrs: Visit by appointment. Schedule of events upon request. Contact: David Sharps. GRADE LEVEL: All grades. GROUP TYPE: All youth groups & homeschoolers. PROGRAM TYPE: Day Trips, Guided Tours, Workshops, Performances. Bilingual Programs in French. MAX. GROUP SIZE: 149. REGISTRATION: Mail, Online, Phone. FOOD: Can bring own food. RECOMM. LENGTH OF VISIT: 1 hour program. RECOMM. RATIO OF STUDENT TO STAFF: 8:1. ARRIVAL TIPS: Bus drop off and pick up at designated entrance. COST: Varies.

A "floating classroom" housed aboard a one-of-a-kind restored covered wooden barge listed on the National Register of Historic Places. A National Park Service "National Maritime Education Initiative" Award Winner. Visitors learn first hand the geography of the New York Harbor, the history of the Tug and Barge "Lighterage Era" (1860-1960) and how food and commercial goods were transported prior to today's bridges and tunnels. Experience the exciting story of the rescue of Barge #79 by a clown and juggler and enjoy the captain's showboat performance. Curriculum available via email. SUPPORTS NY STATE & NYC LEARNING STANDARDS IN: Science, Social Studies. SUPPORTS SCOUT MERIT BADGE ACHIEVEMENT IN: American Heritage. REGION: Kings County, NYC.

SPECTATOR SPORTS

FORDHAM UNIVERSITY ATHLETICS, 441 E. Fordham Rd., Bronx, NY 10458. Tel: 718-817-4300. Email: diazjr@fordham.edu. Website: www.fordhamsports.com. Hrs: 9AM-5PM. Contact: Julio Diaz. GRADE LEVEL: All grades. GROUP TYPE: All youth groups & homeschoolers. PROGRAM TYPE: Day Trips, Guided Activities, Performances. COST: Prices vary, call for details.

Fordham University Athletics is the preeminent NCAA Division I athletic program in the Bronx, NY. The Fordham Rams are a part of the Atlantic 10 Conference for all sports except Football, which competes in the Patriot League. Fordham Men's & Women's Basketball, and Football games provide great spectator sports entertainment at a reasonable price. Other sports such as Men's & Women's Soccer, Volleyball, Baseball & Softball are free to the general public. Parking on campus is $10 per vehicle. For ticket information please call 718-817-4300. Go Rams! SUPPORTS NY STATE & NATIONAL LEARNING STANDARDS IN: Physical Ed/Recreation. SUPPORTS SCOUT MERIT BADGE ACHIEVEMENT IN: Physical Ed/Recreation. REGION: Bronx County, NYC.

NEW YORK YANKEES, Bronx, NY. Tel: For tickets, 718-293-6000. For tours, 718-579-4531. GRADE LEVEL: 1st grade-college. PROGRAM TYPE: Day Trips, Guided Tours. COST: Fee. (See ad under Sports History on page 119, main listing under Social Studies on page 113 and NYC Featured City Page on page 229.) REGION: New York County, NYC.

SPORTS HISTORY

THE NATIONAL TRACK & FIELD HALL OF FAME (AT THE ARMORY), 216 Ft. Washington Ave. @ W. 168th St. in Upper Manhattan, NY, NY 10032. Tel: 212-923-1803 x11. Email: derrick@ArmoryTrack.com. Website: www.Armoryfoundation.org. Hrs: Daily 10AM-5PM. Contact: Derrick Adkins. GRADE LEVEL: K-12th. GROUP TYPE: All youth groups & homeschoolers. PROGRAM TYPE: Day Trips, Guided Activities. COST: Varies.

The National Track & Field Hall of Fame is a modern tri-level 15,000 Sq. ft. interactive experience designed for elementary through high school students celebrating the history, science and sociology of the sport of Track & Field. The visit concludes in the 75,000 sq. ft. New Balance Track & Field Center with its world class track. Students participate in non-competitive abbreviated mini Track & Field events to end the day, including Track & Field events Races, Relays, Throwing & Jumping! SUPPORTS NY STATE & NATIONAL LEARNING STANDARDS IN: Physical Education, Science, Social Studies. SUPPORTS SCOUT MERIT BADGE ACHIEVEMENT IN: Science, Sports & Games. (See ad under Field Days & Recreation on page 91.) REGION: New York County, NYC.

TEAM BUILDING & CHARACTER EDUCATION

ECOLOGY VILLAGE NATIONAL PARK SERVICE, GATEWAY NATIONAL RECRE-ATION AREA, Bldg. 70, Floyd Bennett Field, Brooklyn, NY 11234. Tel: 718-338-4306. Hrs: By appt. 5th-12th grade. Overnight Trips, Guided Activities. An environmentally focused overnight camping experience for schools, scouts and non-profit youth groups that promotes team building. Teachers/Scout Leaders must attend workshop to prepare students for this experience. COST: Free/Fee for camping. REGION: Kings County, NYC.

THEATER · DANCE · MUSIC

KUPFERBERG CENTER PERFORMANCES AT QUEENS COLLEGE, 65-30 Kissena Blvd., Flushing, NY 11367. Tel: 718-793-8080. Fax: 718-261-7063. Email: dfirestone@kupferbergcenter.org. Website: www.Kupferbergcenter.org/revelations. Contact: Dedi Firestone. GRADE LEVEL: K-12th. GROUP TYPE: All youth groups. PROGRAM TYPE: Performances, Workshops. REGISTRATION: Mail, Online, Phone. RECOMM. RATIO OF STUDENT TO STAFF: 15:1. ARRIVAL TIPS: Bus parking, Bus drop off and pick up at designated entrance. COST: Varies.

Kupferberg Center Performances has become the favorite choice of teachers throughout Queens and the metro area. Each year 20,000 children from K-8th grade come to Colden Auditorium to attend inspiring and imaginative Revelations school-time performances of all kinds. Most include workshops! The Jazz Project at Kupferberg Center Performances, a high school residency program, educates music students within their schools, by offering jazz workshops by visiting teaching artists. On weekends, Family Theatre and other special events entertain and delight youngsters of all ages with diverse music, theatre, and dance. SUPPORTS NY STATE & NATIONAL LEARNING STANDARDS IN: The Arts, Language Arts. SUPPORTS SCOUT MERIT BADGE ACHIEVEMENT IN: Music. REGION: Queens County, NYC.

LINCOLN CENTER FOR THE PERFORMING ARTS, 70 Lincoln Center Plaza, New York, NY 10023. Tel: 212-875-5370. Email: mtaschools@lincolncenter.org. Website: www.lincolncenter.org. Hrs: Mon.-Sun. 10AM-5PM. GRADE LEVEL: K-12th. GROUP TYPE: All youth groups & homeschoolers. PROGRAM TYPE: Day Trips, Guided Tours, Guided Activities, Performances, Demonstrations, Lectures / Speakers. REGISTRATION: Mail, Online, Phone. FOOD: Variety of menu selections, Can bring own food, Place to eat on site, Beverages available, Meal vouchers. RECOMM. LENGTH OF VISIT: 2 hours for performance + tour. ARRIVAL TIPS: Expedite check in, Bus parking, Bus drop off and pick up at designated entrance. COST: Prices vary but start as low as $10/head.

Treat your students to a host of engaging activities at the world's leading performing arts center during its 50th anniversary year! Our popular Meet-the-Artist program introduces students to exciting performances ranging from jazz and hip hop, to Broadway, opera, and more! World-class performers show off their talents, share stories of their craft, and encourage participation! Enjoy professionally guided tours of our renowned theaters where children might catch a rehearsal in progress while hearing stories of great artists, architects, and designers. Master Classes invite your group to experience expert instruction from our outstanding chorus masters, maestros, drama coaches, or dance captains. All of our programs are custom designed with school curricula in mind. SUPPORTS NY STATE & NATIONAL LEARNING STANDARDS IN: The Arts. SUPPORTS SCOUT MERIT BADGE ACHIEVEMENT IN: Music, Theater. (See Lincoln Center Featured Theme Page on page 224.) REGION: New York County, NYC.

MANHATTAN CHILDREN'S THEATRE, 52 White St. (Between Broadway & Church Streets), 2 blocks South of Canal Street. Tel: 212-226-4085. Fax: 212-226-3847. Email: manhattanchildrenstheatre@gmail.com Website: www.mctny.org. Office Hrs: Mon.-Fri. 9AM-5PM, Sat. & Sun 11AM-4PM. Contact: Christie Love Santiago. GRADE LEVEL: Pre K-6th grade. GROUP TYPE: All youth groups & homeschoolers. PROGRAM TYPE: Day Trips, Performances. MAX. GROUP SIZE: 90. REGISTRATION: Online, Phone, Prepay. TICKET/VOUCHER RETURN POLICY: Cancellation must be made 3 weeks in advance. FOOD: Can bring own food, Place to eat on site (varies). RECOMM. LENGTH OF VISIT: Shows are 40 to 55 minutes long. RECOMM. RATIO OF STUDENT TO STAFF: 6:1. ARRIVAL TIPS: Bus parking, Bus drop off and pick up at designated entrance. COST: $7-$10 weekdays/$20 weekends. Depends on size of group.

Manhattan Children's Theatre is committed to producing affordable, high quality theatrical entertainment for children and families within the New York City community. Please visit www.mctny.org for all our 2009-2010 Season information. For more information on our programming and scheduling please call Christie Santiago at 212-226-4085. SUPPORTS NY STATE & NATIONAL LEARNING STANDARDS IN: The Arts. SUPPORTS SCOUT MERIT BADGE ACHIEVEMENT IN: Theater. REGION: New York County, NYC.

THE NATIONAL YIDDISH THEATRE - FOLKSBIENE, 135 West 29th St., #504, New York, NY 10001. Tel: 212-213-2120. Fax: 212-213-2186. Email: ashley@folksbiene.org. Website: www.folksbiene.org. Hrs: 10AM-6PM. Contact: Itzy Firestone, Group Sales Manager. GRADE LEVEL: Pre K-12th. GROUP TYPE: All youth groups. PROGRAM TYPE: Performances. MAX. GROUP SIZE: 10. COST: Fee.

The National Yiddish Theatre - Folksbiene. The longest running professional Yiddish theatre in America - 94 years and counting! Join us as we begin our new Season of amazing works! Yearly we present mainstage productions, special events, live concerts, family shows and much more. Please go to our website to find our more information about our theater company as well as our education and outreach programs and special events. Become a member of the Folksbiene now and experience thrilling Yiddish theater that you can't find anywhere else! SUPPORTS NY STATE & NATIONAL LEARNING STANDARDS IN: The Arts, English, Language Arts. REGION: New York County, NYC.

NEW YORK CITY BALLET, 70 Lincoln Center, New York, NY 10023. Tel: 212-870-5636. Email: Education@nycballet.com. Website: nycballet.com. GRADE LEVEL: Pre K-college. GROUP TYPE: All youth groups & homeschoolers. PROGRAM TYPE: Day Trips, Guided Tours, Guided Activities, Performances, Workshops. COST: Varies, free to low cost.

New York City Ballet offers an array of Education Programs. With our curriculum-based school programs and touring programs, students and educators learn that ballet is an accessible and relevant art form. These programs use professional arts educators to promote student- centered, collaborative, and interdisciplinary approaches to learning. Including theater-going opportunities, student groups experience the living processes of creating dance up-close! New York City Ballet also offers Close-Up programs, specially designed to enhance your enjoyment and bring you closer to what you see onstage. For families and individuals, these programs offer behind-the-scenes access and opportunities to interact with Company members. SUPPORTS NY STATE & NATIONAL LEARNING STANDARDS IN: The Arts. SUPPORTS SCOUT MERIT BADGE ACHIEVEMENT IN: The Arts. (See Lincoln Center Featured Theme Page on page 224.) REGION: New York County, NYC.

NEW YORK PHILHARMONIC, 10 Lincoln Center Plaza, New York, NY 10023. Tel: 212-875-5732. Fax: 212-875-5716. Email: education@nyphil.org. Website: nyphil.org/ctd09. Hrs: Vary. Contact: Lynne Mattos. GRADE LEVEL: 3rd-12th. GROUP TYPE: All youth groups. PROGRAM TYPE: Day Trips, Performances, Workshops. REGISTRATION: Mail, Online, Prepay. RECOMM. LENGTH OF VISIT: 1 hour. RECOMM. RATIO OF STUDENT TO STAFF: 10:1. ARRIVAL TIPS: Bus parking, Bus drop off and pick up at designated entrance. COST: $6 per student.

Give your students an unforgettable musical experience – a live performance by the New York Philharmonic! Award-winning School Day Concerts designed and hosted for schools are supported by curriculum, CD, and teacher workshops. Musical Encounters bring students behind-the-scenes at a Philharmonic rehearsal, plus a workshop on the music of the day. Either program, just $6 per student Plus – group discounts on evening and matinee concerts, with coachings by New York Philharmonic musicians available for high-level student ensembles. Visit nyphil.org/ctd09 or call 212-875-5732. SUPPORTS NY STATE & NATIONAL LEARNING STANDARDS IN: The Arts. SUPPORTS SCOUT MERIT BADGE ACHIEVEMENT IN: The Arts, Performing Arts. (See Lincoln Center Featured Theme Page on page 224.) REGION: New York County, NYC.

THE NEW YORK PUBLIC LIBRARY FOR THE PERFORMING ARTS, Dorothy and Lewis B. Cullman Center, 40 Lincoln Center Plaza, New York, NY 10023. Telephone: 212-870-1605. Hrs: Varies. The largest public, circulating performing arts collection in the world. The collection includes all aspects of dance, drama, music, orchestra collection and recorded sound and moving images. It also includes books, films, scores, published plays & screenplays, DVDs, commercial videos, newspaper & magazine articles. The Music Division of the library welcomes class visits and can customize the content to suit particular class needs and provide general introductions to using research. Group tours available by appointment. COST: Free. REGION: New York County, NYC.

THE PAPER BAG PLAYERS, 225 West 99th St., New York, NY 10025. Tel: 800-777-2247/ 212-663-0390. Fax: 212-663-1076. Email: pbagp@verizon.net. Website: thepaperbagplayers.org. Hrs: New York City performances in all five boroughs. GRADE LEVEL: K–3rd. GROUP TYPE: All youth groups and homeschoolers. PROGRAM TYPE: Performances. COST: Varies.

The Paper Bag Players Great Mummy Robbery will have your class laughing, singing, dancing---and sitting on the edge of their seats!   From an expedition to the land of the pyramids in search of that mysterious Mummy by the name of Shirley, to a Paper Bag picnic that turns into a dance-a-thon and the whole audience joins in, to a painting so realistic it comes to life--this show is funny, friendly, and thrilling! Perfect for children in grades K through 3. SUPPORTS NY STATE & NATIONAL LEARNING STANDARDS IN: The Arts, English. SUPPORTS SCOUT MERIT BADGES ACHIEVEMENT IN: Theater. REGION: New York County, NYC.

THE SHADOW BOX THEATRE, 325 West End Ave., #12B, New York, NY 10023. Tel: 212-724-0677. Fax: 212-724-0767. Email: shadowboxtheatre@yahoo.com. Website: www.shadowboxtheatre.org. GRADE LEVEL: Pre K-5th grade. GROUP TYPE: All youth groups & homeschoolers. PROGRAM TYPE: Performances, Workshops, Outreach. MAX. GROUP SIZE: 700. COST: Varies.

Award-winning musical theatre company using shadow, 3D puppets and live performers, serving pre-school and elementary schools for 40 years. Come to our theatres (Manhattan, Brooklyn, Bronx, Queens) or we can come to your school. Our interactive musical shadow puppet shows (7-9 performers) are ideal for up to 500 students. This year's shadow puppet shows are "The African Drum" (sharing African heritage) and "Little is Big" (underwater undersea tale of peace, friendship and courage). We also offer "Storybook Theatre," popular 2- or 3-performer interactive shows of "stories that sing" on Halloween, Thanksgiving, Christmas, Three Kings Day, and multicultural themes. Creative arts workshops for children, professional development workshops for teachers, and storybooks and Read-Along/Move-Along CDs and DVDs based on our shows, are great follow-ups. SUPPORTS NY STATE & NATIONAL LEARNING STANDARDS IN: The Arts, Language Arts, Social Studies. SUPPORTS SCOUT MERIT BADGE ACHIEVEMENT IN: Theater. REGION: New York County, Bronx Country, Kings Country, Queens County, NYC.

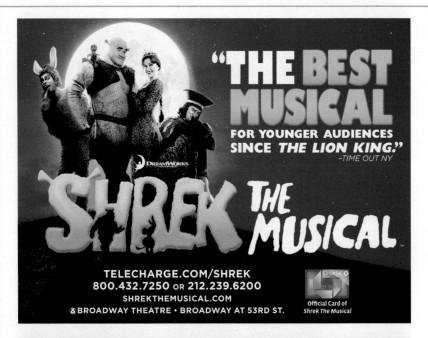

THEATREWORKS USA, 151 West 26th Street, New York, New York 10001. Tel: 800-497-5007. Fax: 800-630-6411. Email: classtrips@twusa.org. Website: www.twusa.org. Hrs: Call for performance dates and times near you. Contact: Box Office. GRADE LEVEL: Pre K-9th. GROUP TYPE: All youth groups & homeschoolers. PROGRAM TYPE: Performances. MAX. GROUP SIZE: 500. REGISTRATION: Mail, Online, Phone, Prepay, Tickets mailed prior to visit. RECOMM. LENGTH OF VISIT: 1 hour. RECOMM. RATIO OF STUDENT TO STAFF: 10:1. COST: Groups of 15 or more - $8 per seat with one free chaperone seat for every 10 paid seats. For groups of fewer than 15 - $10 per seat for all performances.

Get on the bus and supplement your students' curriculum with a Theatreworks USA Class Trips performance: 60-minute plays and musicals based on literature and history including: Aesop's Fables; Charlotte's Web; A Christmas Carol; Click, Clack, Moo; Freedom Train (Harriet Tubman); If You Give a Pig a Pancake; Junie B. Jones; The Lion, the Witch & the Wardrobe; Max & Ruby; Seussical (Dr. Seuss stories); and Tales of a Fourth Grade Nothing. (Not all shows perform in all areas.) Teachers' guides are available, featuring pre and post performance discussions, activity sheets, and more. SUPPORTS NY STATE & NATIONAL LEARNING STANDARDS IN: The Arts, Language Arts. SUPPORTS SCOUT MERIT BADGE ACHIEVEMENT IN: The Arts. REGION: CT, LI, NJ, NY, PA.

THEME RESTAURANTS

B.B. KING BLUES CLUB AND GRILL, 237 W. 42nd Street, New York, NY 10036. Tel: 212-997-4511. Fax: 212-997-4545. Email: melanie@bbkingblues.com. Website: www.bbkingblues.com. Hrs: 11AM-12AM. Contact: Melanie Carroll Shammout. GRADE LEVEL: All grades. GROUP TYPE: All youth groups. PROGRAM TYPE: Day Trips, Performances. MAX. GROUP SIZE: 650. MIN. GROUP SIZE:15. REGISTRATION: Mail, Online, Phone, Prepay. FOOD: Variety of menu selections, Vegetarian, Place to eat on site, Beverages available. RECOMM. LENGTH OF VISIT: 1 hour. COST: Menus starting at $15.00.

Located in the heart of Times Square near all major transportation and Broadway shows, BB King Blues Club offers a one of a kind music experience that's perfect for groups of all ages & sizes. Your group can dine while enjoying free live music, or check out our weekend brunches with Strawberry Fields Beatles Tribute on Saturdays and the world famous Harlem Gospel Choir on Sundays! We make the entire planning process easy with all inclusive menus, special group rates and events as well as flexible time slots offering availability for Breakfast, Lunch and Dinner. SUPPORTS NY STATE & NATIONAL LEARNING STANDARDS IN: The Arts. SUPPORTS SCOUT MERIT BADGE ACHIEVEMENT IN: The Arts, Performing Arts. (See New York City Featured City Page on page 229.) REGION: New York County, NYC.

MARS 2112 RESTAURANT, 1633 Broadway at 51 St., New York, NY 10019. Tel: 212-582-2112. Fax: 212-245-2112. Email: efeliz@mars2112.com. Website: www.Mars2112.com. Hrs: Daily 11:00AM-9PM. Contact: Ericka Feliz. GRADE LEVEL: K-12th. GROUP TYPE: All youth groups & homeschoolers. MAX. GROUP SIZE: 500. MIN. GROUP SIZE: 15. FOOD: Variety of menu selections. RECOMM. LENGTH OF VISIT: 1.5 - 2 hours. ARRIVAL TIPS: Bus drop off and pick up at designated entrance. COST: From $16.00.

Mars 2112 is a spectacular mingling of reality and fantasy, a 35,000 square foot, bi-level multi-dimensional immersive environment that catapults guests to a whole new universe of escape. Get ready for an intergalactic dining adventure that's totally out-of-this-world! An experience for earthlings of all ages! Space travel, intergalactic shuttle, Arcade Game room (Cyberstreet), Martian food, fantasy and more! Mars 2112 invites your school to participate in our "Etiquette For Earthlings" program (check website for details). REGION: New York County, NYC.

LET THE PARTY BEGIN!

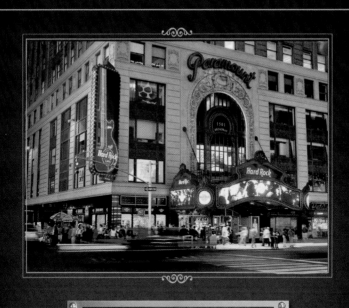

PLANET HOLLYWOOD, 1540 Broadway, New York, NY 10036. Tel: 212-333-7827. Fax: 212-730-2753. Website: www.planethollywood.com. Hrs: Restaurant: Sun.-Thurs. 11AM-12AM, Fri. & Sat. 11AM-1AM; Merchandise Shop: Sun.-Thurs. 10AM-1AM, Fri. & Sat. 10AM-2AM. REGISTRATION: Mail, Online, Phone. FOOD: Variety of menu selections, Kosher, Vegetarian, Place to eat on site, Beverages available, Meal vouchers. RECOMM. LENGTH OF VISIT: 1hour, 15 minutes. ARRIVAL TIPS: Bus parking, Bus drop off and pick up at designated entrance.

Student group menus are offered for breakfast, lunch and dinner. Groups are always seated together and space for exclusive and semi-private events is available. Meal vouchers are available to accommodate all budgets and tastes - from classic burgers to Premiere menu items. Beverages, tax, gratuities, and a special merchandise offer are included! In addition, complimentary meals are provided for escorts/drivers and one complimentary meal is offered for every 20 guests booked! Contact the Sales Team at 212-265-2404 for more information or to book your group today! (Please see contact info for our other locations in our ad above.) (See New York City Featured City Page on page 230.). REGION: New York County, NYC.

TICKETS

SCHOOL THEATRE TICKET PROGRAM, 1560 Broadway, Suite 1113, New York, NY 10036. Tel: 212-354-4722. Fax: 212-575-4740. Website: www.schooltix.com. Contact: Howard Lev/Suzanne Krebs.

Discounts for all groups and individuals to Broadway, off-Broadway shows, music, dance, opera, sporting events, museums and more. To have your facility added to our mailing list to receive discount coupons, visit our web site and fill out an application. We can arrange groups with a minimum of 15 or more (depending on the show) for all Broadway and off-Broadway shows. Discounts vary per show. Call and speak with one of our representatives. To stay up-to-date about our current offers please visit our web site and join our e-mail club. Don't see the show you want? Contact us. REGION: New York County, NYC.

TELECHARGE.COM GROUP SALES, 330 W. 42nd St., 22nd Floor, New York, NY 10036. Tel: 800-432-7780. Fax: 212-302-0997. Email:groupsales@telecharge.com. Website: www.Telecharge.com/groups. Hrs: Mon.–Fri. 9AM–9PM EST, Sat. & Sun. 1–9PM EST. Contact: Dianne Tack. GRADE LEVEL: Late elementary school-college. For schools, scouts, camps, families, adults - groups of all shapes and sizes, Telecharge.com Group Sales makes planning a trip to Broadway a snap. (See main listing on page 87.) REGION: New York County, NYC.

NEW YORK STATE

ADVENTURE SPORTS & OUTDOOR LEARNING

DEER RUN CAMP & RETREAT CENTER, 450 Walker Valley Rd., Pine Bush, NY 12566. Tel: 845-733-5494. Fax: 845-733-5471. Email: info@campdeerrun.org. Website: www.campdeerrun.org. Hrs: Vary. Contact: Camp Director. GRADE LEVEL: 3rd-college. GROUP TYPE: All youth groups & homeschoolers. PROGRAM TYPE: Day Trips, Overnight Trips, Guided Activities, Retreats. MAX. GROUP SIZE: 100. COST: Varies.

Deer Run Camp & Retreat Center provides access to 110 rustic acres of rolling hills, woodlands, meadows, marshes and streams in the southern Catskill region, less than 2 hours driving time from New York City. The camp offers comfortable living and dining accommodations March-November, plus classroom and conference facilities and a small theater. Activities include traditional recreation, plus evidence-based Youth-Development programs centered on our extensive high and low ropes challenge course, climbing wall, environmental education and hiking trails. In addition, Deer Run's Total Adventure Zone™ offers a variety of fun, exciting adventure activities both on-site and off-site. Team-Building, Personal-Development, Drug-Prevention workshops offered. ACA accredited. Licensed by the N.Y.S. Dept. of Health. SUPPORTS NY STATE LEARNING STANDARDS IN: Science, Physical Education. SUPPORTS SCOUT MERIT BADGE ACHIEVEMENT IN: Environmental Science, Sports & Games. REGION: Sullivan County, Catskills Region NY.

HUDSON RIVER RAFTING COMPANY, 1 Main St., North Creek, NY, 12853. Tel: 800-888-7238. Fax: 518-251-2598. Email: raft@hudsonriverrafting.com. Website: www.hudsonriverrafting.com. Hrs: Vary. Contact: Pat Cunningham. GRADE LEVEL: 3rd & Up. GROUP TYPE: All youth groups & homeschoolers. PROGRAM TYPE: Day Trips, Guided Tours, Self-guided Activities. MAX. GROUP SIZE: 300. COST: Fee.

Hudson River Rafting Company (since 1979) offers world class rafting on the Hudson River Gorge (17 miles), one of America's 10 best rafting trips. Raft the Sacandaga River's large dam release; rafting/tubing; excellent for youth groups, 6 trips per day. These rivers are located in North Creek, Lake George and Saratoga. In the western Adirondacks/1000 Island region, try the Black River Canyon for best summer rafting. HRRC provides all river gear: you provide paddle power following guide's commands. Call for pricing and assistance with your river adventure. Base camps have changing rooms, bathrooms, parking, picnic areas. Camping/hiking is nearby. SUPPORTS NY STATE & NATIONAL LEARNING STANDARDS IN: Health & Safety, Physical Education, Science. SUPPORTS SCOUT MERIT BADGE ACHIEVEMENT IN: Camping, Personal Fitness, Physical Education/Recreation, Science. (See Lake George Featured Region Page on page 221 and Regional Highlights on page 16.) REGION: Warren County, Adirondacks Region NY.

JERRY'S 3 RIVER CAMPGROUND, P.O. Box 7, 2333 Rte. 97, Pond Eddy, NY 12770. Tel: 845-557-6078. Fax: 845-557-0878. Website: www.jerrys3rivercampground.com. Hrs: Vary. Contact: Pete Lovelace. GRADE LEVEL: 3rd-college. GROUP TYPE: All youth groups & homeschoolers. PROGRAM TYPE: Day Trips, Overnight Trips, Self-guided Activities. MAX. GROUP SIZE: 350. COST: Varies.

Your students will have a fun-filled adventure while learning to work as a team. Enjoy white water rafting, canoeing, camping on the Delaware River, one of the most scenic and historic areas in the East. River trips range from 3 hours to 3 days depending on your schedule. Riverfront & brookside campsites, include two Pavilions with water and electric, lean-to's, spacious tents, RV Sites, 2 shower houses. On premise recreation canoeing, rafting, volleyball, horseshoes & 1/2 mile river front for fishing (nearby rental of fishing equipment & license). All outdoor activities have inherent risks, waivers required. Family owned and operated for 40-plus years. Competitive rates. SUPPORTS NY STATE & NATIONAL LEARNING STANDARDS IN: Physical Education. SUPPORTS SCOUT MERIT BADGE ACHIEVEMENT IN: Canoeing, Camping, Rafting, Sports & Games. (See Regional Highlights on page 16.) REGION: Sullivan County, Catskills Region NY.

KITTATINNY CANOE, Main Office: 378 Rtes. 6 & 209, Milford, PA 18337. Locations: NY: Barryville; Pond Eddy. PA: Dingman's Ferry; Matamoras; Milford; Smithville Beach. NJ: Delaware-Water-Gap. Tel: 800-FLOAT-KC (356-2852). Email: floatkc@warwick.net. Website: www.kittatinny.com. Hrs: April-Oct. Office for info & reservations open year round. GRADE LEVEL: 4 yrs/40 pounds and up. GROUP TYPE: All youth groups & homeschoolers. PROGRAM TYPE: Day Trips, Overnight Trips, Guided Tours, Self-guided Activities. COST: Varies.

Award winning family owned and operated, offering 69 years of outdoor fun and excitement for all ages and abilities. Kittatinny operates on the Scenic Delaware River, running through two National Parks. All seven of our bases are strategically located to insure the most diverse river trips. No experience is necessary for our white water rafting, kayaking, canoeing or tubing trips. You will however need to be prepared to have a wet fun filled day, as you paddle through crystal clear water with spectacular rock formations and lush forested mountains. A river trip is a wonderful opportunity to enjoy an abundance of wildlife from a new perspective. If that's not enough to entice you we also offer two riverfront campgrounds, paintball fields, and for your convenience we pick up at the Port Jervis Metro North train station or short line bus station. SUPPORTS NY STATE & NATIONAL LEARNING STANDARDS IN: Physical Ed/Recreation, Science, Social Studies. SUPPORTS SCOUT MERIT BADGE ACHIEVEMENT IN: Physical Education, Environmental Science, Water. (See Regional Highlights on page 16.) REGION: NY, PA, NJ.

SACANDAGA OUTDOOR CENTER, One Whitewater Way, Hadley, NY, 12835. Tel: 518-696-RAFT. Fax: 518-691-9240. Email: info@4soc.com. Website: www.4soc.com. Hrs: 9AM-6PM. Contact: John Duncan. GRADE LEVEL: All grades, 5 years and up. GROUP TYPE: All youth groups & homeschoolers. PROGRAM TYPE: Day Trips, Self-guided Tours, Guided Tours, Guided Activities, Workshops. MAX. GROUP SIZE: 150. MIN. GROUP SIZE: 10. COST: Activity dependent.

The Adirondacks premier adventure & fun location. Just minutes from Lake George and Saratoga with spectacular location at the confluence of two rivers. Offering Whitewater Rafting, Tubing, Kayaking, Canoeing, Hiking, Fishing and Mt Biking. Picnic grounds to accommodate your group with lunch packages and bonfire option. All guides are licensed and well trained in all activities. Horseback Riding and Train ride combinations available. We accommodate groups of all sizes and are sensitive to special religious requirements. Our trips range from 2 hours to all day and activities may be combined. SUPPORTS NY STATE & NATIONAL LEARNING STANDARDS IN: Physical Education, Science. SUPPORTS SCOUT MERIT BADGE ACHIEVEMENT IN: Camping, Physical Ed/Recreation, Safety. (See Lake George Featured Region Page on page 222 and Regional Highlights on page 17.) REGION: Saratoga County, Capital Region NY & Warren County, Adirondacks Region NY.

TUBBY TUBES COMPANY - OUTDOOR FUN PARK, 1372 Lake Ave., Lake Luzerne, NY 12846. Tel: 518-696-5454. Fax: 518-696-5405. Email: eric@tubbytubestubing.com. Website: www.tubbytubestubing.com. Hrs: 8:30AM-6PM. Contact: Eric Hamell. GRADE LEVEL: All grades. GROUP TYPE: All youth groups. PROGRAM TYPE: Day Trips, Self-guided Tours, Guided Tours, Self-guided Activities, Guided Activities. MAX. GROUP SIZE: 200. MIN. GROUP SIZE: 10. REGISTRATION: Mail, Online, Phone, Submit Waiver Forms. FOOD: Variety, Kosher, Vegetarian, Can bring own food, Place to eat on site, Beverages available, Meal vouchers. RECOMM. LENGTH OF VISIT: 2-3 hours. RECOMM. RATIO OF STUDENT TO STAFF: 10:1. ARRIVAL TIPS: Expedite check in, Bus Parking, Bus drop off and pick up at designated entrance. COST: Excellent Prices.

Tubby Tubes Co. is the best way for your group to experience the gentle side of the great outdoors. Enjoy our Guided Lazy River Tubing, Rafting and Kayak adventures on the pristine Lower Hudson River Gorge. Cool off, swim, relax and explore nature in the wonderful Adirondacks. Try our unique Floating Classroom and learn the history of the Hudson River and visit historic points along the way. Tubby Tubes Company offers a friendly, safe and organized facility to accommodate your group. We take care of everything you need to have an enjoyable and memorable visit. All ages welcome. SUPPORTS NY STATE & NATIONAL LEARNING STANDARDS IN: Health & Safety, History/Social Studies, Physical Education. SUPPORTS SCOUT MERIT BADGE ACHIEVEMENT IN: Camping, Citizenship, Family Life, Health & Safety, Life Skills, Personal Fitness, Physical Ed/Recreation. (See Lake George Featured Region Page on page 222 and Regional Highlights on page 17.) REGION: Warren County, Adirondacks Region NY.

AMUSEMENT & THEME PARKS

COOPERSTOWN FUN PARK, 4850 State Rte. 28, Cooperstown, NY 13326. Tel: 607-547-2767. Website: www.cooperstownfunpark.com. Hrs: Spring: Sat. 12-9PM, Sun. 12-6PM, Groups can reserve for a weekday in advance; Summer: Mon.-Sun. 10AM-11PM. Contact: Bob Hickey. GRADE LEVEL: All grades. GROUP TYPE: All youth groups & homeschoolers. PROGRAM TYPE: Self-guided Activities. COST: Varies.

At Cooperstown Fun Park, there's something fun for everyone. We feature the only Lazer Tag arena for over 90 miles, a twisting 1/4 mile Go-Kart track, Bumper Boats and a 9 stall Batting Cage. Inside the Fun Park's "main building" we have a Full Arcade with a variety of games, and a kitchen where we serve an array of tasty foods including charbroiled burgers, french fries, chicken fingers, hot dogs and Nestle ice cream novelties. In addition, we have an 18 hole scenic mini golf course located right next to the Fun Park. Visit Cooperstown Fun Park and experience the fun! SUPPORTS NY STATE & NATIONAL LEARNING STANDARDS IN: Physical Education. SUPPORTS SCOUT MERIT BADGE ACHIEVEMENT IN: Physical Ed/Recreation. REGION: Otsego County, Central Leatherstocking Region NY.

PLAYLAND PARK, Playland Parkway, Rye, NY 10580. Tel: 914-813-7016. Website: www.ryeplayland.org. Hrs: Varies. Contact: Group Sales. GRADE LEVEL: All grades. GROUP TYPE: All youth groups & homeschoolers. PROGRAM TYPE: Day Trips, Self-guided Activities. COST: Varies.

Playland has 50 major and Kiddyland rides for children of all ages to enjoy! From the famous and historic Dragon Coaster, and other original treasures, to the latest in high-speed, thrill and water rides, Playland has it all! This picturesque Westchester County-run beach-front property also boasts a beach, boardwalk, pool, pedal boats and mini golf. Built in 1928, this historic Art Deco style amusement park continues to captivate young people from New York City to Connecticut. Conveniently and centrally located on Long Island Sound, Playland is the destination of over one million thrill-seeking visitors annually. SUPPORTS NY STATE & NATIONAL LEARNING STANDARDS IN: Physical Education. SUPPORTS SCOUT MERIT BADGE ACHIEVEMENT IN: Physical Ed/Recreation. (See Regional Highlights on page 11.) REGION: Westchester County, Hudson Valley Region NY.

SUPERSONIC SPEEDWAY FUN PARK, Rte. 145, Durham, NY 12423. Tel: 518-634-7200. Fax: 518-634-7200. E-mail: phandel36@yahoo.com. Hrs: Off-season, Sat.-Sun.; Jun. 27-Labor Day: Daily 10AM-10PM. Groups can make reservations during off hours. Contact: Patty Handel. GRADE LEVEL: All grades. GROUP TYPE: All youth groups. PROGRAM TYPE: Day Trips, Self-guided Activities. MAX. GROUP SIZE: 200. REGISTRATION: Phone. FOOD: Variety of menu selections, Place to eat on site, Beverages available. ARRIVAL TIPS: Bus Parking. COST: Fee.

Located near the Catskills, Supersonic Speedway is an amusement center with fun activities for everyone. At the Speedway you can play mini golf, arcade games, ride the go-carts, use the batting cages, enjoy numerous rides, have a picnic, use the shooting gallery, and much more! And come and visit the restaurant & ice cream shop for a meal and a snack. Your group will have a blast! SUPPORTS NY STATE & NATIONAL LEARNING STANDARDS IN: Physical Education. SUPPORTS SCOUT MERIT BADGE ACHIEVEMENT IN: Physical Ed/Recreation. (See Catskills Featured Region Page on page 214 and Regional Highlights on page 11.) REGION: Greene County,Catskills Region NY.

ANIMALS · AQUARIUMS · ZOOS

ADIRONDACK ANIMAL LAND, State Hwy. 30, Broadalbin, NY 12025. Tel: 518-883-5748. Hrs: Mid-May - Labor Day: Daily 10AM-5PM. K-4th grade. Self-Guided Tours, Guided Tours. Over 500 animals including colorful birds, camels, bear and deer. COST: Fee. REGION: Fulton County, Capital Region NY.

ARMSTRONG'S ELK FARM, 936 Hervey Sunside Rd., Cornwallville, NY 12418. Tel: 518-622-8452. Hrs: Guided Tours, by appt. Educational look into elk farming with Rocky Mountain elk in their natural environment. COST: Free. REGION: Greene County, Catskills Region NY.

ASHVILLE GAME FARM, 468 Lick Springs Rd, Greenwich, NY 12834. Tel: 800-676-5309 or 518-695-4337. Fax: 518-695-4582. Hrs: Daily 10AM-5PM. Website: www.ashvillegamefarm.com. Contact: Jeff Ash or Louise Fairbanks. GRADE LEVEL: All grades. GROUP TYPE: All youth groups and homeschoolers. PROGRAM TYPE: Day Trips, Self-guided Tours, Guided Tours, Performances. REGISTRATION: Online, Phone. FOOD: Can bring own food, Place to eat on site, Beverages available. RECOMM. LENGTH OF VISIT: 1-2 hours. ARRIVAL TIPS: Bus Parking. COST: $11 for adults & $9 for children.

Located in the beautiful country hills of upstate New York, Ashville Game Farm and Exotic Zoo is a fun place for children and adults!! We have everything from monkeys and peacocks to alligators and bears! Our facility is large enough to house a wide variety of animals, yet small enough that it won't take you and your group the entire day to see and enjoy everything. For your convenience, we offer picnic areas and a gift shop where we sell snacks, cold drinks, and hot dogs as well as disposable cameras and neat souvenirs! We are handicap accessible and we offer group rates. SUPPORTS NY STATE & NATIONAL LEARNING STANDARDS IN: Science. SUPPORTS SCOUT MERIT BADGE ACHIEVEMENT IN: Animal Science. REGION: Washington County, Capital Region NY.

BINGHAMTON ZOO AT ROSS PARK, 185 Park Ave., Binghamton, NY 13903. Tel: 607-724-5461. Hrs: Daily 10AM-5PM. Guided Tours, Guided Activities. Set in a lushly wooded park, with animal exhibits, including binturong, grey wolves, tigers, leopards, an aviary, penguins, reindeer and many other animals. COST: Fee. REGION: Broome County, Southern Tier Region NY.

BREEZEWAY FARM PETTING ZOO, 161 Anawana Lake Rd., Monticello, NY 12701. Tel: 845-794-4543. Hrs: Daily 10AM-6PM. Self-guided Tours, Guided Tours. Come pet and feed our friendly farm animals. Pony rides available. COST: Fee. REGION: Sullivan County, Catskills Region NY.

FORSYTH NATURE CENTER, Lucas Ave., Kingston, NY 12401. Tel: 845-339-3053, 845-331-168. Hrs: Seasonal. Pre K-6th grade. Self-guided Tours, Guided Tours. Offers animal exhibits, gardens and environmental educational programs. COST: Free/Fee. REGION: Ulster County, Catskills Region NY.

TREVOR ZOO, 131 Millbrook School Rd., Millbrook, NY 12545. Tel: 845-677-3704. Hrs: Daily 8:30AM-5PM. Self-guided Tours. Home to 80 different species of exotic animals, seven of which are endangered. COST: Fee. REGION: Dutchess County, Hudson Valley Region NY.

UTICA ZOO, 99 Steele Hill Rd., Utica, NY 13501. Tel: 315-738-0472. Hrs: Daily 10AM-5PM. Self-guided Tours, Guided Tours. Collection of over 200 animals including Siberian tigers, Alaskan grizzly bears, and California sea lions. COST: Fee. REGION: Oneida County, Central Leatherstocking Region NY.

ART • ARCHITECTURE • SCULPTURE

BOSCOBEL RESTORATION 1601 Rte. 9D, Garrison, NY 10524. Tel: 845-265-3638. Hrs: Apr.-Oct.: Wed.-Mon. 9:30AM–5PM; Nov.-Dec.: Wed.-Mon. 9:30AM–4PM. Guided Tours. Learn about the lifestyles, furnishings, decorative arts and architecture of the Hudson River in the early 1800s. COST: Fee. REGION: Putnam County, Hudson Valley Region NY.

CORNING MUSEUM OF GLASS, 1 Museum Way, Corning NY 14830. 800-732-6845. Hrs: Daily 9AM-5PM. 3rd grade & up. Self-guided Tours, Guided Tours. More than 45,000 objects trace 3,500 years of glassmaking history, hands-on exhibits and glass blowing demonstrations. COST: Free. REGION: Steuben County, Southern Tier Region NY.

DIA: BEACON, RIGGIO GALLERIES, 3 Beekman St., Beacon, NY 12508. Tel: 845-440-0100. Hrs: Mid-Oct. - Mid-Apr.: Fri.-Mon. 11AM-4PM; Mid-Apr. - Mid-Oct.: Thurs.-Mon. 11AM-6PM. Self-guided Tours, Guided Tours, Workshops. Collection of contemporary art from the 1960s to the present. Works range from Andy Warhol's 1978 Shadows to three of Richard Serra's monumental sculptures. COST: Fee. REGION: Dutchess County, Hudson Valley Region NY.

EMPIRE STATE PLAZA ART COLLECTION, 2978 Corning Tower, Empire State Plaza, Albany, NY 12242. Tel: 518-473-7521. Hrs: Mon.-Fri. 6AM-6PM. Self-guided Tours, Guided Tours, Workshops. Modern art collection features 92 paintings and sculptures by artists who practiced in New York during the 1960s and 70s. COST: Free. REGION: Albany County, Capital Region NY.

FENIMORE ART MUSEUM, 5798 State Hwy. 80, Cooperstown, NY 13326. Tel: 607-547-1410. Hrs: Apr. 1-May 11: Tues.-Sun. 10AM-4PM, May 12-Oct. 12: Daily 10AM–5PM, Oct. 13-Dec. 31: Tues.-Sun. 10AM-4PM. Self-guided Tours, Guided Tours, Workshops. Art and history collections of the New York Historical Association including American Indian art, American folk and fine art. COST: Fee. REGION: Otsego County, Central Leatherstocking Region NY.

FRANCES LEHMAN LOEB ART CENTER, Vassar College, 124 Raymond Ave., Poughkeepsie, NY 12601. Tel: 845-437-5632. Hrs: Tues.-Sat. 10AM-5PM, Sun. 1-5PM. Self-guided Tours, Guided Tours. Collections chart the history of art from antiquity to the present. COST: Free. REGION: Dutchess County, Hudson Valley Region NY.

THE HYDE COLLECTION, 161 Warren St., Glens Falls, NY 12801. Tel: 518-792-1761. Hrs: Tues.-Sat. 10AM-5PM, Sun. 12-5PM. Guided Tours, Workshops. Collection of art works that span the history of western art from the 4th century B.C. through the 20th century. COST: Free/Fee. REGION: Warren County, Adirondacks Region NY.

KATONAH MUSEUM OF ART, Rte. 134 Jay St., Katonah, NY 10536. Tel: 914-232-9555. Hrs: Tues.-Sat. 10AM-5PM, Sun. 12-5PM. Self-guided Tours, Guided Tours, Workshops. 10,000 square foot with two galleries, a Multi-Media Learning Center features original children's book art with hands-on activities, and an outdoor Sculpture Garden. Presents diverse works from around the globe that explore ideas about art, culture and society. Exhibitions range from realism to abstraction, from ancient artifacts to cutting edge contemporary. COST: Fee. REGION: Westchester County, Hudson Valley Region NY.

NEUBERGER MUSEUM OF ART, Purchase College, SUNY, 735 Anderson Hill Rd., Purchase, NY 10577. Tel: 914-251-6110. Fax: 914-251-6101. Website: www.neuberger.org. Email: lauren.piccolo@purchase.edu. Hrs: Tues.-Sat. 10AM-4PM. Tours by appt. only. Contact: Lauren Piccolo. GRADE LEVEL: All grades. GROUP TYPE: All youth groups & home-schoolers. PROGRAM TYPE: Day Trips, Self-guided Tours, Guided Tours. REGISTRATION: Online, Phone, Prepay. FOOD: Place to eat on site, Beverages available. RECOMM. LENGTH OF VISIT: Varies. RECOMM. RATIO OF STUDENT TO STAFF: 10:1. ARRIVAL TIPS: Bus parking, Bus drop off and pick up at designated entrance. COST: Varies.

Introduce your students to the arts and humanities at the Neuberger Museum of Art. In-depth learner-centered tours of 20th-century, contemporary, and traditional African art help students understand the relationship of art to their own ideas and experiences. Discussion and hands-on activities in the galleries are employed to develop students' interpretation and expand the learning experience. Choose from tours of one of the permanent collections (Reframing American Art: Selections from the Roy R. Neuberger Collection or African Art from the Permanent Collection) or the changing exhibitions of contemporary art. Tours are by appointment only Tues.-Fri., 10AM-5PM and Sat. 12-5PM and must be booked three weeks in advance. www.neuberger.org. SUPPORTS NY STATE & NATIONAL LEARNING STANDARDS IN: The Arts. SUPPORTS SCOUT MERIT BADGE ACHIEVEMENT IN: The Arts. REGION: Westchester County, Hudson Valley Region NY.

OLANA STATE HISTORIC SITE, 5720 Rte. 9-G, Hudson, NY 12534. Tel: 518-828-0135. Hrs: Vary. 5th grade & up. Self-guided Tours, Guided Tours. Persian style villa created by Frederic Edwin Church, one of the most renowned American artists of the Hudson River School. COST: Fee. REGION: Columbia County, Hudson Valley Region NY.

ROCKWELL MUSEUM OF WESTERN ART, 111 Cedar St., Corning, NY 14830. Tel: 607-937-5386. Hrs: Mon.-Fri. 8AM-5PM. Guided Tours. American Western and Native American art exhibits based on themes of the American West. COST: Free. REGION: Steuben County, Southern Tier Region NY.

THE STORM KING ART CENTER, Old Pleasant Hill Rd., Mountainville, NY 10953. Tel: 845-534-3115. Hrs: Apr. 1-Oct. 31: Wed.-Sun. 10AM–5:30PM, Nov. 1-15: Wed.-Sun. 10AM-5PM, May 23-Sept 5: Sat. open until 8PM. Self-guided Tours, Guided Tours, Workshops. Five hundred acres of landscaped lawns, fields and woodlands provide the site for postwar sculptures by internationally renowned artists. COST: Fee. REGION: Orange County, Hudson Valley Region NY.

THE THOMAS COLE NATIONAL HISTORIC SITE AT CEDAR GROVE, 218 Spring St., Catskill, NY 12414. Tel: 518-943-7465. Hrs: May-Oct.: Thurs.-Sun. 10AM-4PM and by appt. Guided Tours. Visit the home and original studio building of Thomas Cole, the founder of the art movement known as the Hudson River School. COST: Fee. REGION: Greene County, Catskills Region NY.

ARTS & CRAFTS

POTTERY PLUS FIRED ART STUDIO, 401 Clairmont Ave., Suite 8A, Thornwood, NY 10594. Tel: 845-729-0287. Fax: 845-225-3883. Email: pottery-plus@hotmail.com. Website: www.pottery-plus.biz. Hrs: Vary. Contact: Donna Romaniello. GRADE LEVEL: All grades. GROUP TYPE: All youth groups & homeschoolers. PROGRAM TYPE: Day Trips, Guided Tours, Workshops. MAX. GROUP SIZE: 25. REGISTRATION: Phone. FOOD: Can bring own food. RECOMM. LENGTH OF VISIT: 1.5-2 hours. COST: $15 per student/scout.

Pottery Plus Fired Art Studio - the place to be on rainy days or any day. We are affordable... so everyone from schools to scouts to mom's with one or more children can stop in, paint and even have a snack before they leave! We have affordable Birthday Parties... music, dancing, plus great selections of items to paint. Rainy days? Stop in for some fun painting... with the unlimited selection of paints, including glitter, the possibilities are endless. We also have after-school sessions where we design, paint, and glaze or do hand-building with clay - Mon. & Wed. 4-5:30 pm. Call Today. SUPPORTS NY STATE & NATIONAL LEARNING STANDARDS IN: The Arts. SUPPORTS SCOUT MERIT BADGE ACHIEVEMENT IN: The Arts. REGION: Westchester County, Hudson Valley Region NY.

BEHIND THE SCENE TOURS

ZANARO'S ITALIAN RESTAURANT, One Mamaroneck Ave., White Plains, NY 10601. Tel: 888-244-4022. Fax: 212-262-4050. Email: groupsales@applemetro.com. Website: www.applemetrorestaurants.com. Hrs: Education programs start at 10AM. Regular dining starts at 11AM. GRADE LEVEL: All grades. GROUP TYPE: All youth groups & homeschoolers. PROGRAM TYPE: Guided Tours, Workshops. REGISTRATION: Mail, Online, Phone, Submit Tax Exempt Forms Prior to Visit, Prepay. FOOD: Lunch offered. RECOMM. LENGTH OF VISIT: 90 minutes. RECOMM. RATIO OF STUDENT TO STAFF: 20:1. ARRIVAL TIPS: Bus drop off and pick up at designated entrance. COST: Varies.

Zanaro's Classic Pizza Classes—Fine dining has never been so much fun. Westchester's favorite family style eatery is now perfect for groups. Learn the history of Italy's favorite food – the Pizza. Surprise the students with engaging lessons on food safety and our time-honored recipe for the best pizzas around. Turn simple bread dough into a work of culinary art and lunch. Education programs start at 10AM. Space is limited and subject to availability. For pricing & availability, please call 888-244-4022. Free Pre-Visit Materials Included. SUPPORTS NY STATE & NATIONAL LEARNING STANDARDS IN: Health & Safety. SUPPORTS SCOUT MERIT BADGE ACHIEVEMENT IN: Health & Safety. REGION: Westchester County, Hudson Valley Region NY.

BOAT EXCURSIONS & HARBOR CRUISES

Celebrating 40 years of sailing, singing and award-winning environmental education on the Hudson River

845.454.7673 ext.107
www.clearwater.org

Clearwater

DUTCH APPLE CRUISES, Boarding at Madison Ave. & Broadway, Albany, NY 12201. Tel: 518-463-0220. Hrs: Call for schedule. Guided Tours. Cruise through the scenic and historic Hudson River on one of our many sightseeing cruises. COST: Fee. REGION: Albany County, Capital Region NY.

LAKE GEORGE STEAMBOAT COMPANY, Steel Pier, 57 Beach Rd., P.O. Box 551, Lake George, NY 12845. Tel: 800-553-BOAT/518-668-5777. Fax: 518-668-2015. Email: info@lakegeorgesteamboat.com. Website: www.lakegeorgesteamboat.com. Hrs: Vary. Contact: 518-668-5777, Groups ext. 205; Info ext. 4; Charters ext. 209. GRADE LEVEL: 4th-college. GROUP TYPE: All youth groups & homeschoolers. PROGRAM TYPE: Day Trips, Guided Tours. REGISTRATION: Mail, Online, Phone. FOOD: Variety of menu selections, Place to eat on site, Beverages available. RECOMM. LENGTH OF VISIT: Varies. RECOMM. RATIO OF STUDENT TO STAFF: 10:1. ARRIVAL TIPS: Bus parking, Bus drop off and pick up at designated entrance. COST: Varies.

Cruiseships on Lake George. We invite you to sail with us on Lake George, undoubtedly the most beautiful lake in America. The Lake George Steamboat Company's three large passenger vessels offer: one hour lakefront sailings, daily Paradise Bay trips, 65 mile Discovery cruises, Luncheon, Dinner, Pasta, Pizza and Fireworks Cruises. All sailings from the Steel Pier on 57 Beach Road, Lake George Village. 2009 marks our 192nd year of carrying passengers on Lake George, your enjoyment and safety is our heritage. SUPPORTS NY STATE & NATIONAL LEARNING STANDARDS IN: Social Studies. SUPPORTS SCOUT MERIT BADGE ACHIEVEMENT IN: American Heritage, Social Studies. (See Lake George Featured Region Page on page 222.) REGION: Warren County, Adirondacks Region NY.

CAVES & MINES

HOWE CAVERNS, 255 Discovery Dr., Howes Cave, NY 12092. Tel: 518-296-8900. Email: fun@howecaverns.com. Website: www.howecaverns.com. Hrs: Daily 9AM-6PM; Winter Hrs: Daily 9AM-5PM. Contact: Robert Holt. GRADE LEVEL: All grades. GROUP TYPE: All youth groups and homeschoolers. PROGRAM TYPE: Day Trips, Guided Tours, Guided Activities. COST: $7.56/group member (grades K-12) from the day after Labor Day-June 30.

Continental upheaval. Sedimentation. Ten million years of erosion and calcification. Give your students a lesson in Earth Science they'll never forget. Your journey begins 15 stories beneath the earth's surface where time and the power of water have carved out curious passages and immense galleries. The 80-minute guided tour will lead you through a winding path, along a crystal-clear river and even on an underground lake! Above ground, you can pan for exotic mineral treasures in the gemstone mining center. SUPPORTS NY STATE & NATIONAL LEARNING STANDARDS IN: Science. SUPPORTS SCOUT MERIT BADGE ACHIEVEMENT IN: Science. REGION: Schoharie County, Central Leatherstocking Region NY.

NATURAL STONE BRIDGE AND CAVES PARK, 535 Stone Bridge Rd., Pottersville, NY 12860. Tel: 518-494-2283. Fax: 518-494-7979. Website: www.stonebridgeandcaves.com. Email: stonebridgeandcaves@frontiernet.net. Hrs: Daily 9AM-5PM. Contact: Greg Beckler. GRADE LEVEL: All grades. GROUP TYPE: All youth groups. PROGRAM TYPE: Day Trips, Self-guided Tours, Self-guided Activities, Guided Activities, Workshops. MAX. GROUP SIZE: None. MIN. GROUP SIZE: 10. REGISTRATION: Mail, Online, Phone. FOOD: Variety, Vegetarian, Can bring own food, Place to eat on site, Beverages available. RECOMM. LENGTH OF VISIT: 3 hours. RECOMM. RATIO OF STUDENT TO STAFF: 10:1. ARRIVAL TIPS: Bus Parking, Bus drop off and pick up at designated entrance. COST: $6.00 (K-6th grade) $8.00 (7th-12th grade) One free chaperone for every 10 students.

Two oceans, billions of sea creatures, intense metamorphosis, an unusual fault and melting glaciers exposed some of the oldest marble in North America to form some of the youngest caves in the Adirondacks. A hands-on geological NY wonder and long time favorite of earth science classes, come explore the largest marble cave entrance in the east. Introduction lecture and 90 min exploration of the waterfalls, gorge and caves (using our syllabus) followed by rock/fossil talks will excite any student. Additional activities: Museum grade Petrified Wood, Rock, Fossil & Crystal Displays, Rock Shop. SUPPORTS NY STATE & NATIONAL LEARNING STANDARDS IN: Science. SUPPORTS SCOUT MERIT BADGE ACHIEVEMENT IN: Science/Technology. (See Lake George Featured Region Page on page 222.) REGION: Warren County,Adirondacks Region NY.

CHILDREN'S MUSEUMS

CHILDREN'S MUSEUM OF SARATOGA, 69 Caroline St., Saratoga Springs, NY 12866. Tel: 518-584-5540 Hrs: Vary. Pre K-2nd grade. Self-guided Tours. Interactive exhibits provide opportunities for children to learn about science, history, community living, and the arts. COST: Fee. REGION: Saratoga County, Capital Region NY.

THE CHILDREN'S MUSEUM OF SCIENCE & TECHNOLOGY, 250 Jordan Rd., Troy, NY 12180. Tel: 518-235-2120. Hrs: Sept.-June: Thurs.-Sun. 10AM-5PM, Wed. 1PM-5PM. Groups daily by appt. Ages 5 and under only. Self-guided Tours, Guided Tours, Workshops. Hands-on exhibits for exploring, discovering and imagining the world of science and technology. COST: Fee. REGION: Rensselaer County, Capital Region NY.

DISCOVERY CENTER OF THE SOUTHERN TIER, 60 Morgan Rd., Binghamton, NY 13903. Tel: 607-773-8661. Hrs: Vary. Pre K-5th grade. Self-guided Tours, Workshops. Hands-on exhibits for discovery in the arts, sciences and humanities. COST: Fee. REGION: Broome County, Central Leatherstocking Region NY.

MID-HUDSON CHILDREN'S MUSEUM, 75 N. Water St., Poughkepsie, NY 12601. Tel: 845-471-0589. Hrs: Tues.-Fri 8:30AM-5PM, Sat. & Sun. 11AM-5PM. Pre K-6th grade. Guided Tours. Offers interactive programs on topics including history, the human body, the Hudson River and astronomy. COST: Fee. REGION: Dutchess County, Hudson Valley Region NY.

CIDERING

FROST VALLEY YMCA, 2000 Frost Valley Rd., Claryville, NY 12725. Tel: 845-985-2291. Hrs: Fall Season. Experience apple cidering as part of a one to three day retreat. Contact Bob Eddings for reservations. 845-985-2291. Children have the opportunity to work the cider press and learn about traditions of the farm. (See main listing on page 204.) COST: Fee. REGION: Ulster County, Catskills Region NY.

GREENBURGH NATURE CENTER, 99 Dromore Rd., Scarsdale, NY 10583. Tel: 914-723-3470. COST: Fee. REGION: Westchester County, Hudson Valley Region NY.

TEATOWN LAKE RESERVATION, 1600 Spring Valley Rd., Ossining, NY 10562. Tel: 914-762-2912. COST: Fee. REGION: Westchester County, Hudson Valley Region NY.

DUDE RANCHES & HORSEBACK RIDING

NEW HOPE FARMS EQUESTRIAN PARK, 517 Neversink Dr., Port Jervis, NY 12771. Tel: 845-856-6792. Fax: 845-856-8387. Email: nhfarms@frontiernet.net. Website: www.newhopefarms.com. Hrs: Apr.-Nov.: Tues.-Sun. 10AM- 5PM, closed Mondays; park closed Jan.-Mar. Contact: Mrs. Lesa Ellanson. GRADE LEVEL: All grades. GROUP TYPE: All youth groups. PROGRAM TYPE: Day Trips, Guided Tours, Guided Activities, Lectures/Speakers, Performances, Workshops. MAX. GROUP SIZE: 100. MIN. GROUP SIZE: 10. REGISTRATION: Mail, Online, Phone, Submit Waiver Forms, Prepay. TICKET/VOUCHER RETURN POLICY: 50% refund for cancellations. Inclement weather cancellations 75% refund. FOOD: Can bring own food, Place to eat on site, Beverages available. RECOMM. LENGTH OF VISIT: Dependent upon age group. RECOMM. RATIO OF STUDENT TO STAFF: Varies. ARRIVAL TIPS: Bus Parking. COST: $10/person, half-day (up to 3 hrs), $15/person, all-day (3-6 hrs). (See main listing under Field Days & Recreation on page 142.) REGION: Orange County, Hudson Valley Region NY.

TANGLEWOOD RANCH, 438 Cornwallville Rd., Cornwallville, NY 12418. Tel: 518-622-9531. Hrs: Varies. GRADE LEVEL: All grades. GROUP TYPE: All youth groups. PROGRAM TYPE: Day Trips, Guided Activities, Self-guided Activities. COST: Fee.

Saddle Up Partner! Get your group ready to take a ride through the Catskill Mountains and experience breathtaking views, including a five state view! In addition to horseback riding (Western) along scenic trails, we offer pony rides, horsedrawn hayrides, and all day or 3 hour night rides. Also check out the Indian trading post and craft shop. Call 518-622-9531 for more information and rates. SUPPORTS NY STATE & NATIONAL LEARNING STANDARDS IN: Physical Education. SUPPORTS SCOUT MERIT BADGE ACHIEVEMENT IN: Physical Ed/Recreation. (See Catskills Featured Region Page on page 214.) REGION: Greene County, Catskills Region NY.

FARMS • PICK-YOUR-OWN • MAZES

DR. DAVIES FARM, P.O. Box 146, Rte. 304, Congers, NY 10920. Tel: 845-268-7020. Fax: 845-268-6179. Website: www.drdaviesfarm.com. Hrs: Labor Day - Nov. 10, Daily 10AM-5PM. GRADE LEVEL: Early childhood-2nd. GROUP TYPE: School. PROGRAM TYPE: Day Trips, Self-guided Tours. COST: Varies.

Dr. Davies Farm has over 4,000 apple trees on 40 acres. Only 25 minutes from the GW Bridge. Dr. Davies Farm is perfect for younger children because the apples are accessible to our young pickers. Picnic grounds available. Wagon rides thru beautiful farm with stop at pick-your-own pumpkin field. The Davies family has been serving children with pleasure for over 28 years. Call to schedule a class trip. SUPPORTS NY STATE & NATIONAL LEARNING STANDARDS IN: Science, Social Studies. SUPPORTS SCOUT MERIT BADGE ACHIEVEMENT IN: Plant Life, Nature. REGION: Rockland County, Hudson Valley Region NY.

LAWRENCE FARMS ORCHARD, 39 Colandrea Rd., Newburgh, New York 12550. Telephone: 845-562-4268. Fax: 845-561-7886. Email: jlaw614@aol.com. Website: www.lawrencefarmsorchards.com. Hrs: Daily 9AM-4PM. Contact: Jane Lawrence. GRADE LEVEL: All grades. GROUP TYPE: All youth groups & homeschoolers. PROGRAM TYPE: Day Trips, Self-guided Tours, Guided Tours, Self-guided Activities, Guided Activities. MAX. GROUP SIZE: 100. REGISTRATION: Mail, Online, Phone. FOOD: Variety, Kosher, Vegetarian, Can bring own food, Place to eat on site, Beverages available. RECOMM. LENGTH OF VISIT: 1-3 hours. RECOMM. RATIO OF STUDENT TO STAFF: 5:1. ARRIVAL TIPS: Expedite check in. COST: $10/per child.

At Lawrence Farms Orchards, school children, their teachers and chaperones enjoy picking 24 different Fruits and Vegetables seven days a week from June to October. The School Group Packages include picking containers for each child to pick their fruit into, a Tractor-Pulled Wagon Ride, a short Educational Story about Fruit Growing, Visits with our Animals and play time in our "Little Play Village." Our Country Store is open too with home-made doughnuts, ice-cream and much more. Our visitors enjoy amazing views of the Hudson Valley and our family friendly atmosphere. Visit us at www.lawrencefarmsorchards.com, or call 845-562-4268. SUPPORTS NY STATE & NATIONAL LEARNING STANDARDS IN: Science. SUPPORTS SCOUT MERIT BADGE ACHIEVEMENT IN: Personal Fitness, Science/Technology. REGION: Orange County, Hudson Valley Region NY.

THUNDER RIDGE SKI AREA, Rte. 22, 137 Birch Hill Rd, Patterson, NY 12563. Tel: 845-878-4100 ext. 301. Fax: 845-878-2279. Email: thunderridge@cyburban.com. Website: www.thunderridgeski.com. Hrs: During Oct.: Mon.-Fri. 9AM-4PM. Contact: Meryl DiDio. GRADE LEVEL: Early childhood-3rd. GROUP TYPE: All youth groups & home-schoolers. PROGRAM TYPE: Day Trips, Guided Tours, Workshops. REGISTRATION: Mail, Online, Phone. FOOD: Variety of menu selections, Can bring own food, Place to eat on site, Meal vouchers. RECOMM. LENGTH OF VISIT: 2-3 hours. COST: Varies.

Only 60 minutes north of New York City our Pumpkin Picking Program includes a guided scenic hayride at the top of our 300 acre ski mountain, educational visit to our pumpkin patch, nature scavenger hunt, challenging corn and hay mazes, and farm animals. All children bring home a pumpkin and enjoy a healthy snack. Picnic area and hiking trails also available. We welcome all pre-school and school groups. Please call for more information and reservation. Also visit us for skiing. Ride the Metro-North train and we provide a free shuttle from the Patterson, NY train station. SUPPORTS NY STATE & NATIONAL LEARNING STANDARDS IN: Health & Safety, History, Math, Physical Education, Science, Social Studies. SUPPORTS SCOUT MERIT BADGE ACHIEVEMENT IN: Camping, Family Life, Health & Safety, Life Skills, Personal Fitness, Physical Ed/Recreation, Skiing. (See other listing under Skiing on page 155.) REGION: Putnam County, Hudson Valley Region NY.

FIELD DAYS & RECREATION

ADVENTURE FAMILY FUN CENTER, 1079 Rte 9, Queensbury, New York 12804. Tel: 518-798-7860. Fax: 518-798-7443. Email: adventureracing@nycap.rr.com. Website: www.lakegeorgegocarts.com. Hrs: Daily 10AM-11PM. Contact: Dexter Jenkins. GRADE LEVEL: All grades. GROUP TYPE: All youth groups & homeschoolers. PROGRAM TYPE: Day Trips, Self-guided Activities. MAX. GROUP SIZE: 400. COST: Varies.

Adventure Family Fun Center is the ideal place for your school trip, after prom party or fundraising event. Our 1,000 ft. outdoor go-cart track is the largest in the area. Our 40,000 square foot indoor facility features an indoor track, rock wall, paintball range, multilevel laser tag, bumper cars, dance/ karaoke floor, and huge arcade. Whether you plan on spending an hour or all day, we can accommodate up to 300 people with awesome group rates. SUPPORTS NY STATE & NATIONAL LEARNING STANDARDS IN: Physical Education. SUPPORTS SCOUT MERIT BADGE ACHIEVEMENT IN: Sports & Games. (See Lake George Featured Region Page on page 221.) REGION: Warren County, Adirondacks Region NY.

THE FUN SPOT, 1035 Rte. 9, Queensbury, NY 12804. Tel: 518-792-8989. Fax: 518-792-5073. Email: thefunspot@roadrunner.com. Website: www.thefunspot.net. Hrs: Spring-Fall: open daily, hrs vary; Winter Hrs: Vary. GRADE LEVEL: All grades. GROUP TYPE: All youth groups & homeschoolers. PROGRAM TYPE: Day Trips, Self-guided Activities. REGISTRATION: Phone. FOOD: Variety of menu selections, Can bring own food, Place to eat on site, Beverages available. RECOMM. LENGTH OF VISIT: 2-6 hours. RECOMM. RATIO OF STUDENT TO STAFF: 10:1. ARRIVAL TIPS: Bus parking, Bus drop off and pick up at designated entrance. COST: Varies.

Entertainment for all ages! Gold Rush Adventure Golf featuring cascading waterfalls, streams and caves. Participate in our mining experience and feed our fish. Race on our LeMans Go-Kart track with hairpin turns, bridge and underpass. Go-Karts and Adventure Golf open April through October. Our year round activities include Lasertron Laser Tag, Inflatable Fun on our two Obstacle Courses with 12 foot slides and Bounce House, and Inline/Roller Skating to today's Top Music. Our Snack Bar features both hot and cold food items. Meal Deals and catering options available. Group Rates and Private Party Times available. SUPPORTS NY STATE & NATIONAL LEARNING STANDARDS IN: Physical Education. SUPPORTS SCOUT MERIT BADGE ACHIEVEMENT IN: Physical Ed/Recreation. (See Lake George Featured Region Page on page 221 and Regional Highlights on page 10.) REGION: Warren County, Adirondacks Region NY.

NEW HOPE FARMS EQUESTRIAN PARK, 517 Neversink Dr., Port Jervis, NY 12771. Tel: 845-856-6792. Fax: 845-856-8387. Email: nhfarms@frontiernet.net. Website: www.newhopefarms.com. Hrs: Apr.-Nov.: Tues.-Sun. 10AM- 5PM, closed Mondays; park closed Jan.-Mar. Contact: Mrs. Lesa Ellanson. GRADE LEVEL: All grades. GROUP TYPE: All youth groups. PROGRAM TYPE: Day Trips, Guided Tours, Guided Activities, Lectures/Speakers, Performances, Workshops. MAX. GROUP SIZE: 100. MIN. GROUP SIZE: 10. REGISTRATION: Mail, Online, Phone, Submit Waiver Forms, Prepay. TICKET/VOUCHER RETURN POLICY: 50% refund for cancellations. Inclement weather cancellations 75% refund. FOOD: Can bring own food, Place to eat on site, Beverages available. RECOMM. LENGTH OF VISIT: Dependent upon age group. RECOMM. RATIO OF STUDENT TO STAFF: Varies. ARRIVAL TIPS: Bus Parking. COST: $10/person, half-day (up to 3 hrs), $15/person, all-day (3-6 hrs).

New Hope Farms Equestrian Park is the northeast's finest horse farm. Located ninety minutes from Westchester and less than two hours from Manhattan, we have one of the largest indoor equestrian venues in the nation. In addition to our main show arena, we offer an annexed indoor ring which provides a sheltered instruction environment, which includes guided tours, lectures, even hands-on activities with show horses. For groups and schools we accommodate Pre K through college level. At our spacious 40+ acre facility, we bring the finest care and exceptional instruction. Those who venture to see us are always impressed. Visit us and see why! Open April through November, closed January through March. SUPPORTS NY STATE & NATIONAL LEARNING STANDARDS IN: Health & Safety, History/Social Studies, Physical Education, Science. SUPPORTS SCOUT MERIT BADGE ACHIEVEMENT IN: Animal Science - Horse Option, Dog Care, Environmental Science - Endangered Species, Health & Safety, Horsemanship, Life Skills, Nature - Reptiles and Amphibians, Personal Fitness, Physical Ed/Recreation, Safety, Science/Technology. REGION: Orange County, Hudson Valley Region NY.

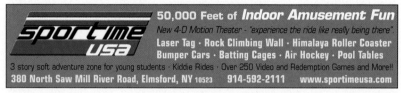
SPORTIME USA, 380 North Saw Mill River Rd., Elmsford, NY 10523. Tel: 914-592-2111. Website: www.sportimeusa.com. Hrs: Open 364 days, Weekdays: 11AM-10PM, Weekends: 10AM-1AM. Contact: Group Sales. GRADE LEVEL: All grades. GROUP TYPE: All youth groups & homeschoolers. PROGRAM TYPE: Day Trips, Overnight Trips, Self-guided Activities. MAX. GROUP SIZE: 750. REGISTRATION: Mail, Phone. FOOD: Variety of menu selections, Kosher, Vegetarian, Can bring own food, Place to eat on site, Beverages available, Meal vouchers. RECOMM. LENGTH OF VISIT: 3 hours (varies). RECOMM. RATIO OF STUDENT TO STAFF: 8:1. ARRIVAL TIPS: Expedite check in, Bus parking, Bus drop off and pick up at designated entrance. COST: Varies.

Sportime USA with 50,000 sq feet of indoor amusement fun offers a very safe environment with some features as our newest attraction: 4-D Motion Theater, "experience the ride like really being there." Other attractions include Lazer Tag, 30 ft rock climbing wall, 9 batting cages, bumper cars, Himalayas roller coaster, 3 story soft adventure zone for young children, kiddie rides, pool tables, air hockey, and over 250 video and redemption games with a super large prize counter area. The ideal place for team building activities and field days. We can accommodate very small to very large groups including rainy day bookings. Free bus parking on premises. Full service restaurant and snack bar capable of handling all types of food needs. Buy lunch or snacks or bring in your own. Fully air-conditioned, Sportime USA is the absolute best place to party and play. "The perfect place for Project Graduation." Conveniently located 2 minutes from the Tappan Zee Bridge and 15 minutes from GW Bridge. (See other listing under Indoor Amusement Centers on page 146.) SUPPORTS NY STATE & NATIONAL LEARNING STANDARDS IN: Physical Education. SUPPORTS SCOUT MERIT BADGE ACHIEVEMENT IN: Sports & Games. REGION: Westchester County, Hudson Valley Region NY.

SURPRISE LAKE CAMP, Winter: 307 Seventh Ave., Suite 900, New York, NY 10001. Camp address: 382 Lake Surprise Rd., Cold Springs, New York 10516. Tel: 212-924-3131. Fax: 212-924-5112. Email: klf@surpriselake.org. Website: www.surpriselake.org. Hrs: Vary. Contact: Ken Freedman. GRADE LEVEL: All grades. GROUP TYPE: School, Scout, Religious Youth groups. PROGRAM TYPE: Overnights/Retreats. MAX. GROUP SIZE: Varies. COST: Varies.

Located only 60 miles from New York City, Surprise Lake Camp sits on nearly 500 beautiful acres surrounding a private, half-mile long lake. The site offers kosher catering, meeting facilities, a 1000-seat amphitheater, sports fields, and overnight accommodations. We have staff available to run programs including low ropes challenge course, climbing tower, hikes, Jewish environmental education programs, and much more. Our beautiful, full-size gymnasium is the perfect place to hold sporting events throughout the year. We are open for rentals from April to early June then from September to October. Surprise Lake Camp can accommodate groups of various sizes for single or multi day programs, depending on the time of year. Housing accommodations vary based on group size and preferences. SUPPORTS NY STATE & NATIONAL LEARNING STANDARDS IN: Physical Education. SUPPORTS SCOUT MERIT BADGE ACHIEVEMENT IN: Physical Ed/Recreation. REGION: Dutchess County, Hudson Valley Region NY.

TANGLEWOOD RANCH, 438 Cornwallville Rd., Cornwallville, NY 12418. Tel: 518-622-9531. Hrs: Varies. GRADE LEVEL: All grades. GROUP TYPE: All youth groups. PROGRAM TYPE: Day Trips, Guided Activities, Self-guided Activities. COST: Fee. (See main listing under Dude Ranches & Horseback Riding on page 140 and Catskills Featured Region Page on page 214.) REGION: Greene County, Catskills Region NY.

VILLA ROMA RESORT AND CONFERENCE CENTER, 356 Villa Roma Rd., Callicoon, NY 12723. Tel: 800-727-8455 ext 7021. Fax: 845-887-4824. Email: kdowdell@villaroma.com. Website: www.villaroma.com. Hrs: 24/7. Contact: Kevin Dowdell. GRADE LEVEL: All grades. GROUP TYPE: All youth groups & homeschoolers. PROGRAM TYPE: Overnight Trips, Self-guided Tours, Self-guided Activities, Guided Activities, Performances, Workshops. COST: Fee.

Villa Roma Resort and Conference Center has an almost unlimited array of facilities and activities perfect for groups and class trips. School trips include deluxe accommodations, meal packages, DJ dance parties, late night snacks, and use of resort facilities which include a game room, sports complex, and pools. Customize your package with the following: Horseback Riding, Mountain Paintball, White Water Rafting, Skiing, and Snow Tubing. From theme parties to sporting events, our staff will provide entertainment for ages 13–18. Other activities include flag football, hemp necklace making, rafting, clay projects, team building events and Beyond Balderdash.™ SUPPORTS NY STATE & NATIONAL LEARNING STANDARDS IN: Physical Education. SUPPORTS SCOUT MERIT BADGE ACHIEVEMENT IN: Personal Fitness, Physical Ed/Recreation. REGION: Sullivan County, Catskills Region NY.

HEALTH & NUTRITION

FIELD TRIP FACTORY, Telephone: 800-987-6409. Fax: 773-342-9513. Email: info@fieldtripfactory.com. Hrs: Mon.-Fri. 8AM-6PM. GRADE LEVEL: Pre K-6th. GROUP TYPE: All youth groups & homeschoolers. PROGRAM TYPE: Day Trips, Guided Tours. COST: Free.

Field Trip Factory offers free community-based field trips. Our learning adventures teach valuable life-skills including health and nutrition, science, responsibility and more. All field trips are grade and age appropriate, meet learning standards, enrich classroom curriculum for teachers and fulfill badge requirements for scouts. See what is available in your area at www.fieldtripfactory.com or call 1-800-987-6409. SUPPORTS STATE LEARNING STANDARDS IN: Health & Safety, Math, Physical Education, Science. SUPPORTS SCOUT BADGE ACTIVITIES IN: Health & Safety, Life Skills, Personal Fitness. (See ad on page 56.) REGION: Throughout all 50 states.

INDOOR AMUSEMENT CENTERS

DAVE AND BUSTER'S, Palisades: 4661 Palisades Center Dr., West Nyack, NY 10994. Tel: 845-353-1555. Email: jessica_foley@daveandbusters.com. Contact: Jessica Foley. Buffalo: Eastern Hills Mall, 4545 Transit Rd., Suite 220 Williamsville, NY 14221. Tel: 716-932-2422. Email: eileen_fox@daveandbusters.com. Contact: Eileen Fox. Website: www.daveandbusters.com. Hrs: Sales office, 9AM-6PM. GRADE LEVEL: K-12th. GROUP TYPE: All youth groups & homeschoolers. PROGRAM TYPE: Self-guided Activities. REGISTRATION: Phone. FOOD: Variety of menu selections, Kosher, Vegetarian, Beverages available. RECOMM. LENGTH OF VISIT: 2-3 hours. RECOMM. RATIO OF STUDENT TO STAFF: 10:1 (before 2:30PM). ARRIVAL TIPS: Expedite check in, Bus parking. COST: Fee.

At Dave & Buster's your group will have a blast! Start out with a delicious meal and then move on to some games in our Million Dollar Midway. Spend an hour with us, or a whole day - at Dave & Buster's it's your call! We have packages for groups of 20 to 2,000; so for your next outing come eat, party & play at Dave & Buster's – your students will thank you! SUPPORTS NY STATE & NATIONAL LEARNING STANDARDS IN: Physical Education. SUPPORTS SCOUT MERIT BADGE ACHIEVEMENT IN: Physical Ed/Recreation. (See ad in New York City on page 96.) REGION: Rockland County, Hudson Valley Region NY.

FUNFUZION AT NEW ROC CITY, 19 Lecount Pl., New Rochelle, NY 10801. Tel: 914-637-7575 x 204. Fax: 914-576-6736. Email: groupsales@funfuziononline.com. Website: www.funfuziononline.com. Hrs: Daily. Contact: Jodi Reynolds. GRADE LEVEL: 3rd-College. GROUP TYPE: All youth groups. PROGRAM TYPE: Day Trips. MAX. GROUP SIZE: 500. MIN. GROUP SIZE: 25. COST: Fee.

Class trips to Funfuzion at New Roc City are the best! Conveniently located off I95 exit 16, and one block from the Metro-North, getting here is easy. Your students will enjoy organized games of bowling, Laser tag, Billiards and Mini-Golf! Also available: amusement rides, go-karts and interactive video games. On-site catering can accommodate groups of any size and budget. Interactive entertainment over the meal period adds to the fun of the day. Exclusive overnight Loc-Ins can be arranged for graduation festivities. Convenient, free bus parking. Safe environment with on-site security. SUPPORTS NY STATE & NATIONAL LEARNING STANDARDS IN: Physical Education. SUPPORTS SCOUT MERIT BADGE ACHIEVEMENT IN: Physical Ed/Recreation. (See ad under Proms & School Celebrations on page 150.) REGION: Westchester County, Hudson Valley Region NY.

KID'S FUN ZONE, 12 Genesee St., New Hartford, NY 13326. Tel: 315-732-ZONE. Website: www.cooperstownfunpark.com. Hrs: Tues.-Thurs. 11AM-7PM, Fri.-Sat. 11AM-8PM, Sun. 11AM-6PM, open Mondays for private parties only. Contact: Bob Hickey. GRADE LEVEL: All grades. GROUP TYPE: All youth groups. PROGRAM TYPE: Self-guided Activities. COST: Varies.

Kid's Fun Zone offers endless entertainment for children of all ages! Kids ages 2-11 will love riding the slides and exploring the tunnels of central New York's largest soft indoor playground, while guests ages 4 and up will enjoy our exciting Lazer Runner laser tag (complete with black lights and techno music!), as well as our arcade, where both high-tech video games and classic arcade games will keep the fun going no matter what your age. With so many adventures to be had here, Kid's Fun Zone is the perfect place to host your school or youth group's next party or special event! SUPPORTS NY STATE & NATIONAL LEARNING STANDARDS IN: Physical Education. SUPPORTS SCOUT MERIT BADGE ACHIEVEMENT IN: Physical Ed/Recreation. REGION: Oneida County, Mohawk Valley Region NY.

SPORTIME USA, 380 North Saw Mill River Rd., Elmsford, NY 10523. Tel: 914-592-2111. Website: www.sportimeusa.com. Hrs: Open 364 days, Weekdays: 11AM-10PM, Weekends: 10AM-1AM. Contact: Group Sales. GRADE LEVEL: All grades. GROUP TYPE: All youth groups & homeschoolers. PROGRAM TYPE: Day Trips, Overnight Trips, Self-guided Activities. MAX. GROUP SIZE: 750. REGISTRATION: Mail, Phone. FOOD: Variety of menu selections, Kosher, Vegetarian, Can bring own food, Place to eat on site, Beverages available, Meal vouchers. RECOMM. LENGTH OF VISIT: 3 hours (varies). RECOMM. RATIO OF STUDENT TO STAFF: 8:1. ARRIVAL TIPS: Expedite check in, Bus parking, Bus drop off and pick up at designated entrance. COST: Varies.

Sportime USA with 50,000 sq feet of indoor amusement fun offers a very safe environment with some features as our newest attraction: 4-D Motion Theater, "experience the ride like really being there." Other attractions include Lazer Tag, 30 ft rock climbing wall, 9 batting cages, bumper cars, Himalayas roller coaster, 3 story soft adventure zone for young children, kiddie rides, pool tables, air hockey, and over 250 video and redemption games with a super large prize counter area. The ideal place for team building activities and field days. We can accommodate very small to very large groups including rainy day bookings. Free bus parking on premises. Full service restaurant and snack bar capable of handling all types of food needs. Buy lunch or snacks or bring in your own. Fully air-conditioned, Sportime USA is the absolute best place to party and play. "The perfect place for Project Graduation." Conveniently located 2 minutes from the Tappan Zee Bridge and 15 minutes from GW Bridge. SUPPORTS NY STATE & NATIONAL LEARNING STANDARDS IN: Physical Education. SUPPORTS SCOUT MERIT BADGE ACHIEVEMENT IN: Sports & Games. (See ad under Field Days and Recreation on page 143.) REGION: Westchester County, Hudson Valley Region NY.

INTERACTIVE LIVING HISTORY

1812 HOMESTEAD FARM & MUSEUM, 112 Reber Rd., Willsboro, NY 12996. Tel: 518-963-4071. Hrs: May-Sept.: 10AM-5PM. Self-guided Tours, Guided Tours. Offers hands-on experience of daily rural life on a farm in the early 1800s. COST: Fee. REGION: Essex County, Adirondacks Region NY.

ERIE CANAL VILLAGE, 5789 Rome New London Rd. (Rtes. 46 & 49), Rome, NY 13440. Tel: 315-337-3999. Hrs: Vary. 2nd grade & up. Self Guided tours. Outdoor living history museum featuring a reconstructed 19th century settlement on the Erie Canal. COST: Fee. REGION: Oneida County, Mohawk Valley Region NY.

THE FARMER'S MUSEUM, 5775 State Hwy. 80, Cooperstown, NY 13326. Tel: 888-547-1450. Hrs: Seasonal. Self-guided Tours, Guided Tours. A Historic Village of a mid-19th-century farming community in Central New York State. COST: Fee. REGION: Otsego County, Central Leatherstocking Region NY.

FORT DELAWARE MUSEUM OF COLONIAL HISTORY, 6615 Rte. 97, Narrowsburg, NY 12764. Tel: Weekday: 845-794-3000, ext. 5002; Weekend: 845-252-6660. Hrs: Weekends Memorial Day-Labor Day; call for hours & special weekday offerings for class trips. 2nd-5th grade. Self-guided Tours, Performances. Authentic depiction of the life of the Delaware Company Pioneers with demonstrations of 18th century life skills. COST: Fee. REGION: Sullivan County, Catskills Region NY.

FORT TICONDEROGA, 30 Fort Rd., Ticonderoga, NY 12883. Tel: 518-585-2821. Hrs: May 21-Oct 20: Daily 9AM-5PM. Self-guided Tours, Guided Tours, Workshops. Site of the French & Indian War and American Revolution. Enjoy a reenactment of Ethan Allen's capture in 1777; students get mustered into the Green Mountain Boys and taught to march and handle a musket. COST: Fee. REGION: Essex County, Adirondacks Region NY.

FORT WILLIAM HENRY MUSEUM, 48 Canada St., Lake George, NY 12845. Tel: 518-668-5471. Hrs: May 2-Oct.: Daily 9AM-6PM. Self-Guided Tours, Guided Tours, Performances. Learn about the weapons and warfare of the 18th century, through cannon firing and musket ball molding demonstrations and museum exhibits. COST: Fee. REGION: Warren County, Adirondacks Region NY.

HISTORIC CHERRY HILL, 523 1/2 S. Pearl St., Albany, NY 12202. Tel: 518-434-4791. Hrs: Call for hours. Guided Tours, Workshops. Collection of one family's material possessions spanning five generations and over three hundred years of American history. Tours focus on how the family dealt with social, economic, and historical changes over the years. COST: Fee. REGION: Albany, Capital Region NY.

MUSEUM VILLAGE, 1010 Rte. 17M, Monroe, NY 10950. Tel: 845-782-8248. Hrs: Groups are scheduled Sept.-Nov. & Apr.-June: Weekdays 10AM-2PM. Self-guided Tours, Workshops. A living history museum in which children can explore many buildings and perform the tasks of life as it was in the 19th century. COST: Fee. REGION: Orange County, Hudson Valley Region NY.

MAPLE SUGARING

Follow the maple sugaring process from sap to syrup. Season runs February-March; confirm times with venue. Reserve in the Fall.

ARROWHEAD FARM, 5941 Rte. 209, Kerhonkson, NY 12446. Tel: 845-626-7293. COST: Free. REGION: Ulster County, Catskills Region NY.

FROST VALLEY YMCA, 2000 Frost Valley Rd., Claryville, NY 12725. Tel: 845-985-2291. (See main listing on page 203.) COST: Fee. REGION: Ulster County, Catskills Region NY.

GREENBURGH NATURE CENTER, 99 Dromore Rd., Scarsdale, NY 10583. Tel: 914-723-3470. COST: Fee. REGION: Westchester County, Hudson Valley Region NY.

TACONIC OUTDOOR EDUCATION CENTER, 75 Mountain Laurel Ln., Cold Spring, NY 10516. Tel: 845-265-3773. COST: Fee. REGION: Putnam County, Hudson Valley Region NY.

TRAILSIDE NATURE MUSEUM, Ward Poundridge Reservation, Cross River, NY 10518. Tel: 914-864-7322. COST: Fee. REGION: Westchester County, Hudson Valley Region NY.

WOOD'S MAPLE SUGAR BUSH, 1470 Rte. 23, Chateaugay, NY 12920. Tel: 518-497-6387. Visitors experience maple syrup production. COST: Free. REGION: Franklin County, Adirondacks Region NY.

MULTICULTURAL

HAMMOND MUSEUM & JAPANESE STROLL GARDEN, 28 Deveau Rd., North Salem, NY 10560. Tel: 914-669-5033. Hrs: Wed.-Sat. 12-4PM. Guided Tours, Workshops, Performances. Garden is based on traditional Japanese design and museum collections include Eastern art, fans and photographs. COST: Fee. REGION: Westchester County, Hudson Valley Region NY.

HOLOCAUST MUSEUM AND STUDY CENTER, 17 S. Madison Ave., Spring Valley, NY 10977. Tel: 845-356-2700. Hrs: Mon.-Wed. 9:30AM-4PM, Thurs. 9:30AM-7PM, Sun 12-4PM. 6th-12th grade. Guided Tours, Workshops. Permanent and rotating exhibits documenting the story of the Holocaust with authenticity, dignity, and compassion. COST: Fee. REGION: Rockland County, Hudson Valley Region NY.

THE IRISH AMERICAN HERITAGE MUSEUM, 2267 Rte. 145, East Durham, NY 12423. Tel: 518-634-7497. Hrs: Memorial Day-Labor Day: Wed.-Sun. 12-4PM. Guided Tours. Learn about the contributions of the Irish people and their culture in America. COST: Fee. REGION: Greene County, Catskills Region NY.

IROQUOIS INDIAN MUSEUM, 324 Caverns Rd., Howes Cave, NY 12092. Tel: 518-296-8949. Hrs: Vary. 4th-12th grade. Workshops. Features contemporary Iroquois art and archeological artifacts. Programs allow students to learn about the Iroquois relationship to nature and identify archeological artifacts. COST: Fee. REGION: Schoharie County, Central Leatherstocking Region NY.

THE MICHAEL J. QUILL IRISH CULTURAL & SPORTS CENTER, 2119 Rte. 145, Weldon House, East Meadow, NY 12423. Tel: 518-634-2224. Hrs: Varies. Guided Tours. Promotes and preserves the cultural and artistic heritage of the Irish and those of Irish descent. COST: Fee. REGION: Greene County, Catskills Region NY.

MULTIDIMENSIONAL

ADIRONDACK MUSEUM, Rtes. 28N and 30 just north of Blue Mountain Lake, NY 12812. Tel: 518-352-7311, ext. 116. Hrs: May 22-Oct. 18: Daily 10AM-5PM. Self-guided Tours, Guided Tours. An open air museum with 22 exhibit spaces and galleries tell the stories of the men and women who have lived, worked and played in the Adirondacks. COST: Fee. REGION: Hamilton County, Adirondacks Region NY.

ALBANY INSTITUTE OF HISTORY & ART. 125 Washington Ave. Albany, NY 12210. Tel: 518-463-4478. Museum Hrs: Wed.-Sat.10AM-5PM, Sun. 12–5PM. 2nd grade & up. Self-guided Tours, Guided Tours. Collection of art works and historical artifacts that document the life and culture of the Upper Hudson Valley region from the late 17th century to the present. COST: Fee. REGION: Albany County, Capital Region NY.

ASHOKAN CENTER INC., 477 Beaverkill Rd., Olivebridge, NY 12461. Tel: 845-657-8333. Hrs: Vary. Guided Tours, Workshops. Outdoor/environmental education and living history programs. COST: Fee. REGION: Ulster County, Catskills Region NY.

HUDSON RIVER MUSEUM, 511 Warburton Ave., Yonkers, NY 10701. Tel: 914-963-4550. Hrs: Call for reservation. Self-guided Tours, Guided Tours. Includes six art galleries, the Andrus Planetarium, and Glenview Mansion, a historic house museum of 1876. COST: Fee. REGION: Westchester County, Hudson Valley Region NY.

MUSEUM OF EARTH, 1259 Trumansburg Rd./Rte. 96, Ithaca, NY 14850. Tel: 607-273-6620. Hrs: Mon.-Sat. 10AM-5PM, Sun. 11AM-5PM, closed Tues. & Wed. during the winter. Self-guided Tours, Guided Tours, Workshops. Features science and art exhibits and programs that cover the history of the Earth and its life, with a particular focus on the Northeastern United States. COST: Fee. REGION: Tompkins County, Finger Lakes Region NY.

NEW YORK STATE MUSEUM, 264 Madison Ave., Albany, NY 12210. Tel: 518-474-5877. Hrs: Daily 9:30AM-5PM. Self-guided Tours, Guided Tours. Learn about geology, biology, anthropology, and history through exhibits and programs that investigate the past, present and future of New York State. COST: Free. REGION: Albany County, Capital Region NY.

ROBERSON MUSEUM & SCIENCE CENTER, 30 Front St., Binghamton, NY 13905. 888-269-5325. Tel: 607-772-0660. Hrs: Wed., Thurs., Sat., Sun. 12-5PM; Fri. 12-9PM. Self-guided Tours, Guided Tours. Features exhibitions on 19th and 20th-century art, history, folk life, science and natural history. Planetarium programs also available. COST: Fee. REGION: Broome County, Southern Tier Region NY.

PLANETARIUMS

Please call for planetarium show times. Experience a realistic and scientifically accurate simulation of the night sky in a domed theater.

THE CHILDREN'S MUSEUM OF SCIENCE & TECHNOLOGY, 250 Jordan Rd. (in Rensselaer Technology Park), Troy, NY 12180. Tel: 518-235-2120. COST: Fee. REGION: Rensselaer County, Capital Region NY.

HENRY HUDSON PLANETARIUM, The Albany Heritage Area Visitors Center, 25 Quackenbush Sq., Albany, NY 12207. Tel: 518-434-0405. Hrs: Vary. COST: Fee. REGION: Albany County, Capital Region NY.

HUDSON RIVER MUSEUM, 511 Warburton Ave., Yonkers, NY 10701. Tel: 914-963-4550. COST: Fee. REGION: Westchester County, Hudson Valley Region NY.

ROBERSON MUSEUM & SCIENCE CENTER, 30 Front St., Binghamton, NY 13905. Tel: 888-269-5325. COST: Fee. REGION: Broome County, Southern Tier Region, NY.

SCHENECTADY MUSEUM & SUITS-BUECHE PLANETARIUM, 15 Nott Terrace Heights, Schenectady, NY 12308. Tel: 518-382-7890. COST: Fee. REGION: Schenectady County, Capital Region NY.

PROMS & SCHOOL CELEBRATIONS

SCIENCE & ENVIRONMENTAL EDUCATION

AGROFORESTRY RESOURCE CENTER, Cornell Cooperative Extension of Greene County Tree Farm, 6055 Rte. 23, Acra, NY 12405. Tel: 518-622-9820. Hrs: Mon.-Fri. 8:30AM-4:30PM. Guided Tours, Workshops. Educational center and model forest offering programs in wildlife, forest stewardship, gardening and agriculture. COST: Fee. REGION: Greene County, Catskills Region NY.

CARY INSTITUTE OF ECOSYSTEM STUDIES, 2801 Sharon Tpke. (Rte. 44), Millbrook, NY 12545. Tel: 845-677-5343. Hrs: Vary. Workshops. 2,000 acre ecological research site; offers educational programs on ecological systems. COST: Fee. REGION: Dutchess County, Hudson Valley Region NY.

CATSKILL FLY FISHING CENTER & MUSEUM, 1031 Old Rte. 17, Livingston Manor, NY 12758. Tel: 845-439-4810. Hrs: Vary. 4th grade & up. Guided Tours. Preserving America's flyfishing heritage; teaching its future generations of flyfishers; and protecting its flyfishing environment. COST: Free/Fee. REGION: Sullivan County, Catskills Region NY.

CLEARWATER, 112 Little Market St., Poughkeepsie, NY 12601. Tel: 845-454-7673. Fax: 845-454-7953. Email: sailcoord@clearwater.org. Website: www.clearwater.org. Hrs: 9AM-5PM. Contact: Catherine Stankowski. GRADE LEVEL: 4th-college. PROGRAM TYPE: Day Trips, Guided Tours, Guided Activities. GROUP TYPE: All youth groups. MAX. GROUP SIZE: 50. MIN. GROUP SIZE: 20. REGISTRATION: Mail, Online, Phone. FOOD: No food offered. RECOMM. LENGTH OF VISIT: 3 hours. COST: $1,250 per group.

Clearwater has been providing high-quality environmental education programs onboard our 106 ft. sloop for over 40 years. Students become part of the lesson by raising the 3,000 lb. mainsail, sampling and identifying Hudson River life, and testing the waters for signs of pollution. Students are also connected to the important heritage of the Hudson Valley through traditional sea chanteys and river songs. Lessons are tied to NYS learning standards and are highly interactive. Clearwater sails from various docks between Albany, NYC and Long Island Sound from mid-April to the end of October. Most field trips consist of three-hour sails with longer sails available. Clearwater and her crew comply with all US Coast Guard regulations. SUPPORTS NY STATE & NATIONAL LEARNING STANDARDS IN: Math, Health & Safety, History/Social Studies, Physical Education, Science, Technology. SUPPORTS SCOUT MERIT BADGE ACHIEVEMENT IN: Health & Safety, Life Skills, Personal Fitness, Physical Ed/Recreation, Safety, Social Studies, Science/Technology. (See ad under Boat Excursions & Harbor Cruises on page 138.) REGION: Hudson Valley, NYC, northern NJ, LI Sound.

DEER RUN CAMP & RETREAT CENTER, 450 Walker Valley Rd., Pine Bush, NY 12566. Tel: 845-733-5494. Fax: 845-733-5471. Email: info@campdeerrun.org. Website: www.campdeerrun.org. Contact: Camp Director. GRADE LEVEL: 3rd -college. GROUP TYPE: All youth groups & homeschoolers, adults. PROGRAM TYPE: Day

Trips, Overnight Trips, Guided Activities, Retreats. MAX. GROUP SIZE: 100. COST: Varies. (See main listing under Adventure Sports on page 131 and Overnights and Retreats on page 202.) REGION: Sullivan County, Catskill Region, NY.

EMPIRE STATE AEROSCIENCES MUSEUM, 250 Rudy Chase Dr., Glenville, NY 12302. Tel: 518-377-2191. Hrs: Vary. K-9th grade. Self-guided Tours, Guided Tours. Learn about the history of flight and New York State's impact on the development of aviation. COST: Fee. REGION: Schenectady County, Capital Region NY.

FROST VALLEY YMCA, 2000 Frost Valley Rd., Claryville, NY 12725. Tel: 845-985-2291. Fax: 845-985-0056. Email: info@frostvalley.org. Website: www.FrostValley.org. Hrs: Daily. Contact: Environmental Education Director. GRADE LEVEL: 1st grade-college. GROUP TYPE: All youth groups & homeschoolers. PROGRAM TYPE: Day Trips, Overnight Trips, Guided Activities, Workshops. MAX. GROUP SIZE: 420 (overnight), 80 (day). REGISTRATION: Mail, Phone. FOOD: Kosher, Vegetarian, Place to eat on site, Beverages available. RECOMM. RATIO OF STUDENT TO STAFF: 10:1. COST: Varies. (See main listing under Overnights and Retreats on page 203.) REGION: Sullivan & Ulster Counties, Catskills Region NY.

GREENBURGH NATURE CENTER, 99 Dromore Rd., Scarsdale, NY 10583. Tel: 914-723-3470. Hrs: Mon.-Thurs. 9:30AM-4:30PM, Sat.-Sun. 10AM-4:30PM. Self-guided Tours, Workshops. Features a woodland preserve with live animals, a museum, a greenhouse with botanical exhibits, and a hands-on discovery room. COST: Fee. REGION: Westchester County, Hudson Valley Region NY.

GREENKILL OUTDOOR ENVIRONMENTAL EDUCATION & RETREAT CENTER, YMCA Camping Services, 300 Big Pond Rd., Huguenot, NY 12746. Tel: 845-858-2200. Fax: 845-858-7823. Email: camps@ymcanyc.org. Website: www.ymcanyc.org. Hrs: Year round. Contact: Hillary Gallacher. GRADE LEVEL: All grades to adult. GROUP TYPE: All youth groups & homeschoolers. PROGRAM TYPE: Day Trips, Overnight Trips, Guided Activities, Retreats. MAX. GROUP SIZE: 200. COST: Varies.

Situated on 1,100 beautiful acres, 90 miles from NYC. Residential outdoor environmental education program provides 2-5 day hands-on experiences through interdisciplinary learning. 20+ classes offered by instructors in Environmental Sciences, Outdoor Skills, Environmental History & Challenge Education-team building courses, low & high ropes course, and climbing wall. One day programs also available. Retreat center provides groups the perfect setting for weekend retreats. Double occupancy accommodation for up to 36. Larger groups utilize rooms with bunks for 4-10. Groups enjoy natural peaceful setting, hiking trails, lakes for boating, winter tubing and XC-skiing, sports center & program buildings. Camp Talcott & McAlister offer seasonal facilities for rustic experience for 10-200. SUPPORTS NY STATE & NATIONAL STATE LEARNING STANDARDS IN: Math, Science & Technology, Social Studies, Physical Education, Language Arts. SUPPORTS SCOUT MERIT BADGE ACHIEVEMENT IN: Physical Education/Recreation, Science. REGION: Ulster County, Hudson Valley Region NY.

HIGH FALLS GORGE, P.O. Box 1678, Lake Placid, NY 12946. Tel: 518-946-2278. Fax: 518-946-7293. Email: info@highfallsgorge.com. Website: www.highfallsgorge.com. Hrs: Daily 9AM-4:30PM. Contact: Kathryn Reiss. GRADE LEVEL: All grades. GROUP TYPE: All youth groups & homeschoolers. PROGRAM TYPE: Day Trips, Self-guided Tours, Guided Tours, Self-guided Activities. MAX. GROUP SIZE: 150. MIN. GROUP SIZE: 20. REGISTRATION: Phone. FOOD: Variety, Can bring own food, Place to eat on site, Beverages available. RECOMM. LENGTH OF VISIT: 45 minutes - 2 hours. RECOMM. RATIO OF STUDENT TO STAFF: 10:1. ARRIVAL TIPS: Bus Parking. COST: Fee, $5-$7 - driver/director free w/ group reservation.

Students witness erosion in action, where four splendid waterfalls flow into a deep crevice carved over a billion years by ice, water and wind. On a one-half mile walk, informational signs tell our geologic story, while surrounding forests reveal plant species that have remained unchanged for thousands of years. Open nearly year-round, each season offers a different experience, including ice formations and snow-shoeing in the winter. SUPPORTS NY STATE & NATIONAL LEARNING STANDARDS IN: Science. SUPPORTS SCOUT MERIT BADGE ACHIEVEMENT IN: Personal Fitness, Science/Technology. REGION: Essex County, Adirondacks Region NY.

HUDSON HIGHLANDS NATURE MUSEUM, 2 locations: Wildlife Education Center, 25 Boulevard, Cornwall-on-Hudson, NY. Tel: General: 845-534-7781. Ed Programs: 845-534-5506, ext 206. Hrs: Vary. Guided Tours, Workshops. Wildlife and ecology exhibits and Native American programs. Outdoor Discovery Center, 100 Muser Drive, off Angola Road, Cornwall, NY. Explore the natural environment of the Hudson Valley, including a wetlands area, two farm ponds, several hiking trails, and more. COST: Fee. REGION: Orange County, Hudson Valley Region NY.

KOPERNIK OBSERVATORY & SCIENCE CENTER, 698 Underwood Rd., Vestal, NY 13850. Tel: 607-748-3685. Fax: 607-748-3222. Email: info@Kopernik.org. Website: www.kopernik.org. Hrs: Vary. Contact: Kristen Gordon. GRADE LEVEL: K-12th. GROUP TYPE: School. PROGRAM TYPE: Day Trips, Overnight Trips, Guided Activities, Performances, Workshops. COST: Varies.

The Kopernik Observatory, located just 13 miles Southwest of Binghamton, New York, is a regional Science Center for K-12 students. From its 1,700 foot hilltop, the Center offers three domed observatories and four classroom labs for specified subjects such as: space science, physics, earth science and computers. The general public, students, and educators may attend a diverse selection of science classes, workshops, and special events at this educational facility. Friday night public programs include hands-on activities for children, telescope viewing weather permitting, and informative presentations by Observatory staff and visiting lecturers. School groups may schedule private programs. SUPPORTS NY STATE & NATIONAL LEARNING STANDARDS IN: Science, Technology. REGION: Broome County, Central Leatherstocking Region NY.

LANDIS ARBORETUM, 174 Lape Rd., Esperance, NY 12066. Tel: 518-875-6935. Hrs: Daily dawn until dusk. Self-guided Tours, Guided Tours, Workshops. Public garden includes activities on botany, astronomy and bird and owl watching sessions. COST: Free. REGION: Schoharie County, Central Leatherstocking Region NY.

LOWER HUDSON VALLEY CHALLENGER CENTER, 225 Rte. 59, Airmont, NY 10901. Tel: 845-357-3416. Fax: 845-369-3523. Email: director@LHVCC.com. Website: www.LHVCC.com. Hrs: Vary. Contact: John Huibregtse. GRADE LEVEL: K-7th. GROUP TYPE: All youth groups & homeschoolers. PROGRAM TYPE: Day Trips, Workshops, Performances. REGISTRATION: Phone. FOOD: Can bring own food, Place to eat on site, Beverages available. RECOMM. LENGTH OF VISIT: 2-3 hours. ARRIVAL TIPS: Bus parking, Bus drop off and pick up at designated entrance. COST: Vary by type of program.

Be an astronaut for a day! By combining learning with fun, the Lower Hudson Valley Challenger Learning Center allows elementary and middle school students to experience what it is like to be an astronaut. Simulated but realistic space missions take students on a journey they will never forget. Student-astronauts conduct research, solve emergencies, and perform hands-on scientific experiments as they voyage to the Moon, to Mars, or to a Comet. The Challenger Center's space missions are designed to provide authentic science and technology learning experiences within a cooperative, group-learning atmosphere underscored by teamwork, communication, problem-solving, and decision making. A mission at the Challenger Center is an entertaining learning experience that will last a lifetime. Exploring. Learning. Inspiring. It's our Mission. SUPPORTS NEW YORK STATE & NATIONAL LEARNING STANDARDS IN: Science. SUPPORTS SCOUT MERIT BADGE ACHIEVEMENT IN: Science. REGION: Rockland County, Hudson Valley Region NY.

MOHONK PRESERVE, 3197 Rte. 44/55, Gardiner, NY 12525. Tel: 845-255-0919. Hrs: Visitor Center: Daily 9AM-5PM. Self-guided Tours, Guided Tours. 6,500 acres in the Shawangunk Mountains–including cliffs, forests, fields, ponds, and streams. COST: Fee. REGION: Ulster County, NY.

NATIONAL BOTTLE MUSEUM, 76 Milton Ave., Ballston Spa, NY 12020. Tel: 518-885-7589. Hrs: Vary. Self-guided Tours, Guided Tours. Learn about early bottle making methods and view the surviving hand tools, a miniature model of a typical 1800's glass furnace and exhibits of hand made bottles COST: Fee. REGION: Saratoga County, Capital Region NY.

NEW YORK POWER AUTHORITY, 3 locations: Niagara: 866-697-2386; Blenheim-Gilboa: 800-724-0309; St. Lawrence-FDR: 800-262-6972. Hrs: Vary. Self-guided Tours, Guided Tours, Performances. The Authority's 3 visitors centers feature hands-on exhibits about energy, the environment and local history. COST: Free. REGIONS: Schoharie County, Central Leatherstocking Region NY; Niagara County, Greater Niagara Region NY; St. Lawrence County, Thousand Islands Region NY.

OSWEGATCHIE EDUCATION RETREAT CENTER, 9340 Long Pond Rd., Croghan, NY 13327. Tel: 315-346-1222. Hrs: Vary. Guided Tours, Workshops. Offers environmental education in a natural setting which includes four bodies of water, various streams, wetlands, open fields, and woodlands for hiking. COST: Fee. REGION: Lewis County, Adirondacks Region NY.

POK-O-MACCREADY OUTDOOR EDUCATION CENTER, 1391 Reber Rd., Willsboro, NY 12996. Tel: 518-963-7967. Fax: 518-963-4165. Email: director@pmoec.org. Website: www.pmoec.org. Hrs: Aug.-Jun. Contact: Stites McDaniel. GRADE LEVEL: 3rd-college. GROUP TYPE: All youth groups. PROGRAM TYPE: Day Trips, Overnight Trips, Guided Activities, Workshops. MAX. GROUP SIZE: 120, MIN. GROUP SIZE: 10. REGISTRATION: Mail, Online, Phone. FOOD: Variety of menu selections, Kosher, Vegetarian, Can bring own food, Place to eat on site. RECOMM. LENGTH OF VISIT: 1-5 days. RECOMM. RATIO OF STUDENT TO STAFF: 10:1. COST: Varies.

Since 1974, PMOEC has hosted overnight or day trips to schools or groups seeking an educational, fun, and memorable outdoors experience. PMOEC offers classes in Teambuilding, Natural Science, Living History, and High Adventure. Our campus, with our own waterfront for boating and pond ecology classes, is over 300 acres and lies inside the beautiful 6 million acre Adirondack Park. PMOEC has cross-county skiing, mountain biking, hiking, and nature trails. Open from August through June, PMOEC can host groups of up to 120 students and teachers in four winterized dormitories. The center became a not-for-profit organization in October 2008. SUPPORTS NY STATE & NATIONAL LEARNING STANDARDS IN: The Arts, English, History/Social Studies, Language Arts, Physical Education, Science. SUPPORTS SCOUT MERIT BADGE ACHIEVEMENT IN: Camping, Personal Fitness, Physical Ed/Recreation. (See Lake Champlain Featured Region Page on page 220.) REGION: Essex County, Adirondacks Region NY.

RAMSHORN/LIVINGSTON SANCTUARY, Dubois Road, Catskill, NY 12414. Tel: 518-678-3248. Hrs: Daily Dawn to Dusk. Self-guided Tours, Guided Tours. Visit a major feeding area for heron, waterfowl and migratory birds as well as a breeding ground and nursery for American shad and bass at Hudson River's largest tidal swamp forest. Contains miles of walking trails and a twenty-eight-foot wildlife observation tower. COST: Fee. REGION: Greene County, Catskills Region NY.

SCHENECTADY MUSEUM & SUITS-BUECHE PLANETARIUM, 15 Nott Terrace Heights, Schenectady, NY 12308. Tel: 518-382-7890. Hrs: Tues.-Sat., 10AM-5PM. Self-guided Tours, Guided Tours. Explores the area's rich technological heritage with interactive exhibits including a vast General Electric archive with early televisions and kitchen appliances. Also, view the sky from any location on Earth and any place in the solar system with the GOTO Star Machine at the Planetarium. COST: Fee. REGION: Schenectady County, Capital Region NY.

STONY KILL FARM ENVIRONMENTAL EDUCATION CENTER, 79 Farmstead Ln., Wappingers Falls, NY 12590. Tel: 845-831-8780. Hrs: Vary. Self-guided Tours, Guided Tours, Workshops. Features miles of nature trails, an 18th century stone farmhouse and 19th century barn, and learning center. COST: Free/Fee. REGION: Dutchess County, Hudson Valley NY.

TACONIC OUTDOOR EDUCATION CENTER, 75 Mountain Laurel Ln., Cold Spring, NY 10516. Tel: 845-265-3773. Hrs: Vary. Guided Tours. Located in the Fahnestock Memorial State Park offers environmental education, outdoor recreation and maple sugaring. COST: Fee. REGION: Putnam County, Hudson Valley Region NY.

TEATOWN LAKE RESERVATION, 1600 Spring Valley Rd., Ossining, NY 10562. Tel: 914-762-2912. Hrs: Tues.-Sun. 9AM-5PM. Self-guided Tours, Guided Tours, Workshops. Features hiking trails, a nature center with a live animal collection, an island refuge with native and endangered species of wildflowers, and diverse habitats including forests, lakes, streams, and farmland. COST: Fee. REGION: Westchester County, Hudson Valley Region NY.

TRAILSIDE NATURE MUSEUM, Ward Pound Ridge Reservation, Rtes. 35 & 121, Cross River, NY 10518. Tel: 914-864-7322. Hrs: Wed-Sun 9AM-4PM. Self-guided Tours, Guided Tours, Workshops. Presents exhibits that focus on the natural world and the human history of the Reservation, and offers programs on Native American life, archaeology, maple sugaring, and other topics. COST: Free/Fee. REGION: Westchester County, Hudson Valley Region NY.

WESTCHESTER COUNTY DEPARTMENT OF PARKS, RECREATION, AND CONSERVATION NATURE CENTERS, 25 Moore Ave., Mt. Kisco, NY 10549. Tel: 914-864-7000. Self-guided Tours, Guided Tours, Workshops. Sites: CRANBERRY LAKE PRESERVE, Old Orchard St. (off Rte. 22), North White Plains, NY. Tel: 914-428-1005; CROTON POINT PARK, Croton Point Ave., Croton-on-Hudson, NY. Tel: 914-862-5297; EDITH G. READ WILDLIFE SANCTUARY, Playland Pkwy, Rye, NY. Tel: 914-967-8720; LENOIR PRESERVE, 19 Dudley St., Yonkers, NY. Tel: 914-968-5851; MARSHLANDS CONSERVANCY, Rt. 1, Rye, NY. Tel: 914-835-4466.

WESTMORELAND SANCTUARY, 260 Chestnut Ridge Rd., Bedford Corners, NY 10549. Tel: 914-666-8448. Guided Activities. Hrs: Mon-Fri. 9AM-5PM, Sat 9AM-5PM, Sun. 10:30AM-5PM. Museum and nature center offering hands-on programs which include bluebird house building, bird banding with live native birds, insects, pond study and mammals. COST: Free/Fee. REGION: Westchester County, Hudson Valley Region NY.

THE WILD CENTER, 45 Museum Dr., Tupper Lake, New York 12986. Tel: 518-359-7800. Hrs: Daily 10AM-6PM. Guided Tours, Performances. A natural history museum located on a 31-acre site near the geographic center of the Adirondack Park. There are walking trails, naturalist guides, movies, live exhibits including more than 900 live animals, live otters, and a wealth of information about the natural world of the Adirondacks. COST: Fee. REGION: Franklin County, Adirondacks Region NY.

SKIING & SNOWBOARDING

THUNDER RIDGE SKI AREA, Rte. 22, 137 Birch Hill Rd, Patterson, NY 12563. Tel: 845-878-4100 ext. 301. Fax: 845-878-2279. Email: thunderridge@cyburban.com. Website: www.thunderridgeski.com. Hrs: Mon.-Fri. 10AM-9PM, Sat. 9AM-9PM, Sun. 9AM-5PM. Contact: Meryl DiDio or Ellie Taylor. GRADE LEVEL: All grades. GROUP TYPE: All youth groups & homeschoolers. PROGRAM TYPE: Day Trips, Overnight Trips, Self-guided Activities, Guided Activities. REGISTRATION: Mail, Online, Phone. FOOD: Variety of menu selections, Can bring own food, Place to eat on site, Meal vouchers. RECOMM. LENGTH OF VISIT: 4-5 hours. COST: Varies.

Only 60 minutes north of New York City, we offer skiing and snowboarding for all ability levels from novice to expert! 30 trails and 3 lifts. Day and night skiing and riding. Lesson and equipment rental packages available, helmets included. Cafeteria available. Please call for more information and reservation. Ride the Metro-North train and we provide a free shuttle from the Patterson, NY train station. SUPPORTS NY STATE & NATIONAL LEARNING STANDARDS IN: Health & Safety, History, Math, Physical Education, Science, Social Studies. SUPPORTS SCOUT MERIT BADGE ACHIEVEMENT IN: Camping, Family Life, Health & Safety, Life Skills, Personal Fitness, Physical Ed/Recreation, Skiing. (See other listing under Farms - Pick Your Own on page 141.) REGION: Putnam County, Hudson Valley Region NY.

SOCIAL STUDIES

BRONCK MUSEUM, 90 County Rt. 42, Coxsackie, NY 12051. Tel: 518-731-6490. Hrs: Memorial Day weekend-Oct. 15, call for hours. Guided Tours. Tour a complex of Dutch Colonial dwellings and 19th century barns, including the oldest surviving Dutch House in the Hudson Valley. COST: Fee. REGION: Greene County, Catskills Region NY.

D & H CANAL HISTORICAL SOCIETY, 23 Mohonk Rd., High Falls, NY 12440. Tel: 845-687-9311. Hrs: Vary. Workshops. Learn about the Delaware and Hudson Canal and 19th century life through models, photographs, and artwork. COST: Fee. REGION: Ulster County, Catskills Region NY.

ELEANOR ROOSEVELT HISTORIC SITE AT VAL KILL, Rte. 9G, Hyde Park, NY 12538. Tel: 845-229-0174. Hrs: Oct.-May: Daily 9AM 5PM. Guided Tours. 2nd-12th grade. The historic home where Eleanor Roosevelt pursued her political and social interests. COST: Free. REGION: Dutchess County, Hudson Valley Region NY.

FRANKLIN D. ROOSEVELT HOME NATIONAL HISTORIC SITE, 4097 Albany Post Rd., Hyde Park, NY 12538. Contact Park Service Reservationist Anne Murray 845-486-1966. Hrs: Daily 9AM-5PM. 2nd-12th grade. Guided Tours. Visit the Roosevelt family home, FDR Library & Museum and the Rose Garden burial site. COST: Free. REGION: Dutchess County, Hudson Valley Region NY.

GEORGE WASHINGTON'S HEADQUARTERS AT TAPPAN, 20 Livingston St., Tappan, NY 10983. Tel: 845-359-1359. Hrs: Tues.-Sun. 10AM-4PM. Self-guided Tours, Guided Tours. Visit the oldest surviving structure in Rockland County and learn about George Washington and the American Revolutionary War. COST: Free. REGION: Rockland County, Hudson Valley Region NY.

GLENN H. CURTISS MUSEUM, 8419 State Rte. 54, Hammondsport, NY 14840. Tel: 607-569-2160. Hrs: May 1-Oct. 31: Mon.-Sat. 9AM-5PM, Sun. 10AM-5PM; Nov.1-Apr. 31: Mon.-Sun. 10AM-4PM. Self-guided Tours, Guided Tours. Dedicated to the memory of pioneer aviator, Glenn Curtiss, the museum contains a collection and interactive center relating to early aviation and local history. COST: Fee. REGION: Steuben County, Finger Lakes Region NY.

HANFORD MILLS MUSEUM, Route 12, East Meredith, NY 13757. Tel: 607-278-5744. Hrs: May 15-Oct. 15: Tues.-Sun. 10AM-5PM. Guided Tours, Workshops. Learn about the evolution of power generation and technology by visiting a working water powered sawmill and gristmill woodworking shop. COST: Fee. REGION: Delaware County, Catskills Region NY.

HISTORIC HUDSON VALLEY, 150 White Plains Rd., Tarrytown, NY 10591. Tel: 914-631-8200. Hrs: Vary. Guided Tours, Workshops. Discover the history, architecture, landscape, and material culture of the Hudson Valley through a museum of 7 historic sites including buildings, landmarks and living history programs. COST: Fee. REGION: Westchester County, Hudson Valley Region NY.

HISTORICAL SOCIETY OF ROCKLAND COUNTY, 20 Zukor Rd., New City, NY 10956. Tel: 845-634-9629. Hrs: Tues.-Sun. 1-5PM. Self-guided Tours, Guided Tours, Workshops. 2nd-6th grade. Exhibitions, tours, and artifacts relating to the history of Rockland County, from the earliest Native Americans through the present. COST: Fee. REGION: Rockland County, Hudson Valley Region NY.

HUDSON-ATHENS LIGHTHOUSE, Middle of Hudson River, Athens NY 12015. Tel: 518-828-5294. Hrs: Vary. Guided Tours. Learn about the historic lighthouse built in the late 1800s to aid navigation of the Hudson River. COST: Fee. REGION: Greene County, Catskills Region NY.

HUDSON RIVER MARITIME MUSEUM, 50 Rondout Landing, Kingston, NY 12401. Tel: 845-338-0071. Hrs: May-Oct.: Thurs.-Mon. 12-6PM. Self-guided Tours, Guided Tours, Workshops. Indoor and outdoor exhibits on Hudson River maritime history. COST: Fee. REGION: Ulster County, Hudson Valley Region NY.

JOHN BROWN FARM STATE, 115 John Brown Rd., Lake Placid, NY 12946. Tel: 518-523-3900. Hrs: May-Oct.: Daily 10AM-5PM (closed Tues). Guided tours. Learn about abolitionist John Brown at his home which has been restored to its late 1800s condition. COST: Fee. REGION: Essex County, Adirondacks Region NY.

JOHN JAY HOMESTEAD, 400 Jay St., Katonah, NY 10536. Tel: 914-232-5651. Hrs: Vary. Guided Tours, Workshops. Learn about one of our founding fathers as well as farm life in the 19th century at the Homestead's 62-acre grounds. COST: Fee. REGION: Westchester County, Hudson Valley Region NY.

MUSCOOT FARM COMPLEX, Rte. 100, Somers, NY 10536. Tel: 914-864-7282. Hrs: Daily 10AM-4PM. Pre K-6th. Self-guided Tours, Guided Tours. Includes a Dairy Barn, Milk House, Ice House, Blacksmith Shop and several other barns and buildings where visitors discover what farm life was like in the 1920's. COST: Fee. REGION: Westchester County, Hudson Valley Region NY.

NEW WINDSOR CANTONMENT STATE HISTORIC SITE, 374 Temple Hill Rd. (Rte. 300), Vails Gate, NY 12584. Tel: 845-561-1765. Hrs: Wed.-Sat. 10AM-5PM, Sun. 1-5PM, Mon. 10AM-5PM. Guided Tours, Workshops. Location of the final encampment of George Washington's Army and home to the National Purple Heart Hall of Honor. Visitors will find staff in reproduction period dress and uniforms demonstrating musket drills and camp life activities. COST: Fee. REGION: Orange County, Hudson Valley Region NY.

THE SCARSDALE HISTORICAL SOCIETY, Cudner-Hyatt House and the 1828 Quaker Meeting House, 937 Post Rd., Scarsdale, NY 10583. Tel: 914-723-1744. Hrs: Mon.-Fri. 10AM-4PM. Guided Tours. See the tools, textiles and furnishings of the mid-19th century and exhibitions focusing on the history, culture, architecture and art of the 18th- 20th centuries. COST: Fee. REGION: Westchester County, Hudson Valley Region NY.

THE STATE CAPITOL, Albany, NY. Guided Tours. Senate & Assembly Chambers: 518-474-2418. MEET WITH YOUR ASSEMBLY & SENATE REPRESENTATIVES. Directory of assembly members: 518-455-4100. Directory of senate representatives: 518-455-2800. Call your representative's office 4-8 weeks in advance to arrange group meetings with your rep. or a staff member. THE GOVERNOR'S MANSION: 518-473-7521. Hrs: Guided tours on Thursdays only, with reservations 2 weeks in advance. Groups of 10-30. COST: Free. REGION: Albany County, Capital Region NY.

STRONG NATIONAL MUSEUM OF PLAY, One Manhattan Sq., Rochester, NY 14607. Tel: 585-263-2700. Hrs: Mon.-Thurs. 10AM-5PM, Fri. & Sat. 10AM-8PM, Sun.12-5PM. Pre K-8th grade. Self-guided Tours. Educational, hands-on museum dedicated to the study of play and American culture. Exhibits include butterfly garden, classic toys, historic carousel and more. COST: Fee. REGION: Monroe County, Finger Lakes Region NY.

USS SLATER, 141 Broadway, Albany, NY 12202. Tel: 518-431-1943. Hrs: Vary. Guided Tours. The only destroyer escort remaining afloat in the U.S. Museum displays artifacts such as uniforms, photos and documents. COST: Fee. REGION: Albany County, Capital Region NY.

VAN WYCK HOMESTEAD MUSEUM, 504 Rte. 9, Fishkill, NY 12524. Tel: 845-896-9560. Hrs: Vary. Guided Tours. Tour a Dutch Colonial home used as officers' headquarters during the Revolutionary War, and view artifacts from the 18th century and Hudson Valley portraits. COST: Fee. REGION: Dutchess County, Hudson Valley Region NY.

WASHINGTON'S HEADQUARTERS STATE HISTORIC SITE, 84 Liberty St., Newburgh, NY 12550. Tel: 845-562-1195. Hrs: Vary. Self-guided Tours, Guided Tours. Tour the rooms where American history was made and learn about General George Washington's most important contributions to shaping the American republic. COST: Fee. REGION: Orange County, Hudson Valley Region NY.

TEAM BUILDING & CHARACTER EDUCATION

DEER RUN CAMP & RETREAT CENTER, 450 Walker Valley Rd., Pine Bush, NY 12566. Tel: 845-733-5494. Fax: 845-733-5471. Email: info@campdeerrun.org. Website: www.campdeerrun.org. Hrs: Vary. Contact: Camp Director. GRADE LEVEL: 3rd-college. GROUP TYPE: All youth groups & homeschoolers, adults. PROGRAM TYPE: Day Trips, Overnight Trips, Guided Activities, Retreats. MAX. GROUP SIZE: 100. COST: Varies. (See main listing under Adventure Sports and Overnights and Retreats on pages 131 and 202.) REGION: Sullivan County, Catskills Region NY.

THEATER · DANCE · MUSIC

THE PAPER BAG PLAYERS, 225 West 99th St., New York, NY 10025. Tel: 800-777-2247/ 212-663-0390. Fax: 212-663-1076. Email: pbagp@verizon.net. Website: thepaperbagplayers.org. Hrs: New York State performances in Buffalo and Tarrytown. GRADE LEVEL: K–3rd grade. GROUP TYPE: All youth groups and homeschoolers. PROGRAM TYPE: Performances. COST: Varies.

The Paper Bag Players Great Mummy Robbery will have your class laughing, singing, dancing---and sitting on the edge of their seats! From an expedition to the land of the pyramids in search of that mysterious Mummy by the name of Shirley, to a Paper Bag picnic that turns into a dance-a-thon and the whole audience joins in, to a painting so realistic it comes to life--this show is funny, friendly, and thrilling! Perfect for children in grades K through 3. SUPPORTS NY STATE & NATIONAL LEARNING STANDARDS IN: The Arts, English. SUPPORTS SCOUT MERIT BADGES ACHIEVEMENT IN: Theater. REGION: Erie, Westchester Counties, NY.

WESTCHESTER BROADWAY THEATRE, 1 Broadway Plaza, Elmsford, New York 10523. Tel: 800-729-7469 and 914-592-2225. Fax: 914-592-6047. Website: www.broadwaytheatre.com. Contact: Heidi Giarlo. GRADE LEVEL: All grades. GROUP TYPE: All youth groups & homeschoolers. PROGRAM TYPE: Performances, Workshops. MAX. GROUP SIZE: 500. COST: Varies.

Professional, live Broadway musicals and special entertainment events coupled with fine dining in one comfortable, safe, state-of-the-art facility. 2009/ 2010 Mainstage: 42nd Street, The Christmas Voyager, The 25th Annual Putnam County Spelling Bee, and Rent. Matinees Wednesdays, Thursdays and Sundays. Q & A session following performances by request. Educational Theatre Workshops of the WBT offers specialized classes in Theatre Arts. Longest-running, year-round Equity Theatre in NY State. SUPPORTS NEW YORK STATE & NATIONAL LEARNING STANDARDS IN: The Arts. SUPPORTS SCOUT MERIT BADGE ACHIEVEMENT IN: Theater. REGION: Westchester County , Hudson Valley Region NY.

TRIP SERVICES

MTA METRO-NORTH RAILROAD, Group Travel Department, Graybar Building, 420 Lexington Avenue-9th Floor, New York, NY 10017. Tel: 212-499-4398. Email: groupsales@mnr.org.

MTA Metro-North Group Travel offers substantial savings for groups of ten or more. And since free parking is available on weekends at most Metro-North Railroad stations, you'll save even more. Relax in comfort while enjoying scenic views, historic landmarks, and the excitement of rail travel. Whether it's a class trip, family outing, or a company picnic, Metro-North's friendly Group Travel staff can suggest fun trips to New York City, upstate New York, and Connecticut, and even help you create one of your own. It all starts with a safe, easy, memorable train ride. Call Metro-North Group Travel today at 212-499-4398. (See ad under Transportation Services and Charter Buses on page 7.)

LONG ISLAND

AMUSEMENT & THEME PARKS

ADVENTURELAND AMUSEMENT PARK, 2245 Rte. 110, Farmingdale, NY 11735. Tel: 631-694-6868. Fax: 631-694-6816. Email: Mail@Adventureland.us. Website: www.Adventureland.us. GRADE LEVEL: All grades. GROUP TYPE: All youth groups & homeschoolers. PROGRAM TYPE: Day Trips, Self-guided Activities. REGISTRATION: Phone. FOOD: Variety of menu selections, Place to eat on site. RECOMM. LENGTH OF VISIT: 2.5 – 4 hours. RECOMM. RATIO OF STUDENT TO STAFF: 20:1. ARRIVAL TIPS: Bus parking. COST: Varies.

Adventureland Caters To Kids Of All Ages From 2 – 102; Groups of all sizes From 20 – 2000. For the past 45 plus years the Adventureland Family has been creating miles of smiles for so many school, scout and youth groups across Long Island, Queens and N.Y.C. From Roller Coasters to Ferris Wheels, From the Big Kid "Adventure Falls" Log Flume Ride to the Lil' Kid "Lil Dipper" Log Flume Ride, From A Large sit down fast food style restaurant to Relaxing games of chance. Adventureland Has It All!! Dreaming of an exclusive group outing - where it is just your school or scout council - Adventureland will help make your dream come true. Are you organizing a fund raiser for your school, church or organization? There are many ways Adventureland can assist you in accomplishing your goals. Let the Adventureland Family continue to create fun filled memories for your youth group. SUPPORTS NY STATE & NATIONAL LEARNING STANDARDS IN: Physical Education. SUPPORTS SCOUT MERIT BADGE ACHIEVEMENT IN: Physical Ed/Recreation. (See Regional Highlights on page 10.) REGION: Suffolk County, LI.

ANIMALS • AQUARIUMS • ZOOS

THE ANIMAL FARM PETTING ZOO, 296 Wading River Rd., Manorville, NY 11949. Tel: 631-878-1785. Hrs: Mon.-Fri. 10AM-5PM, Sat.-Sun. 10AM-6PM. Self-guided Tours. Exotics, reptiles, wildlife, farm animals and babies. See, feed and pet the animals. Pony and Train rides. COST: Fee. REGION: Suffolk County, LI.

BROOKHAVEN ECOLOGY CENTER & ANIMAL PRESERVE, 249 Buckley Rd., Holtsville, NY 11742. Tel: 631-758-9664. Hrs: Mon.-Sun. 9AM-4PM. Self-guided Tours, Guided Tours. A nature preserve and ecology center with ecology exhibits and greenhouses. Over 100 injured or non-releasable wild and farm animals. COST: Free. REGION: Suffolk County, LI.

ATLANTIS MARINE WORLD AQUARIUM, 431 East Main St., Riverhead, NY 11901. Tel: 631-208-9200, ext. 105. Fax: 631-208-0466. Website: www.atlantismarineworld.com. Hrs: Open 364 days a year (Closed December 25), 10AM-5PM. GRADE LEVEL: All grades. GROUP TYPE: All youth groups & homeschoolers. PROGRAM TYPE: Day Trips, Overnights/Retreats, Self-guided Tours, Guided Tours, Self-guided Activities, Guided Activities, Performances, Workshops, Outreach Programs, Demonstrations, Exhibits, Lectures/Speakers, Special Events / Festivals, Teacher Workshops, Other. REGISTRA-TION: Mail, Phone, Prepay, Tickets mailed prior to visit. FOOD: Variety of menu selections, Can bring own food, Place to eat on site, Beverages available. RECOMM. LENGTH OF VISIT: 3-4 hours. RECOMM. RATIO OF STUDENT TO STAFF: 10:1. ARRIVAL TIPS: Expedite check in, Bus parking, Bus drop off and pick up at designated entrance. COST: Varies.

Next class trip, take your students on a voyage of discovery at Atlantis Marine World Aquarium. Named a Top 10 Aquarium by Parents Magazine, it's more than one million gallons of exhibits and interactive adventures designed to educate and captivate. Located along the Peconic River, Atlantis Marine World features more than 100 exhibits and interactive experiences, including the 120,000-gallon Lost City of Atlantis Shark Exhibit, North America's largest all-living Coral Reef display, Penguin Pavilion, Ray Bay, Shark Reef Lagoon, Sea Lion Shows, Japanese Snow Monkeys, Atlantis Explorer tour boat, Interactive Salt Marsh, the archaeological dig site - Unearthing Atlantis, and the newest exhibit, North American River Otters - Otter Falls. Also: Social and Corporate Catered Affairs including team-building programs, sleepovers, birthday parties, Summer/Winter Adventure Days, arcade, cafe, ice cream shop, and playground (with 25-foot climbing wall). Convenient parking/wheelchair accessible. SUPPORTS NY STATE & NATIONAL LEARNING STANDARDS IN: Science. SUPPORTS SCOUT MERIT BADGE ACHIEVEMENT IN: Science. (See Regional Highlights on page 12.) REGION: Suffolk County, LI.

COLD SPRING HARBOR FISH HATCHERY & AQUARIUM, 1660 Rte. 25A Cold Spring Harbor, NY 11724. Tel: 516-692-6768. Hrs: Daily 10AM-5PM. Self-guided Tours, Workshops. Largest collection of New York State fresh water turtle, fish and amphibians housed in two buildings and outdoor ponds. COST: Fee. REGION: Suffolk County, LI.

INTERNATIONAL FAUNA SOCIETY, 213 East Main St., Riverhead, NY 11901. Tel: 631-722-5488. Hrs: Daily 11AM-6PM. Self-guided Tours. The Serpentarium is a live reptile exhibit located in Downtown Riverhead. Come encounter huge lizards, giant snakes, amazing frogs and more. Live animal presentations throughout the day. COST: Fee. REGION: Suffolk County, LI.

LONG ISLAND GAME FARM, 638 Chapman Blvd., Manorville, NY 11949. Tel: 631-878-6644. Hrs: Weekdays 10AM-4:30PM, Weekends 10AM-5:30PM. Self-guided Tours. The largest combined children's zoo and wildlife park on Long Island. COST: Fee. REGION: Suffolk County, LI.

THE PET DEN'S PARTY JUNGLE, 6230 Jericho Tpke., Commack, NY 11725. Tel: 631-499-0276. Fax: 631-499-0313. Website: www.petden.com/partyjungle.html. Email: info@petden.com. Hrs: Vary. GRADE LEVEL: All grades. GROUP TYPE: All youth groups & homeschoolers. PROGRAM TYPE: Guided Activities, Outreach Programs. COST: Fee.

The Pet Den's Party Jungle is an all-inclusive private party center decorated with beautiful hand painted jungle murals, where children will learn about the wonderful world of the animal kingdom as our staff performs an exciting, educational, hands-on exotic animal demonstration. Our staff members are friendly, knowledgeable, and experienced in working with animals and children. It's a perfect educational activity for school field trips and scouting programs. Special rate packages are available for these groups and there are many to choose from and can be tailored to accommo-date your educational needs. We also offer the "Pet Zoo on Wheels," an exciting pro-gram where we bring unique exotic animals to your location. SUPPORTS NY STATE & NATIONAL LEARNING STANDARDS IN: Science. SUPPORTS SCOUT MERIT BADGE ACHIEVEMENT IN: Science, Animals. REGION: Suffolk County, LI.

RIVERHEAD FOUNDATION FOR MARINE RESEARCH AND PRESERVATION, 467 East Main St., Riverhead, NY 11901. Tel: 631-369-9840. Hrs: Vary. Guided Tours. Dedicated to the rescue, rehabilitation, and release of seals, sea turtles, whales, dol-phins, and porpoises. Provides tours of the facility, seal cruises, ecology walks, and beach cleanups to foster good stewardship of the environment. COST: Fee. REGION: Suffolk County, LI.

TACKAPAUSHA MUSEUM AND PRESERVE, 2225 Washington Ave., Seaford, NY 11783. Tel: 516-571-7443. Hrs: Wed.-Sat. 10AM-4PM, Sun. 1-4PM. Self-guided Tours, Guided Tours. Exhibits on Long Island wildlife and their habitats. Surrounding the muse-um is a large preserve for nature walks. COST: Fee. REGION: Nassau County, LI.

ART • ARCHITECTURE • SCULPTURE

HECKSCHER MUSEUM OF ART, 2 Prime Ave., Huntington, NY 11743. Tel: 631-351-3250. Hrs: Tues.-Fri. 10AM-5PM, Sat.-Sun. 1-5PM, Holidays & Mondays 10AM-5PM. Self-guided Tours, Guided Tours. Features 15th to 20th century European and American paintings, sculpture and works on paper. COST: Fee. REGION: Suffolk County, LI.

ISLIP ART MUSEUM, 50 Irish Ln., East Islip, NY 11730. Tel: 631-224-5402. Hrs: Wed.-Sat. 10AM-4PM, Sun. 12-4PM. Self-guided Tours. Collection of works by lead-ing contemporary artists, focusing on those with ties to Long Island. COST: Free. REGION: Suffolk County, LI.

NASSAU COUNTY MUSEUM OF ART, One Museum Dr., Roslyn Harbor, NY 11576. Tel: 516-484-9338. Hrs: Tues.-Sun. 11AM-4:45PM. Guided Tours. 19th and 20th cen-tury European and American art, encompassing all types of media. COST: Fee. REGION: Nassau County, LI.

POLLOCK-KRASNER HOUSE & STUDY CENTER, 830 Springs-Fireplace Rd., East Hampton, NY 11937. Tel: 631-324-4929. Hrs: Vary. Guided Tours. Visit the fhome and studio of artists Jackson Pollock and his wife, Lee Krasner and see how they lived and worked. COST: Fee. REGION: Suffolk County, LI.

BOTANICAL GARDENS & NATURE CENTERS

CLARK BOTANIC GARDEN, 193 I.U. Willets Rd., Albertson, NY 11507. Tel: 516-484-8600. Hrs: Daily 10AM-4PM. Self-guided Tours, Guided Tours, Workshops. 12 acres of shrubs, ponds, small trees, unusual annuals, perennials and roses, and 3 beehives. COST: Free. REGION: Nassau County, LI.

OLD WESTBURY GARDENS, 71 Old Westbury Rd., P.O. Box 430, Old Westbury, NY 11568. Tel: 516-333-0048. Fax: 516-333-6807. Website: www.oldwestburygardens.org. Hrs: Mid-Apr - Oct. 31: Daily (except Tuesdays) 10AM-5PM; Sundays in Nov.; December Holiday Celebration; Special Days in Winter. Contact: Angela Savino, Group Tour Coordinator, ext. 310. GRADE LEVEL: All grades. GROUP TYPE: All youth groups & homeschoolers. PROGRAM TYPE: Day Trips, Self-guided Tours, Guided Tours, Performances, Workshops. COST: Varies. Special rates for group tours.

Enjoy nature walks on trails throughout 200 acres. Explore scenic woodlands, gardens, an enchanting Thatched Cottage, ponds, lakes, and wide open spaces on the former estate of John S. Phipps, his wife, Margarita Grace Phipps, and their four children. Special events, April through December, include Family Fridays, Storytime, indoor and outdoor concerts, shows, Kidsfest, painting, photography, and horticulture classes, Scottish Games, antique auto shows, Teddy Bear Picnics, and Doll Teas. Visit the Gift Shop and Plant Shop. Picnic or enjoy refreshments in the Gardens' outdoor café. Tour Westbury House, a magnificent Charles II-style mansion, filled with fine antique furniture, art, and decorative arts. Special rates for group tours. SUPPORTS NY STATE & NATIONAL LEARNING STANDARDS IN: Arts, Science, Social Studies. SUPPORTS SCOUT MERIT BADGE ACHIEVEMENT IN: Gardening, Science, Social Studies. (See Regional Highlights on page 13.) REGION: Nassau County, LI.

PLANTING FIELDS ARBORETUM STATE HISTORIC PARK, Planting Fields Rd., Oyster Bay, NY 11771. Tel: 516-922-8600. Hrs: Vary. Self-guided Tours. 409 acre estate with 160 acres of garden, plants and trees, many from Europe and Asia. COST: Free/Fee for parking. REGION: Nassau County, LI.

CHILDREN'S MUSEUMS

CHILDREN'S MUSEUM OF THE EAST END, 376 Bridgehampton Sag Harbor Tpke., Bridgehampton, NY 11932. Tel: 631-537-8250. Hrs: Mon.-Sun. 9AM-5PM, closed Tues. Pre K-4th grade. Self-guided Tours, Guided Tours. Interactive and hands-on exhibits that focus on the unique history and diversity of the eastern end of Long Island. COST: Fee. REGION: Suffolk County, LI.

LONG ISLAND CHILDREN'S MUSEUM, 11 Davis Ave., Garden City, NY 11530. Tel: 516-224-5800. Website: www.limc.org Hrs: Public: Tues.-Sun. 10AM-5PM. Field Trips: Tues.-Fri. 10-11:30AM or 12-1:30PM. Contact: Rebecca Elioseff at 516-224-5869. GRADE LEVEL: Pre K-6th. GROUP TYPE: All youth groups & homeschoolers. PROGRAM TYPE: Day Trips, Self-guided Tours, Guided Tours, Self-guided Activities, Performances, Workshops. COST: $8 per student for Guided Tours, $7 for Self-Guided Tours, $10 Regular Admission. (Additional fees for workshops & performances may apply.)

Long Island Children's Museum is a learning laboratory where 14 hands-on exhibits invite children to experiment, explore and play. Through lively interdisciplinary activities, children and adults can share in the excitement of the learning process as they explore our world. The museum offers six content and age-specific field trip programs designed for children from Pre K-6th grade. Theme-based field trips include: Machines, Mapping, Patterns and Structure and Function. LICM also offers scout workshops, birthday parties and outreach programs on subjects such as folklore, animal sciences, architecture, biology, history, art…and bubbles; bringing the museum to your school, library or community center. Museum field trips support New York State Learning Standards. Scout Workshops support Scout Merit Badge Achievements. SUPPORTS NY STATE & NATIONAL LEARNING STANDARDS IN: The Arts, Science, Social Studies. SUPPORTS SCOUT MERIT BADGE ACHIEVEMENT IN: Arts, Science, Social Studies. REGION: Nassau County, LI.

CIRCUS

BIG APPLE CIRCUS. Performances: New Jersey, Fall 2009; Lincoln Center, NYC, Oct. 2009-Jan. 2010; Queens, NYC, May 2010; Long Island, NY, Jun. 2010. Mailing address: Slifka Family Creative Center, 39 Edmunds Ln., Walden, NY 12586. Tel: 800-922-3772 Fax: 845-778-4542. Website: www.bigapplecircus.org. GRADE LEVEL: All grades. GROUP TYPE: All youth groups & homeschoolers. PROGRAM TYPE: Day Trips, Performances. MAX GROUP SIZE: 700. REGISTRATION: Phone, Prepay, Tickets mailed prior to visit. TICKET/VOUCHER RETURN POLICY: Prices and schedule subject to change. All sales final. FOOD: Variety of menu selections, Can bring own food, Place to eat on site, Beverages available, Meal vouchers. RECOMM. LENGTH OF VISIT: 2 hours 15 minutes. COST: Tickets starting as low as $13.00.

"America's Best Circus for Children!" - Parents Magazine. Big Apple Circus presents our all-new 2010 Season Tour. We welcome the opportunity to work with your group to create a field trip full of fun, laughter and joy. We offer: Special Discounts for School Groups and Senior Groups, Scout packages with badges available, Wheelchair Accessible Seating. Purchase orders accepted. For tickets and further information call 800-922-3772. SUPPORTS NY STATE & NATIONAL LEARNING STANDARDS IN: The Arts. SUPPORTS SCOUT MERIT BADGE ACHIEVEMENT IN: Performing Arts. (See ad under Circus in New York City on page 88.) REGION: New York, Queens, Nassau Counties, NYC, New Jersey.

FARMS • PICK-YOUR-OWN • MAZES

BENNER'S FARM, 56 Gnarled Hollow Rd., East Setauket, NY 11733. Tel: 631-689-8172. Hrs: Seasonal. Pre K-6th grade. Guided Tours. Fifteen-acre family homestead with hands-on activities, gives visitors a sense of what it is like to live on a small farm . COST: Fee. REGION: Suffolk County, LI.

FORT SALONGA FARM, 30 Meadow Glen Rd., Northport, NY 11768. Tel: 631-269-9666. Hrs: Aug.-Oct. PYO: Apples, pumpkins, raspberries. COST: Fee. REGION: Suffolk County, LI.

HALLOCKVILLE MUSEUM FARM, 6038 Sound Ave., Riverhead, NY 11901. Tel: 631-298-5292. Hrs: Fri.-Sun. 11AM-4PM. K-8th grade. Guided Tours. Hstoric buildings and gardens. Experience real farming in the fields and meet the farm's cows, sheep and chickens. COST: Fee. REGION: Suffolk County, LI.

SCHMITT'S FAMILY FARM, 26 Pinelawn Rd., Melville, NY 11747. Tel: 631-271-3276. Hrs: Seasonal. PYO: Pumpkins. COST: Fee. REGION: Suffolk County, LI.

SUFFOLK COUNTY FARM, 350 Yaphank Ave., Yaphank, NY 11980. Tel: 631-852-4607. Hrs: Daily 9AM-3PM. PYO: Pumpkins. COST: Fee. REGION: Suffolk County, LI.

WICKHAM'S FRUIT FARM, 28700 Rte. 25, Cutchogue, NY 11935. Tel: 631-734-6441. Email: wickhamsfruitfarm@yahoo.com. Website: www.wickhamsfruitfarm.com. Hrs: Mon.-Sat. 9AM-4PM for tours, closed Sun. GRADE LEVEL: Pre K-High School. GROUP TYPE: All youth groups & homeschoolers. PROGRAM TYPE: Guided Tours, Guided Activities. MAX. GROUP SIZE: 200. MIN. GROUP SIZE: 10. REGISTRATION: Mail, Online, Phone. FOOD: Can bring own food, Place to eat on site, Beverages available. RECOMM. LENGTH OF VISIT: 2 hours. RECOMM. RATIO OF STUDENT TO STAFF: Varies. ARRIVAL TIPS: Expedite check in, Bus parking, Bus drop off and pick up at designated entrance. COST: See website.

We can customize a tour to suit your group needs, emphasizing agricultural, historical, agribusiness, or food production aspects. Tours feature our historic, bicentennial farm that is set against the beautiful waters of Peconic Bay on Eastern Long Island. Take a ride on our wagons over land that has been farmed as early as 1661 by Indians as manifested by Indian arrowheads dug up over the years. We also feature pick-your-own fruits in season, and observation of a real beehive where visitors can understand the importance of pollination and nature's little creatures in the sequence of food production. Complete your excursion in the country with a picnic on the farm surrounded by orchards and open fields, the blue sky and the sea. SUPPORTS NY STATE & NATIONAL LEARNING STANDARDS IN: History/Social Studies, Physical Education, Science. SUPPORTS SCOUT MERIT BADGE ACHIEVEMENT IN: Physical Ed/Recreation, Social Studies, Science/Environmental. REGION: Suffolk County, LI.

HEALTH & NUTRITION

FIELD TRIP FACTORY, Telephone: 800-987-6409. Fax: 773-342-9513. Email: info@fieldtripfactory.com. Website: www.fieldtripfactory.com. Hrs: Mon.-Fri. 8AM-6PM. GRADE LEVEL: Pre K-6th. GROUP TYPE: All youth groups & homeschoolers. PROGRAM TYPE: Day Trips, Guided Tours. COST: Free.

Field Trip Factory offers free community-based field trips. Our learning adventures teach valuable life-skills including health and nutrition, science, responsibility and more. All field trips are grade and age appropriate, meet learning standards, enrich classroom curriculum for teachers and fulfill badge requirements for scouts. See what is available in your area at www.fieldtripfactory.com or call 1-800-987-6409. SUPPORTS STATE LEARNING STANDARDS IN: Health & Safety, Math, Physical Education, Science. SUPPORTS SCOUT BADGE ACTIVITIES IN: Health & Safety, Life Skills, Personal Fitness. (See ad on page 56.) REGION: Throughout all 50 states.

INDOOR AMUSEMENT CENTERS

ACTIVE KIDZ LONG ISLAND, 210 Forest Dr., East Hills, NY 11548. Tel: 516-621-6600. Fax: 516-621-6603. Email: activekidz@verizon.net. Website: www.activekidzlongisland.com. Hrs: Daily 10AM-5PM. Contact: Andy Oelbaum. GRADE LEVEL: All grades. GROUP TYPE: All youth groups & homeschoolers. PROGRAM TYPE: Day Trips, Self-guided Activities. MAX. GROUP SIZE: 100. REGISTRATION: Phone. FOOD: Variety, Kosher, Place to eat on site. RECOMM. LENGTH OF VISIT: 1-2 hours. COST: Varies.

Located in East Hills, NY, Active Kidz Long Island is one of the top sports and entertainment centers, an 8,400 square foot facility with a gymnasium, rock climbing wall, and 3 level Adventure Maze. We will create a program designed especially for your group. We hope to add more fun attractions including a new high bounce room and a state of the art themed laser tag arena. Call us at 516-621-6600 for more about our sports classes, holiday camp and group visits. Group rates are available. SUPPORTS NY STATE & NATIONAL LEARNING STANDARDS IN: Physical Education. SUPPORTS SCOUT MERIT BADGE ACHIEVEMENT IN: Personal Fitness, Physical Ed/Recreation. REGION: Nassau County, LI.

DAVE AND BUSTER'S, Westbury: 1504 Old Country Rd., Westbury, NY 11590. Tel: 516-542-6916. Fax: 516-542-9042. Email: karen_kelly@daveandbusters.com. Contact: Karen Kelly. Farmingdale: 261 Airport Plaza Blvd., Farmingdale, NY 11735. Tel: 631-249-0708. Email: nicole_catanzaro@daveandbusters.com. Contact: Nicole Catanzaro. Islandia: 1856 Veteran's Memorial Hwy., Islandia, NY 11749. Tel: 631-582-6615. Email: Hillary_Epstein@daveandbusters.com. Contact: Hillary Epstein. Hrs: Sales office, 9AM-6PM. Website: www.daveandbusters.com. GRADE LEVEL: K-12th. GROUP TYPE: All youth groups & homeschoolers. PROGRAM TYPE: Self-guided Activities. REGISTRATION: Phone. FOOD: Variety of menu selections, Kosher, Vegetarian, Beverages available. RECOMM. LENGTH OF VISIT: 2-3 hours. RECOMM. RATIO OF STUDENT TO STAFF: 10:1 (before 2:30PM). ARRIVAL TIPS: Expedite check in, Bus parking. COST: Fee.

At Dave & Buster's your group will have a blast! Between our great food, amazing Midway full of arcade games and 12 lanes of bowling (bowling not available at Islandia location), the fun doesn't stop at D & B! Whether you are looking to spend an hour with us, or a whole day, we have packages for groups of 20 to 2,000. So for your next outing come eat, party & play at Dave & Buster's – your students will thank you. SUPPORTS NY STATE & NATIONAL LEARNING STANDARDS IN: Physical Education. SUPPORTS SCOUT MERIT BADGE ACHIEVEMENT IN: Physical Ed/Recreation. (See ad in New York City on page 96.) REGION: Nassau County, LI.

KARTS INDOOR RACEWAY, 701 Union Pkwy., Ronkonkoma, NY 11779. Tel: 631-737-5278. Fax: 631-737-5460. Email: info@karts1.com. Website: www.karts1.com. Hrs: Mon.-Thurs. 11AM-10PM, Fri.-Sat. 11AM-1AM, Sun. 11AM-8PM. Contact: Ann Keller, Len Elkins. GRADE LEVEL: Varies by height. GROUP TYPE: All youth groups. PROGRAM TYPE: Day Trips. MAX. GROUP SIZE: 100. MIN. GROUP SIZE: 25. REGISTRATION: Phone, Submit Waiver Forms, Prepay. TICKET/VOUCHER RETURN POLICY: No refunds. FOOD: Variety, Place to eat on site, Beverages available, Meal vouchers. RECOMM. LENGTH OF VISIT: 1.5 hours. RECOMM. RATIO OF STUDENT TO STAFF: 6:1. ARRIVAL TIPS: Expedite check in, Bus Parking. COST: Please call for details.

Perfect affordable fun for your school or summer camp and open rain or shine, Karts Indoor Raceway's 27,000 square foot facility is Long Island's First & only Indoor Go-Kart Racing arena. Offering two incredible tracks built for non-stop action for both young racers 40"-53" tall and more experienced racers 54" and taller. "Karts" also has: Slot-car racing, Roller Bowling and awesome Arcade Games and don't forget to take a break at the Pit Stop Cafe where you will find something for everyone! Contact us on the web at: www.karts1.com or call us directly at: 631-737-5278 with any questions you may have. SUPPORTS NY STATE & NATIONAL LEARNING STANDARDS IN: Physical Education. SUPPORTS SCOUT MERIT BADGE ACHIEVEMENT IN: Physical Ed/Recreation. REGION: Suffolk County, LI.

MAPLE SUGARING

SCIENCE MUSEUM OF LONG ISLAND, 1526 North Plandome Rd., Plandome, NY 11030. Tel: 516-627-9400. Hrs: Feb.- Mid-Mar., hrs vary. COST: Fee. REGION: Nassau County, LI.

MULTICULTURAL

AFRICAN AMERICAN MUSEUM, 110 N. Franklin St., Hempstead, NY 11550. Tel: 516-572-0730. Hrs: Wed.-Sat. 10AM-5PM. Self-guided Tours, Guided Tours. Long Island's only African American history museum. Focuses on the history of African-Americans on Long Island and their contribution to the social and cultural development of American society. COST: Fee. REGION: Nassau County, LI.

HOLOCAUST MEMORIAL & TOLERANCE CENTER OF NASSAU COUNTY, Welwyn Preserve, 100 Crescent Beach Rd., Glen Cove, NY 11542. Tel: 516-571-8040. Hrs: Mon.-Fri. 9:30AM-4:30PM, Sun. 12-4PM. 5th-12th grade. Self-guided Tours, Guided Tours, Workshops. Educating people about the Holocaust and the lessons that can be drawn from it. The Center's Tolerance Workshops demonstrate the destructive nature of prejudice, apathy, bullying, and hatred. COST: Free. REGION: Nassau County, LI.

SHINNECOCK NATION CULTURAL CENTER & MUSEUM, 100 Montauk Hwy., Southampton, NY 11968. Tel: 631-287-4923. Hrs: Thurs.-Sat. 11AM-4PM, Sun. 12-4PM. Self-guided Tours, Guided Tours, Workshops. Experience the art, history and culture of the Shinnecock Native Americans, indigenous to New York. Highlights include a mural that depict the journey of the People from pre-historic times to the present. COST: Fee. REGION: Suffolk County, LI.

MULTIDIMENSIONAL

THE FOLLOWING LISTINGS HAVE MULTIPLE FOCUSES IN THEIR EXHIBIT HALLS COVERING ANTHROPOLOGY, ART, SCIENCE, CULTURE, OR HISTORY.

THE LONG ISLAND MUSEUM, 1200 Rte. 25A, Stony Brook, NY 11790. Tel: 631-751-0066. Hrs: Wed.-Sat. 10AM-5PM, Sun. 12-5PM. Self-guided Tours, Guided Tours. Displays items dating from the late 1700s to the present, including American artifacts of everyday life, works of art and nearly 200 historic carriages. COST: Fee. REGION: Suffolk County, LI.

PARRISH ART MUSEUM, 25 Job's Ln., Southampton, NY 11968. Tel: 631-283-2118. Hrs: Mon.-Sat. 11AM-5PM, Sun. 1-5PM. Self-guided Tours, Guided Tours. Dedicated to American art from the 19th century to the present, with a focus on Long Island's East End. COST: Fee. REGION: Suffolk County, LI.

SUFFOLK COUNTY VANDERBILT MUSEUM, 180 Little Neck Rd., Centerport, NY 11721. Tel: 631-854-5539. Fax: 631-854-5530. Website: www.vanderbiltmuseum.org. Hrs: Tues.-Sun. 12-5PM, summer hours 10AM-5PM. Contact: Reservationist. GRADE LEVEL: All grades. GROUP TYPE: All youth groups & homeschoolers. PROGRAM TYPE: Day Trips, Guided Tours, Performances, Workshops. COST: Varies. Teachers & chaperones are free with groups of students over 200 and 1 complimentary ticket to each group of 25 students.

The Suffolk County Vanderbilt Museum is the former summer residence of William K. Vanderbilt II, great-grandson of Cornelius Vanderbilt, founder of the Staten Island Ferry and New York Central Railroad. William Vanderbilt traveled the world and amassed a unique collection of marine specimens and cultural artifacts for his museum which he entrusted to Suffolk County in his will. A planetarium was added to the estate by Suffolk County to expand the programming opportunities for educating the public. SUPPORTS NY STATE & NATIONAL LEARNING STANDARDS IN: Art, Science, Social Studies. SUPPORTS SCOUT MERIT BADGE ACHIEVEMENT IN: Art, Science, Social Studies. REGION: Suffolk County, LI.

PLANETARIUMS

SUFFOLK COUNTY VANDERBILT MUSEUM & PLANETARIUM, 180 Little Neck Rd., Centerport, NY 11721. Tel: 631-854-5555. Hrs: Call for show times. (See ad and main listing above.) COST: Fee. REGION: Suffolk County, LI.

SCIENCE & ENVIRONMENTAL EDUCATION

CRADLE OF AVIATION MUSEUM, Charles Lindbergh Blvd., Garden City, NY 11530. Tel: 516-572-4066. Fax: 516-572-4065. Email: info@CradleOfAviation.org. Website: www.CradleOfAviation.org. Hrs: Tues.-Sun. 9:30AM-5PM, closed Mon. GRADE LEVEL: 1st-college. GROUP TYPE: All youth groups & homeschoolers. PROGRAM TYPE: Day Trips, Self-guided Tours, Guided Tours, Workshops. COST: Varies.

When school groups visit the museum there is magic in the air as students and teachers experience Long Island's amazing aerospace heritage of discovery. Science, technology and history core curriculum standards can be fulfilled in exciting ways though our guided school programs, IMAX movies and Aerospace Quest. Each of our eight galleries deliver a "wow" experience as students travel through time seeing 70 air and space craft from hot air balloons or an actual lunar module. With the Leroy R. and Rose W. Grumman IMAX Dome Theater and the Red Planet Café, a visit to the museum is an exciting and educational field trip, right in your backyard. The Cradle of Aviation is a 130,000-square-foot safe, spacious environment operated by Museums at Mitchel, a non-profit educational corporation, in partnership with the County of Nassau. SUPPORTS NY STATE & NATIONAL LEARNING STANDARDS IN: Science, Technology, History. SUPPORTS SCOUT MERIT BADGE ACHIEVEMENT IN: Gardening, Science, Social Studies. REGION: Nassau County, LI.

HICKSVILLE GREGORY MUSEUM, One Heitz Pl., Hicksville, NY 11801. Tel: 516-822-7505. Hrs: Tues.-Fri. 9:30AM-4:30PM, Sat.-Sun. 1-5PM. Self-guided Tours, Guided Tours, Workshops. The collections include butterflies, moths, rocks, fossils and minerals and offers activities in Earth Sciences. COST: Fee. REGION: Nassau County, LI.

LONG ISLAND CHILDREN'S MUSEUM, 11 Davis Ave., Garden City, NY 11530. Tel: 516-224-5800. Website: www.limc.org. Hrs: Public: Tues.-Sun. 10AM-5PM; Field Trips: Tues.-Fri. 10-11:30AM or 12-1:30PM. Contact: Rebecca Elioseff at 516-224-5869. GRADE LEVEL: Pre K-6th. GROUP TYPE: All youth groups & homeschoolers. PROGRAM TYPE: Day Trips, Self-guided Tours, Guided Tours, Self-guided Activities, Performances, Workshops. COST: $8 per student for Guided Tours, $7 for Self-Guided Tours, $10 Regular Admission. (Additional fees for workshops & performances may apply.)

Long Island Children's Museum is a learning laboratory where 14 hands-on exhibits invite children to experiment, explore and play. Through lively interdisciplinary activities, children and adults can share in the excitement of the learning process as they explore our world. The museum offers six content and age-specific field trip programs designed for children from Pre K-6th grade. Theme-based field trips include: Machines, Mapping, Patterns and Structure and Function. LICM also offers scout workshops, birthday parties and outreach programs on subjects such as folklore, animal sciences, architecture, biology, history, art…and bubbles; bringing the museum to your school, library or community center. Museum field trips support New York State Learning Standards. Scout Workshops support Scout Merit Badge Achievements. SUPPORTS NY STATE & NATIONAL LEARNING STANDARDS IN: The Arts, Science, Social Studies. SUPPORTS SCOUT MERIT BADGE ACHIEVEMENT IN: Arts, Science, Social Studies. REGION: Nassau County, LI.

SCIENCE MUSEUM OF LONG ISLAND, 1526 North Plandome Rd., Plandome, NY 11030. Tel: 516-627-9400. Hrs: Vary. Workshops. Offers over 50 hands-on Science workshops. COST: Fee. REGION: Nassau County, LI.

SUFFOLK COUNTY MARINE ENVIRONMENTAL LEARNING CENTER, 3690 Cedar Beach Rd., Southold, NY 11971. Tel: 631-852-8660. Hrs: Mon.-Fri. 9AM-5PM. Guided Tours. Features marine & environmental education programs, touch tanks, and salt marshes. COST: Fee. REGION: Suffolk County, LI.

SUNKEN FOREST, The Fire Island National Seashore, Fire Island, NY. Tel: 631-597-6183. Tours: 631-687-4765. Self-guided Tours, Guided Tours. At 300 years, the Sunken Forest represents stability in an extremely dynamic environment--a barrier island. Learn about how a well developed forest was formed just a few hundred yards from Fire Island's sandy beaches and pounding surf. COST: Fee. REGION: Suffolk County, LI. REGION: Suffolk County, LI.

SWEETBRIAR NATURE CENTER, 62 Eckernkamp Dr., Smithtown, NY 11787. Tel: 631-979-6344. Hrs: Vary. Self-guided Tours, Guided Tours, Workshops. 54 acres of varied garden, woodland, field and wetland habitats and a butterfly house. COST: Fee. REGION: Suffolk County, LI.

SEAPORTS & LIGHTHOUSES

FIRE ISLAND LIGHTHOUSE, east of Robert Moses State Park, NY. Tel: 631-661-4876. Hrs: Seasonal. Self-guided Tours, Guided Tours. Learn about the history of the Fire Island Lighthouse and visit the observatory and museum. COST: Fee. REGION: Suffolk County, LI.

MONTAUK POINT LIGHTHOUSE MUSEUM, 2000 Montauk Hwy., Montauk, NY 11954. Tel: 631-668-2544. Hrs: Seasonal. 4-12th grade. Self-guided Tours, Guided Tours. Visit the oldest lighthouse in New York State and view an assortment of many historical documents and photographs. COST: Fee. REGION: Suffolk County, LI.

SOCIAL STUDIES

AMERICAN AIRPOWER MUSEUM, 1230 New Hwy., Farmingdale, NY 11735. Tel: 631-293-6398. Hrs: Thurs.-Sun. 10:30AM-4PM. Self-guided Tours, Guided Tours. Features operational World War II aircrafts. COST: Fee. REGION: Suffolk County, LI.

COLD SPRING HARBOR WHALING MUSEUM, 301 Main St., Cold Spring Harbor, NY 11724. Tel: 631-367-3418. Hrs: Vary. Guided Tours, Workshops. Collects, preserves, and exhibits objects and documents pertinent to whaling, especially the regional whaling history of Long Island, whale conservation, and the history of Cold Spring Harbor as a maritime port. COST: Fee. REGION: Suffolk County, LI.

GARVIES POINT MUSEUM AND PRESERVE, 50 Barry Dr., Glen Cove, NY 11542. Tel: 516-571-8010. Hrs: Tues.-Sat. 10AM-4PM. Guided Tours. Exhibits focus on geology of Long Island and how LI was formed when glaciers deposited debris in the area. There are exhibits on plate tectonics and LI's geology, with samples of local rocks and minerals. The museum is also a research facility, and there is a large scale model of the archaeological excavations in the area. In addition there are exhibits on the local Native Americans' history and culture, from the Paleo-Indians to the later inhabitants of LI. Explore one of the many scenic trails in the preserve behind the museum. COST: Fee. REGION: Nassau County, LI.

THE LONG ISLAND MARITIME MUSEUM, 86 West Ave., West Sayville, NY 11796. Tel: 631-854-4974. Hrs: Mon-Sat. 10AM-4PM, Sun. 12-4PM. 2nd-12th grade. Self-guided Tours, Guided Tours. Learn about Long Island's maritime history and heritage through collections of boats, vessels and related equipment having to do with past and present maritime activities COST: Fee. REGION: Suffolk County, LI.

OLD BETHPAGE VILLAGE RESTORATION, 1303 Round Swamp Rd., Old Bethpage, NY 11804. Tel: 516-572-8400. Hrs: Wed.-Fri. 10AM-4PM, Sat. & Sun. 10AM-5PM. 3rd-12th grade. Self-guided Tours, Performances. Recreates the atmosphere of a pre-Civil War Long Island Village, featuring more than 55 historic buildings and costumed interpreters illustrating agricultural, domestic and commercial activities. COST: Fee. REGION: Nassau County, LI.

SAGAMORE HILL NATIONAL HISTORIC SITE, 20 Sagamore Hill Rd., Oyster Bay, NY 11771. Tel: 516-922-4788. Hrs: Vary. Guided Tours. Exhibits and audio-visual programs on Theodore Roosevelt's family life and career. COST: Free. REGION: Nassau County, LI.

WALT WHITMAN BIRTHPLACE STATE HISTORIC SITE AND INTERPRETIVE CENTER, 246 Old Walt Whitman Rd., Huntington Station, NY 11746. Tel: 631-427-5240. Hrs: Vary. Guided Tours. Newly restored farmhouse, birthplace of America's greatest poet, built c.1819 by Whitman's father. Interpretive Center exhibits: 130 Whitman portraits, original letters, manuscripts, artifacts, Whitman's voice on tape, and schoolmaster's desk. COST: Fee. REGION: Suffolk County, LI.

WATER MILL MUSEUM, 41 Old Mill Rd., Water Mill, NY 11976. Tel: 631-726-4625. Hrs: Vary. Guided Tours. Learn about milling and Colonial life and visit a working 17th century water powered grist mill. At the water-powered grist mill, learning how the corn is ground and about ice harvesting in Water Mill. At the Corwith Windmill on the Village Green, learning how the sails are turned into the wind and some of the history of the area. COST: Fee. REGION: Suffolk County, LI.

THEATRE · DANCE · MUSIC

THE PAPER BAG PLAYERS, 225 West 99th St., New York, NY 10025. Tel: 800-777-2247/ 212-663-0390. Fax: 212-663-1076. Email: pbagp@verizon.net. Website: thepaperbagplayers.org. Hrs: Long Island performances in Hempstead. GRADE LEVEL: K–3rd grade. GROUP TYPE: All youth groups and homeschoolers. PROGRAM TYPE: Performances. COST: Varies.

The Paper Bag Players Great Mummy Robbery will have your class laughing, singing, dancing---and sitting on the edge of their seats! From an expedition to the land of the pyramids in search of that mysterious Mummy by the name of Shirley, to a Paper Bag picnic that turns into a dance-a-thon and the whole audience joins in, to a painting so realistic it comes to life--this show is funny, friendly, and thrilling! Perfect for children in grades K through 3. SUPPORTS NY STATE & NATIONAL LEARNING STANDARDS IN: The Arts, English. SUPPORTS SCOUT MERIT BADGES ACHIEVEMENT IN: Theater. REGION: Nassau County, NY.

PENNSYLVANIA

ADVENTURE SPORTS & OUTDOOR LEARNING

BUCKS COUNTY RIVER COUNTRY, 2 Walters Ln., Point Pleasant, PA 18950. Tel: 215-297-5000. Fax: 215-297-5643. Email: info@rivercountry.net. Website: www.rivercountry.net. Hrs: May-Oct.: 8:30AM-7PM. GRADE LEVEL: All grades. GROUP TYPE: All youth groups & homeschoolers. PROGRAM TYPE: Day Trips, Self-guided Tours. REGISTRATION: Mail, Online, Phone, Prepay. FOOD: Variety of menu selections, Kosher, Vegetarian, Can bring own food, Place to eat on site, Beverages available. RECOMM. LENGTH OF VISIT: 2.5 hours-all day. RECOMM. RATIO OF STUDENT TO STAFF: 10:1. ARRIVAL TIPS: Bus parking. COST: Varies.

Family oriented river adventures on the Historic Delaware River. Since 1969 we've been offering 2-hour to full day Tubing, Rafting, Canoeing, Kayaking trips on the clean, 1-4' deep, 80 degree (average) Delaware River. A fun way to enjoy nature. We offer you an unforgettable adventure enjoying nature with prices that are made to fit School, Scout and Youth Groups budgets. Food combos are available or bring your own. Early morning Tubing $10, check web for details. All you can eat Bar-B-Que, check web for details. Reserve On-line, no waiting. SUPPORTS PA STATE LEARNING STANDARDS IN: Physical Education, Science. SUPPORTS SCOUT MERIT BADGE ACHIEVEMENT IN: Canoeing, Water. (See Bucks County Featured Region Page on page 213 and Regional Highlights on page 16.) REGION: Bucks County, South East PA.

JUNIATA RIVER ADVENTURES, INC., RR 3 Box 566, Mifflintown, PA 17059. Tel: 717-320-1102. Fax: 717-320-1105. Email: adventures@juniatariveradventures.com. Website: www.juniatariveradventures.com. Hrs: 7AM-1PM. Contact: Skip Sanderson. GRADE LEVEL: 6th-college. GROUP TYPE: All youth groups & homeschoolers. PROGRAM TYPE: Day Trips, Overnight Trips, Self-guided Tours, Self-guided Activities. MAX. GROUP SIZE: 120. COST: Group Rates.

Our small town location and low overhead will save you big dollars; just compare our rates with other outfitters. We outfit dozens of youth groups annually. We offer group friendly accommodations, flexible schedules and arrangements. 2 hour to overnight river trips available on a scenic, leisurely flowing river. Trips offer students a variety of outdoor river activities including wildlife, fishing and swimming. Primitive camping available along the river or at our site. Beach volley court and picnic tables on site. We can help plan for additional activities to complete your trip. SUPPORTS PA STATE & NATIONAL LEARNING STANDARDS IN: Health & Safety, Physical Education. SUPPORTS SCOUT MERIT BADGE ACHIEVEMENT IN: Camping, Health & Safety, Physical Ed/Recreation, Safety. (See Regional Highlights on page 16.) REGION: Juniata County, Central PA.

KITTATINNY CANOE, Main Office: 378 Rts. 6 & 209, Milford, PA 18337. Locations: NY: Barryville, Pond Eddy. PA: Dingman's Ferry, Matamoras, Milford, Smithville Beach. NJ: Delaware-Water-Gap. Tel: 800-FLOAT-KC (356-2852). Email: floatkc@warwick.net. Website: www.kittatinny.com. Hrs: Apr.-Oct. Office open year round for info & reservations. 4 yrs/40 lbs & up. GRADE LEVEL: 4 yrs/40 pounds and up. GROUP TYPE: All youth groups & homeschoolers. PROGRAM TYPE: Day Trips, Overnight Trips, Guided Tours, Self-guided Activities. COST: Varies. (See main listing under Adventure Sports in New York State on page 132 and Regional Highlights on page 16.) REGION: NY, PA, NJ.

POCONO WHITEWATER ADVENTURES, 1519 State Rte. 903, Jim Thorpe, PA 18229. Tel: 1-800-WHITEWATER (1-800-944-8392). Fax: 570-325-4097. Website: www.PoconoWhitewater.com. Email: Info@PoconoWhitewater.com. Hrs: Daily, Year Round. Contact: Nikki Hurley. GRADE LEVEL: All grades. GROUP TYPE: All youth groups. PROGRAM TYPE: Day Trips, Overnight Trips, Self-guided Tours, Guided Tours, Self-guided Activities, Guided Activities. MAX. GROUP SIZE: 1000. MIN. GROUP SIZE: 4. REGISTRATION: Mail, Online, Phone. FOOD: Variety, Kosher, Vegetarian, Can bring own food, Place to eat on site, Beverages available. RECOMM. LENGTH OF VISIT: 1 day. ARRIVAL TIPS: Expedite check in, Bus Parking, Bus drop off and pick up at designated entrance. COST: Fee.

This year take your class outdoors! We offer mild to wild rafting, scenic rail-trail biking, and exciting Skirmish paintball games. Make it a day trip or combine our activities for an overnight getaway with free Camping!! We also have an Outdoor Classroom Program, in conjunction with DCNR (Dept. of Conservation & Natural Resources) that combines our outdoor adventures with ecological and historic awareness. Get Outside, Explore, & Learn with Pocono Whitewater - We're Green, Healthy, Fun, Close, and Affordable! SUPPORTS PA STATE & NATIONAL LEARNING STANDARDS IN: Physical Education. SUPPORTS SCOUT MERIT BADGE ACHIEVEMENT IN: Physical Ed/Recreation, Safety. (See Regional Highlights on page 17.) REGION: Carbon County, North East PA.

AMUSEMENT & THEME PARKS

HERSHEYPARK, 100 W. Hersheypark Dr., Hershey, PA 17033. Tel: 800-242-4236. Email: hersheyparkgroups@hersheypa.com. Website: www.hersheypark.com/groups. Hrs: Call for hours. GRADE LEVEL: All grades. GROUP TYPE: All youth groups & homeschoolers. PROGRAM TYPE: Day Trips. REGISTRATION: Mail, Phone, Prepay, Tickets mailed prior to visit. FOOD: Variety of menu selections, Kosher, Vegetarian, Place to eat on site, Beverages available, Meal vouchers. RECOMM. LENGTH OF VISIT: 4+ hours. RECOMM. RATIO OF STUDENT TO STAFF: 10:1. ARRIVAL TIPS: Bus parking. COST: Group rates: Savings! Your school can save up to 45% off regular rates and we offer one free chaperone ticket for every 10 tickets purchased. Bus parking is free!

Hersheypark, located in Central Pennsylvania, is home to more than 65 rides and attractions including 11 roller coasters, The Boardwalk at Hersheypark, award-winning live entertainment, and our newest water feature - The SEAquel. Included with your admission is ZooAmerica North American Wildlife Park, our 11 acre walk-through zoo. Also, visit Hershey's Chocolate World to learn about the chocolate making process. Catered meals and/or discounted meal tickets are available for groups of 20 or more. Call today to request a Group Planner and ask about our Educational Days and free Educational guides. For further information, please call 1-800-242-4236, e-mail hersheyparkgroups@hersheypa.com, or visit www.hersheypark.com/groups. SUPPORTS PA STATE & NATIONAL LEARNING STANDARDS IN: Physical Education and Science. SUPPORTS SCOUT MERIT BADGE ACHIEVEMENT IN: Science, Sports & Games. (See Gettysburg Feature City Page on page 218 and Regional Highlights on page 10.) REGION: Dauphin County, South East PA.

For more additional information on class trips,
please visit us at
ClassTrips.com

SESAME PLACE, 100 Sesame Rd., Langhorne, PA 19047. Tel: 866-GO-4-ELMO. Fax: 215-741-5315. Email: groupsales@sesameplace.com. Website: www.sesameplace.com. Hrs: Vary. Contact: Gayle Kennedy. GRADE LEVEL: Pre K-3rd. GROUP TYPE: All youth groups & homeschoolers. PROGRAM TYPE: Day Trips, Performances. MAX. GROUP SIZE: None. MIN. GROUP SIZE: 15. COST: Group rates available.

Sesame Place is the nation's only theme park based entirely on the award-winning television show Sesame Street. Share in the spirit of imagination with your students-where you can experience together through whirling rides, colorful shows and furry friends. This Spring, Sesame Place is offering Sesame Street - My World is Green and Growing, an education program focused completely on the environment and Conservation! Call for details. Located just 30 minutes north of Philadelphia and 90 minutes south of New York City, Sesame Place is the place for kids and the kid in all of us. For more information visit sesameplace.com or call 1-866-GO-4-ELMO. SUPPORTS PA STATE & NATIONAL LEARNING STANDARDS IN: Science and Environmental Studies, and Physical Ed/Recreation. SUPPORTS SCOUT MERIT BADGE ACHIEVEMENT IN: Recreation, Sports & Games. (See Bucks County Featured Region Page on page 213 and Regional Highlights on page 11.) REGION: Bucks County, South East PA.

ANIMALS • AQUARIUMS • ZOOS

ANIMALAND ZOOLOGICAL PARK, 4181 Rte. 660 W., Wellsboro, PA 16901. Tel: 570-724-4546. Hrs: Seasonal. Self-guided Tours. Home to over 200 wild, exotic, and domestic animals. COST: Fee. REGION: Tioga County, Central PA.

CLAWS 'N' PAWS WILD ANIMAL PARK, 1475 Ledgedale Rd., Lake Ariel, PA 18436. Tel: 570-698-6154. Hrs: May 1-late Oct.: Daily 10AM-6PM. Self-guided Tours. 300 animal representing 120 species on 30 acres. COST: Fee. REGION: Wayne County, North East PA.

CLYDE PEELING'S REPTILAND, 18628 US Rte. 15, Allenwood, PA 17810. Tel: 570-538-1869. Hrs: Sept, Oct, April, May: Daily 10AM-6PM; Nov-March: Daily 10AM-5 PM; Memorial Day-Labor Day: Daily 9AM-7PM. Self-guided Tours, Performances. Zoo specializing in reptiles and amphibians. COST: Fee. REGION: Union County, Central PA.

ELMWOOD PARK ZOO, 1661 Harding Blvd., Norristown, PA 19401. Tel: 610-277-3825. Hrs: Daily 10AM-5PM. Self-guided Tours. 150 animals on 16 acres including children's petting barn. COST: Fee. REGION: Montgomery County, South East PA.

LAKE TOBIAS WILDLIFE PARK, 760 Tobias Rd., Halifax, PA 17032. Tel: 717-362-9126. Fax: 717-362-9993. Email: ltwp@pa.net. Website: www.laketobias.com. Hrs: Seasonal: May-Oct. Contact: Pam Jury, Office Manager/Reservations. GRADE LEVEL: All grades. GROUP TYPE: All youth groups & homeschoolers. PROGRAM TYPE: Day Trips, Self-guided Tours, Guided Tours. MIN. GROUP SIZE: 25. COST: Park Admission (includes Zoo Exhibits and Petting Zoo) - $3.00 (all ages 3 yrs. & up); Safari Tour - $4.00 (all ages 3 yrs. & up); Reptile Building - $1.00 (all ages 3 yrs. & up).

Over 100 acres of rolling hills are scattered with herds of buffalo, deer, yak, watusi and more. Our guided safari tours take you among the roaming herds on an informative adventure. Monkeys, tigers, ostriches and many interesting creatures reside along 50 acres of zoo-type setting continuously educating and entertaining park visitors. For those who wish to get a closer look, we offer the Petting Zoo. Alligators, snakes and other surprises will thrill you in our Reptile Building. Eye-opening presentations given throughout the day enlighten you on these fascinating creatures. SUPPORTS PA STATE & NATIONAL LEARNING STANDARDS IN: Science. SUPPORTS SCOUT MERIT BADGE ACHIEVEMENT IN: Science. (See Regional Highlights on page 12.) REGION: Dauphin County, South Central PA.

LEHIGH VALLEY ZOO, 5150 Game Preserve Rd., Schnecksville, PA 18078. Tel: 610-799-4171. Hrs: Apr.-Oct. 1: Daily 10AM-4PM; Nov. 1-Mar. 31: Daily 10AM-3PM. Self-guided Tours, Guided Tours. Home to approximately 55 different species of wildlife from around the world. COST: Fee. REGION: Lehigh County, South East PA.

PHILADELPHIA ZOO, 3400 W. Girard Ave., Philadelphia, PA 19104. Tel: 215-243-1100. Hrs: Mar. 1-Nov.1: Daily 9:30AM-5PM; Nov. 2-Feb. 28: Daily 9:30AM-4PM. Self-guided Tours, Guided Tours. 42-acre Victorian garden is home to more than 1,300 animals, many of them rare and endangered. COST: Fee. REGION: Philadelphia County, South East PA.

RED DEER FARM, 63 Pinnacle Dr., Catawissa, PA 17820. Tel: 570-356-7482. Hrs: Jun.-Aug.: Tue.-Sat. 10AM-6PM; Sep.-Nov.: Fri. & Sat. 10AM-5PM. Guided Tours. Located on 200 acres that raise Red Deers. Tour the farm on a guided hayride, learn about the farming operations and get a chance to feed the deers. COST: Fee. REGION: Columbia County, Central PA.

WOLF SANCTUARY OF PENNSYLVANIA, 465 Speedwell Forge Rd., Lititz, PA 17543. Tel: 717-626-4617. Hrs: Vary. Guided Tours. Home of more than 20 wolves on 24 acres of natural woodland. COST: Fee. REGION: Lancaster County, Southern PA.

ZOOAMERICA NORTH AMERICAN WILDLIFE PARK, 100 W. Hersheypark Dr., Hershey, PA 17033. Tel: 717-534-3860. Hrs: Daily 10AM-5PM; Summer: 10AM-8PM. Self-guided Tours, Guided Tours. Over 200 animals from five regions of North America. COST: Fee. REGION: Dauphin County, South East PA.

ART · ARCHITECTURE · SCULPTURE

ALLENTOWN ART MUSEUM, 31 N. 5th St., Allentown, PA 18101. Tel: 610-432-4333. Hrs: Wed.-Sat. 11AM-5PM, Sun. 12-5PM. Self-guided Tours, Guided Tours. Presents over 10,000 works of art, most of which are European based. COST: Fee. REGION: Lehigh County, South East PA.

A.R.T. RESEARCH ENTERPRISES, 3050 Industry Dr., Lancaster, PA 17603. Tel: 717-290-1303. Fax: 717-290-1309. Email: mail@thinksculpture.com. Website: www.thinksculpture.com. Hrs: 9AM-3PM. Contact: Ben Blaney. GRADE LEVEL: K-College. GROUP TYPE: All youth groups & homeschoolers. PROGRAM TYPE: Guided Tours. MAX. GROUP SIZE: 85. MIN. GROUP SIZE: 2. REGISTRATION: Mail, Phone, Prepay, Tickets mailed prior to visit. RECOMM. LENGTH OF VISIT: 1.5 hours. RECOMM. RATIO OF STUDENT TO STAFF: Varies. ARRIVAL TIPS: Bus parking. COST: $6 students, $12 adults.

If you've been curious about how sculpture is made, this is the tour for you! Our one hour guided tour includes the history and projects of ART Research Enterprises, the mold room where originals are molded, the wax room showing the process of recreating the original in wax, possibly a hot metal pour or fabrication, the finishing room where technicians assemble the metal sculpture and patina them, our Sculpture garden & Koi pond, and the ART gift shop. Every tour is different as we make custom art from small to monumental for international artists. Contact us 717-290-1303. SUPPORTS PA STATE & NATIONAL LEARNING STANDARDS IN: Arts. SUPPORTS SCOUT MERIT BADGE ACHIEVEMENT IN: Arts. (See Pennsylvania Dutch Country Featured Region Page on page 232.) REGION: Lancaster County, South East PA.

BRANDYWINE RIVER MUSEUM, U.S. Rte. 1 & Creek Rd., Chadds Ford, PA 19317. Tel: 610-388-2700. Hrs: Daily 9:30AM-4:30PM. Self-guided Tours, Guided Tours, Workshops. Features American art with primary emphasis on the art of the Brandywine region, American illustration and still life painting. COST: Fee. REGION: Delaware County, South East PA.

FONTHILL MUSEUM, E. Court St. & Swamp Rd. (Rte. 313), Doylestown, PA 18901. Tel: 215-348-9461. Hrs: Mon.-Sat. 10AM-5PM, Sun. 12-5PM. 1st-12th grade. Guided Tours. The collection includes several thousand European and American prints, and decorative ceramic tiles from Europe, Asia, North Africa and the Middle East. Many of these tiles are inset into Fonthill's walls and ceilings. COST: Fee. REGION: Bucks County, South East PA.

JAMES A. MICHENER ART MUSEUM, 138 S. Pine St., Doylestown, PA 18901. Tel: 215-340-9800, ext. 124. Hrs: Tues.-Fri. 10AM-4:30PM, Sat. 10AM-5PM, Sun. 12-5PM. Self-guided Tours, Guided Tours. Dedicated to preserving, interpreting and exhibiting the art and cultural heritage of the Bucks County region. The museum is now home to a world class collection of Pennsylvania Impressionist paintings. COST: Fee. REGION: Bucks County, South East PA.

PENNSYLVANIA ACADEMY OF THE FINE ARTS, 118 N. Broad St., Philadelphia, PA 19102. Tel: 215-972-7600. Hrs: Tues.-Sat. 10AM-5PM, Sun. 11AM-5PM. Self-guided Tours, Guided Tours, Workshops. Collections of 19th and 20th century American paintings, sculptures, and works on paper. COST: Fee. REGION: Philadelphia County, South East PA.

PHILADELPHIA MUSEUM OF ART, 26th St. & Benjamin Franklin Pkwy., Philadelphia, PA 19130. Tel: 215-763-8100. Hrs: Tues.-Sun. 10AM-5PM, Fri. until 8:45PM. Self-guided Tours, Guided Tours, Workshops. Its collections include more than 225,000 objects, with over 200 galleries spanning 2,000 years. COST: Fee. REGION: Philadelphia County, South East PA.

RODIN MUSEUM, 22nd St. & Benjamin Franklin Pkwy., Philadelphia, PA 19130. Tel: 215-568-6026. Hrs: Tues.-Sun. 10AM-5PM. Self-guided Tours, Guided Tours. Houses 124 sculptures including bronze casts by the artist, Auguste Rodin. COST: Fee. REGION: Philadelphia County, South East PA.

THE SUSQUEHANNA ART MUSEUM, 301 Market St., Harrisburg, PA 17101. Tel: 717-233-8668. Hrs: Tues., Wed., Fri. & Sat. 10AM-4PM; Thurs. 4-8PM; Sat. 12-5PM; Sun. 1-4PM. Self-guided Tours, Guided Tours, Workshops. Three exhibits each year featuring works of nationally and internationally recognized artists as well as exhibits which reflect the diverse cultural heritage of the Susquehanna region. COST: Free/Fee. REGION: Dauphin County, South East PA.

WOODMERE ART MUSEUM, 9201 Germantown Ave., Philadelphia, PA 19118. Tel: 215-247-0476. Hrs: Tues.-Sat. 10AM-5PM, Sun. 1-5PM. Self-guided Tours, Guided Tours, Workshops. More than 2500 works of art, much of it celebrating the art and artists of the Philadelphia region. COST: Fee. REGION: Philadelphia County, South East PA.

ARTS & CRAFTS

BLACK SHEEP POTTERY, CLAY STUDIO & CERAMIC ART CENTER, 4038 Skippack Pike, PO Box 393, Skippack, PA 19474. Tel: 610-584-5877. Fax: 917-591-5498. Email: blacksheeppottery@mac.com. Website: www.blacksheeppottery.org. Hrs: Tues.-Sun. 12-9PM, Mon by appt. Contact: Nicole Dubrow, Managing Director. GRADE LEVEL: All grades. GROUP TYPE: All youth groups & homeschoolers. PRO-GRAM TYPE: Day Trips, Guided Tours, Guided Activities, Workshops. MAX. GROUP SIZE: 24. MIN. GROUP SIZE: 4. REGISTRATION: Mail, Online, Phone, Submit Waiver Forms, Prepay. TICKET/VOUCHER RETURN POLICY: No refunds. If notice of cancella-tion within 48 hours, exchanges are good toward any service or goods, less a $5 materials processing fee per participant. FOOD. Can bring own food, Place to eat on site. RECOMM. LENGTH OF VISIT: 2-3 hours. RECOMM. RATIO OF STUDENT TO STAFF: 6:1. ARRIVAL TIPS: Bus Parking, Bus drop off and pick up at designated entrance. COST: Call for details.

Black Sheep Pottery Ceramic Art Center clay programs invite Pre K-adult groups to experience the real living art of a working production pottery and contemporary clay studio. Pre/post visit material and discussion topics available to enrich visitor experi-ence in Historic Skippack Village. Individual hands-on wheel & handbuilding life skills learned in master workshop and pottery tour; option of prepared ceramic production ware available for custom painting. Prices vary by project. 100% Green/sustainable studio practices recycled clay & glaze resources program. Private/Group classes & events year round. Bus Parking available. SUPPORTS PA STATE & NATIONAL LEARN-ING STANDARDS IN: The Arts, Math, History/Social Studies, Science. SUPPORTS SCOUT MERIT BADGE ACHIEVEMENT IN: The Arts, Life Skills. REGION: Montgomery County, South East PA.

BEHIND THE SCENE TOURS

THE CRAYOLA FACTORY at Two Rivers Landing, 30 Centre Sq., Easton, PA 18042. Tel: 610-515-8000. Hrs: Tues.-Fri. 9:30AM-3PM, Sat. 9:30AM-5PM, Sun 12-5PM. PreK-6th grade. Self-guided Tours. Experience more than a dozen hands-on activities as well as learn how Crayola Crayons® and Markers are made.COST: Fee. REGION: Northampton County, PA.

HARLEY-DAVIDSON FACTORY TOUR, 1425 Eden Rd., York, PA 17402. Tel: 877-883-1450. Hrs: Vary. 12 yrs & older. Guided Tours. Features exhibits that detail the plant's history and guide visitors through the manufacturing and assembly processes. COST: Fee. REGION: York County, South Central PA.

HERR'S SNACK FACTORY TOUR, 271 Old Baltmore Pike Herr Dr., Nottingham, PA 19362. Tel: 800-63-SNACK. Hrs: Mon.-Thurs. 9-11AM & 1-3PM, Fri. 9-11AM. Guided Tours. Visit the factory and experience first-hand how Herr's produces their snacks. COST: Free. REGION: Chester County, South East PA.

HERSHEY'S CHOCOLATE WORLD, 100 W. Hershey Park Ave., Hershey, PA 17033. Tel: 800-HERSHEY. Hrs: Vary. Self-guided Tour. The free tour experience shows you HERSHEY'S chocolate making process! The tour concludes with a FREE HERSHEY'S product sample.COST: Fee. REGION: Dauphin County, PA.

MACY'S CENTER CITY, 1300 Market St., Philadelphia, PA 19107. Tel: 212-494-7430. Fax: 212-494-2118. Email: jennifer.h.gothelf@macys.com. Website: www.macys.com. Hrs: Mon.-Sat. 10AM-8PM, Sun. 11AM-7PM. Contact: Jennifer Gothelf. GRADE LEVEL: All grades. GROUP TYPE: All youth groups & homeschoolers. PROGRAM TYPE: Guided Tours, Guided Activities. MIN. GROUP SIZE: 5. REGISTRATION: Phone, Prepay. TICKET/VOUCHER RETURN POLICY: No returns accepted. FOOD: Place to eat on site, Can bring own food. RECOMM. LENGTH OF VISIT: 1/2 day. RECOMM. RATIO OF STUDENT TO STAFF: 10:1. ARRIVAL TIPS: Expedite check in, Bus parking. COST: $8.00 Historical Tour.

Macy's Center City located within the historic Wanamaker Building has been a Philadelphia destination for many years. Historical Tours of the Wanamaker Building with narratives on the history of the building, Macy's, and the business of fashion retailing are available for groups. Beauty and Fashion Programs are also offered for group itineraries and include a private presentation with a Macy's expert in beauty or fashion, refreshments & fun! Reservations required in advance for all group programs. Group members also receive a Macy's Visitor Savings Pass to save 10% throughout the store (exclusions apply). SUPPORTS PA STATE & NATIONAL LEARNING STANDARDS IN: The Arts, History/Social Studies. SUPPORTS SCOUT MERIT BADGE ACHIEVEMENT IN: Social Studies. REGION: Philadelphia County, South East PA.

PHILADELPHIA EAGLES, 1 NovaCare Way, Philadelphia, PA 19145. Tel: 267-570-4510. Email: bstanko@eagles.nfl.com. Website: www.philadelphiaeagles.com. Hrs: Mon.-Sat. 10AM-8PM, Sun. 11AM-7PM. Contact: Brea Webster Stanko. GRADE LEVEL: All grades. GROUP TYPE: All youth groups & homeschoolers. PROGRAM TYPE: Day Trips, Guided Tours. MAX. GROUP SIZE: None. MIN. GROUP SIZE: 10 REGISTRATION: Mail, Phone, Submit waiver forms prior to visit, Prepay. FOOD: Can bring own food, Place to eat on site. RECOMM. LENGTH OF VISIT: 1.5 hours. RECOMM. RATIO OF STUDENT TO STAFF: 20:1. ARRIVAL TIPS: Bus parking, Bus drop off and pick up at designated entrance. COST: $7 Adults, $5 Students.

Looking for a field trip that is unique, historical and educational? Lincoln Financial Field, home of the Philadelphia Eagles, Stadium Tour is perfect! Take a first hand look at one of the premier stadiums in the NFL. View state-of-the-art equipment, Press Box, Broadcast Booth, Field Level, Eagles Locker Room and more! Students will learn fascinating stadium facts, marketing techniques, and different careers in sports management. This is truly an event that every age will enjoy! SUPPORTS PA STATE & NATIONAL LEARNING STANDARDS IN: History/Social Studies, Technology. SUPPORTS SCOUT MERIT BADGE ACHIEVEMENT IN: Science/Technology. (See Philadelphia Featured City Page on page 235.) REGION: Philadelphia County, South East PA.

QVC STUDIO TOUR, 1200 Wilson Dr., West Chester, PA 19380. Tel: 800-600-9900. Hrs: Daily 10AM-5:30PM. 3rd grade & up. Guided Tours. See how QVC programs are sourced, tested, brought to life on air, and delivered to QVC customers. The QVC Studio Tour is a one-of-a-kind guided walking tour through the fantastic world of electronic retailing. At this state-of-the-art broadcasting facility, guests will see and experience how QVC products are sourced, tested, brought to life on air, and delivered to millions of QVC customers. COST: Fee. REGION: Chester County, South East PA.COST: Fee. REGION: Chester County, South East PA.

BOTANICAL GARDENS & NATURE CENTERS

BARTRAM'S GARDEN, 54th St. & Lindbergh Blvd., Philadelphia, PA 19143. Tel: 215-729-5281. Hrs: Vary. Guided Tours, Workshops. Botanical garden features an 18th century farmstead, native plants, wildflower meadow, and wetland. America's oldest living botanical garden features an 18th century farmstead, native plants, wildflower meadow, and wetland. Colonial naturalist John Bartram's 45-acre farm on the grassy banks of the Schuylkill River provides a unique and fun outdoor classroom for quality education programs in natural history, colonial history, and environmental science. Seasonal programs including tree identification, cider-making, botanical illustration, apiculture, ornithology, colonial food preparation, medicinal herbs, and more. COST: Fee. REGION: Philadelphia County, South East PA.

BOWMAN'S HILL WILDFLOWER PRESERVE, 1635 River Rd., New Hope, PA 18938. Tel: 215-862-2924. Hrs: Daily 9AM-5PM. Self-guided Tours, Guided Tours. 134 acres featuring hundreds of species of native plants, in a setting of woodlands, meadows, a pond and a creek. A group tour of Bowman's Hill Wildflower Preserve is an ideal way to bring classroom lessons to life. Tours will be geared to the needs of your class, with an emphasis on the Academic Standards for Environment and Ecology. Some of our popular programs include "Seed Study", "Trees" and "Exploring Wetlands." "Feed the Birds" is always a winner with pre-school and kindergarten groups. COST: Fee. REGION: Bucks County, South East PA.

BENJAMIN RUSH MEDICINAL PLANT GARDEN, The College of Physicians of Philadelphia, 19 S. 22nd St., Philadelphia, PA 19103. Tel: 215-563-3737. Hrs: Daily 10AM-5PM. 4th-12th grade. Self-guided Tours, Guided Tours. The garden contains more than fifty different kinds of herbs, illustrating their medicinal value historically, as well as their value in contemporary medical therapy. COST: Fee. REGION: Philadelphia County, South East PA.

CAMDEN CHILDREN'S GARDEN, 3 Riverside Dr., Camden, NJ 08103. Located on the Camden Waterfront across from Philadelphia. Tel: 856-365-8733. Fax: 856-365-9750. Email: info@camdenchildrensgarden.org. Website: www.CamdenChildrensGarden.org. Hrs: 10AM-4PM. Contact: Cate Rigoulot. GRADE LEVEL: Pre K-8th. GROUP TYPE: All youth groups. PROGRAM TYPE: Day Trips, Self-guided Tours, Guided Activities, Workshops. MAX. GROUP SIZE: 500. MIN. GROUP SIZE: 10. REGISTRATION: Mail, Phone, Prepay. FOOD: Can bring own food, Beverages available. RECOMM. LENGTH OF VISIT: 2 hours. RECOMM. RATIO OF STUDENT TO STAFF: 5:1. ARRIVAL TIPS: Bus Parking, Bus drop off and pick up at designated entrance. COST: $6.00 Child; Group Rate $5.50 for additional chaperones. (See main listing in New Jersey on page 49 and Regional Highlights on page 13.) REGION: Camden County, Southern NJ.

LONGWOOD GARDENS, US Rte. 1, PO Box 501, Kennett Square, PA 19348. Tel: 610-388-1000. Fax: 610-388-2294. Email: mjennings@longwoodgardens.org. Website: www.longwoodgardens.org. Hrs: Daily 9AM-5PM. Contact: Michelle Jennings. GRADE LEVEL: All grades. GROUP TYPE: All youth groups. PROGRAM TYPE: Self-guided Tours, Guided Tours, Self-guided Activities, Guided Activities. MIN. GROUP SIZE: 15. REGISTRATION: Mail, Phone, Fax. FOOD: Variety of menu selections, Vegetarian, Can bring own food, Place to eat on site, Beverages available, Meal vouchers. RECOMM. LENGTH OF VISIT: 2-3 hours. RECOMM. RATIO OF STUDENT TO STAFF: 10:1. ARRIVAL TIPS: Expedite check in, Bus parking. COST: $5.00 per student.

Longwood Gardens is a place of unparalleled beauty, offering a new experience every day of the year with one-of-a kind events, wonderful concerts, and delicious fine and casual cuisine. Our exciting School & Youth Programs nurture student curiosity while focusing on learning. Our hands-on curriculum-based programs are cultivated to expand learning beyond the classroom walls! Tailored to grades K-12, each 90 minute program features people and places that are unique to Longwood, while connecting to national education standards for learning. We look forward to welcoming you and your students for an unforgettable day of learning and fun at Longwood Gardens! SUPPORTS PA STATE & NATIONAL LEARNING STANDARDS IN: The Arts, English, Math, History/Social Studies, Language Arts, Science. SUPPORTS SCOUT MERIT BADGE ACHIEVEMENT IN: The Arts, Social Studies, Science/Technology. (See Philadelpia Featured City Page on page 235 and Regional Highlights on page 13.) REGION: Chester County, South East PA.

THE MARYWOOD UNIVERSITY ARBORETUM, 2300 Adams Ave., Scranton, PA 18509. Tel: 570-348-6218. Hrs: Daily, sunrise to sunset. Self-guided Tours, Guided Tours. 42 species of trees that contain 103 varieties, and a comparable number of shrubs, as well as ornamental grasses, perennial, biennial and annual blooms. COST: Free. REGION: Lackawanna County, North East PA.

CAVES & MINES

CRYSTAL CAVE PARK, 963 Crystal Cave Rd., Kutztown, Pennsylvania 19530. Tel: 610-683-6765. Hrs: Vary. Guided Tours. Discovered in 1871, Crystal Cave is Pennsylvania's oldest operating cave. View milky white stalactites, stalagmites, and dropstone formations. COST: Fee. REGION: Berks County, PA.

LACKAWANNA COUNTY COAL MINE, McDade Park, Scranton, PA 18504. Tel: 800-238-7245, Tickets: 570-963-6463. Hrs: Daily 10AM-4:30PM. Guided Tours. Explore 300 feet beneath the earth, an anthracite coal mine originally opened in 1860. COST: Fee. REGION: Lackawanna County, North East PA.

LINCOLN CAVERNS, INC., 7703 William Penn Hwy. (US Rte. 22), Huntingdon, PA 16652. Tel: 814-643-0268. Hrs: Vary. Guided Tours. Explore winding passageways and rooms containing massive flowstones, thousands of delicate stalactites, pure white calcite and sparkling crystals. COST: Fee. REGION: Huntingdon County, Central PA.

LOST RIVER CAVERNS, 726 Durham St., Hellertown, Pennsylvania 18055. Tel: 610-838-8767. Hrs: Memorial Day-Labor Day 9AM-6PM, Remainder of the year 9AM-5PM. Five cavern chambers have an abundance of stalactites, stalagmites, and other crystal formations along with fluorescent minerals. COST: Fee. REGION: Northampton County, PA.

PIONEER TUNNEL COAL MINE & STEAM TRAIN, Rts. 61 & 54, Ashland, PA 17921. Tel: 570-875-3850. Hrs: Vary. Guided Tours. Visit a real Anthracite Coal Mine and take a ride on an old-fashioned narrow gauge Steam Train. COST: Fee. REGION: Schuylkill County, South East PA.

CHILDREN'S MUSEUMS

CHILDREN'S MUSEUM, 2 W. 7th St., Bloomsburg, PA 17815. Tel: 570-389-9206. Hrs: Tues-Sat. 10AM-4PM. Pre K-6th grade. Self-guided Tours. Offers interactive exhibits on various topics including health, art, science & history. COST: Fee. REGION: Columbia County, Central PA.

HANDS-ON HOUSE, CHILDREN'S MUSEUM OF LANCASTER, 721 Landis Valley Rd., Lancaster, PA 17601. Tel: 717-569-KIDS. Hrs: Mon.-Thurs. & Sat. 10AM-5PM, Fri. 10AM-8PM, Sun. 12-5PM. Pre K-2nd grade. Self-guided Tours. Features interactive exhibits which encourage learning through play and imagination. COST: Fee. REGION: Lancaster County, South East PA.

PETER J. MCGOVERN LITTLE LEAGUE MUSEUM, 525 U.S. Rte. 15 Hwy., South Williamsport, PA 17702. Tel: 570-326-3607. Email: dhall@LittleLeague.org, jogurcak@LittleLeague.org. Website: www.LittleLeague.org/museum. Hrs: Labor Day-Memorial Day: Fri.-Sat. 10AM-5PM, Sun.-Thurs. appt. only; Memorial Day-Jun. 31: Mon., Thurs., Fri., Sat. 10AM-5PM, Sun. 12-5PM, Tues.-Wed. appt. only; Jul. 1-Labor Day: Mon.-Sat. 10AM-5PM, Sun. 12-5PM. Contact: Janice L. Ogurcak, Museum Director. GRADE LEVEL: All grades. GROUP TYPE: All youth groups & homeschoolers. PROGRAM TYPE: Day Trips, Self-guided Tours, Guided Tours. REGISTRATION: Online, Phone. FOOD: Can bring own food, Place to eat on site. RECOMM. LENGTH OF VISIT: 1.5-2 hours. RECOMM. RATIO OF STUDENT TO STAFF: 10:1. ARRIVAL TIPS: Bus parking, Bus drop off and pick up at designated entrance. COST: General Admission: $5 general, $3 senior citizens 62 yrs+, $1.50 children 13 yrs & under; group rates available.

The Peter J. McGovern Little League Museum includes many educational and fun displays. Learn how a glove is made, how much yarn goes into a baseball, and the history of equipment safety. Race the clock to time yourself running from home plate to first base. Don't miss the Hall of Excellence, a part of the museum dedicated to former Little Leaguers who have been successful in many fields, including George W. Bush, the first Little League graduate elected President of the United States. Smithsonian Institution Traveling Exhibition "Beyond Baseball: The Life of Roberto Clemente" scheduled for Fall 2010. SUPPORTS PA STATE & NATIONAL LEARNING STANDARDS IN: History. SUPPORTS SCOUT MERIT BADGE ACHIEVEMENT IN: Citizenship, Social Studies. REGION: Lycoming County, North Central PA.

PLEASE TOUCH MUSEUM at Memorial Hall, Fairmount Park, 4231 Ave. of the Republic, Philadelphia, PA 19131. Tel: 215-963-0667. Hrs: Mon.-Sat. 9AM-5PM, Sun. 11AM-5PM. Pre K-2nd grade. Self-guided Tours. Interactive exhibit zone, with varying themes. COST: Fee. REGION: Philadelphia County, South East PA.

FARMS • PICK-YOUR-OWN • MAZES

LINVILLA ORCHARDS, 137 W. Knowlton Rd., Media, PA 19063. Tel: 610-876-7116. Hrs: Vary. Pre K-3rd grade. PYO: Apples, berries, peaches, grapes, pears & vegetables. Straw bale and corn maze. COST: Fee. REGION: Delaware County, South East PA.

MAST FARMS, 242 Twin County Rd., Morgantown, PA 19543. Tel: 610-286-5537. Hrs: Mon, Thurs, Fri. 12-7PM; Sat 9AM-7PM. PYO: Pumpkins. COST: Fee. REGION: Lancaster County, South East PA.

SHADY BROOK FARM, 931 Stony Hill Rd., Yardley, PA 19067. Tel: 215-968-1670. Hrs: Vary. PYO: Berries, peaches, apples. COST: Fee. REGION: Bucks County, South East PA.

WEAVER'S ORCHARD & FARM MARKET, 40 Fruit Ln., Morgantown, PA 19543. Tel: 610-856-7300. Hrs: Vary. Pre K & K. PYO: Berries, cherries, peaches, apples. COST: Fee. REGION: Berks County, South East PA.

FIELD DAYS • RECREATION • SKATING

ADVENTURE SPORTS IN HERSHEY, 3010 Elizabethtown Rd., Hershey, PA 17033. Mailing address: 2905 Church Rd., Elizabethtown, PA 17022. Tel: 717-533-7479. Website: www.adventurehershey.com. Hrs: Open Apr.-Oct.; Memorial Day - Labor Day 10AM-10PM. May open for private parties of 50 or more in the off season. GRADE LEVEL: All grades. GROUP TYPE: All youth groups & homeschoolers. PROGRAM TYPE: Day Trips, Self-guided Activities. COST: Varies.

Adventure Sports in Hershey is a great way to fill in a two to five hour block of time. Our Family entertainment center features go-karts, bumper boats with squirt guns, scenic miniature golf with fountains and waterfalls, batting range for baseball and softball, golf driving range, golf instruction available, arcade and snack bar. Group and birthday parties packages available. Picnic pavilion. Some age and height restrictions apply. Minutes from Hershey attractions. Located on Route 743 just three miles south of Hershey. SUPPORTS PA STATE & NATIONAL LEARNING STANDARDS IN: Physical Education. SUPPORTS SCOUT MERIT BADGE ACHIEVEMENT IN: Sports & Games. (See Pennsylvania Dutch Country Featured Region Page on page 232.) REGION: Dauphin County, South East PA.

DOYLESTOWN ROCK GYM & ADVENTURE CENTER, 3853 Old Easton Rd., Doylestown, Pennsylvania 18902. Tel: 215-230-9085. Fax: 215-230-6920. Email: info@doylestownrockgym.com. Website: www.doylestownrockgym.com. Hrs: Mon.-Thurs. 4-10PM, Fri. 12-10PM, Sat. & Sun. 10AM-9PM. Contact: Dana Caracciolo. GRADE LEVEL: All grades. GROUP TYPE: All youth groups & homeschoolers. PROGRAM TYPE: Day Trips, Overnights/Retreats, Self-guided Activities, Guided Activities, Workshops. COST: Group packages are available.

The Doylestown Rock Gym & Adventure Center is the area's premier adventure facility, with over 12,000 sq ft of climbing area. You can walk in the door and start climbing for as little as $15. We offer group and private instructional packages. Other programs include birthday parties, climbing club, summer camp, and teambuilding programs. For even more excitement, join outside on the real rocks. Our expert guides provide you with a safe and enjoyable outing, no experience necessary. If you want to develop your skills further, we offer technical outdoor instruction. Start your climbing adventure today! SUPPORTS PA STATE & NATIONAL LEARNING STANDARDS IN: Physical Education. SUPPORTS SCOUT MERIT BADGE ACHIEVEMENT IN: Camping, Safety and Sports & Games. (See Bucks County Featured Region Page on page 213.) REGION: Bucks County, South East PA.

ICEWORKS SKATING COMPLEX, 3100 Dutton Mill Rd., Aston, PA 19014. Tel: 610-497-2200. Fax: 610-485-7540. Email: lshaw@iceworks.net. Website: www.iceworks.net. Hrs: Daily 6:30AM-1AM. Contact: Lisa Shaw, ext. 117. GRADE LEVEL: All grades. GROUP TYPE: All youth groups & homeschoolers. PROGRAM TYPE: Day Trips, Self-guided Activities, Guided Activities. COST: Varies.

IceWorks is a state-of-the-art four surface ice skating facility. We are located off I-95 just south of the Philadelphia International Airport and just north of Wilmington, Delaware. Our complex includes one Olympic rink and three NHL sized rinks. We offer two restaurants, two game rooms, hockey and figure skating pro shop, many party and banquet rooms. Open 363 days a year and approximately 20 hours a day. IceWorks can accommodate any size group and will customize your skating event to make it great. Discounts, fundraising programs, group tours/meals are available through group sales. Accommodations available at IceWorks' rates. SUPPORTS PA STATE & NATIONAL LEARNING STANDARDS IN: Physical Education. SUPPORTS SCOUT MERIT BADGE ACHIEVEMENT IN: Skating, Sports & Games. REGION: Delaware County, South East PA.

LEHIGH VALLEY PAINTBALL, 307 Swartley Rd., Hatfield, PA 19440. Tel: 215-997-7877. Email: info@lvpsouth.com. Website: www.lvpsouth.com. Hrs: Field hours: Thurs.-Sun. Contact: Mike Crotsley. GRADE LEVEL: All grades. GROUP TYPE: All youth groups. PROGRAM TYPE: Day Trips, Self-guided Activities. REGISTRATION: Phone. FOOD: Place to eat on site, Beverages available. ARRIVAL TIPS: Bus Parking. COST: Call for group rates.

We accommodate every type of player from beginner to experienced. We offer indoor/outdoor speedball fields, and over 25 acres of woodsball fields. Private groups including birthday parties, church groups, park & rec, corporate events, college and youth groups. We have a knowledgeable and trained staff with an emphasis on safety. You can contact us at www.lvpsouth.com or (215) 997-7877. SUPPORTS PA STATE & NATIONAL LEARNING STANDARDS IN: Physical Education. SUPPORTS SCOUT MERIT BADGE ACHIEVEMENT IN: Physical Ed/Recreation. (See Lehigh Valley Featured Region Page on page 223.) REGION: Montgomery County, South East PA.

STEEL ICE CENTER, 320 E. 1st St., Bethlehem, PA 18015. Tel: 610-625-4774. Fax: 610-625-4775. Email: aroesch@ptd.net. Website: www.steelicecenter.com. Hrs: Vary. Contact: Angela Roesch-Davis. GRADE LEVEL: All grades. GROUP TYPE: All youth groups & homeschoolers. PROGRAM TYPE: Day Trips, Guided Activities, Self-guided Activities. MAX. GROUP SIZE: None. COST: Varies.

The Steel Ice Center is the premier ice skating facility in the Lehigh Valley. At the Ice Center we have a dynamic mix of programs that will suit both beginner and advanced skaters. Our mission at the Ice Center is to provide an excellent skating experience by providing a clean, safe facility with well supported activities through attention to customer service. The Steel Ice Center is the perfect place for private or public school class trips. We tailor our programs to your group's specific needs and bring your group together for an experience you will never forget. SUPPORTS PA STATE & NATIONAL LEARNING STANDARDS IN: Physical Education. SUPPORTS SCOUT MERIT BADGE ACHIEVEMENT IN: Physical Ed/Recreation. REGION: Northampton County, South East PA.

WATER'S EDGE MINI GOLF, 230 North Ronks Rd., Bird-in-Hand, Pennsylvania 17505. Tel: 717-768-4653. Fax: 717-768-0203. Email: watersedgem@aol.com. Website: www.watersedgegolf.net. Hrs: 10AM-10PM. GRADE LEVEL: All grades. GROUP TYPE: All youth groups & homeschoolers. PROGRAM TYPE: Day Trips, Overnight Trips. REGISTRATION: Phone. FOOD: Place to eat on site, Beverages available. RECOMM. LENGTH OF VISIT: 1 hour. ARRIVAL TIPS: Bus Parking. COST: $6.75 per person.

Come to Water's Edge Mini Golf, two beautifully landscaped, water-filled miniature golf courses located in Bird-in-Hand, PA. Waters Edge is a family fun destination that is both challenging and relaxing. Come test your golf skills amid cascading waterfalls, gently rolling streams and serene ponds. Putt for par as you stroll through gardens bursting with colorful plants, shubbery and water, water everywhere. Then take a break in our spacious snack bar and arcade area, where friendly atmosphere and fast service make you feel right at home. Situated in the heart of lovely Lancaster County. SUPPORTS PA STATE & NATIONAL LEARNING STANDARDS IN: Physical Education. SUPPORTS SCOUT MERIT BADGE ACHIEVEMENT IN: Physical Ed/Recreation. (See Pennsylvania Dutch Country Featured Region Page on page 233.) REGION: Lancaster County, South East PA.

GROUP FRIENDLY RESTAURANTS

BUCA DI BEPPO. Locations: Allentown: 610-264-3389; Cherry Hill: 856-779-3288; East Norriton: 610-272-BUCA; Exton: 610-524-9939; Philadelphia: 215-545-2818; Reading: 610-374-3482; Pittsburgh-Robinson Town Centre: 412-788-8444; Pittsburgh-Station Square: 412-471-9463. Website: www.Bucadibeppo.com. Hrs: Daily, hrs vary. GROUP TYPE: All youth groups & homeschoolers. COST: Varies.

Buca di Beppo gets to the heart of fresh Italian cooking with recipes like Chicken Carbonara using imported Italian spaghetti. At Buca, we serve family-style food in two portion sizes. Buca Small feeds two to three and Buca Large feeds an average-size country. Well, actually it feeds four to six. At Buca, groups of all sizes and ages step into Little Italy and enjoy a variety of group menus to satisfy everyone's palate and budget. Whether you're celebrating a special occasion or planning a group event, Buca di Beppo is the perfect place for great Italian food and fun! (See Philadelphia Featured City Page on page 234.) REGION: Throughout PA.

DAVE AND BUSTER'S, Locations: 325 N. Columbus, Philadelphia, PA 19106. Tel: 215-413-1951; 500 W. Germantown Pike, Ste 2195, Plymouth Meeting, PA 19462. Tel: 610-832-9200; Franklin Mills Mall, 1995 Franklin Mills Circle, Philadelphia, Pennsylvania 19154. Tel: 215-632-0333. Website: www.daveandbusters.com. Hrs: Sales office, 9AM-6PM. GRADE LEVEL: K-12th. COST: Fee. (See main listing under Indoor Entertainment Centers on page 186, Philadelphia Featured City Page on page 234 and ad in New York City on page 96.) REGION: PA.

GENERAL PICKETT'S BUFFET, 571 Steinwehr Ave., Gettysburg, PA 17325. Tel: 717-334-7580. Fax: 717-334-3701. Email: gpbuffet@embarqmail.com. Website: www.generalpickettsbuffets.com. Hrs: 11AM-8PM. Contact: Deborah Pyles, Reservations Manager. GRADE LEVEL: All grades. GROUP TYPE: All youth groups & homeschoolers. Conveniently located 1/2 mile from the new Gettysburg Visitor's Center, General Pickett's Buffet features lunch and dinner buffets. COST: Special scout troop pricing. REGION: Adams County, PA.

HEALTH & NUTRITION

FIELD TRIP FACTORY, Telephone: 800-987-6409. Fax: 773-342-9513. Email: info@fieldtripfactory.com. Website: www.fieldtripfactory.com. Hrs: Mon.-Fri. 8AM-6PM. GRADE LEVEL: Pre K-6th. GROUP TYPE: All youth groups & homeschoolers. PROGRAM TYPE: Day Trips, Guided Tours. COST: Free.

Field Trip Factory offers free community-based field trips. Our learning adventures teach valuable life-skills including health and nutrition, science, responsibility and more. All field trips are grade and age appropriate, meet learning standards, enrich classroom curriculum for teachers and fulfill badge requirements for scouts. See what is available in your area at www.fieldtripfactory.com or call 1-800-987-6409. SUPPORTS STATE LEARNING STANDARDS IN: Health & Safety, Math, Physical Education, Science. SUPPORTS SCOUT BADGE ACTIVITIES IN: Health & Safety, Life Skills, Personal Fitness. (See ad on page 56.) REGION: Throughout all 50 states.

HISTORIC RAILROAD EXCURSIONS

NEW HOPE & IVYLAND RAILROAD, 32 Bridge St., New Hope, PA 18938. Tel: 215-862-2332. Fax: 215-862-2150. Website: www.newhoperailroad.com. Hrs: Jan.-Mar.: Weekends; Apr.-May: Fri., Sat. & Sun.; Memorial Day weekend-end of Oct.: Daily; Nov.: Fri., Sat., Sun; Dec.: Thurs-Sun. & the weeks around Christmas. GRADE LEVEL: Pre K-12th. GROUP TYPE: All youth groups & homeschoolers. PROGRAM TYPE: Day Trips, Guided Tours. COST: Group rates, School Rates, and Camp Rates available. Not valid with any other offer.

All aboard the New Hope & Ivyland railroad. Enjoy a 45 minute narrated train ride through the beautiful Hills and Valleys of Bucks County aboard one of our antique passenger cars. Seasonal theme trains include: Song & Story Hour, Easter Bunny Express, Halloween Trains, and Santa Trains. Boxed Lunches are available for picnicking before, during, and after your train ride. We are only 30 minutes away from popular destinations such as Sesame Place & Philadelphia. SUPPORTS PA STATE & NATIONAL LEARNING STANDARDS IN: Social Studies. SUPPORTS SCOUT MERIT BADGE ACHIEVEMENT IN: Social Studies. (See Bucks County Featured Region Page on page 213.) REGION: Bucks County, South East PA.

STEAMTOWN NATIONAL HISTORIC SITE, Lackawanna & Cliff Sts., Scranton, PA 18503. Tel: 570-340-5200. Hrs: Jan.-Apr.: 10AM-4PM; May-Dec.: 9AM-5PM. Train rides seasonal. Self-guided Tours, Guided Tours. Steamtown offers a Technology Museum and History Museum that explore the people, history, technology and lore of steam railroading, the Locomotion Shop and a short train excursion. COST: Fee. REGION: Lackawanna County, North East PA.

STOURBRIDGE LINE RAIL EXCURSIONS, Wayne County Chamber of Commerce, 32 Commercial St., Honesdale, PA 18431. Tel: 570-253-1960. Hrs: Vary. Guided Tours. Themed rides. COST: Fee. REGION: Wayne County, North East PA.

INDOOR AMUSEMENT CENTERS

ARNOLD'S FAMILY FUN CENTER, V2200 West Dr., Oaks, PA 19456. Tel: 610-666-0600. Fax: 610-666-1500. Website: www.arnoldsfamilyfuncenter.com. Hrs: See Website. Contact: Holly Brinton. GRADE LEVEL: All grades. GROUP TYPE: All youth groups & homeschoolers. PROGRAM TYPE: Day Trips, Self-Guided Activities. COST: No Entry Fee, pay as you go.

Arnold's Family Fun Center is Pennsylvania's premier indoor Family Fun Center. With 120,000 square feet of action-packed adventure, fun-seekers of all ages will enjoy endless excitement on rides such as Bumper Cars, Krazy Cars, and Moonbounces. Or, try a real challenge with a thrilling race on our Go-Karts. Arnold's offers an enormous selection of games, from a classic Pin Ball Arcade to Lasertag. Hungry? Arnold's offers a pizza buffet with exceptional pizzas, a gourmet soup and salad bar, and delicious desserts! SUPPORTS PA STATE & NATIONAL LEARNING STANDARDS IN: Physical Education. SUPPORTS SCOUT MERIT BADGE ACHIEVEMENT IN: Physical Ed/Recreation, Sports & Games. (See Philadelphia Featured City Page on page 234.) REGION: Montgomery County, South East PA.

DAVE AND BUSTER'S, Locations: 325 N. Columbus, Philadelphia, PA 19106. Tel: 215-413-1951; 500 W. Germantown Pike, Ste 2195, Plymouth Meeting, PA 19462. Tel: 610-832-9200; Franklin Mills Mall, 1995 Franklin Mills Circle, Philadelphia, PA 19154. Tel: 215-632-0333. Website: www.daveandbusters.com. Hrs: Sales office, 9AM-6PM. GRADE LEVEL: K-12th. GROUP TYPE: All youth groups & homeschoolers. PROGRAM TYPE: Self-guided Activities. REGISTRATION: Phone. FOOD: Variety of menu selections, Kosher, Vegetarian, Beverages available. RECOMM. LENGTH OF VISIT: 2-3 hours. RECOMM. RATIO OF STUDENT TO STAFF: 10:1 (before 2:30PM). ARRIVAL TIPS: Expedite check in, Bus parking. COST: Fee.

At Dave & Buster's your group will have a blast! Start out with a delicious meal and then move on to some games in our Million Dollar Midway. 18 lane bowling alley (only at Franklin Mills Mall.) Spend an hour with us, or a whole day - at Dave & Buster's it's your call! We have packages for groups of 20 to 2,000; so for your next outing come eat, party & play at Dave & Buster's – your students will thank you! SUPPORTS PA STATE & NATIONAL LEARNING STANDARDS IN: Physical Education. SUPPORTS SCOUT MERIT BADGE ACHIEVEMENT IN: Physical Ed/Recreation. (See Philadelphia Featured City Page on page 234 and ad in New York City on page 96.) REGION: PA.

OZZY'S FAMILY FUN CENTER, 5411 Pottsville Pike, Leesport, PA 19533. Tel: 610-926-6162. Email: info@playozzys.com. Website: www.playozzys.com. Hrs: Vary. Contact: Gary Seibert. GRADE LEVEL: All grades. GROUP TYPE: All youth groups. PROGRAM TYPE: Day Trips, Overnight Trips, Self-guided Activities, Guided Activities, Workshops. REGISTRATION: Phone. FOOD: Variety, Vegetarian, Place to eat on site, Beverages available, Meal vouchers. RECOMM. LENGTH OF VISIT: 4 hours. RECOMM. RATIO OF STUDENT TO STAFF: 15:1. ARRIVAL TIPS: Expedite check in, Bus Parking, Bus drop off and pick up at designated entrance. COST: Fee.

Along with Fun for Everyone, Ozzy's Family Fun Center, Leesport, PA, promotes Excitement and Challenges to anyone who treads on its 10 acres of activities. Whether it's Roller Skating, Laser Tag, Arcade Games, Mini Golf, Go-Karts, Bumper Boats, Chip-it Golf, Rock Climbing or Funsters Cafe there is something for everyone at Ozzy's. For more than 25 years, Ozzy's has been the funnest place in town. Ozzy's is also Berks County's number one Company Picnic Facility and Team Building Facilitators. No one is too old or too young to enjoy the year round plethora of activities at Ozzy's. Funtastic!! SUPPORTS PA STATE & NATIONAL LEARNING STANDARDS IN: Physical Education. SUPPORTS SCOUT MERIT BADGE ACHIEVEMENT IN: Life Skills, Personal Fitness, Physical Ed/Recreation. REGION: Berks County, South East PA.

INTERACTIVE LIVING HISTORY

AMERICAN CIVIL WAR MUSEUM, 297 Steinwehr Ave., Gettysburg, PA 17325. Tel: 717-334-6245. Hrs: Mar.-Dec.: Daily 9AM-5PM. Extended spring & summer hrs. Self-guided Tours. Presents the history of the Civil War era and Battle of Gettysburg with life-sized dioramas. Experience a re-creation of the Battle of Gettysburg in the digitally enhanced Battle room exhibit, followed by an animated Abraham Lincoln's deliverance of the Gettysburg Address. COST: Fee. REGION: Adams County, South Central PA.

BRANDYWINE BATTLEFIELD, 1491 Baltimore Pike, Chadds Ford, PA 19317. Tel: 610-459-3342. Hrs: Tues.-Sat. 9AM-5PM, Sun. 12-5PM. Guided Tours. Brings to life the largest engagement of the Revolutionary War between the Continental Army led by General George Washington and the British forces headed by General William Howe. COST: Fee. REGION: Delaware County, South East PA.

COLONIAL PENNSYLVANIA PLANTATION, 3900 North Sandy Flash Dr., Newtown Square, PA 19073. Tel: 610-566-1725. Hrs: Vary. Guided Tours, Workshops. Experience 18th century Pennsylvania farm life. 3rd grade & up. The 3 1/2 hour Sampler Workshop is the ultimate hands-on experience. Participants cook a colonial dessert over the open hearth, complete farm chores and make a colonial craft. Candle-making, stenciling, carding & spinning wool, a school lesson, and colonial toys are the current craft choices. COST: Fee. REGION: Delaware County, South East PA.

CORNWALL IRON FURNACE, 94 Rexmont Rd. Cornwall, PA 17016. Tel: 717-272-9711. Hrs: Tues.-Sat. 9AM-5PM, Sun. 12-5PM. 4th grade & up preferred. Guided Tours. Visit a fully intact 19th century charcoal fueled iron-making complex. COST: Fee. REGION: Lebanon County, South East PA.

EPHRATA CLOISTER, 632 W. Main St., Ephrata, PA 17522. Tel: 717-733-6600. Hrs: Mon.-Sat. 9AM-5PM, Sun. 12-5PM. Self-guided Tours, Guided Tours. One of America's earliest religious communities, the Ephrata Cloister was founded in 1732 by German settlers seeking spiritual goals rather than earthly rewards. COST: Fee. REGION: Lancaster County, South East PA.

GHOST TOUR OF PHILADELPHIA, 42 Main St., Monocacy, PA 19542. Tel: 610-587-8308. Fax: 866-692-9332. Email: ghosttour@ghosttour.com. Website: www.ghosttour.com. Hrs: Year round. GRADE LEVEL: 3rd-12th. GROUP TYPE: All youth groups & homeschoolers. PROGRAM TYPE: Day Trips, Guided Tours. MAX. GROUP SIZE: 250. REGISTRATION: Mail, Online, Phone. RECOMM. LENGTH OF VISIT: 2 hours. COST: Varies.

Ghost Tour of Philadelphia...Candlelight Walking Tour or Haunted Trolley in America's most historic...and most haunted city! Put some mystery in your history and watch it come alive on this entertaining adventure through Independence Park and Society Hill. Does Benjamin Franklin still linger at his old haunts? Who lurks in the chambers of Independence Hall? What beautiful woman awaits Benedict Arnold at the Powel House? Join us as we push aside the cobwebs for a unique and fascinating look at our nation's history. Allow 90 minutes. Also available: Ghost Tour of Lancaster, PA in the heart of the Pennsylvania Dutch Country 610-587-8308. SUPPORTS PA STATE & NATIONAL LEARNING STANDARDS IN: Government & History. SUPPORTS SCOUT MERIT BADGE ACHIEVEMENT IN: American Heritage. (See Philadelphia Featured City Page on page 235.) REGION: Philadelphia County, South East PA.

HISTORIC FARNSWORTH HOUSE INN GHOST/HISTORY TOURS & BUFFETS: 401 Baltimore St., Gettysburg, Pennsylvania 17325. Telephone: 717-334-8838. Email: farnsworthhousemarketing@comcast.net. Website: www.farnsworthhouseinn.com. Hrs: Vary. Contact: Rene Staub. GRADE LEVEL: All grades. GROUP TYPE: All youth groups & homeschoolers. PROGRAM TYPE: Day Trips, Guided Tours, Performances. REGISTRATION: Mail, Online, Phone. FOOD: Variety of menu selections, Vegetarian, Place to eat on site, Beverages available. RECOMM. LENGTH OF VISIT: Varies. RECOMM. RATIO OF STUDENT TO STAFF: 25:2. ARRIVAL TIPS: Expedite check in, Bus parking, Bus drop off and pick up at designated entrance. COST: Fee/Call for pricing.

One of the most recognized buildings in Gettysburg /over 100 bullet holes in house. One of the most haunted inns in America with variety of candlelight ghost walks & stories in cellar for anytime of day. They are the origins of Gettysburg Ghost Storytelling/Featured on Food Network, Discovery, History, Sci Fi, & Travel Channels. Vacant Chair Dinner Theatre offers buffet with period songs/superstitions & ghost stories. Historical presentations available including house tour or "The Soldier's Life". PA Dutch & period fare served by period dressed servers delivers Civil War dining experience. Buffets available for groups of 25 or more. Boxed lunches available for a day on the battlefield. On-site bus parking available. SUPPORTS PA STATE & NATIONAL LEARNING STANDARDS IN: History/Social Studies. SUPPORTS SCOUT MERIT BADGE ACHIEVEMENT IN: Social Studies. (See Gettysburg Featured City Page on page 218.) REGION: Adams County, South Central PA.

HISTORIC PHILADELPHIA, INC., 116 S. Third St., Philadelphia, PA 19106. Tel: 215-629-5801, ext. 209. Fax: 215-629-5814. E-mail: melissa@historicphiladelphia.org. Website: www.historicphiladelphia.org. Hrs: On demand. Contact: Melissa Nast. GRADE LEVEL: 4th-college. GROUP TYPE: All youth groups. PROGRAM TYPE: Day Trips, Overnight Trips, Guided Tours, Guided Activities, Performances. MAX. GROUP SIZE: 250. MIN GROUP SIZE: 20. COST: $15.00 - $71.00 (ask about complimentary policies).

Make History with Your Group! Don't just see the Liberty Bell & Independence Hall...Do it all! Historic Philadelphia's tours & performances make history exciting and fun with the Lights of Liberty sound & light show, Colonial Kids Quest, a "whodunit" with puppets, Founding Fathers & Famous Figures performances, The Condensed American Revolution - a comedic journey through our nation's birth and much more! Great for groups of all ages, Historic Philadelphia is guaranteed to entertain, educate and engage your students! Come to Historic Philadelphia, where History Speaks to You! SUPPORTS PA STATE & NATIONAL LEARNING STANDARDS IN: History/Social Studies. SUPPORTS SCOUT MERIT BADGE ACHIEVEMENT IN: Social Studies. (See Philadelphia Featured City Page on page 235 and Regional Highlights on page 14.) REGION: Philadelphia County, South East PA.

LIVING THE EXPERIENCE, 512 E. Strawberry St., Church Towne of Lancaster, PA 17602. Tel: 1-800-510-5899, ext. 113. Fax: 717-396-8382. Email: liveitbethel@aol.com. Website: www.bethelamelancaster.org. Hrs: Tues.-Fri. 10AM, 11AM, 1PM. Contact: Phoebe Bailey. GRADE LEVEL: 1st-8th. GROUP TYPE: Schools, religious youth groups, & homeschoolers. PROGRAM TYPE: Day Trips, Guided Tours, Guided Activities, Workshops, Films, Outreach Programs, Exhibits, Performances, Teacher Workshops, Book Readings, Lectures/Speakers. MAX. GROUP SIZE: 175. COST: $10 w/o meal & $16.50 with meal.

"Living The Experience"® is a reenactment of the Underground Railroad in Lancaster, PA. Our guests go back into the period of the 1800's, hearing inspiring stories as they participate in helping to tell the stories by standing in as historic figures and partici-pating as an enslaved African being brought over on a slave ship, then to auction, then to bondage, then to their freedom. Join us after the show for a wonderful Soulful meal. During dessert learn about the use of Spirituals & the encoded mes-sages hidden in them. SUPPORTS PA STATE & NATIONAL LEARNING STANDARDS IN: Social Studies, Communication Arts, and Theater. SUPPORTS SCOUT MERIT BADGE ACHIEVEMENT IN: Social Studies, Arts. (See Pennsylvania Dutch Country Featured Region Page on page 233 and Regional Highlights on page 14.) REGION: Lancaster County, South East PA.

OLD BEDFORD VILLAGE, 220 Sawblade Rd., Bedford, PA 15522. Tel: 814-623-1156. Hrs: Vary. Self-guided Tours, Guided Tours, Workshops. Experience what life was like in 18th and 19th century Pennsylvania. COST: Fee. REGION: Bedford County, South Central PA.

PETER WENTZ FARMSTEAD, Shearer Rd., Worcester, PA 19490. Tel: 610-584-5104. Hrs: Tues.-Sat. 10AM-4PM, Sun. 1-4PM. An 18th century living farmstead with farm animals. Guided Tours. COST: Fee. REGION: Montgomery County, South East PA.

QUIET VALLEY LIVING HISTORICAL FARM, 1000 Turkey Hill Rd., Stroudsburg, PA 18360. Tel: 570-992-6161. Hrs: Vary. Guided Tours, Workshops. Recreation of the life of the original Pennsylvania German family who lived on the farm from the 1760s to 1913. COST: Fee. REGION: Monroe County, North East PA.

ROTH LIVING FARM MUSEUM, Delaware Valley College, Rte. 202 & Hancock Rd., North Wales, PA 19454. Tel: 215-699-3994. Hrs: Vary. Guided Tours, Workshops. Dedicated to providing historical information on farming practices with an emphasis on 19th and early 20th-century farming through hands-on activities and demonstrations. COST: Fee. REGION: Montgomery County, South East PA.

SLEEPY HOLLOW OF GETTYSBURG CANDLELIGHT GHOST TOURS, Tel: 717-337-9322. Fax: 717-337-9327. Email: ghostwalks@embarqmail.com. Website: www.sleepyhollowofgettysburg.com. Hrs: Call for hours. GRADE LEVEL: All grades. GROUP TYPE: All youth groups & homeschoolers. PROGRAM TYPE: Day Trips, Guided Tours. COST: Fee.

Why just read about ghosts, wouldn't you rather look for them instead? Sleepy Hollow of Gettysburg Candlelight Ghost Tours allow you to walk into the realm of the unknown, escorted by a period dressed guide, back in time down the very streets soldiers walked over a century ago. Our storytellers, who have over 50 years of combined storytelling experience, share tales and legends that are blended with bits of human interest and historical fact, making them entertaining & educational for all ages. Our Ghost Walks have entertained very small groups to extremely large groups with completely unscripted, interactive storytelling. SUPPORTS PA STATE & NATIONAL LEARNING STANDARDS IN: History/Social Studies. SUPPORTS SCOUT MERIT BADGE ACHIEVEMENT IN: Social Studies. (See Gettysburg Featured City Page on page 218.) REGION: Adams County, South Central PA.

MULTICULTURAL

AFRICAN AMERICAN MUSEUM IN PHILADELPHIA, 701 Arch St., Philadelphia, PA 19106. Tel: 215-574-0380. Fax: 215-574-3110. Email: info@aampmuseum.org. Website: www.aampmuseum.org. Hrs: Tues.-Sat. 10AM-5PM, Sun. 12-5PM. GRADE LEVEL: All grades. GROUP TYPE: All youth groups & homeschoolers. MAX. GROUP SIZE: Varies. MIN. GROUP SIZE: 20. PROGRAM TYPE: Exhibits, Guided Tours, Self-guided Tours, Workshops. COST: Fee.

Enjoy a face-to-face encounter with the bold and fearless people who helped form our nation with "Audacious Freedom: African Americans in Philadelphia 1776-1876, presented by PECO" at the African American Museum in Philadelphia. This state-of-the art exhibition employs innovative use of sound, light and cutting edge technology and is a must see on your trip to historic Philadelphia. Founded in 1976, the African American Museum in Philadelphia is the first institution funded and built by a major municipality to preserve, interpret and exhibit the heritage of African Americans. For more information call 215-574-0380 or visit www.aampmuseum.org. SUPPORTS PA STATE & NATIONAL LEARNING STANDARDS IN: History/Social Studies. SUPPORTS SCOUT MERIT BADGE ACHIEVEMENT IN: Social Studies. (See Philadelphia Featured City Page on page 234.) REGION: Philadelphia County, South East PA.

NATIONAL MUSEUM OF AMERICAN JEWISH HISTORY, Independence Mall East, 55 N. 5th St., Philadelphia, PA 19106. Tel: 215-923-3811. Hrs: Mon.-Thurs. 10AM-5PM, Fri. 10AM-3PM, Sun. 12-5PM. Self-guided Tours, Guided Tours, Workshops. Dedicated exclusively to collecting, preserving and interpreting artifacts pertaining to the American Jewish experience. COST: Fee. REGION: Philadelphia County, South East PA.

PEARL S. BUCK HOUSE, 520 Dublin Rd., Perkasie, PA 18944. Tel: 215-249-0100. Hrs: Vary. 1st-12th grade. Guided Tours, Workshops. Promotes the legacy of Pearl S. Buck and cross-cultural appreciation. COST: Fee. REGION: Bucks County, South East PA.

POCONO INDIAN MUSEUM, Rte. 209, Bushkill, PA 18324. Tel: 570-588-9164. Hrs: Seasonal. Self-guided Tours, Guided Tours. Focusing on the history of the Delaware Indian. COST: Free/Fee. REGION: Pike County, North East PA.

SHOFUSO: THE JAPANESE HOUSE AND GARDEN, Horticultural Dr., W. Fairmount Park, Philadelphia, PA 19131. Tel: 215-878-5097. Hrs: Vary. Guided Tours. Authentic 17th century style Japanese house and garden with koi pond. COST: Fee. REGION: Philadelphia County, South East PA.

MULTIDIMENSIONAL

THE FOLLOWING LISTINGS HAVE MULTIPLE FOCUSES IN THEIR EXHIBIT HALLS COVERING ANTHROPOLOGY, ART, SCIENCE, CULTURE, OR HISTORY.

EVERHART MUSEUM, 1901 Mulberry St., Scranton, PA 18510. Tel: 570-346-7186. Hrs: Mon., Thurs. & Fri. 12-4PM; Sat. 10AM-5PM; Sun. 12-5PM. Self-guided Tours, Guided Tours. Focuses on natural history, science and art with emphasis on northeast Pennsylvania's unique heritage. COST: Fee. REGION: Lackawanna County, South East PA.

STATE MUSEUM OF PENNSYLVANIA, 300 North St., Harrisburg, PA 17120. Tel: 717-787-4979. Hrs: Tues.-Sat. 9AM-5PM, Sun. 12-5PM. Self-guided Tours. Three floors of exhibits on archaeology, history, and art, plus planetarium. COST: Fee. REGION: Dauphin County, South East PA.

WHITAKER CENTER FOR SCIENCE AND ARTS, Harsco Science Center, 222 Market St., Harrisburg, PA 17101. Tel: 717-214-ARTS. Hrs: Tues.-Sat. 9:30AM-5PM, Sun. 11:30AM-5PM. Pre K-12th grade. Self-guided Tours, Guided Tours. Three floors of hands-on galleries and traveling exhibits in science and art. COST: Fee. REGION: Dauphin County, South East PA.

PLANETARIUMS

Please call for planetarium show times. Experience a realistic and scientifically accurate simulation of the night sky in a domed theater.

FRANKLIN INSTITUTE SCIENCE MUSEUM, 222 N. 20th St., Philadelphia, PA 19103. Tel: 215-448-1200. COST: Fee. REGION: Philadelphia County, South East PA.

READING PUBLIC MUSEUM, 500 Museum Rd., Reading, PA 19611-1425. 610-371-5850. COST: Fee. REGION: Berks County, South East PA.

STATE MUSEUM OF PENNSYLVANIA, 300 North St., Harrisburg, PA 17120. Tel: 717-787-4979. COST: Fee. REGION: Dauphin County, South Central PA.

SCIENCE & ENVIRONMENTAL EDUCATION

ACADEMY OF NATURAL SCIENCES, 1900 Benjamin Franklin Pkwy., Philadelphia, PA 19103. Tel: 215-299-1000. Hrs: Mon.-Fri. 10AM-4:30PM, Sat. & Sun. 10AM-5PM. Self-guided Tours, Guided Tours, Workshops. Natural history museum. COST: Fee. REGION: Philadelphia County, South East PA.

BUCKS COUNTY AUDUBON SOCIETY, HONEY HOLLOW ENVIRONMENTAL EDUCATION CENTER, 2877 Creamery Rd., New Hope, PA 18938. Tel: 215-297-5880. Hrs: Mon.-Fri. 9AM-5PM. Guided Tours. Located on the Honey Hollow Watershed in Solebury Township. Dedicated to conserving wildlife, promoting awareness of environmental problems, watching birds, understanding the interdependence of humans and their world. COST: Fee. REGION: Bucks County, South East PA.

BUSHKILL FALLS, Rte. 209 Bushkill Falls Rd., Bushkill, PA 18324. Tel: 570-588-6682. Hrs: Seasonal. Self-guided Tours. Series of eight waterfalls, towering 100-foot Main Falls, nestled deep in the wooded Pocono Mountains, is accessible through a network of hiking trails and bridges. COST: Fee. REGION: Pike County, North East PA.

DA VINCI SCIENCE CENTER, 3145 Hamilton Blvd. Bypass, Allentown, PA 18103. Tel: 484-664-1002, ext. 121. Fax: 484-664-1002. Email: ContactUs@davinci-center.org. Website: www.davinci-center.org. Hrs: Mon.-Sat. 9:30AM-5PM., Sun. 12-5PM. Contact: Guest Services. GRADE LEVEL: Pre K-8th. GROUP TYPE: All youth groups. PROGRAM TYPE: Day Trips, Self-guided Tours, Guided Tours, Workshops. REGISTRATION: Phone, Prepay. TICKET/VOUCHER RETURN POLICY: Contact Guest Services for information. FOOD: Can bring own food, Place to eat on site, Beverages available. RECOMM. LENGTH OF VISIT: 3-4 hours. RECOMM. RATIO OF STUDENT TO STAFF: 5:1 for Pre K-2nd grade; 10:1 for 3rd grade and up. ARRIVAL TIPS: Expedite check in, Bus Parking, Bus drop off and pick up at designated entrance. COST: School Groups of 10 or more: $7.95 per student.

Science comes alive for students at the Da Vinci Science Center when they explore the robotic dinosaur, freeze their shadow on a wall, touch live ocean animals, and deliver their own weather forecast. The Center's exciting programs and hands-on exhibits engage students in captivating experiences seldom available in the classroom and reinforce PDE science and math assessment anchors. Boxed Chick-fil-A lunches available for advanced purchase by school groups (min. 15 lunches). For more information, visit www.davinci-center.org. SUPPORTS PA STATE & NATIONAL LEARNING STANDARDS IN: Math, Science. SUPPORTS SCOUT MERIT BADGE ACHIEVEMENT IN: Science/Technology. (See Lehigh Valley Featured Region Page on page 223.) REGION: Lehigh County, South East PA.

DELAWARE RIVER STEAMBOAT FLOATING CLASSROOM, Lamberville, NJ & New Hope, PA. Telephone: 609-921-6612. Fax: 609-258-1113. Email: info@SteamboatClassroom.org. Website: www.SteamboatClassroom.org. Hrs: by Appt. Contact: Professor Bart Hoebel. GRADE LEVEL: All grades. GROUP TYPE: All youth groups & homeschoolers. PROGRAM TYPE: Day Trips, Guided Tours, Workshops. MAX. GROUP SIZE: 49 per boat trip, AM/PM trips - 98 per day. REGISTRATION: Mail, Online, Phone, Submit waiver forms prior to visit. FOOD: Can bring own food, Place to eat on site. RECOMM. LENGTH OF VISIT: 3-5 hours. RECOMM. RATIO OF STUDENT TO STAFF: 5:1. ARRIVAL TIPS: Bus parking. COST: $19/person, $695 minimum, subsidies may be available.

Come to the steamboat "SPLASH" (acronym for "Student Participation in Learning Aquatic Science & History"). As the whistle blows, this authentic stern-wheeler goes on a 2-hr voyage of fun and learning, featuring environment-based science, social studies and technology. SPLASH is a Coast Guard certified steamboat, boarding in Lambertville NJ. Students, scouts and campers will hear the story of Washington's crossing the Delaware River, see where canal boats crossed, wildlife flourishes and millions of people get drinking water. SPLASH carries 49 passengers, with special activities for school, camp or youth groups, featuring clean-water ecology, including interactive watershed model, invertebrate identification, water physics, water safety, bird spotting, historical role-playing. SUPPORTS NJ STATE & NATIONAL LEARNING STANDARDS IN: Science, History. SUPPORTS SCOUT MERIT BADGE ACHIEVEMENT IN: Electricity, Environmental Science, Water. REGIONS: Central NJ & Bucks County PA, NYC & Philadelphia.

FLORENCE SHELLY PRESERVE, Rte. 171, Thompson, PA 18465. Tel: 570-756-2429. Hrs: Daily dawn-dusk. Self-guided Tours, Guided Tours. 300 acres of fields, woodlands, a stream, and a glacial pond surrounded by a floating bog. COST: Free. REGION: Susquehanna County, North East PA.

FRANKLIN INSTITUTE SCIENCE MUSEUM, 222 N. 20th St., Philadelphia, PA 19103. Tel: 215-448-1200. Hrs: 9:30AM-5PM. Exhibits on science and technology. COST: Fee. REGION: Philadelphia County, South East PA.

POCONO ENVIRONMENTAL EDUCATION CENTER, RR2, Box 1010, Dingman's Ferry, PA 18328. Tel: 570-828-2319. Fax: 570-828-9695. Email: peec@ptd.net. Website: www.peec.org. Hrs: Daily. GRADE LEVEL: All grades. GROUP TYPE: All youth groups. PROGRAM TYPE: Day Trips, Overnights/Retreats, Guided Activities, Outreach, Teacher Workshops. REGISTRATION: Mail, Online, Phone. FOOD: Variety of menu selections, Kosher, Vegetarian, Place to eat on site, Beverages available. RECOMM. LENGTH OF VISIT: 1-5 days. RECOMM. RATIO OF STUDENT TO STAFF: 14:1. ARRIVAL TIPS: Bus parking, Bus drop off and pick up at designated entrance. COST: Varies.

PEEC is a special place for students, teachers, scouts, families and groups interested in learning about the natural world in a beautiful setting. Day and residential programs offer a unique well-rounded experience for everyone! Participants enjoy pond and stream explorations, interpretive nature programs, astronomy, field studies, bird watching, outdoor recreation, energy and sustainability studies, team building and more. Outreach for local schools. Facility Rentals, Conference, Retreat & Reunion opportunities with new modern facilities and meeting rooms. For more information, call PEEC at (570) 828-2319 or visit www.peec.org. PEEC is close to home, where learning comes "naturally!" SUPPORTS NJ, NY, PA CURRICULUM: Physical Ed/Recreation, Science. SUPPORTS SCOUT MERIT BADGE ACHIEVEMENTS: Physical Ed/Recreation, Science. REGION: Pike County, North East PA.

LANCASTER SCIENCE FACTORY, 454 New Holland Ave., Lancaster, PA 17602. Tel: 717-509-6363. Hrs: Tues.-Sat. 10AM-5PM, Sun. 12-5PM. Summer: Mon.-Sat. 10AM-5PM & Sun. 12-5PM. 3rd-8th grade. Self-guided Tours. Exhibits relating to the physical sciences, engineering, technology and mathematics. COST: Fee. REGION: Lancaster County, South East PA.

PENN'S CAVE AND WILDLIFE PARK, 222 Penns Cave Rd., Centre Hall, PA 16828. Tel: 814-364-1664. Hrs: Daily 9AM-7PM. Guided Tours. Water cavern and wildlife park. COST: Fee. REGION: Centre County, Central PA.

UNIVERSITY OF PENNSYLVANIA MUSEUM OF ARCHAEOLOGY AND ANTHROPOLOGY, 3260 South St., Philadelphia, PA 19104. Tel: General: 215-898-4000; Group Tours: 215-746-6774. Hrs: Tues.-Sat. 10AM-4:30PM, Sun. 1-5PM. Self-guided Tours, Guided Tours, Workshops. Three gallery floors feature materials from ancient Egypt, Mesopotamia, the Bible Lands, Mesoamerica, Asia and the ancient Mediterranean World, as well as artifacts from native peoples of the Americas, Africa and Polynesia. COST: Fee. REGION: Philadelphia County, South East PA.

WAGNER FREE INSTITUTE OF SCIENCE, 1700 W. Montgomery Ave., Philadelphia, PA 19121. Tel: 215-763-6529. Hrs: Tues.-Fri. 9AM-4PM. A natural history museum. Guided Tours. COST: Free. REGION: Philadelphia County, South East PA.

SOCIAL STUDIES

AARON AND JESSICA'S BUGGY RIDES, 3121 Old Philadelphia Pike (Rte. 340), Bird-in-Hand, PA 17505. Tel: 717-768-8828. Email: aaron.n.jessica@hotmail.com. Website: www.amishbuggyrides.com. Hrs: Apr.-Nov.: Mon.-Sat. 8AM-Sunset; Dec.-Mar.: Mon.-Sat. 10AM-4:30PM. Contact: Aaron Petersheim. GRADE LEVEL: All grades. PROGRAM TYPE: Day Trips, Guided Tours, Guided Activities. MAX. GROUP SIZE: 500. COST: $6 for students and teachers.

Aaron and Jessica's Buggy Rides is operated by Amish, Mennonite and Brethren. Our regular ride passes by an Amish village and through our cousin's Amish farm. We offer 5 different routes of 3 to 4 miles and longer rides as well. All the farms you pass on our regular ride are Amish farms. No other ride can offer you that. You see real Amish life. Our basic ride lasts about 25 to 35 minutes long with knowledgeable drivers who are real horsemen, who will guide your tour and answer your questions. Also enjoy home made cookies, pretzels, lemonade and root beer! SUPPORTS PA STATE & NATIONAL LEARNING STANDARDS IN: History/Social Studies. SUPPORTS SCOUT MERIT BADGE ACHIEVEMENT IN: Social Studies. (See Pennsylvania Dutch Country Featured Region Page on page 232.) REGION: Lancaster County, South East PA.

AMISH FARM & HOUSE, 2395 Rte. 30 East, Lancaster, PA 17602. Tel: 717-394-6185. Hrs: Seasonal. Self-guided Tours, Guided Tours. Focuses on historical and contemporary Amish culture in Lancaster. COST: Fee. REGION: Lancaster County, South East PA.

ANTHRACITE HERITAGE MUSEUM, 22 Bald Mountain Rd., McDade Park, Scranton, PA 18504. Tel: 570-963-4804. Hrs: Mon.-Sat. 9AM-5PM, Sun. 12-5PM. Guided Tours. Tells the story of the people who came from Europe to work in the anthracite mining and textiles industries. COST: Fee. REGION: Lackawanna County, North East PA.

ARTILLERY RIDGE CAMPGROUND, 610 Taneytown Rd., Gettysburg, PA 17325. Tel: 717-334-1288. Fax: 717-334-0855. Email: artilleryridge@comcast.net. Hrs: 8AM-9PM. Website: www.artilleryridge.com. Contact: Susan Conover. GRADE LEVEL: All grades. GROUP TYPE: All youth groups. PROGRAM TYPE: Day Trips, Overnight Trips, Guided Tours, Guided Activities. REGISTRATION: Mail, Phone, Submit Waiver Forms. FOOD: Can bring own food, Beverages available. RECOMM. RATIO OF STUDENT TO STAFF: 5:1. ARRIVAL TIPS: Bus Parking, Bus drop off and pick up at designated entrance. COST: Different pricing options available.

We are the closest camping to the Battlefield. We have full service sites as well as a group tenting area. We offer horseback riding on the battlefield. A 1 hour trail ride or a 2 hour history tour also available. While camping and riding with us you get a complimentary Diorama showing the entire Battlefield in miniature with a 35 minute light and sound show. We also offer camping with your own horse. We have 19 covered boxstalls over 20 two horse corrals and 25 single corrals all close to camp sites. For reservations please call 1-717-334-1288 for camping or riding and 1-717-334-6408 for Diorama. SUPPORTS PA STATE & NATIONAL LEARNING STANDARDS IN: History/Social Studies, Physical Education. SUPPORTS SCOUT MERIT BADGE ACHIEVEMENT IN: Camping, Social Studies, Physical Ed/Recreation. (See Gettysburg Featured City Page on page 218.) REGION: Adams County, South Central PA.

BETSY ROSS HOUSE, 239 Arch St., Philadelphia, PA 19106. Tel: 215-686-1252. Hrs: Daily 10AM-5PM. Self-guided Tours. Tour the home of America's most famous Flagmaker and learn about her life and times. COST: Fee. REGION: Philadelphia County, South East PA.

CAPITOL, 3rd St. & State St., Harrisburg, PA 17120. For a free tour of Pennsylvania's Capitol building & State Supreme Court, call General Assembly's Office of Capitol Visitor Services at 800-TOUR-N-PA. Hrs: Mon.-Fri. 8:30AM-4PM, Sat.-Sun. tours at 9AM, 11AM, 1PM, 3PM. Self-guided Tours, Guided Tours. Tours subject to change without notice. Reserve your tour as far in advance as possible. Allow 40 minutes for a tour. Explore the Pennsylvania government at work by visiting the Welcome Center at the Capitol. Learn about the Pennsylvania Government—and have fun in the process—by reading, listening, touching, and interacting with 18 colorful and informative exhibits. To arrange a meeting with your local representative or his/her staff, call your representative's office 4-8 weeks in advance. Tel: 717-787-2372 for representatives' contact information. COST: Free. REGION: Dauphin County, South Central PA.

DANIEL BOONE HOMESTEAD, 400 Daniel Boone Rd., Birdsboro, PA 19508. Tel: 610-582-4900. Hrs: Mar.-Dec.: Tues.-Sat. 9AM-5PM, Sun. 12-5PM; Jan.-Feb.: Sat. 9AM-5PM, Sun. 12-5PM. 2nd-12th grade. Self-guided Tours, Guided Tours. Tells the story of Daniel's youth and the saga of the region's 18th century settlers by contrasting their lives and cultures. COST: Fee. REGION: Berks County, South East PA.

ECKLEY MINERS' VILLAGE, 2 Eckley Main St., Weatherly, PA 18255. Tel: 570-636-2070. Hrs: Mon.-Sat. 9AM-5PM, Sun. 12-5PM. 2nd-12th grade. Guided Tours. Preserves the life of a company mining towns built in the anthracite region of Pennsylvania during the 19th century. COST: Fee. REGION: Luzerne County, North East PA.

EDGAR ALLAN POE NATIONAL HISTORIC SITE, 532 N. 7th St., Philadelphia, PA 19123. Tel: 215-597-8780. Hrs: Wed.-Sun. 9AM-5PM. 6th-12th grade. Guided Tours. A 3-building complex where Poe lived from 1843-1844. His life and work are portrayed through a tour, an exhibit area and a short video. COST: Free. REGION: Philadelphia County, South East PA.

EISENHOWER NATIONAL HISTORIC PARK, 1195 Baltimore Pike, Gettysburg, PA 17325. Tel: 717-338-9114. Hrs: Daily 9AM-4PM. Guided Tours. The home and farm of President Dwight D. Eisenhower. Located adjacent to the Gettysburg Battlefield, the farm served the President as a weekend retreat and a meeting place for world leaders. COST: Fee. REGION: Adams County, South Central PA.

ELFRETH'S ALLEY & MUSEUM, 124-26 Elfreth's Alley, Philadelphia, PA 19106. Tel: 215-574-0560. Hrs: Nov.-Feb.: Thurs.-Sat. 10AM-5PM, Sun. 12-5PM; Mar.-Oct.: Tues.-Sat. 10AM-5PM, Sun. 12-5PM. Guided Tours. Consists of 32 historic houses, dating back to the first days of the eighteenth century. Learn about Philadelphia's working class households in the 18th & 19th centuries. The Museum tells several unique stories about early Philadelphia, revealing the lives of early American women, workers, and the transformations that came with the age of factories and industry. COST: Fee. REGION: Philadelphia County, South East PA.

FORT MIFFLIN ON THE DELAWARE, Fort Mifflin & Hog Island Rds., Philadelphia, PA 19153. Tel: 215-685-4167. Hrs: Wed-Sun. 10AM-4PM. Guided Tours, Performances. The only Revolutionary War battlefield completely intact includes 14 authentic restored buildings. COST: Fee. REGION: Philadelphia County, South East PA.

HALL OF PRESIDENTS AND FIRST LADIES, 789 Baltimore St., Gettysburg, PA 17325. Tel: 717-334-5717. Hrs: Seasonal. Self-guided Tours, Guided Tours. A wax gallery of presidents and their wives. Through light and sound, the wax figures tell the story of America from their perspective. COST: Fee. REGION: Adams County, South Central PA.

INDEPENDENCE NATIONAL HISTORICAL PARK, 143 South 3rd St., Philadelphia, PA 19106. Tel: 215-965-2305. Hrs: Seasonal. Self-guided Tours, Guided Tours. The site of Benjamin Franklin's home includes an underground museum, which highlights the life and accomplishments of Ben Franklin. COST: Free/Fee. REGION: Philadelphia County, South East PA.

INDEPENDENCE NATIONAL HISTORICAL PARK & VISITOR CENTER, 520 Market St., between 5th St. and 6th St., Philadelphia, PA 19106. Tel: 215-965-2305. Reservations: 877-444-6777. Hrs: Seasonal. 4th-12th. Self-guided Tours, Guided Tours. Arrange for a guided tour of the historical park, the scene of the adoption of the Declaration of Independence and drafting of the United States Constitution. The Visitor Center contains exhibits and 2 films: "Independence," a 28-minute film on the call for independence and the drafting of the Constitution and "Choosing Sides," a 20-minute film based on diaries and historical accounts depicting the thoughts and feelings of young people as they reflect on the Revolutionary War and their freedom. COST: Free/Fee. REGION: Philadelphia County, South East PA.

INDEPENDENCE SEAPORT MUSEUM, Penn's Landing Waterfront, 211 S. Columbus Blvd. & Walnut St., Philadelphia, PA 19106. Tel: 215-413-8630. Hrs: Daily 10AM-5PM. Self-guided Tours, Guided Tours, Workshops. Showcases the region's maritime history with two floors of exhibit galleries, a wooden boat workshop, the National Historic Landmark 1892 Cruiser Olympia and the WWII Submarine Becuna. COST: Fee. REGION: Philadelphia County, South East PA.

THE LIBERTY BELL & CENTER: INDEPENDENCE NATIONAL HISTORICAL PARK, 526 Market St., between 6th St. and Market St., Philadelphia, PA 19106. Tel: 215-965-2305. Hrs: Seasonal. Self-guided Tours, Guided Tours. The Center offers a video presentation and exhibits about the Liberty Bell, focusing on its origins and its modern day role as an international icon of freedom. The Liberty Bell itself is displayed in a magnificent glass chamber. COST: Free/Fee. REGION: Philadelphia County, South East PA.

NATIONAL CONSTITUTION CENTER, 525 Arch St., Independence Mall, Philadelphia, PA 19106. Tel: 866-917-1787. Hrs: Mon.-Fri. 9:30AM-5PM, Sat. 9:30AM-6PM, Sun. 12-5PM. Guided Tours. The only museum devoted to the U.S. Constitution and its impact on American history. COST: Fee. REGION: Philadelphia County, South East PA.

NATIONAL LIBERTY MUSEUM, 321 Chestnut St., Philadelphia, PA 19106. Tel: 215-925-2800, ext. 144. Fax: 215-925-3800. Email: tours@libertymuseum.org. Website: www.libertymuseum.org. Hrs: Tues.-Sun. 10AM-5PM, daily in summer. Contact: Education Dept., ext. 129. GRADE LEVEL: All grades. GROUP TYPE: All youth groups & homeschoolers. PROGRAM TYPE: Day Trips, Guided Tours, Workshops. MAX. GROUP SIZE: 140. COST: Varies.

The National Liberty Museum was created to help defuse violence and bigotry by celebrating America's heritage of freedom and the wonderful diverse society it has produced. The Museum honors the accomplishments of 2,000 men, women, and young people of every background and nationality; teaches character education and peaceful solutions to conflict; and highlights the rights and responsibilities of living in a democracy. Your students will see eight galleries of exhibits, interactives, videos and art, including a collection of beautiful, contemporary glass sculptures that serves as a metaphor for the fragility of freedom. Other popular exhibits include two life-size children made entirely of jelly beans; a shredder machine that devours cruel worlds; a polling station with electronic voting equipment and much more. The National Liberty Museum also offers Teacher Training for educators and is available for facility rentals for groups large and small. SUPPORTS PA STATE & NATIONAL LEARNING STANDARDS IN: Social Studies. SUPPORTS SCOUT MERIT BADGE ACHIEVEMENT IN: Understanding Yourself and Others, Citizenship in the Community. (See Philadelphia Featured City Page on page 235.) REGION: Philadelphia County, South East PA.

RAILROAD MUSEUM OF PENNSYLVANIA, 300 Gap Rd., Strasburg, PA 17579. Tel: 717-687-8628. Hrs: Mon.-Sat. 9AM-5PM (closed Mon. Nov.-Mar), Sun. 12-5PM. Self-guided Tours, Guided Tours. Displays over 100 locomotives and cars from the mid-19th and 20th centuries and houses one of the most significant collections of historic railroad artifacts in the world. COST: Fee. REGION: Lancaster County, South East PA.

VALLEY FORGE NATIONAL HISTORICAL PARK, 1400 N. Outer Line Dr., King of Prussia, PA 19406. Tel: 610-783-1077. Education: 610-783-1066. Hrs: Grounds open daily 6AM-10PM; Museum open daily 9AM-5PM. The newly renovated Washington's Headquarters was the place where General George Washington and his staff lived and worked for the six months of the Valley Forge winter encampment is open for tours. The historical Park includes a Visitors Center, the Muhlenberg Brigade encampment; Knox Estate (Park Library); Varnum's Quarters; Washington Memorial Chapel. The Park also includes 3,500-acres with a variety of habitats that students can explore. COST: Free/Fee. REGION: Chester and Montgomery Counties, South East PA.

THEATER · DANCE · MUSIC

AMERICAN MUSIC THEATRE, 2425 Lincoln Hwy. East, PO Box 10757, Lancaster, PA 17605. Tel: 717-397 700. Hrs: 10:30AM or schedule a schooltime performance. Guided Tours, Performances. COST: Fee. REGION: Lancaster County, South East PA.

DUTCH APPLE DINNER THEATRE, 510 Centerville Rd., Lancaster, PA 17601. Hrs: Vary. Performances. Broadway style show for middle and high school students. The Theatre for Young Audiences, for Pre K and elementary program is available four times each year featuring classic stories and traditional fairy tales. Both include a buffet lunch. COST: Fee. REGION: Lancaster County, South East PA.

THE PAPER BAG PLAYERS, 225 W. 99th St., New York, NY 10025. Performance locations: Bethelem, Philadelphia, Glenside, Upper Darby. Tel: 800-777-2247/212-663-0390. Fax: 212-663-1076. Email: pbagp@verizon.net. Website: thepaperbagplayers.org. Hrs: Vary. GRADE LEVEL: K–3rd. GROUP TYPE: All youth groups & homeschoolers. PROGRAM TYPE: Performances. COST: Varies. (See ad and main listing in New York City on page 125.) REGION: Philadelphia County, Northampton County, Montgomery County, Delaware County.

THE PHILADELPHIA ORCHESTRA SCHOOL CONCERTS, 260 South Broad St., Philadelphia, PA 19102. Hrs: Vary. Website: www.philorch.org/schoolconcerts. GRADE LEVEL: 3rd-8th. GROUP TYPE: All youth groups. PROGRAM TYPE: Day Trips, Performances. REGISTRATION: Online, Prepay, Tickets mailed prior to visit. FOOD: No food offered. TICKET/VOUCHER RETURN POLICY: The Orchestra must have a confirmed number of paid participants 4 weeks before the concert date. ARRIVAL TIPS: Bus Parking, Bus drop off and pick up at designated entrance. COST: $8 per person.

Held on weekdays, Philadelphia Orchestra School Concerts are 45-minute programs open to school groups and homeschools throughout the Greater Philadelphia Area. For the 2009-10 school year, the Orchestra introduces a new, single-concert format created in collaboration with area music and classroom teachers, school administrators, and teaching artists. Join host Jamie Bernstein as she guides your students through an interactive performance designed to inspire, entertain, and educate. Concert Dates: 10/23/09, 12/1/09, 1/27/10, 2/9/10, 3/2/10. SUPPORTS PA STATE & NATIONAL LEARNING STANDARDS IN: The Arts, English, History/Social Studies, Language Arts. SUPPORTS SCOUT MERIT BADGE ACHIEVEMENT IN: The Arts, Performing Arts. REGION: Philadelphia County, South East PA.

OVERNIGHTS & RETREATS

OVERNIGHTS & RETREATS

ADIRONDACK MOUNTAIN CLUB, PO Box 867, Lake Placid, New York 12946. Tel: 518-523-3480 Ext. 19. Fax: 518-523-3518. Email: workshops@adk.org. Website: www.adk.org. Hrs: Year Round. Contact: Ryan Doyle, Group Outreach Coordinator. Grade Level: All grades. Group TYPE: All youth groups, Homeschoolers. PROGRAM TYPE: Day Trips, Overnight Trips, Retreats, Guided Activities. COST: Varies.

The Adirondack Mountain Club (ADK) works with groups year-round creating programs centered around responsible recreation, outdoor skills, environmental literacy, reflective writing, natural history, and most importantly, developing a healthy, active lifestyle. All programs offer the chance to develop self-reliance, outdoor skills, responsibility, teamwork, confidence, compassion, and environmental stewardship. SUPPORTS NY & NATIONAL STATE LEARNING STANDARDS IN: Science, Physical Education. SUPPORTS SCOUT MERIT BADGE ACHIEVEMENT IN: Science. REGION: Essex County, Adirondacks NY.

BEAR CREEK CAMP, PO Box 278, Bear Creek, PA 18602. Tel: 570-472-3741. Fax: 570-472-3742. Email: campinfo@bearcreekcamp.org. Website: www.bearcreekcamp.org. Hrs: 9AM-5PM. Contact: Tracey O'Day. GRADE LEVEL: All grades. GROUP TYPE: All youth groups. PROGRAM TYPE: Day Trips, Overnight Trips. MAX. GROUP SIZE: 92. MIN. GROUP SIZE: 15. REGISTRATION: Mail, Online, Phone. TICKET/VOUCHER RETURN POLICY: Varies, deposit non-refundable. FOOD: Variety, Vegetarian, Can bring own food, Place to eat on site, Beverages available. RECOMM. LENGTH OF VISIT: 1 day-1 week. RECOMM. RATIO OF STUDENT TO STAFF: 8:1. ARRIVAL TIPS: Bus Parking, Bus drop off and pick up at designated entrance. COST: Contact for more details.

With our 3,000 acres we have a wide variety of habitats and programming opportunities for children to "get-away" and enjoy time in a beautiful, pristine natural setting. Our programs center on children using experiential programs, and nurture opportunities for growth in leadership skills. We offer Environmental Programming, High and Low Ropes, and a lake with swimming and watercraft. Open to all groups regardless of race, creed, or religious affiliation, we have a variety of levels of housing, from platform tents to enclosed cabins. We take reservations up to 18 months in advance. We also have a full summer residential program from late June through mid August. SUPPORTS PA STATE & NATIONAL LEARNING STANDARDS IN: Science. SUPPORTS SCOUT MERIT BADGE ACHIEVEMENT IN: Science. REGION: Luzerne County, North East PA.

BRYN MAWR RETREAT AND CONFERENCE CENTER, 593 Bryn Mawr Rd., Honesdale Pennsylvania 18431. Tel: 570-253-8900. Fax: 570-253-1342. Email: eventcenter@brynmawrmountain.com. Website: www.brynmawrmountain.com. Hrs: Sep.-June. Contact: Corie Beilman or Pilar Beam. GRADE LEVEL: All grades. GROUP TYPE: All youth groups and homeschoolers. PROGRAM TYPE: Overnights/Retreats, Self-guided Activities, Guided Activities, Workshops, Special Events/Festivals. MAX. GROUP SIZE: 500. COST: Varies.

Nestled high in the hills of beautiful Wayne County, Bryn Mawr Mountain Retreat & Conference Center is a destination of choice for school trips. Dozens of schools visit Bryn Mawr each year for outdoor experience, teambuilding and character development programs. Students learn teamwork, problem-solving and critical thinking skills that they take back to the classroom to help them approach learning and leadership in new ways. Activities include hiking, biking, kayaking, ropes course, talent shows, campfires, dances, boat races, and much more. We are pleased to offer a variety of programs that will meet your school's specific needs. Our flexible curricula and facilities allow us to accommodate any age group at any time of year. SUPPORTS PA STATE & NATIONAL LEARNING STANDARDS IN: Physical Education. SUPPORTS SCOUT MERIT BADGE ACHIEVEMENT IN: Physical Ed/Recreation, Team Building. REGION: Wayne County, North East PA.

CAMP SPEERS-ELJABAR YMCA, 143 Nichecronk Rd., Dingmans Ferry, PA 18328. Tel: 570-828-2329. Fax: 570-828-2984. Email: speerys@campspeersymca.org. Website: www.campspeersymca.org. Contact: Cherie Hammond. GRADE LEVEL: All grades. GROUP TYPE: School, Scout, After-school. PROGRAM TYPE: Overnights/Retreats, Guided Activities, Workshops. MAX. GROUP SIZE: 400. REGISTRATION: Mail, Online, Phone. FOOD: Variety of menu selections, Vegetarian. RECOMM. LENGTH OF VISIT: 2 nights/3 days. RECOMM. RATIO OF STUDENT TO STAFF: 12:1. ARRIVAL TIPS: Expedite check in, Bus parking, Bus drop off and pick up at designated entrance. COST: Fee.

Our extensive facilities and close proximity to the Philadelphia and NYC areas make us the ideal location for school, club, church, family, college, and recreation groups of all kinds. 1,100 acres of mountain woodlands feature a 100 acre bog, a 42 acre spring fed glacial lake, miles of trails, fields and more to create the perfect setting. Log cabins (some with in-cabin showers & toilets) can accommodate up to 14 people. Other log cabin style buildings provide a variety of indoor spaces. Spring & Fall activities include climbing towers, high ropes, horseback riding, team building, conflict resolution, cultural diversity, wildlife ecology, animal tracking, canoeing and more. Winter activities include cross country skiing, ice skating & fishing, stargazing, winter habitat studies, and more. Campfires, night hikes and nature presentations fill the evenings with fun. Our professional staff customize programs to meet your needs. SUPPORTS PA STATE & NATIONAL LEARNING STANDARDS IN: Physical Education, Science. SUPPORTS SCOUT MERIT BADGE ACHIEVEMENT IN: Camping, Physical Ed/Recreation, Science/Environmental, Team Building. REGION: Pike County, North East PA.

CAPE COD SEA CAMPS, 3057 Main St. / PO BOX 1880, Brewster, MA 02631. Tel: 508-896-3451. Fax: 508-896-8272. Email: groups@capecodseacamps.com. Website: www.capecodfieldtrips.com. Hrs: 9AM-4PM, year round. Contact: Garran Peterson. GRADE LEVEL: All grades. GROUP TYPE: All youth groups. PROGRAM TYPE: Day Trips, Overnight Trips, Self-guided Tours, Self-guided Activities, Workshops. MAX. GROUP SIZE: 700. MIN. GROUP SIZE: 20. REGISTRATION: Mail, Phone, Submit Waiver Forms, Prepay. FOOD: Variety, Vegetarian, Can bring own food, Place to eat on site, Beverages available. RECOMM. RATIO OF STUDENT TO STAFF: 10:1. ARRIVAL TIPS: Bus Parking, Bus drop off and pick up at designated entrance. COST: Per Person Rates.

The Cape Cod Sea Camps provides group rentals April – June & August - October and have been catering to school groups, educational tours, sports camps, and retreat groups for well over 30 years, offering full meals and accommodations on Cape Cod! With 60 acres of property and 600 feet of beachfront right on Cape Cod Bay, our location offers an excellent outdoor classroom for interactive science lessons. In addition, there are local whale watches, the Cape Cod National Seashore, Woods Hole Oceanographic Institute, Plimoth Plantation, Pilgrim Monument, and much more! Come explore Cape Cod! SUPPORTS MA STATE & NATIONAL LEARNING STANDARDS IN: English, History/Social Studies, Physical Education, Science. SUPPORTS SCOUT MERIT BADGE ACHIEVEMENT IN: Physical Ed/Recreation, Social Studies, Science/Environmental. (See Plymouth/Cape Cod Featured Region Page on page 236.) REGION: Barnstable County, South East MA.

DEER RUN CAMP & RETREAT CENTER, 450 Walker Valley Rd., Pine Bush, NY 12566. Tel: 845-733-5494. Fax: 845-733-5471. Email: info@campdeerrun.org. Website: www.campdeerrun.org. Contact: Camp Director. GRADE LEVEL: 3rd-college. GROUP TYPE: All youth groups & homeschoolers. PROGRAM TYPE: Day Trips, Overnights/Retreats, Guided Activities. MAX. GROUP SIZE: 100. COST: Varies.

Deer Run Camp & Retreat Center provides access to 110 rustic acres of rolling hills, woodlands, meadows, marshes and streams in the southern Catskill region, less than 2 hours driving time from New York City. The camp offers comfortable living and dining accommodations March-November, plus classroom and conference facilities and a small theater. Activities include traditional recreation, plus evidence-based Youth-Development programs centered on our extensive high and low ropes challenge course, climbing wall, environmental education and hiking trails. In addition, Deer Run's Total Adventure Zone™ offers a variety of fun, exciting adventure activities both on-site and off-site. Team-Building, Personal-Development, Drug-Prevention workshops offered. ACA accredited. Licensed by the N.Y.S. Dept. of Health. SUPPORTS NY STATE LEARNING STANDARDS IN: Science, Physical Education. SUPPORTS SCOUT MERIT BADGE ACHIEVEMENT IN: Environmental Science, Sports & Games. REGION: Sullivan County, Catskills Region NY.

DIAMOND RIDGE CONFERENCE CENTER, PO Box 297, Jamison, PA 18929. Tel: 215-343-8840. Fax: 215-343-8849. Email: info@diamondridgeconferencecenter.com. Website: www.diamondridgeconferencecenter.com. Hrs: Daily. Contact: Steven Bernstein. GRADE LEVEL: All grades. GROUP TYPE: All youth groups. PROGRAM TYPE: Day Trips, Overnight Trips, Guided Activities. MAX. GROUP SIZE: 225. MIN. GROUP SIZE: 35. REGISTRATION: Mail, Phone. FOOD: Variety of menu selections. COST: Varies.

Diamond Ridge Conference Center is available mid-August through mid-June for recreational class trips, team building programs and school retreats. Our 33-acre campus is located approximately 1 hour and 45 minutes from NYC and 1 hour from Philadelphia. We can accommodate 225 guests in comfortable cabins and semi-private lodges. Our popular team building programs, led by professional facilitators, combine high ropes, low ropes and group initiatives. Diamond Ridge offers a number of environmental education, outdoor adventure and orienteering programs. SUPPORTS PA STATE & NATIONAL LEARNING STANDARDS IN: Geography, Physical Education, Science. SUPPORTS SCOUT MERIT BADGE ACHIEVEMENT IN: Physical Ed/Recreation, Orienteering, Science. REGION: Bucks County, South East PA.

ECOLOGY VILLAGE NATIONAL PARK SERVICE, GATEWAY NATIONAL RECREATION AREA, Bldg. 70, Floyd Bennett Field, Brooklyn, NY 11234. Tel: 718-338-4306. Hrs: By appt. 5th-12th grade. Overnight Trips, Guided Activities. An environmentally focused overnight camping experience for schools, scouts and non-profit youth groups that promotes team building. Teachers/Scout Leaders must attend workshop to prepare students for this experience. COST: Free/Fee for camping. REGION: Kings County, NYC.

Offers students in grades 4-8 the only curriculum-based overnight camping program in the New York City. During the camping trip, students explore nature in the urban outback, prepare meals outdoors, practice teamwork, and participate in hands-on environmental stewardship. This inquiry-based program has recently been revised to reflect NYC learning standards, as well as new scope and sequence in science. A free 30-hour training course is required to bringing classes camping at Ecology Village. Programmatic and logistical information and instruction will be provided by National Park Service Rangers and NYC DOE teachers to ensure that the camping experience is enriching and educational for your students and meets classroom learning objectives. Topics covered include: Camping skills, logistics, and safety; Team-building techniques; Pre- and post-visit environmental and marine science activities; Introduction to onsite student programs.

FAIRVIEW LAKE YMCA CAMPS, 1035 Fairview Lake Rd., Newton, NJ 07860. Tel: 800-686-1166. Fax: 973-383-6386. Email: fairviewlake@metroymcas.org. Website: www.fairviewlakeymca.org. Hrs: Daily. GRADE LEVEL: All grades. GROUP TYPE: School, Scout, Weekend. PROGRAM TYPE: Day Trips, Overnights/Retreats, Guided Activities, Workshops. MAX. GROUP SIZE: 325. REGISTRATION: Mail, Phone. FOOD: Variety of menu selections, Vegetarian, Can bring own food, Place to eat on site, Beverages available. RECOMM. LENGTH OF VISIT: 1-5 days. RECOMM. RATIO OF STUDENT TO STAFF: 15:1. COST: Varies.

We design programs to meet each groups' specific environmental education, conference, or recreational needs and budget. Then we inject the right amount of cooperation, enthusiasm, and the expertise you need to have a successful trip. Six hundred acres of unspoiled woodlands, a 110-acre lake, running streams, open fields, modern cabins, meeting rooms, an outdoor amphitheater, an outdoor sports complex, and excellent food service merge to create an unparalleled site for fun and learning. Offering highlights: Boating, High and Low Ropes, three climbing walls, archery, arts and crafts, campfires, and cross country skiing. Environmental studies include Animals, Apple Cidering, Biology, Birding, Botany, Colonial Period, Critical Thinking Skills, Geology, Maple Sugaring, Multicultural, Native American Indians, Natural Resources, Observation Skills, Recycling, Water Cycle, and Weather. We also do Teacher Workshops and Outreach Programs to schools including a portable planetarium. Facility Rental. Visit our website at www.fairviewlake.org for in-depth information or call for a brochure. SUPPORTS NJ & NY STATE CURRICULUM IN: Physical Education, Science. REGION: Sussex County, Northern NJ.

FROST VALLEY YMCA, 2000 Frost Valley Rd., Claryville, NY 12725. Tel: 845-985-2291. Fax: 845-985-0056. Email: info@frostvalley.org. Website: www.FrostValley.org. Hrs: Daily. Contact: Environmental Education Director. GRADE LEVEL: 1st-college. GROUP TYPE: All youth groups & homeschoolers, School. PROGRAM TYPE: Day Trips, Overnight Trips, Guided Activities, Workshops. MAX. GROUP SIZE: 420 (overnight), 80 (day). REGISTRATION: Mail, Phone. FOOD: Kosher, Vegetarian, Place to eat on site, Beverages available. RECOMM. RATIO OF STUDENT TO STAFF: 10:1. COST: Varies.

Frost Valley YMCA is located in New York State's Catskill Mountains Region, 2-1/2 hours from NYC. Year round programs and activities take place at our 6,000 acre camp with the goal of promoting a sense of environmental stewardship. We specialize in outdoor/experiential education and offer leadership through team building programs for all ages and abilities. Seasonal maple sugaring, ice cutting, apple cidering. Frost Valley also offers Summer Camp, Weekend Family Getaways and Conferencing facilities, Adventure Trips, Corporate Team-Building, Leadership and Teacher's Training. SUPPORTS NY, NJ & NATIONAL STATE LEARNING STANDARDS IN: Science, Math, and Physical Education, Wellness, Adventures Sports and Outdoor Exploration. SUPPORTS SCOUT MERIT BADGE ACHIEVEMENT IN: Environmental Science and Equestrian Arts. REGION: Sullivan & Ulster Counties, Catskills Region NY.

JERRY'S 3 RIVER CAMPGROUND, P.O. Box 7, 2333 Rte. 97, Pond Eddy, NY 12770. Tel: 845-557-6078. Fax: 845-557-0878. Website: www.jerrys3rivercampground.com. Hrs: Vary. Contact: Pete Lovelace. GRADE LEVEL: 3rd-college. GROUP TYPE: All youth groups & homeschoolers. PROGRAM TYPE: Day Trips, Overnight Trips, Self-guided Activities. MAX. GROUP SIZE: 350. River trips range from 3 hours to 3 days depending on your schedule. Riverfront & brookside campsites, include two Pavilions with water and electric, lean-to's, spacious tents, RV Sites, 2 shower houses. On premise recreation canoeing, rafting, volleyball, horseshoes & 1/2 mile river front for fishing (nearby rental of fishing equipment & license). All outdoor activities have inherent risks, waivers required. Family owned and operated for 40-plus years. Competitive rates. COST: Varies. (See main listing on page 132.) REGION: Sullivan County, Catskills Region NY.

KITTATINNY CANOE, Main Office: 378 Routes 6 & 209, Milford, PA 18337. Locations: NY: Barryville; Pond Eddy. PA: Dingman's Ferry; Matamoras; Milford; Smithville Beach. NJ: Delaware-Water-Gap. Tel: 800-FLOAT-KC (356-2852). Email: floatkc@warwick.net. Website: www.kittatinny.com. Hrs: April-Oct. Office for info & reservations open year round. GRADE LEVEL: 4 yrs/40 pounds and up. GROUP TYPE: All youth groups & homeschoolers. PROGRAM TYPE: Day Trips, Overnight Trips, Guided Tours, Self-guided Activities. COST: Varies. (See main listing under Adventure Sports in New York State on page 132 and Regional Highlights on page 16.) REGION: NY, PA, NJ.

POLLACE'S RESORT, 71 Landon Ave., Catskill, NY 12414. Tel: 518-943-3710. Fax: 518-943-7725. Email: fun@pollaces.com. Website: www.pollaces.com. Hrs: Vary. Contact: Charlie Serro. GRADE LEVEL: All grades. GROUP TYPE: All youth groups & homeschoolers. PROGRAM TYPE: Day Trips, Overnight Trips, Guided Tours, Guided Activities, Performances. MAX. GROUP SIZE: 100. REGISTRATION: Mail, Online, Phone. FOOD: Variety, Vegetarian, Place to eat on site, Beverages available. ARRIVAL TIPS: Expedite check in, Bus Parking, Bus drop off and pick up at designated entrance. COST: Varies.

This is the land of Rip van Winkle, the historic Hudson River, and the majestic Catskill Mts. This area has been the inspiration for famous authors, artists, historians, ecologists and such. Your overnight or day trip will include a visit and tour of our historic and educational sites, Living World Animal Wildlife Show, group activities, delicious meals and overnight accommodations at Pollace's Resort. See our website for details - www.pollaces.com, and click on bus trips. The Pollace family would like to have their facility become your field trip destination. Let us personalize your trip with the many educational and exciting activities available. SUPPORTS NY STATE & NATIONAL LEARNING STANDARDS IN: The Arts, History/Social Studies. SUPPORTS SCOUT MERIT BADGE ACHIEVEMENT IN: The Arts, Social Studies. (See Catskills Featured Region Page on page 214.) REGION: Greene County, Catskills Region NY.

QUINIPET CAMP & RETREAT CENTER, 99 Shore Rd./PO Box 549, Shelter Island Heights, NY 11965. Tel: 631-749-0430. Fax: 631-749-3403. Email: info@quinipet.org. Website: www.quinipet.org. Hrs: Daily. Contact: Director of Environmental and Adventure Programming. GRADE LEVEL: 2nd-college. GROUP TYPE: All youth groups. PROGRAM TYPE: Day Trips, Overnight Trips, Self-guided Tours, Guided Activities, Workshops. MAX. GROUP SIZE: 175 (overnight) 90 (day). MIN. GROUP SIZE: 25. REGISTRATION: Phone, Submit waiver forms. FOOD: Variety, Can bring own food. RECOMM. LENGTH OF VISIT: 1-4 day overnight trips. RECOMM. RATIO OF STUDENT TO STAFF: 12:1. ARRIVAL TIPS: Bus Parking. COST: Varies.

Quinipet Camp & Retreat is located on picturesque Shelter Island just a brief ferry ride away from the North Fork or Sag Harbor on the South Fork. Year round programs and activities take place at our waterfront retreat facility with planned excursions to nearby Shelter Island and East End locations. We specialize in outdoor experiential education with a focus on environmental education, marine studies and teambuilding programs. We have an aquaculture project, low ropes course and real rock climbing onsite. Quinipet also offers summer camp, sailing programs and year round retreat rentals. SUPPORTS NY STATE & NATIONAL LEARNING STANDARDS IN: Math, History/Social Studies, Physical Education, Science. SUPPORTS SCOUT MERIT BADGE ACHIEVEMENT IN: Physical Ed/Recreation. REGION: Suffolk County, LI.

RHODES GROVE CAMP & CONFERENCE CENTER, 7693 Browns Mill Rd., Chambersburg, PA 17202. Tel: 717-375-4162. Fax: 717-375-4634. Email: info@rhodesgrove.com. Website: www.rhodesgrove.com. Hrs: Vary. Contact: Angela Monn. GRADE LEVEL: All grades. GROUP TYPE: All youth groups. PROGRAM TYPE: Overnight Trips, Self-guided Activities, Guided Activities. MAX. GROUP SIZE: 300. REGISTRATION: Online, Phone, Submit Waiver Forms, Prepay. FOOD: Variety, Vegetarian, Place to eat on site, Beverages available. RECOMM. LENGTH OF VISIT: Varies. RECOMM. RATIO OF STUDENT TO STAFF: Varies. ARRIVAL TIPS: Expedite check in, Bus Parking, Bus drop off and pick up at designated entrance. COST: Varies.

Rhodes Grove is a naturally pleasing center. Nestled in the beautiful Cumberland Valley of South-Central, PA we are located in a quaint farming village with nostalgic charm but just minutes off Interstate-81 with plentiful amenities. Our environment offers a satisfying combination of peaceful retreat facilities and modern conveniences and recreational activities. A value packed experience, expectations are surpassed through excellent facilities, superior food service, and on call staff. Our rates are sensible, competitive and all-encompassing. Come join our community of fellowship, renewal and enrichment. SUPPORTS SCOUT MERIT BADGE ACHIEVEMENT IN: Camping, Citizenship, Family Life, Health & Safety, Life Skills, Personal Fitness, Physical Ed/Recreation, Safety. (See Gettysburg Featured City Page on page 218.) REGION: Franklin County, South Central PA.

VACAMAS PROGRAMS FOR YOUTH, 256 Macopin Rd., West Milford, NJ 07480. Tel: 973-838-2568. Fax: 973-838-7534. Email: conference@vacamas.org. Website: www.vacamas.org. Hrs: Year Round, 24 hrs/day depending on residential or day trips. Contact: Conference Center Coordinator. GRADE LEVEL: All grades. GROUP TYPE: All youth groups & homeschoolers. PROGRAM TYPE: Day Trips, Overnight Trips, Workshops. MAX. GROUP SIZE: 400. COST: Fee. (See main listing under Field Days & Recreation in NJ on page 54.) REGION: Passaic County, Northern NJ.

WOODLOCH RESORT, RR 1 Box 280, Hawley, PA 18428. Tel: 800-784-3466. Fax: 570-685-8092. Email: kathy.hummel@woodloch.com. Website: www.woodloch.com. GRADE LEVEL: All grades. GROUP TYPE: All youth groups & homeschoolers. PROGRAM TYPE: Day Trips, Overnights/Retreats, Self-guided Activities, Guided Activities, Workshops. MAX. GROUP SIZE: 300. COST: Varies.

Woodloch Resort, nestled in the picturesque Northeast Pocono Mountains, extends an invitation for you to enjoy our stimulating class trip packages! Recognized by Better Homes & Gardens as "One of America's Best Resorts," Woodloch offers year-round excitement. Fun for all ages, enjoy our all-inclusive plans featuring lunch, indoor pool facilities and abundant group activities, such as go-carts, bumper cars and our beautiful lake with beachfront activities (weather permitting). Woodloch offers a special Spirit of Scouting program that focuses on competition, creativity and nature. Let your scouts earn their exclusive Woodloch patch! All of our packages may be customized. Let our professional staff help you coordinate a special experience designed especially for your group! SUPPORTS PA STATE NATIONAL LEARNING STANDARDS IN: Physical Education. SUPPORTS SCOUT MERIT BADGE ACHIEVEMENT IN: Created a "Woodloch Badge" with the Scouting Association-includes Art, Nature & Team Building. REGION: Pike County, North East PA.

**For additional information on trips and group savings
and special offers for youth groups please visit**

ClassTrips.com

YMCA CAMP SHAND, Box 339, Cornwall, PA 17016. Tel: 717-272-8001. Fax: 7I7-272-2633. Email: csmith@lancasterymca.org. Website: www.ymcacampshand.org. Hrs: Daily, year round. Contact: Christine Smith. GRADE LEVEL: All grades. GROUP TYPE: All youth groups. PROGRAM TYPE: Day Trips, Overnight Trips, Self-guided Activities, Guided Activities, Workshops. MAX. GROUP SIZE: 120. REGISTRATION: Online, Phone. FOOD: Variety, Vegetarian, Can bring own food, Beverages available. RECOMM. LENGTH OF VISIT: Varies. RECOMM. RATIO OF STUDENT TO STAFF: 8:1. ARRIVAL TIPS: Bus Parking. COST: Depends on services needed.

YMCA Camp Shand: Over 120 years of history make this beautiful wooded setting a wonderful place for all ages and group sizes. 120 acres of woods, fields and nature trails, private pond and streams. Adirondack style cabins accommodate up to 120 children and adults and offer modern bathroom facilities with private shower stalls. Full service dining hall. Activities range from canoeing, ropes course, rock wall climbing, hiking, environmental education programs, swimming, campfires, baseball, fishing, volleyball, basketball, talent shows. Groups can work on team and confidence building, and problem solving through a variety of activities. SUPPORTS PA STATE & NATIONAL LEARNING STANDARDS IN: Physical Education. SUPPORTS SCOUT MERIT BADGE ACHIEVEMENT IN: Camping, Life Skills, Physical Ed/Recreation. (See Pennsylvania Dutch Country Featured Region Page on page 233.) REGION: Lebanon County, South East PA.

ZOAR OUTDOOR, 7 Main St., Charlemont, MA 01339. Tel: 800-532-7483. Fax: 413-337-8436. Email: info@zoaroutdoor.com. Website: www.zoaroutdoor.com. Hrs: 9AM-5PM. Contact: Bruce Lessels. GRADE LEVEL: K-12th. GROUP TYPE: All youth groups & homeschoolers. PROGRAM TYPE: Day Trips, Overnight Trips, Self-guided Tours, Guided Tours, Self-guided Activities, Guided Activities, Performances, Workshops. REGISTRATION: Online, Phone, Prepay. TICKET/VOUCHER RETURN POLICY: More than 30 days in advance - $10 per person cancellation fee, 30 days or less in advance - cost forfeited. Money forfeited may not be applied to any outstanding balances. FOOD: Variety, Vegetarian, Place to eat on site, Beverages available. RECOMM. LENGTH OF VISIT: 1-5 days. RECOMM. RATIO OF STUDENT TO STAFF: 8:1. ADMISSION: Expedite check in, Bus Parking, Bus drop off and pick up at designated entrance. COST: Fee.

Zoar Outdoor is New England's Outdoor Adventure Resort, offering whitewater rafting, canoeing, kayaking, zip line canopy tours, fly fishing, biking and rock climbing on the Deerfield River in western Massachusetts. Our friendly professional staff, comfortable base camp with onsite camping and lodging and top-notch equipment ensure that your adventure will be memorable. From half-day family raft trips to week-long whitewater kayak clinics we can match your schedule and your desire for adventure. SUPPORTS MA STATE & NATIONAL LEARNING STANDARDS IN: Physical Education. SUPPORTS SCOUT MERIT BADGE ACHIEVEMENT IN: Physical Ed/Recreation. (See Berkshires Featured Region Page on page 210 and Regional Highlights on page 17.) REGION: Franklin County, North West MA.

DESTINATIONS

- Baltimore
- Berkshires
- Boston
- Bucks County
- Catskills
- Coastal Maine
- Disney Youth Group Programs
- Gettysburg
- Kennebec
- Lake Champlain
- Lake George
- Lehigh Valley
- Lincoln Center
- New London
- New York City
- Orlando/Kissimmee
- Pennsylvania Dutch Country
- Philadelphia
- Plymouth/Cape Cod
- Salem
- Tampa
- Virginia: Highlights
- Washington, D.C.
- Wilmington

BALTIMORE HIGHLIGHTS

Where learning and fun is around every corner. For further information please contact: Baltimore Tourism Association - www.baltimoretourism.com.

BALTIMORE SPIRIT CRUISES, 561 Light St., Baltimore, MD 21202. A unique Baltimore educational experience! Baltimore Spirit Cruises has a variety of student-friendly cruises replete with food, music and history aboard our vessels. The Spirit of Baltimore and Inner Harbor Spirit sail from berths in the Inner Harbor in front of the new Visitors Center. Enjoy our  2 hr buffet lunch cruise, or 3 hr buffet dinner cruises. All with a DJ! Or take our 1 hour educational sightseeing tours of the historic Inner Harbor. 800-695-BOAT. www.spiritcruises.com.

GEPPI'S ENTERTAINMENT MUSEUM AT CAMDEN YARDS, 301 W. Camden St., Baltimore, Maryland 21201. Take a memorable trip through the history of American pop culture. Experience a timeline of nostalgic toys, comics and other collectibles highlighting familiar characters. Interactive exhibits include cast iron mechanical banks, famous comic book stories and vintage radio clips. The Mickey Mouse, Superman, Elvis, Barbie, G.I. Joe and others mark historic milestones. 410-625-7060. www.geppismuseum.com.

HARD ROCK BALTIMORE, 601 E. Pratt St., Baltimore, MD 21202. Looking for a new twist for your groups this year? Why not try the Hard Rock Café in Baltimore? We offer great menu options, convenient motor coach drop-off, complimentary meals, and are guaranteed to be a hit with any member of the group. Hey, where else are you encouraged to sing with your mouth full and dance in the dining room? 410-347-7625. www.hardrock.com.

NATIONAL AQUARIUM IN BALTIMORE, Pier 3, 501 E. Pratt St., Baltimore, MD 21202. Discover the secrets behind the weird lives of over 16,000 animals at the National Aquarium in Baltimore. Learn about the quality and quantity of marine life while traveling through diverse exhibits; from the Chesapeake to the Amazon, from the Pacific reef to the tropical rain forest. For group reservations and tickets to the Aquarium, including Animal Planet Australia: Wild Extremes, daily dolphin shows and the new 4-D experience, call 410-576-3833 or visit www.aqua.org.

PORT DISCOVERY CHILDREN'S MUSEUM, 35 Market Pl., Baltimore, MD 21202. Three floors of fun and educational exhibits and programs for ages 2-10 and ranked among the TOP 5 children's museums in the U.S. Enjoy KidWorks, our three-story tree house; explore 1920's Egypt in search of a Pharaoh's tomb; solve the mystery of Miss Perceptions Mystery House, make a splash in our new Wonders of Waters exhibit and more! 410-727-8120. www.portdiscovery.org.

RIDE THE DUCKS, 25 Light St., Baltimore, MD 21202. Laugh and learn by land and sea on Baltimore's original Duck Tour! See the USS Constellation, the Star-Spangled Banner Flag House, the Washington Monument, Mount Vernon, Federal Hill, Fells Point and much more in a way that goes beyond the textbook. The fun really starts when the Duck splashes down in the Inner Harbor for a spectacular view of the city. 410-727-3825. www.baltimoreducks.com.

STAR-SPANGLED TRAILS. Baltimore, "A National Heritage Area." Explore Baltimore's heritage, history and cultural institutions through guided walking tours. Choose from Discover Heritage Walk, Mount Vernon Cultural Walk, Pennsylvania Ave Heritage Trails and Historic Fell's Point tours. Students will see more than 20 of the city's distinct landmarks, including the Flag House, Star-Spangled Banner Museum, the Carroll Mansion, the Jewish Museum, and more. www.starspangledtrails.org or call 443-984-2369 or visit www.baltimore.org.

TOBY'S DINNER THEATRE OF BALTIMORE, 5625 O'Donnell St., Baltimore, MD 21224. Located in the city of Baltimore, Toby's Dinner Theatre offers award-winning Broadway and original musicals with an exceptional buffet-style dinner. From our customer's first contact with our Group Sales staff to watching our servers transform into the glamorous, talented performers on stage, our commitment to your students' enjoyable Toby's experience is first and foremost. 410-649-1660 or 1-866-99TOBYS. www.tobysdinnertheatre.com.

THE UNITED STATES NAVAL ACADEMY. Undergraduate college of the U.S. Navy and U.S. Marine Corps, is located in historic Annapolis, MD, only 45 minutes from Washington, DC and Baltimore, MD. The Armel-Leftwich Visitor Center provides educational tours for grades 4-12, Navy Way Boot Camps for grades 1-5 and A Path to Leadership tour for grades 10-12. Call 410-293-8687 or email tourinfo@usna.edu for information.

BERKSHIRES HIGHLIGHTS

ABSOLUTELY EXPERIENTIAL offers onsite and off-site programming for student and Staff development. Programs work in public and private schools, as well as Residential Treatment facilities; they are based on the concept that people learn best through doing. We design all of our programs to be fun and engaging while meeting specific goals developed to meet your school's needs such as: Social Skills development, Peer Leadership Training, Peer Mediation and At-Risk Youth programs. 'Fun Day' packages available. 413-443-8383. www.absolutelyexperiential.com. REGION:Berkshire County, Western MA.

HERMAN MELVILLE'S ARROWHEAD is an 18th century farmhouse where the author lived and wrote for thirteen years, completing his most famous novel, Moby Dick, as well as other great works. Today Arrowhead is a house museum interpreting the life of the Melville family in the Berkshires. The author's study, piazza, the original fireplace and restored barn are all open to the public. 413-442-1793. www.mobydick.org. REGION: Berkshire County, Western MA.

MOXIE OUTDOOR ADVENTURES, Charlemont, MA; Forks, ME. We specialize in whitewater adventures in New England. Enjoy the thrill of white water and the team building experience, with our professional staff. Mild to wild, we offer some of the most exciting youth river adventures in Massachusetts and Maine. We will spend as much time as you need to put together an exciting learning experience for your group. 800-866-6943. www.moxierafting.com. Locations in: MA, ME. (See Regional Highlights on page 16.) REGION: Franklin County, Western MA & Somerset County, Central ME.

ZOAR OUTDOOR offering whitewater rafting, canoeing, kayaking, zip line canopy tours, fly fishing, biking and rock climbing on the Deerfield River in western Massachusetts. Our friendly professional staff, comfortable base camp with onsite camping and lodging and top-notch equipment ensure that your groups' adventure will be memorable. Charlemont, MA 01339. 800-532-7483. www.zoaroutdoor.com. (See main listing on page 206 and Regional Highlights on page 17.) REGION: Franklin County, Western MA. "

BOSTON HIGHLIGHTS

BAY COLONY HISTORICAL TOURS, Boston's premier guide service since 1977, offers customized tours, educational and fun. Walk Boston's Freedom Trail, 16 historic sites of American Independence. Visit the Paul Revere House, Old North Church, "Old Ironsides" and climb the Bunker Hill Monument. Night Activity: Boston Ghost Tour: Murder, Mystery & Mayhem. Explore the Macabre & Mysterious. Contact: Kiki Kneeland, One Cordis Street, Charlestown, MA 02129. Call 617-523-7303 or email: kikiboston@aol.com.

BLUE MAN GROUP BOSTON. Performing at the Charles Playhouse located at 74 Warrenton St., Boston, MA 02116. Blue Man Group is an exciting and outrageous experience that leaves the entire audience in a blissful, euphoric state. This unique theatrical experience is a form of entertainment like nothing else, guaranteed to be an outing your students will never forget! Contact Kirstin Beal, Group Sales Manager, at 617-542-6700 ext. 3. www.blueman.com.

BOSTON HARBOR CRUISES AND WHALE WATCHING. Experience everything from Whale Watching, narrated Sightseeing and Sunset Cruises to Boston's only Hi-Speed Thrill Boat Ride Codzilla. We have Boston's only three-hour whale watch cruise on our high-speed catamarans. We will get you there in half the time, which allows you more time to watch the whales. Our catamarans feature 3 outside decks for optimum viewing as you visit Stellwagen Bank, the East Coast's most famous whale watching destination. 877-SEE-WHALE. www.bostonharborcruises.com.

COCO KEY INDOOR WATER RESORT, 50 Ferncroft Rd., Danvers, MA 01923. Stay, party, play for the day at New England's largest indoor water resort. 65,000 sq. ft of wet and wild water adventures under one roof and 84 degrees all year! Outrageous water slides, body flumes, an Adventure River, and much more. Located 30 minutes North of Boston near historic coastal villages such as Salem. Direct# 978-777-2500. Ext# 6299, WaterPark Sales. www.cocokeywaterresort.com/boston. (See ad in CT on page 24 and Regional Highlights on page 10.)

CONCORD BIKE TOURS, Concord, MA. Visit the historic sites of where the Revolutionary War began, or the homes and resting places of Thoreau, Alcott, Hawthorne and Emerson. These bike tours are educational and fun! Tours include: bikes, helmets, water & tour guide. Hrs: Seasonal, April-November. Contact: Sue Merlino. 978-697-1897. info@concordbiketours.com. www.concordbiketours.com

THE FREEDOM TRAIL. Take in the rich history of America's Revolution — the events that lead up to the historic break from Britain and the brave people who shaped our national government. The Freedom Trail is a 2.5 mile red-brick walking trail that leads you to 16 nationally significant historic sites, every one an authentic American treasure. 617-357-8300. www.thefreedomtrail.org.

ROWES WHARF WATER TRANSPORT is a full service water transportation company, which offers a wide variety of vessels to a number of destinations. Whether you are looking for an island hopping adventure in the Boston Harbor Islands, a sunset cruise, or a tour of the USS Constitution, many different boats are available to choose from. Group discounts available; call for more information. 617-406-8584. www.roweswharfwatertransport.com.

UNOFFICIAL TOURS, the Home of the "Hahvahd Tour," was created by Harvard alumni to capture and share the Harvard legacy through the eyes of current Harvard students. The award-winning tour has been lauded by national media including NBC, NY Times, and NPR. This 70 minute walking tour inspires young and old, and informs about a successful college experience. The tour insures that you are ready to apply to college, and the "Harvard" of your choice: 617-674-7788 or tours@unofficialtours.com.

OTHER PLACES OF INTEREST:

BOSTON CHILDREN'S MUSEUM. Provides exhibits and hands-on activities that spark the imagination. 617-426-8855 • MUSEUM OF FINE ARTS. A collection of approximately 450,000 objects. 617-267-9300 • MUSEUM OF SCIENCE. More than 400 interactive exhibits, from astronomy to zoology. 617-723-2500 • NEW ENGLAND AQUARIUM. Over 70 exhibits featuring aquatic animals from around the world. 617-973-5200.

Visit the BUNKER HILL MONUMENT, tour the USS CONSTITUTION & MUSEUM. The museum, located adjacent to USS Constitution, brings to life the stories of the individuals who authorized, built, served on and preserved USS Constitution. 617-241-7575 • FANEUIL HALL MARKETPLACE. An unparalleled urban marketplace. 617-523-1300 • JOHN F. KENNEDY PRESIDENTIAL LIBRARY AND MUSEUM. Dedicated to the study and understanding of the 35th president's life and career. 617-514-1600 • MAPPARIUM AT THE MARY BAKER EDDY LIBRARY. 3-dimensional perspective that illustrates how ideas have traversed time and geography, and changed the world. 888-222-3711.

BUCKS COUNTY HIGHLIGHTS

BUCKS COUNTY RIVER COUNTRY. Since 1969 we've been offering 2 hour to full day Tubing, Rafting, Canoeing, Kayaking trips on the clean, 1-4' deep, 80 degree (average) Delaware River. An educational, fun way to enjoy nature. We offer your students an unforgettable educational adventure enjoying nature with prices that are made to fit School, Scout and Youth Group budgets. Food combos are available or bring your own. 215-297-5000. www.rivercountry.net. (See main listing on page 172 and Regional Highlights on page 16.)

DOYLESTOWN ROCK GYM & ADVENTURE CENTER, 3853 Old Easton Rd, Doylestown, PA 18902. Offers indoor and outdoor climbing, an indoor challenge course and a variety of programs for all ages and ability levels. Choose from walk-in programs, classes, summer camps, youth climbing club, outdoor trips, private lessons, technical outdoor instruction, adventure race training and more. 215-230-9085. www.doylestownrockgym.com. (See main listing on page 183.)

NEW HOPE & IVYLAND RAILROAD, 32 W. Bridge St., New Hope, PA 18938. Climb aboard the New Hope & Ivyland Railroad and relax as you travel through the rolling hills and valleys of historic Bucks County, Pennsylvania and experience, first hand, the sights, sounds and romance of the Golden Era of Steam Railroading. Located in downtown New Hope, one block west of Main Street. 215-862-2332 or visit us online at www.newhoperailroad.com. (See main listing on page 185.)

SESAME PLACE, 100 Sesame Rd., Langhorne, PA 19047. All new Environmental Education Program! Share in the spirit of imagination with your students at Sesame Place - where you can experience Sesame Street together through whirling rides, water slides, colorful shows and furry friends. When a class trip is this fun, it's something they'll remember forever. 866-GO-4-ELMO. www.sesameplace.com. (See main listing and ad on page 174 and Regional Highlights on page 11.)

At **THE WASHINGTON CROSSING HISTORIC PARK**, costumed interpreters/demonstrators can give your students various information and interactive activity sessions regarding different topics of the Colonial era, specifically the story of Washington's Crossing. Sessions can include open-hearth cooking, military rations and daily life, sailors in the boat barn discussing the Crossing of the River, Colonial medicine, children's games and more. Washington Crossing, PA. 215-493-4076.

CATSKILLS HIGHLIGHTS

FROST VALLEY YMCA is located in New York State's Catskill Mountains Region, 2-1/2 hours from NYC. We specialize in outdoor/experiential education and offer leadership through team building programs for all ages and abilities. Seasonal maple sugaring, ice cutting, apple cidering. Frost Valley also offers Adventure Trips, Leadership and Teacher's Training. 845-985-2291 www.FrostValley.org. REGION: Sullivan & Ulster Counties, NY. (See main listing on page 203.)

POLLACE'S RESORT is located in the land of Rip van Winkle, the historic Hudson River, and the majestic Catskill Mts. Your overnight or day trip will include a visit and tour of our historic and educational sites, Living World Animal Wildlife Show, group activities, and delicious meals. Let us personalize your field trip with the many educational and exciting activities available. 518-943-3710. www.pollaces.com. REGION: Greene County, NY. (See main listing on page 204.)

SUPERSONIC SPEEDWAY FUN PARK is an amusement center with fun activities for everyone. At the Speedway you can play mini golf, arcade games, ride the go-carts, use the batting cages, enjoy numerous rides, have a picnic, use the shooting gallery, and much more! And come and visit the restaurant & ice cream shop for a meal and a snack. Your group will have a blast! 518-634-7200. www.blackthorneresort.com. REGION: Greene County, NY. (See Regional Highlights on page 11 and main listing on page 134.)

TANGLEWOOD RANCH, 438 Cornwallville Rd., Cornwallville, NY 12418. Saddle Up Partner! Get your group ready to take a ride through the Catskill Mountains and experience breathtaking views, including a five state view! In addition to horseback riding (Western) along scenic trails, we offer pony rides, horsedrawn hayrides, and all day or 3 hour night rides. Also check out the Indian trading post and craft shop. Call 518-622-9531. REGION: Greene County, NY. (See main listing on page 140.)

WINDHAM MOUNTAIN is a winter resort where skiers and snowboarders "come out and play" in the snow. Just a 2 1/2 hour drive from New York City, we offer beginners, intermediates and experts the chance to experience its two adjoining mountain peaks. It's the kind of place where students love to explore the varied terrain in a safe environment. 518-734-4300. www.windhammountain.com. REGION: Greene County, NY.

COASTAL MAINE HIGHLIGHTS

ACADIA NATIONAL PARK. Bar Harbor, ME. Junior Ranger Program includes hands-on activities to explore the park's plants, animals, and history. Take a Ranger-Narrated Boat Cruise. Play in the Sand, Go for a Hike or a Bike Ride. 207-288-3338. REGION: Hancock County, South East ME.

THE CASCO BAY LINES. Explore the Maine coast most visitors never see aboard America's oldest continually operating ferry service. Seven different cruises, private charters, and daily commuter service to six different islands. See what the islands of Casco Bay have to offer. 207-774-7871. www.cascobaylines.com. REGION: Cumberland County, Southern ME.

COLONIAL PEMAQUID STATE HISTORIC SITE (FT. WILLIAM HENRY). Host interpretive tours and learn about the native people who camped on this once-remote peninsula dating back to the mid-1620s. The museum houses artifacts unearthed from the grounds. Explore Fort William Henry and visit Pemaquid Lighthouse Park - The lighthouse built in 1827 above spectacular granite cliffs, and the adjoining keeper's house is home to the Pemaquid Fishermen's Museum. Park season: 207-677-2423. Off season: 207-624-6080. REGION: Lincoln County, South Central ME.

LUCKY CATCH CRUISES. Captain Tom will guide you through the daily routines of a Maine lobsterman, while enjoying close-up views of historic lighthouses, civil war forts and seals. See how that tasty treat gets from the bottom of the ocean to your dinner plate. REGION: Cumberland County, Southern ME. 207-761-0941.

MUSEUM HIGHLIGHTS IN PORTLAND: HOME OF HENRY WADSWORTH LONGFEL-LOW. 207-774-1822 • MAINE NARROW GAUGE RR CO & MUSEUM. 207-828-0814 • PORTLAND MUSEUM OF ART. 207-775-6148.

THE WHALE CAMP on Grand Manan Island off Maine Coast. Simply no other program offers you as many face-to-face encounters to closely observe & Study Whales, Dolphins, Porpoises, Seals & Puffins in their natural habitat. Through direct observation, data collection and hands-on experience with marine science equipment, The Whale Camp is where exploration & inspiration abound. 1-888-54WHALE. www.whalecamp.com.

DISNEY YOUTH GROUP PROGRAMS

HIGHLIGHTS:

Disney Youth Education Series (Y.E.S.) Website: www.DisneyYES.com/ct GRADE LEVEL: K-12 GROUP TYPE: School, Scout, Home School, Church, or other organized youth group. *Disney Y.E.S.* offers educational field trip programs and academic journeys year-round. Participants find enrichment, inspiration, and pure fun as they see how principles they're learning in the classroom are making exciting things happen around the *Walt Disney World*® Resort and *Disneyland*® Resort. On any day, *Disney Y.E.S.* students can be found swirling through G-force motion to test the laws of physics, experiencing what life is like on the other side of the globe, and checking out careers from business to acting. 19 curriculum-based, educational field trip programs focused on Arts & Humanities, Life Management & Careers, Natural and Physical Sciences are offered at *Walt Disney World* and five programs centered around Arts & Humanities, Life Management & Careers, Physical Science and California History are available at *Disneyland*. *Disney Y.E.S.* grade-level content and specially designed materials are the perfect enhancement to just about any classroom curriculum. Programs are developed by Disney Institute and Disney's Animal Program Educators and are aligned with National Standards.

Disney Performing Arts

Website: www.DisneyPerformingArts.com/ct GRADE LEVEL: Variety of Grade Levels. GROUP TYPE: Student or Performing Group, see website for details.

Disney Magic Music Days offers year-round programs to instrumental, dance, vocal, and other performing groups to perform at magical locations throughout the *Walt Disney World*® and *Disneyland*® Theme Parks and Resorts.

Disney Performing Arts Workshops are an exciting way to sharpen performance skills by exposing groups to different teaching styles, interpretations, and instructional techniques, taught by Disney professionals.

Festival Disney at Walt Disney World®, is an exhilarating Disney produced music festival where middle, junior, and senior high school choirs, bands, orchestras, and auxiliary ensembles compete for top awards.

Disney Jazz Celebration at Walt Disney World®, brings together student jazz bands with the leaders in jazz education and jazz celebrities during this annual festival.

MENC: The National Association for Music Education officially endorses *Disney Magic Music Days Performances*, *Disney Performing Arts Workshops*, *Disney Jazz Celebration* and *Festival Disney*.

Disney Theme Park Adventures

GRADE LEVEL: All Grade Levels. GROUP TYPE: Any organized School, Scout, Religious group or Youth organization. *Disney Theme Park Adventures* is a year-round program offering reduced price Disney Theme Park tickets for qualifying youth groups. Website: www.DisneyThemeParkAdventures.com/ct

Disney Grad Nite

Website: www.DisneyGradNite.com/ct. GRADE LEVEL: 12. GROUP TYPE: High School Seniors *Disney Grad Nite* is the ultimate senior class celebration with concert performances by top artists, exclusive use of Disney attractions and high-energy dance parties.

Visit www.DisneyYouthGroups.com/ct today!

GETTYSBURG HIGHLIGHTS

ARTILLERY RIDGE CAMPGROUND, 610 Tanettown Rd., Gettysburg, PA 17325. We are the closest camping to the Battlefield. We offer horse back riding over the battlefield and a 3- dimensional viewing of the entire battlefield. National Riding Stables and Gettysburg Diorama. Please contact us for your reservations. 717-334-1288 or 717-334-6408. Visit our website at www.artilleryridge.com. (See main listing on page 195.)

GETTYSBURG NATIONAL MILITARY PARK offers ranger led battlefield walks, evening campfire programs, living history programs and storytelling. During the winter months the park offers a special series of indoor hands-on programs that address high points of the battle and the army commanders. 717-334-1124, extension 8023.

HISTORIC FARNSWORTH HOUSE INN GHOST/HISTORY TOURS & BUFFETS. One of the most haunted inns in America with a variety of candlelight ghost walks and presentations including Candlelight Ghost Walks, Ghost Stories in our cellar, and our new Vacant Chair Dinner Theatre with buffet, period songs and ghost stories. Historical presentations available including house tour and/or The Soldier's Life. Civil War Buffets available for groups of 25 or more. Boxed lunches for a day on the battlefield. On-site bus parking available. 717-334-8838. www.farnsworthhouseinn.com. (See main listing on page 188.)

RHODES GROVE CAMP & CONFERENCE CENTER, 7693 Browns Mill Rd., is located in Chambersburg, PA, 17202. Nestled in the beautiful Cumberland Valley we are just minutes off of I-81. With Gettysburg, Harrisburg, and Antietam close by you are sure to enjoy the option of exciting day trips around the area. You can contact us by calling 717-375-4162, or on the web, www.rhodesgrove.com. (See main listing on page 205.)

SLEEPY HOLLOW OF GETTYSBURG CANDLELIGHT GHOST TOURS. Why just read about ghosts, wouldn't you rather look for them instead? Walk into the realm of the unknown, escorted by a period dressed guide, back in time down the very streets soldiers walked over a century ago. Our Ghost Walks have entertained very small groups to extremely large groups with completely unscripted, interactive storytelling. 717-337-9322. www.sleepyhollowofgettysburg.com. (See main listing on page 190.)

Nearby, **HERSHEYPARK**, "The cleanest, greenest theme park in America," with over 65 rides and attractions, including 11 roller coasters, The Boardwalk and award-winning live entertainment. 1-800-242-4236, hersheyparkgroups@hersheypa.com or visit www.Hersheypark.com/groups. (See main listing on page 173 and Regional Highlights on page 10.)

KENNEBEC & MOOSE RIVER VALLEYS HIGHLIGHTS

LONG REACH CRUISES, 870 Washington St., Bath, ME 04530 (Office). Several types of cruises are available, all of which offer great views of the beautiful Maine landscape, as well as excellent opportunities for lighthouse viewing and wildlife watching. Passengers are also treated to interesting and lively narration from a friendly captain and crew throughout the trip. 888-538-6786. www.longreachcruises.com. REGION: Sagadahoc County, South Central ME.

MAINE STATE MUSEUM. Experience Maine's history where you can see what the earliest Maine inhabitants hunted, what they ate, how they made tools, and what they left behind. The four floors offer animal habitats, a functioning water-powered mill, an early steam locomotive, and Maine products from ships to guns and from cars to glass. Augusta, ME. 207-287-2301. www.maine.gov/museum/. REGION: Kennebec County, South West ME.

MOXIE OUTDOOR ADVENTURES, Forks, ME; Charlemont, MA. We specialize in whitewater adventures in New England. Enjoy the thrill of white water and the team building experience, with our professional staff. Mild to wild, we offer some of the most exciting youth river adventures in Massachusetts and Maine. We will spend as much time as you need to put together an exciting learning experience for your group. 800-866-6943. www.moxierafting.com. Locations in: MA, ME. (See Regional Highlights on page 16.) REGION: Franklin County, Western MA & Somerset County, Central ME.

NORTH COUNTRY RIVERS offers daily whitewater rafting trips in Maine (Apr-Oct) on the Kennebec, Penobscot and Dead Rivers. Rafting packages are available with all trips and include Camping, Cabin Lodging and Meals. One day, multi-day & overnight trips. No experience necessary, all equipment & guides provided. 25 Years Experience as Maine's Premier Rafting Outfitter. Call 1-800-348-8871 for reservations & information. (See Regional Highlights on page 17.) REGION: Somerset County, Central ME.

OLD FORT WESTERN, built in 1754, is America's oldest surviving wooden fort. Group tours with hands-on theme based activities. Program Highlights: History of the Fort; A Day in the Life of a Fort Soldier; Pilgrims and Indians at Cushnoc; Introduction to Archaeology. Augusta, ME. 207-626-2385. www.oldfortwestern.org. REGION: Kennebec County, South West ME.

PINE TREE STATE ARBORETUM promotes the knowledge and appreciation of Maine's trees and other flora by offering educational, recreational, and inspirational opportunities. The six-mile, year round trail system is open to hiking, jogging, bird watching, non-motorized biking and horseback riding. 207-621-0031. www.pinetreestatearboretum.org. REGION: Kennebec County, South West ME.

LAKE CHAMPLAIN, NY & VT HIGHLIGHTS

1812 HOMESTEAD, a working farm and museum of the 1800's, includes "Hands on" experiences including dipping candles, woodwork, feeding the animals, attending lessons in the schoolhouse, baking on the hearth, spinning wool, pressing cider, boiling maple syrup, making soap and cheese, blacksmithing, and learning Native American lore and skills. Willsboro, NY. 518-963-4071. REGION: Essex County, Adirondacks NY.

ECHO LAKE AQUARIUM AND SCIENCE CENTER
Explore the wonder, beauty, and science of the Lake Champlain Basin! We offer a dynamic staff, 70 live animals, and over 100 interactive exhibits to engage curious minds. Choose a self-guided experience or register your group for a staff program. $30 for a 1/2 hour program plus the price of admission. 1-877-ECHOFUN, www.echovermont.org. REGION: Chittenden County, Western VT.

FAMILY FUN & ENTERTAINMENT CENTER consists of a Driving Range with 30 stations, a sand trap and 10 natural grass tees, Batting Cages with 6 stations of various speeds and an 18 hole mini golf surrounded by waterfalls, fountains, a cave and mountain views. REGION: Chittenden County, Western VT. 802-872-8858.

THE LAKE CHAMPLAIN MARITIME MUSEUM, Vergennes, VT. Offers hands-on experiences at our on-site programs at Basin Harbor, touring our replica schooner, taking students out in boats and exploring our exciting exhibits. The special program On-Water, begins with a short presentation on the history and archaeology of the lake, focused on how archaeologists discover and record the shipwrecks that are found. Students then go aboard the tour boat EScape and head out to the shipwreck, viewing it live with the ROV. 802-475-2022. REGION: Addison County, Western VT.

POK-O-MACCREADY OUTDOOR EDUCATION CENTER. Started in 1974, PMOEC is the only Outdoor Education Center in Adirondack Park. The center offers classes in Teambuilding, Natural Science, Living History, and High Adventure. Our 300 acre campus is located on beautiful Long Pond and surrounded by mountains. Fun and exciting activities are sure to give your students lasting memories! The center became a not-for-profit organization in October 2008. 518-963-7967. Director@pmoec.org. www.pmoec.org. (See main listing on page 154.) REGION: Essex County, Adirondacks NY.

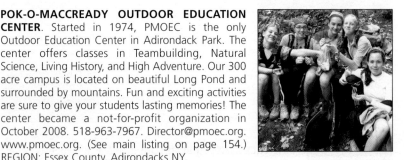

THE SHELBURNE MUSEUM, one of New England's most diverse art museums, contains 150,000 works of art, Americana, and design contained on 45 scenic acres and in 39 historic buildings. 802-985-3346. REGION: Chittenden County, Western VT.

LAKE GEORGE HIGHLIGHTS

ADIRONDACK MUSEUM, Rte. 28N & 30, Blue Mountain Lake, NY 12812. The Museum expands public understanding of Adirondack history and the relationship between people and the Adirondack wilderness. Located on 32 acres overlooking the Blue Mountain Lake with 22 buildings and historic structures. Exhibits located in the beauty of the outdoors. 518-352-7311. www.adkmuseum.org. REGION: Hamilton County, NY.

ADVENTURE FAMILY FUN CENTER is the ideal place for your school trip, after prom party or fund raising event. Our 1,000 ft. outdoor go-cart track is the largest in the area. Our 40,000 square foot indoor facility features an indoor track, rock wall, paintball range, multi-level laser tag, bumper cars, dance/karaoke floor, and huge arcade. Awesome group rates! 518-798-7860. www.lakegeorgegocarts.com. (See main listing on page 142.) REGION: Warren County, NY.

FORT TICONDEROGA, P.O. Box 390, Ticonderoga, NY 12883. Fort Ticonderoga is one of the most important historic sites in America, site of the French & Indian War and American Revolution. Students get mustered into the Green Mountain Boys and taught to march and handle a musket. They also get to reenact the siege of the Fort by Ethan Allen and Benedict Arnold. Lecture hall, classrooms, student and scout programs available. 518-585-2821. www.fort-ticonderoga.org. REGION: Essex County, NY.

THE FUN SPOT. Entertainment for all ages! Gold Rush Adventure Golf featuring cascading waterfalls, streams and caves. LeMans Go-Kart Raceway and Mini-Racers (Open April thru October). Year round activities include Lasertron Laser Tag; Inline/Roller Skating to today's Top Music; Inflatable Fun on our two Obstacle Courses with 12 foot slides and Bounce House. Snack Bar, Meal Deals and Catering. Group Rates and Private Party Times Available. www.thefunspot.net. 518-792-8989. (See main listing on page 142 and Regional Highlights on page 10.) REGION: Warren County, NY.

HUDSON RIVER RAFTING COMPANY (since 1979) offers world class rafting on the Hudson River Gorge (17 miles), one of America's 10 best rafting trips. Raft the Sacandaga River's large dam release; rafting/ tubing; excellent for youth groups, 6 trips per day. These rivers are located in North Creek, Lake George and Saratoga. In the western Adirondacks/1000 Island region, HRRC provides all river gear. Base camps have changing rooms, bathrooms, parking, picnic areas. Camping/hiking is

nearby. 800-888-7238. www.hudsonriverrafting.com. (See main listing and ad on page 131 and Regional Highlights on page 16.) REGION: Warren County, NY.

LAKE GEORGE STEAMBOAT COMPANY invites you to sail with us on Lake George, undoubtedly the most beautiful lake in America. The Lake George Steamboat Company's three large passenger vessels offer: one hour lakefront sailings, daily Paradise Bay trips, 65 mile Discovery cruises, Luncheon, Dinner, Pasta, Pizza and Fireworks Cruises. All sailings from the Steel Pier on 57 Beach Road, Lake George Village. 2009 marks our 192nd year of carrying passengers on Lake George, your enjoyment and safety is our heritage. 800-553-BOAT or 518-668-5777. www.lakegeorgesteamboat.com. (See main listing on page 138.) REGION: Warren County, NY.

NATURAL STONE BRIDGE AND CAVES PARK. A hands-on geological NY wonder and long time favorite of earth science classes, come explore the largest marble cave entrance in the east. Introduction lecture and 90 min exploration of the waterfalls, gorge and caves (using our syllabus) followed by rock/fossil talks will excite any student. Additional activities: Museum grade Petrified Wood, Rock, Fossil & Crystal Displays, Rock Shop.

518-494-2283. stonebridgeandcaves@frontiernet.net. www.stonebridgeandcaves.com. (See main listing on page 139) REGION: Warren County, NY.

SACANDAGA OUTDOOR CENTER,1 Whitewater Way, Hadley, NY 12835. The premier adventure center in the Adirondacks since 1987, offering great activities from 2 hours to all day for children 5 years and up. Our licensed guides make the difference with years of experience accompanying youth groups of all ages. Spectacular setting at the confluence of two rivers. 866-696-RAFT or 518-696-RAFT. info@4soc.com. www.4soc.com. (See main listing on page 132-133 and Regional Highlights on page 17.) REGION: Saratoga County, NY.

TUBBY TUBES COMPANY - OUTDOOR FUN PARK. Enjoy Lazy River Tubing, Rafting and kayaking on the Lower Hudson River Gorge. The river is clean, sandy and averages 2-3 feet deep. All ages welcome. Located at 1372 Lake Ave. Lake Luzerne, NY 12846 (1 mile from Lake George). 518-696-5454. www.tubbytubes.com. (See main listing on page 133 and Regional Highlights on page 17.) REGION: Warren County, NY.

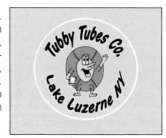

LEHIGH VALLEY HIGHLIGHTS

BURNSIDE PLANTATION was an integral part of the Moravian farming system, which demonstrates farming methods used between 1748 and 1848, a time of great change in agriculture. Through the two and a half-hour "A Century at Burnside Plantation" program discover what daily life was like on an early Bethlehem farm. 610-691-6055. www.historicbethlehem.org.

THE CRAYOLA FACTORY, 30 Centre Sq., Easton, PA 18042. You can color, draw, paint and create with the latest Crayola products. See how Crayola Crayons and Markers are made. Learn about the history of the Crayola brand. Come and explore dozens of interactive projects and activities. 610-515-8000.

CRYSTAL CAVE is an underground wonder, visited by millions since its discovery in 1871. The 45-minute Educational Underground Tours consist of an 8 minute video presentation and a 125 foot descent underground to experience the amazing stone sculpture including The Cathedral Chamber, The Natural Bridge and The Crystal Ballroom, among other marvels. 610-683-6765. www.crystalcavepa.com.

DA VINCI SCIENCE CENTER, 3145 Hamilton Blvd. Bypass, Allentown, PA 18103. Science comes alive for students at the Da Vinci Science Center. The Center's exciting programs and hands-on exhibits engage students in captivating experiences seldom available in the classroom and reinforce PDE science and math assessment anchors. 484-664-1002. www.davinci-center.org. (See main listing on page 192.)

INDEPENDENCE FAMILY FUN CENTER welcomes all youth groups for a day of active and exciting activities. Our 19,000 square foot facility includes a rock-climbing tower, a roller skating rink, laser tag, mini-bowling lanes, arcade games, and even a moon bounce! Special group rates are available for what is sure to be a fun, active, and unforgettable day for kids of all ages! 610-769-5811. www.familyfunoff309.com.

LEHIGH VALLEY PAINTBALL is located at 307 Swartley Rd. in Hatfield, PA. We accommodate every type of player from beginner to experienced. We offer indoor/outdoor speedball fields, and over 25 acres of woodsball fields. You can contact us at www.lvpsouth.com or 215-997-7877. (See main listing on page 183.)

NATIONAL CANAL MUSEUM & BOAT RIDES. The only museum in the country dedicated to telling the story of America's historic towpath canals. The museum features four galleries filled with hands-on exhibits. Combine museum visit with a boat ride on the Josiah White II Canal Boat Ride. REGION: Easton, PA. 610-559-6613.

LINCOLN CENTER HIGHLIGHTS

LINCOLN CENTER FOR THE PERFORMING ARTS. Great way to introduce young people to the world of performing arts during our 50th anniversary year! Our popular Meet-the-Artist program actively involves your students in exciting 1-hour performances ranging from jazz and hip hop, to Broadway, opera, and more! Each is followed by a professionally guided tour of our renowned theaters where children might catch a rehearsal in progress. Also, arrange for group Master Classes in all disciplines. 212-875-5370 or mtaschools@lincolncenter.org. (See main listing on page 122).

NEW YORK CITY BALLET offers an array of Education Programs. With our school and touring programs, students and educators learn that ballet is an accessible and relevant art form. Our interactive Close-Up programs offer behind-the-scenes access and opportunities to interact with members of the Company. Through Education programs at NYCB, you'll be sure to see the ballet in a whole new light! Please email education@nycballet.com or call 212-870-5636! (See main listing on page 124).

NEW YORK PHILHARMONIC. Give your students an unforgettable musical experience – a live performance by the New York Philharmonic! Award-winning School Day Concerts designed and hosted for schools are supported by curriculum, CD & teacher workshops. Musical Encounters go behind-the-scenes at a Philharmonic rehearsal, plus a workshop. Just $6/student at Avery Fisher Hall at Lincoln Center. Visit nyphil.org/ctd09 or call 212-875-5732. (See main listing and ad on page 124).

THE NEW YORK PUBLIC LIBRARY FOR THE PERFORMING ARTS, Dorothy and Lewis B. Cullman Center, 40 Lincoln Center Plaza, New York, NY 10023. The largest public, circulating performing arts collection in the world. The collection includes all aspects of dance, drama, music, orchestra collection and recorded sound and moving images. It also includes books, films, scores, published plays & screenplays, DVDs, commercial videos, newspaper & magazine articles. The Music Division of the library welcomes class visits and can customize the content to suit particular class needs and provide general introductions to using research. Group tours available by appointment. 212-870-1605.

NEW LONDON HIGHLIGHTS

HISTORIC SHIP NAUTILUS/SUBMARINE FORCE MUSEUM, 1 Crystal Lake Rd., Groton, CT 06439-5501. Tour the world's first nuclear-powered submarine, and the first ship ever to reach the North Pole, Historic Ship NAUTILUS, and visit the Navy's official submarine museum. Free admission. Open year round, call for hours. Buses & RVs welcome. Toll free 800-343-0079, or 860-694-3174, www.submarinemuseum.org, contact Mike Riegel. (See main listing on page 33.)

MASHANTUCKET PEQUOT MUSEUM & RESEARCH CENTER. Students journey back in time to see and feel history come alive as never before. Exploring new worlds, they descend a glacial crevasse, walk through a 16th century Native American village, and stand next to life-size figures of the first people of New England as they hunt a herd of caribou. 860-396-6839. www.pequotmuseum.org. (See main listing on page 25, ad on page 34 and Regional Highlights on page 14.)

MYSTIC AQUARIUM, 55 Coogan Blvd., Mystic, CT 16355. 70 exhibits with over 12,000 fishes, invertebrates, and marine mammals, representing 425 species from around the world. Focus is to inform the public about marine animals, the habitats that support them, and the historical and scientific significance of deep sea exploration. Hands-on activities and demonstrations. 860-572-5955.

MYSTIC SEAPORT. Immerse yourself in American maritime history at Mystic Seaport - The Museum of America and the Sea. Explore a re-created 19th-century maritime village, discover stars under the planetarium dome, see a working shipyard in action, and climb aboard authentic tall ships. Discover the crafts and industries of a thriving coastal community while getting involved in hands-on demonstrations. 860-572-5322. www.mysticseaport.org. (See main listing and ad on page 34 and Regional Highlights on page 15.)

PROJECT OCEANOLOGY. A one-of-a-kind, hands-on, minds-on science immersion experience. Typical student activities include a 2 1/2 hour oceanographic cruise aboard our fully-equipped, U.S. Coast Guard certified research vessel using scientific instruments. Back on shore,

students can explore tidal marshes, rocky intertidal zones, sandy beaches and near shore fishes. 860-445-9007. www.oceanology.org. (See main listing on page 29.)

NEW YORK CITY HIGHLIGHTS

ACCOMMODATIONS

DAYS HOTEL BROADWAY, 215 West 94th St., New York, NY 10025. Located on Manhattan's upper west side in exciting New York City. As a "walking city" with an infinite variety of neighborhoods, New York has something to offer everyone from educational pursuits to just plain fun! Our location on Manhattan's vibrant upper west side is the perfect base from which to explore them. 212-864-6400. www.daysinn.com. (See main listing and ad on page 72.)

NEW YORK YMCA GUEST ROOMS, Reservation Sales Center - 5 West 63rd St., New York, NY 10023. The New York YMCA's have been providing affordable lodging facilities for student groups for over thirty years. Contact the Reservation Office for information on any of our five guest room properties - West Side, Vanderbilt, Harlem, Flushing & Greenpoint. Special group rates are available. The YMCA is a nonprofit, tax-exempt organization. 212-579-7730. www.ymcanyc.org/reservation. (See main listing on page 72.)

ATTRACTIONS & RECREATION

BESTOFBROADWAY.COM'S BROADWAY SCHOOLROOM. We offer a vast variety of workshops which utilize experienced Broadway professionals who tailor each program for your group(s) by using themes and issues of shows that focus on practical hands-on learning, creating collaborations to dynamically enhance team building both on and off stage, and foster opportunities to obtain and/or fine tune technical, theatrical and life skills. 212-398-8383/800-223-7565. www.BestOfBroadway.com & www.BestOfBroadway.com/Schoolroom. (See main listing on page 84 and ad on page 130.)

BILLY ELLIOT THE MUSICAL is the new show that has captured Broadway's heart, delighted the critics and swept the awards--winning 10 Tony Awards® including Best Musical! Called "Extraordinarily uplifting" by Time Out New York and "The freshest and most inspiring show in years" by The New York Times, "Billy Elliot" is a joyous, exciting and feel-good celebration of one boy following his heart and making his dreams come true. Call Telecharge.com at 212-239-6262. www.billyelliotgroups.com. (See main listing on page 84 and ad on page 120.)

BLUE MAN GROUP, 434 Lafayette St., NYC. The critically acclaimed and award-winning Blue Man Group creates theatrical experiences that defy categorization. Three bald and blue characters take the audience on a multimedia journey that is funny, intelligent, and visually stunning. A dynamic live band accompanies them with haunting tribal rhythms, driving the show to its unforgettable climax. "A Sensation!" raves Time Magazine. 212-260-8993. groupsnyc@blueman.com. www.blueman.com. (See main listing on page 84-85 and ad on page 120.)

CITY ICE PAVILION. Discover how great it is to skate at the City Ice Pavilion, New York's newest NHL Size Ice Rink. Ideally located on a rooftop in Long Island City…just 2 miles from midtown over the 59th Street Bridge. The City Ice Pavilion Staff is there to help everyone learn. Look no further for a School, Holiday or Corporate Event…or a super special Birthday Party. Fri. Evening 7:30-10PM, Sat. 12-4pm, Sat. Night 7-10PM, Sun. 12-3PM. 718-706-6667. www.Cityicepavilion.com. (See main listing and ad on page 95.)

EMPIRE STATE BUILDING OBSERVATORY. Discover the world's most exciting classroom—the Empire State Building Observatory. With customized lesson plans developed with the Bank Street College of Education, students of all ages will love learning from the highest point in New York. ESB also offers a variety of specialty curriculums dealing with its historic construction and its place in popular culture. Take education to amazing heights at the Empire State Building. www.esbnyc.com. Call 212-736-3100 for group sales. (See main listing on page 108 and ad on page 109.)

THE LION KING, The Minskoff Theatre, Broadway & 45th St., New York, NY 10036. Hailed by Newsweek as "a landmark event in entertainment," "The Lion King" is a breathtaking adventure that stretches the boundaries of Broadway, from the heart of Africa to the plains of your imagination. See it now. Remember it forever. Book your Group direct with Disney On Broadway Group Sales: 212-703-1040 or 1-800-439-9000. Group sales email: groupsales@disneyonbroadway.com. www.disneyonbroadway.com. (See main listing on page 85 and ad on page 121.)

Photo of Sierra Boggess by Per Briegehagen ©Disney

THE LITTLE MERMAID, Lunt-Fontanne Theatre, Broadway & 46th St., New York, NY 10036. Take a journey to the wonderful world under the sea and beyond your wildest dreams. Disney's "The Little Mermaid" combines a timeless tale, state-of-art stagecraft and irresistible songs. It adds up to what Time Magazine calls "one of the most ravishing shows ever seen on a Broadway stage." Book your Group direct with Disney on Broadway Group Sales. 212-703-1040 or 1-800-439-9000. groupsales@disneyonbroadway.com. www.disneyonbroadway.com. (See main listing on page 85 and ad on page 121.)

MADAME TUSSAUDS NEW YORK, 234 West 42nd St., New York, NY 10036. Hrs: Open 365 days a years from 10AM. May close early for special events, please call ahead for updated closing times. Groups visit themed environments filled with an exceptional showcase of incredibly life-like wax figures – a veritable who's who of entertainment, music, sports, politics and world history. 888-923-0334 or 212-512-9600 ext. 607. groupsales@madametussaudsny.com. www.madame-tussauds.com. GROUP RATES: 15+. For general information, please call 800-246-8872. (See main listing and ad on page 111.)

MARY POPPINS, New Amsterdam Theatre, 214 West 42nd St., New York, NY 10036. Believe in the magic of "Mary Poppins," the perfectly magical musical from producers Disney and Cameron Macintosh that's guaranteed to lift your spirits to new heights. Book your Group direct with Disney On Broadway Group Sales: 212-703-1040 or 1-800-439.9000. groupsales@disneyonbroadway.com. www.disneyonbroadway.com. (See main listing on page 86 and ad on page 121.)

NEW YORK YANKEES, Bronx, NY. Tour Yankee Stadium and learn about American history from a new and fun perspective, as the evolution of one of the most storied sports teams in the nation comes to life. Tour Highlights: Yankees Museum, Monument Park, dugout area and field, clubhouse and batting cage area. All sites subject to current availability. For tour information: 718-977-TOUR (8687), or: www.yankees.com. (See main listing on page 113 and ad on page 119.)

RIPLEY'S BELIEVE IT OR NOT! TIMES SQUARE, 234 West 42nd St. btw 7th & 8th Avenues, New York, NY 10036. New York's most fascinating, unique and exciting destination. Open everyday from 9AM; experience 500+ astonishing artifacts and be captivated by dozens of interactive exhibits, innovative scavenger hunts and educational content. Witness our incredible collection of the world's most remarkable elements of science, history, the arts, tolerance and humanity. Group Rates for 15 or more. 212-398-3133. groupsales@ripleysnewyork.com. www.ripleysnewyork.com. (See main listing and ad on page 114-115.)

SHREK THE MUSICAL. "The best musical for younger audiences since The Lion King!" (Time Out NY). Based on the Oscar®-winning DreamWorks film that started it all, this spectacular new production brings the hilarious story of everyone's favorite ogre to life on the Broadway stage. Full of big laughs, great dancing and breathtaking scenery, "Shrek The Musical" is part romance, part twisted fairy tale and all irreverent fun for students of all ages. 212-239-6262 or 800-432-7780 (outside NY Metro area). www.ShrekTheMusical.com. (See main listing on page 86 and ad on page 126.)

TOP OF THE ROCK OBSERVATION DECK, 30 Rockefeller Plaza, New York, NY 10111. Discover Top of the Rock Observation Deck, a 3-tiered observation deck atop 30 Rockefeller Plaza, New York City's most amazing attraction! The unforgettable experience includes a multi-media theater exhibit, glass ceiling elevator ride to the top and a panoramic 360-degree, unobstructed view from the 70th floor observatory, 850 feet in the sky! 212-698-2000. info@topoftherocknyc.com. www.topoftherocknyc.com. (See main listing on page 106 and ad on page 117.)

THEME RESTAURANTS

B.B. KING BLUES CLUB. Located in the heart of Times Square near all major transportation and Broadway shows, B.B. King Blues Club offers a one of a kind music experience that's perfect for groups of all ages & sizes. Dine while enjoying free live music, or check out our weekend brunches with Strawberry Fields Beatles Tribute on Saturdays and the world famous Harlem Gospel Choir on Sundays! Availability for Breakfasts, Lunches and Dinners. 212-997-4511. www.bbkingblues.com. (See main listing and ad on pages 92 and 127.)

DAVE AND BUSTER'S, 234 West 42nd St., New York, NY 10036. At Dave & Buster's your group will have a blast! Start out with a delicious meal and then move on to some games in our Million Dollar Midway. Spend an hour with us, or a whole day - at Dave & Buster's it's your call! We have packages for groups of 20 to 2,000; so for your next outing come to Dave & Buster's – your students will thank you! 646-495-2015. www.daveandbusters.com. (See ad on page 96 and main listing on page 92.)

ESPN ZONE NYC, 1472 Broadway (42nd & Broadway), New York, NY 10036. More than just a meal on the run, ESPN Zone is the hottest stop in the city with great food, high energy and a 10,000 sq. ft. sports arena filled with sports-themed games and interaction. ESPN Zone takes the concept of sports entertainment to a whole new level, and delivers an experience you won't find anywhere else. 212-921-3776 (ESPN). Espnzone.com. (See ad on pages 90 and 128.)

HARD ROCK CAFE NY is one of the city's largest entertainment destinations, featuring a 708-seat restaurant perfect for tour groups dining breakfast, lunch & dinner. Hard Rock boasts a 1,800-square-foot Rock Shop with authentic Hard Rock merchandise, a Live concert venue and a unique outdoor space above the building's historic marquee, where guests can host private parties amid the lights and excitement of Times Square. 212-343-3355. www.hardrock.com. (See ad on page 129.)

PLANET HOLLYWOOD. For breakfast, lunch or dinner, small groups to large, there's no place like the Planet. Let us roll out the red carpet for you and your guests at the ultimate Hollywood event. To book a group event, contact the Sales Team at: New York 212-265-2404, Orlando 407-827-7836, Myrtle Beach 843-916-9501, Las Vegas 702-791-7827, Cancun 011-52-998-883-0643, Honolulu 808-924-7406. (See main listing and ad on page 130.)

SIGHTEEING TOURS

BIKE AND ROLL. Bike tours are a great way to explore NYC. Our tours are led by knowledgeable guides who always have safety as their first concern. You'll be awed by views of the city. Why spend your time sitting on a tour bus? With Bike and Roll your group's trip to NYC will be the highlight of their trip - active, safe, educational and fun! 212-260-0400. www.bikeandroll.com. (See main listing and ad on page 80.)

GRAY LINE NEW YORK SIGHTSEEING - GROUPS AND CHARTERS. 85-seat open-top double decker bus—climate controlled lower level, accompanied by NY Licensed Tour Guide. 49-seat and 55-seat deluxe motor coach—comfortable seating with lavatory facility and audio-visual equipped. 28-seat trolleys—beautiful brass trimmed interior equipped w/ PA system. 16-seat mini-coach Vehicles are climate controlled. We proudly serve New York City and other areas upon request. 212-445-0848, ext. 4. (See main listing and ad on page 6.)

HARBOR EXPERIENCE COMPANIES is the leading waterborne tour and landside recreation company in New York City. Experience the harbor your way for an educational and fun time. All cruises depart from South Street Seaport where you will find Water Taxi Beach for lunch and fun with miniature golf, skeeball and ping pong. We have something for every taste and every budget. 866-983-2542. www.harborexperience.com. (See main listing and ad on page 81.)

NY WATERWAY TOURS, Pier 78 (W 38th & 12th Ave), New York, NY 10018. NYC tours including Skyline Cruise, City Lights Cruise, Specialty and Baseball Cruises. Tour Guides provide interesting facts for your Student Tour Group about NYC sights including the Statue of Liberty, Empire State Building, the South Street Seaport and the Brooklyn Bridge. Schedules vary by season. Ask about our History & Architecture Cruise which each take a more detailed looked at NYC from two distinct angles. 800-533-3779. nywaterwaytours.com. (See main listing on page 81.)

ORLANDO/KISSIMMEE HIGHLIGHTS

BOGGY CREEK AIRBOAT RIDES, 2001 E. Southport Rd., Kissimmee, FL 34746. Discover territory that remains unaltered by man in the wilderness of the Central Florida Everglades. Ride with a certified U.S. Coast Guard Captain and see Florida alligators, turtles, birds and more in their natural environment. 407-344-9550. www.bcairboats.com.

DISNEY YOUTH GROUP PROGRAMS. Organized schools, scouts, faith based groups, and community youth groups are invited to participate in the exciting and enriching experiences of Disney Youth Group Programs. From field studies and competitions to live stage performances and awesome celebrations, there's no other place on the planet as prepared to engage and encourage the dreams of your youth as the Walt Disney World® Resort in Florida and Disneyland® Resort in California. For more information visit www.DisneyYouthGroups.com/ct or call toll-free 877-939-6884. (See main listing and ad on pages 216-217.)

KENNEDY SPACE CENTER, SR 405, Orsino, FL. Visitors get the unique chance to tour – up close – NASA's launch and landing facilities. Experience interactive simulators, live shows and jaw-dropping encounters with massive rockets, as well as have the opportunity to meet a real member of NASA's Astronaut Corps. Only 45 minutes from Orlando. 321-449-4400. www.kennedyspacecenter.com.

MEDIEVAL TIMES DINNER & TOURNAMENT. Travel through the mists of time to a forgotten age and tale of devotion, courage, and love. Experience heroic knights on spirited horses displaying astounding athletic feats and thrilling swordplay. Enjoy a "hands-on" feast, as the sweeping musical score and brilliant lights provide a fabulous backdrop for an experience that blurs the boundary between fairy tale and spectacle! 866-543-9637. www.medievaltimes.com.

SEAWORLD ORLANDO offers a variety of fun, educational youth programs ranging from 1-day field trips to sleepovers at the park. Whether you spend time with a SeaWorld Instructor or chart your own course, you'll find inspiration in SeaWorld's animal shows and attractions and pick up some valuable lessons along the way. 7007 SeaWorld Drive, Orlando, FL. Visit SeaWorld.org or call 1-800-406-2244 for more information.

PENNSYLVANIA DUTCH COUNTRY HIGHLIGHTS

AARON AND JESSICA'S BUGGY RIDES, 3121 Old Philadelphia Pike, Bird-in-Hand, PA 17505. We offer 5 different routes through real, non-commercial Amish farms on private roads, with no cars. See real Amish life. Our basic ride lasts about 25 to 35 minutes long with Amish drivers who are real horsemen, who will give your tour and answer your questions. 717-768-8828. www.amishbuggyrides.com. (See main listing on page 194.)

ADVENTURE SPORTS IN HERSHEY, 3010 Elizabethtown Rd., Hershey, PA 17033. Entertainment center featuring go-karts, bumper boats with squirt guns, scenic miniature golf with fountains and waterfalls, batting range for baseball and softball, golf driving range, golf instruction available, arcade and snack bar. Group packages available. Picnic pavilion. Some age and height restrictions apply. Minutes from Hershey attractions. Located on Route 743 just three miles south of Hershey. 717-533-7479. www.adventurehershey.com. (See main listing on page 182.)

THE AMISH FARM AND HOUSE, 2395 Covered Bridge Dr., Lancaster, PA 17602. Explore the history and modern-day customs of the Old Order Amish at Lancaster's most complete Amish attraction! Learn about this unique lifestyle as you tour our historic 1805 farmhouse with a knowledgeable guide. Discover our 15-acre farm - complete with barns, exhibits, and a wide variety of farm animals, Willow Lane One-Room School, demonstrators, enjoy a buggy ride and more! 717-394-6185. www.amishfarmandhouse.com.

A.R.T. RESEARCH ENTERPRISES, INC., 3050 Industry Dr., Lancaster, PA 17603. If you've been curious about how sculpture is made, our one hour tour guides you through the process of making custom sculpture from small to monumental from artists around the world. Tours of the entire process can also be highlighted by a hot metal pour. Sculpture Garden and Koi pond included. Every tour is different. Contact us at 717-290-1303. (See main listing on page 176.)

DUTCH APPLE DINNER THEATRE is a 386-seat theater located in the heart of Pennsylvania Dutch Country. Children's theatre productions are available for children of all ages throughout the year. 2009 children's shows include Alice in Wonderland, Stuart Little and The Jungle Book. A kid-style meal is planned for each children's theatre production. Group rates available for 16 or more. 717-898-1900. www.dutchapple.com.

GHOST TOURS OF LANCASTER, Downtown Lancaster City, PA. In the tradition of storytelling, we bring history back to life! Join us for a fascinatingly entertaining tour in one of America's oldest Colonial-era towns where tales from the Opera House to the countryside are presented as you've never heard them before. Hear the seldom-told tales of Pennsylvania Dutch folklore and age-old legends that have passed from generation to generation for more than 300 years. 610-587-8308. lancaster@ghosttour.com. www.ghosttour.com.

LIVING THE EXPERIENCE®, 450-512 East Strawberry St., ChurchTowne of Lancaster, PA. "Living the Experience" (LTE) is a famed reenactment about the life and times of free and enslaved Africans of Lancaster City and County. This Underground Railroad living history program is presented interactively in first person interpretation in an effort to bring alive the people, places, and events of Lancaster. 1-800-510-5899, ext. 113. (See main listing on page 189 and Regional Highlights on page 14.)

WATER'S EDGE MINI GOLF, 230 North Ronks Rd., Bird-in-Hand, PA 17505. Come visit Waters Edge Mini Golf, two beautifully landscaped, water filled miniature golf courses located in Bird-in-Hand, PA. Take a break in our snack bar or a walk around the pond on our walking path. Situated in the heart of Lancaster County, Water's Edge has something for everyone. 717-768-4653. www.watersedgegolf.net. (See main listing on page 184.)

YMCA CAMP SHAND. A great place to stay and play while visiting PA Dutch Country. 120 acres of woods, fields, nature trails, private pond and streams. Adirondack style cabins accommodate up to 120. Modern bathrooms. Full service dining hall. Canoeing, ropes course, rock wall, hiking, environmental education programs, swimming, campfires, sports, fishing, talent shows. Team building and problem solving. Cornwall, PA. www.ymcacampshand.org. 717-272-8001. (See main listing on page 206.)

Nearby, **HERSHEYPARK**, "The cleanest, greenest theme park in America," with over 65 rides and attractions, including 11 roller coasters, The Boardwalk and award-winning live entertainment. 1-800-242-4236, hersheyparkgroups@hersheypa.com or visit www.Hersheypark.com/groups. (See main listing on page 173 and Regional Highlights on page 10.)

PHILADELPHIA HIGHLIGHTS

AFRICAN AMERICAN MUSEUM IN PHILADELPHIA. Enjoy a face-to-face encounter with the bold and fearless people who helped form our nation with "Audacious Freedom: African Americans in Philadelphia 1776-1876 presented by PECO" at the African American Museum in Philadelphia. This state-of-the art exhibition employs innovative use of sound, light and cutting edge technology and is a must see on your trip to historic Philadelphia. For more information call 215-574-0380 or visit www.aampmuseum.org. 215-574-0380. www.aampmuseum.org. (See main listing and ad on page 190.)

ARNOLD'S FAMILY FUN CENTER has a brand new and exciting look!! Located in Oaks, Pennsylvania, Arnold's indoor entertainment venue offers over 120,000 square feet of attractions ranging from an incredible Go-Kart racetrack to Duck Pin Bowling and Arcade games, just to name a few! For more information contact us at 610-666-0600 or visit our Web site at www.arnoldsfamilyfuncenter.com. (See main listing and ad on page 186.)

BUCA DI BEPPO gets to the heart of fresh Italian cooking with family-style favorites like Chicken Parmigiana, Ravioli Pomodoro and housemade Lasagna. Dishes are served with generous portion sizes meant to be shared by everyone at the table. At Buca, groups of all sizes and ages step into Little Italy and enjoy a variety of group menus to satisfy everyone's palate and budget. 215-545-2818. www.Bucadibeppo.com. (See main listing on page 184.)

DAVE & BUSTER'S. At Dave & Buster's your group will have a blast! Start out with a delicious meal and then move on to some games in our Million Dollar Midway. Spend an hour with us, or a whole day - at Dave & Buster's it's your call! We have packages for groups of 20 to 2,000; so for your next outing come to Dave & Buster's – your students will thank you! Philadelphia, 325 North Columbus, Philadelphia, PA 19106. 215-413-1951; Plymouth Meeting, 500 W. Germantown Pike, Suite 2195, Plymouth Meeting, PA 19462. 610-832-9200; Franklin Mills Mall, 1995 Franklin Mills Circle, Philadelphia, PA 19154. 215-632-0333. www.daveandbusters.com. (See ad in New York City on page 96 and main listing on page 186.)

FORT MIFFLIN ON THE DELAWARE, Fort Mifflin & Hog Island Roads, Philadelphia, PA 19153. Experience history with your students/ scouts/group and interact with living history interpreters in our exciting Education programs. Be a Continental Army soldier, a surgeon on the Civil War battlefield caring for the sick or wounded, or learn about how the American flag evolved into the stars and stripes of today. 215-685-4167. www.fortmifflin.us.

GHOST TOUR OF PHILADELPHIA...Candlelight Walking Tour or Haunted Trolley in America's most historic...and most haunted city! Put some mystery in your history and watch it come alive on this entertaining adventure in Independence Park and Society Hill. Does Benjamin Franklin still linger at his old haunts? Who lurks in the chambers of Independence Hall? Join us as we push aside the cobwebs for a unique and fascinating look at our nation's history. 610-587-8308. ghosttour@ghosttour.com. www.ghosttour.com. (See main listing and ad on page 188.)

 **HISTORIC PHILADELPHIA, INC.**, 116 S. Third St., Philadelphia, PA 19106. Make History with Your Group! Don't just see the Liberty Bell & Independence Hall...Do it all! Historic Philadelphia's tours & performances make history exciting & fun with a sound & light show, a "whodunit" with puppets, Founding Fathers & Famous Figures, a comedic romp through our nation's birth and much more! Call Melissa Nast 215-629-5801 ext. 209. www.historicphiladelphia.org. (See main listing on page 189 and Regional Highlights on page 14.)

LONGWOOD GARDENS, US Route 1, Kennett Sq., PA 19348. A place of unparalleled beauty, offering a new experience every day of the year with one-of-a kind events, wonderful concerts, and delicious fine and casual cuisine. The 1050 acres of natural woodlands, majestic gardens, opulent conservatories and dancing fountains are open every day of the year! 610-388-1000. www.longwoodgardens.org. (See Regional Highlights on page 13 and main listing and ad on page 180.)

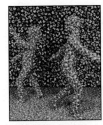 **THE NATIONAL LIBERTY MUSEUM** was created to help defuse violence and bigotry by celebrating America's heritage of freedom and the wonderful diverse society it has produced. The Museum honors the accomplishments of 2,000 men, women, and young people of every background and nationality; teaches character education and peaceful solutions to conflict; and highlights the rights and responsibilities of living in a democracy. 215-925-2800, ext. 144. www.libertymuseum.org. (See main listing and ad on page 197.)

PHILADELPHIA EAGLES. Looking for a field trip that is unique, historical & educational? Lincoln Financial Field, home of the Philadelphia Eagles, Stadium Tour is perfect! Learn interesting stadium facts, state-of-the-art equipment, and more. Visit the Press Box, Field Level, Interview Room, Eagles Locker Room and much more! Adults are $7 and Students are $5. Tour Hotline: 267-570-4510. bstanko@eagles.nfl.com. www.philadelphiaeagles.com. (See main listing on page 178.)

PHILADELPHIA MUSEUM OF ART. One of the largest museums in the United States, the Philadelphia Museum of Art invites visitors from around the world to explore its renowned collections, acclaimed special exhibitions, and enriching programs. 215-763-8100. www.philamuseum.org.

PLYMOUTH/CAPE COD HIGHLIGHTS

ART'S DUNE TOURS' professional guides escort your youth group on a tour of the historic sand dunes on the Provincetown Cape Cod National Seashore protected lands. We offer a wide variety of ecological and historic theme tours. Try one of our traditional New England Clam Bake dinners served picnic style. Cape Cod, MA. 508-487-1950/ 800-894-1951.

BIKE AND THE LIKE. Take a "nooks and crannies" style bike tour to discover the uniqueness of Cape Cod and nearby areas. Experienced tour guides provide personal, in-depth exploration of the Cape, Nantucket and Martha's Vineyard. Trips include food, lodging, and luggage transportation. Cape Cod, MA. 877-776-6572. www.bikeandthelike.com.

CAPE COD SEA CAMPS provides group rentals April-June & August-October and has been catering to school groups, educational tours, sports camps, and retreat groups for well over 30 years, offering full meals and accommodations on Cape Cod! With 60 acres of property and 600 feet of beachfront right on Cape Cod Bay, our location offers an excellent outdoor classroom for interactive science lessons. 508-896-3451. groups@capecodseacamps.com. www.capecodfieldtrips.com. (See main listing and ad on page 201.)

CAPTAIN JOHN BOATS & WHALE WATCHING. Come aboard one of our vessels and learn about Cape Cod Bay and the Stellwagen Bank National Marine Sanctuary, and how these waters attract whales and seabirds close to shore. Cruise Plymouth Harbor aboard the Pilgrim Belle, a Mississippi-style paddlewheeler, where you'll get a narrated account of this historic town and seaport and a mariner's view of many historic sites. 1-800-242-2469. www.captainjohn.com.

CRANBERRY BOG TOURS: A.D. MAKEPEACE COMPANY, 158 TIHONET RD., WAREHAM, MA 02571. TEL: 508-295-1000. WWW.ADMAKE-PEACE.COM. FLAX POND CRANBERRY COMPANY, 58 POND ST., CARVER, MA 02330. 508-866-2162. WWW.FLAXPONDFARMS.COM. GUIDED TOURS OF CRANBERRY BOGS. LEARN ABOUT THE CRANBERRY GROWING PROCESS, METHODS OF HARVESTING, AND THE HISTORY OF CRANBERRIES IN NORTH AMERICA.

DOLPHIN FLEET WHALE WATCH takes your class to Stellwagen Bank National Marine Sanctuary from Provincetown, Cape Cod, Massachusetts for a science-based viewing of humpbacks, finback and minke whales, guided by experienced naturalists. There's also an opportunity to learn about pelagic (lives at sea) birdlife, pinnipeds (seals) and sea turtles. Pre-trip orientation at your accommodations and data follow-up sent directly to your classroom. 800-826-9300. www.whalewatch.com.

GREAT MARSH KAYAK TOURS. Experience the Cape in a new, exciting way with guided kayak tours. Afterwards, visit the Zooquarium, which offers an aquarium, seal & sea lion show, petting zoo, touch tidal pool, wildlife, and the Zoorific Outdoor Theater. Lunch and mini golf top off the day. Winter: 508-328-7064, Summer: 508-775-6447. www.greatmarshkayaktours.com

HYANNIS WHALE WATCHER CRUISES. Our expert naturalists will share an intriguing look into the "wonderful world of whales," answering any questions your students might have. Students are also provided with our "Explorer's Journal," which serves to document their adventure as well as to stimulate their imaginations. We also offer dinner cruises that last 2 1/2 hours, BBQ as well as Clambake. 888-942-5392. www.whales.net.

MUSEUMS: CAPE COD MUSEUM OF NATURAL HISTORY. 508-896-3867 • JABEZ HOWLAND HOUSE. 508-746-9590 • JOHN F. KENNEDY HYANNIS MUSEUM FOUNDATION. 508-790-3077 • NATIONAL MARINE LIFE CENTER. 508-743-9888 • PILGRIM HALL MUSEUM. 508-746-1620 • SANDWICH GLASS MUSEUM. 508-888-0251.

OCEANQUEST HANDS-ON MARINE EDUCATION. Oceanography comes alive for all ages! Discover the wonders of ocean science during a 2-hour Hands-On Discovery Cruise aboard a fully certified & equipped research vessel. Add a Coastal Ecology field trip to expand the at-sea program. The hands-on teaching and learning techniques provide high quality, relevant & fun experiences. Woods Hole, MA. 508-385-7656. oceanquest.org.

PLIMOTH PLANTATION, Plymouth, MA. Plimoth Plantation, a Smithsonian Institution affiliate, is a living history museum located in Plymouth, Massachusetts. Our four major exhibits include the Wampanoag Homesite, 1627 English Village, Crafts Center, and Mayflower II, a reproduction ship modeled after the 17th century sailing vessel that brought the colonists to Plymouth in 1620. Open daily 9AM–5PM, March 24 through Thanksgiving. 508-746-1622. www.plimoth.org.

SALEM HIGHLIGHTS

7 SEAS WHALE WATCH, located in Gloucester, is in close proximity to two major feeding areas for a variety of species of great whales. Every 7 Seas Whale Watch cruise is accompanied by an experienced marine biologist who will provide insight into the lives of the great whales and the particular whale behaviors you observe. 800-745-9594. www.7seaswhalewatch.com.

THE HOUSE OF THE SEVEN GABLES. Enable your students to visualize and more fully understand early Colonial life at Salem's premier classroom—The House of the Seven Gables. Engage learners through an experience with a "living textbook" by which economics, geography, history, literature, mathematics, and science come to life. 978-744-0991. www.7gables.org.

PEABODY ESSEX MUSEUM. Brings art, architecture, and culture together in new ways. It's collections encompass twenty-two historic buildings, including four National Historic Landmarks, six National Register buildings, and our most recent architectural acquisition, Yin Yu Tang, the only complete Qing Dynasty house located outside China. 866-745-1876. www.pem.org.

THE SALEM FERRY, 10 Blaney St., Salem, MA. Experience coastal New England on a scenic, 45-minute trip aboard a high-speed catamaran. Round-trip service between Salem and downtown Boston. 978-741-0220. www.salemferry.com.

STUDENT TOURS offers customized itineraries that showcase Greater Boston's rich American Heritage from colonial seaports and farmland to an independent nation. Follow the "Red Coat Trail" along the Battle Road to Lexington and Concord, where Minutemen fought to keep their Liberties. Visit Salem and explore its rich Maritime History and the Hysteria of 1692 as you walk the Witch Trial Trail. Contact Kiki Kneeland, One Cordis Street, Charlestown, MA 02129-3302. 617-523-7303 or email: kikiboston@aol.com.

THE WITCH DUNGEON MUSEUM, 16 Lynde St., Salem, MA 01970. An award winning live reenactment of a 1692 witch trial followed by a guided tour of the dungeon. The presentation is historically accurate, educational and fun filled. An interactive experience where you can ask your tour guide questions. The Witch Dungeon has been featured on Good Morning America, the Discovery Channel and Fox TV. 978-741-3570. www.witchdungeon.com.

TAMPA • CLEARWATER • ST. PETERSBURG HIGHLIGHTS

BUSCH GARDENS encompasses opportunities that offer teachers ways to combine education, conservation and fun among one of North America's largest zoos and world-class thrill rides. Choose from Physics Day, discounted group tickets or even sleeping next to the tigers at our educational (and fun) sleepovers. 3000 Busch Blvd. in Tampa. Visit buschgardens.org or call 1-877-248-2267 for more information.

CALYPSO QUEEN CRUISES, 25 Causeway Blvd., Slip #18, Clearwater Beach Marina, Clearwater, FL 33767. Tropical Fun on the Water! Enjoy the beauty of the intra-coastal waterways of Clearwater Harbor as the captain comments on the history of the area and points out present day sights. Rain won't spoil this day - 2 enclosed decks. 1 1/2 hour cruise with Kids Lunch. Daily Departures. 727-461-3113. www.CalypsoQueen.com.

GHOST TOUR OF ST. PETERSBURG & TAMPA BAY, 535 1st St. NE, St. Petersburg, FL 33701. Discover the mysteries that lurk in the shadows of Florida's "Sunshine Coast" on a guided walking tour of St. Petersburg or Tampa. Hear the seldom-told tales of Native Americans, Spanish Conquistadors, early pioneers, land barons, and Tampa Bay's quirky characters as we bring history back to life! Allow 90 minutes. 727-894-4678. ghosttour@ghosttour.net. www.ghosttour.com.

SALVADOR DALI MUSEUM is home to the largest collection of Salvador Dali's work outside of Spain, with over 2,000 original works, including paintings, drawings, and sculptures. In addition to our permanent collection, the museum also frequently showcases other artists in temporary exhibits. 727-823-3767. www.salvadordalimuseum.org.

YBOR CITY STATE MUSEUM & WALKING TOURS. Once a community of cigar manufacturing workers from Spain, Cuba, and Italy, the city is now a nationally recognized historic neighborhood where visitors can explore the history and culture of a most unique immigrant community. School groups are welcome, and educators will find helpful tools on our website for preparing students to visit and to help them retain what they learned. 813-247-1434. www.ybormuseum.org.

VIRGINIA - HISTORIC HIGHLIGHTS

ASH LAWN-HIGHLAND (1000 James Monroe Pkwy., Charlottesville, VA) was the home of President James Monroe and wife Elizabeth from 1799 until 1823. Today Ash Lawn-Highland provides visitors a unique look into the life of the 5th president. Tour the Monroe House, stroll the lush grounds and exquisite boxwood gardens. Also visit the plantation's farm animals and enjoy the peacocks. 434-293-8000. www.al-h.us. REGION: Albemarle County, Central VA.

COLONIAL WILLIAMSBURG is America's largest living history experience! Beautifully restored colonial buildings, talented historical re-enactors, and countless museums and special demonstrations bring 18th Century America to life for visitors of all ages. Colonial Williamsburg offers a multitude of age-appropriate special programs for students from kindergarten through high school, all of which teach students about life in Colonial times and the history of the nation's beginnings. 757-229-1000. www.history.org. REGION: Hampton Roads Region, Eastern VA.

JAMESTOWN 4-H EDUCATIONAL CENTER. Safe and bus-friendly, our 16-acre Campus is ideal for student and youth groups visiting the Historic Triangle of Virginia. Cabins and Lodges provide bunk beds for 216 people. Outdoor Education programming includes environmental education, low ropes, archery, canoeing and kayaking, outdoor living skills, campfire programming, pier fishing, wetlands walkway tours, and pool swimming. 757-253-4931. www.jamestown4h.ext.vt.edu. REGION: Hampton Roads Region, Eastern VA.

JAMESTOWN SETTLEMENT is a living history museum where students and other visitors will learn about the first permanent English colony in the Americas. Features of the Settlement include replicas of the English ships that landed in Virginia in 1607, re-creations of a colonists' Fort and a Powhatan village, various gallery exhibits, and a number of educational activities. 888-593-4682. www.historyisfun.org. REGION: Hampton Roads Region, Eastern VA.

MONTICELLO. Once home to our nation's third president, Thomas Jefferson, Monticello is now a museum where students can learn all about Jefferson's life and work in politics, science, and architecture. The unusual main house, gardens, and plantation are all open for the public to learn more about this most important historical figure. 434-984-9822. www.monticello.org. REGION: Albemarle County, Central VA.

MOUNT VERNON. Located 16 miles south of Washington, D.C., Mount Vernon was once home to George Washington. In addition to the mansion and gardens, visitors are welcome to explore a demonstration farm and gristmill Washington used in his innovative farming techniques. 703-780-2000. www.mountvernon.org. REGION: Fairfax County, Northern VA.

RICHMOND, VIRGINIA is the state capital of Virginia and a city rich in American history. Here, visitors can explore the White House of the Confederacy, tour Civil War battlefields, and visit St. John's Episcopal Church, where Patrick Henry famously declared, "Give me liberty, or give me death." To start planning your class's historical adventure, contact the Richmond Metropolitan Convention and Visitors Bureau. 1-800-370-9004. REGION: Greater Richmond Region, Central VA.

RIPLEY'S BELIEVE IT OR NOT!® MUSEUM AND 4-D THEATER, 1735 Richmond Rd., Williamsburg, VA 23185. Your destination for the amazing, unusual, and bizarre! The Museum features eleven galleries and over 300 exhibits, including a 500 pound gorilla made entirely from nails! Pair the Museum up with our 4D Theater for a year round experience that's Unbelievable. Ask about our "Overnight at the Odditorium" and discounted Group Rates! 757-220-9220. www.WilliamsburgRipleys.com. REGION: Hampton Roads Region, Eastern VA.

WILLIAMSBURG KOA CAMPGROUND, 4000 Newman Rd., Williamsburg, VA 23188. Come camp on our 370 site campground. We are close to Colonial Williamsburg, Busch Gardens, Jamestown, and Yorktown. Your group will love our Jumping Pillow! We have a heated pool, 43 Kabins, 6 Lodges, Wi-Fi, cable, pavilions, and game rooms for your class trip. Bring a tent or try a Lodge or Kabin. 1-800-562-1733 www.williamsburgkoa.com. REGION: Hampton Roads Region, Eastern VA.

WATER COUNTRY USA, Williamsburg, VA. There is a new reason this season to visit the mid-Atlantic's largest water park. Water Country USA debuts a new area called "Rock 'n' Roll Island" featuring new slides, a pool and a lazy river. Celebrate the great music of the 1950's and '60s in the water and under the sun. Please check out watercountryusa.com or call 800-343-7946

WASHINGTON DC HIGHLIGHTS

LEARN THE WORKINGS OF OUR GOVERNMENT BY VISITING:

ARLINGTON NATIONAL CEMETERY. 703-607-8000 • BUREAU OF ENGRAVING AND PRINTING. 202-874-3108 • LIBRARY OF CONGRESS. 202-707-9779 • NATIONAL ARCHIVES GUIDED TOUR. 202-357-5450 • PENTA-GON TOUR. 703-697-1776 • SUPREME COURT. 202-479-3030 • U.S. CAPITOL. 202-225-6827 • WHITE HOUSE TOUR. 202-456-7041.

MEMORIALS & MONUMENTS: For information on the following monuments call 202-426-6841: FRANKLIN DELANO ROOSEVELT MEMORIAL • HOLOCAUST MEMORIAL • JEFFERSON MEMORIAL • LINCOLN MEMORIAL   WASHINGTON MONUMENT • NATIONAL WORLD WAR II MEMORIAL   VIETNAM VETERANS MEMORIAL.

MUSEUMS • GARDENS • ZOOS

FREER GALLERY OF ART. 202-633-4880 • HIRSHHORN MUSEUM AND SCULPTURE GAR-DEN. 202-633-1000 • INTERNATIONAL SPY MUSEUM. 202-654-0930 • NATIONAL AIR AND SPACE MUSEUM. 202-633-1000 • NATIONAL GALLERY OF ART. 202-737-4215 • NATIONAL MUSEUM OF AFRICAN ART. 202-633-4600 • NATIONAL MUSEUM OF NAT-URAL HISTORY. 202-633-1000 • NATIONAL MUSEUM OF THE AMERICAN INDIAN. 202-633-1000 • NATIONAL MUSEUM OF WOMEN IN THE ARTS. 202-783-5000 • NATIONAL PORTRAIT GALLERY. 202-633-8300 • NATIONAL ZOO. 202-633-3038 • THE UNITED STATES NATIONAL ARBORETUM. 202-245-2726 • U.S. HOLOCAUST MEMORIAL MUSEUM. 202-488-0400.

TOURS

BIKE AND ROLL. Bike tours are a great way to explore D.C. Our tours are led by knowledgeable guides who always have safety as their first concern. You'll be awed by views of the city and its monu-ments. Why spend your time sitting on a tour bus? With Bike and Roll your group's trip to D.C. will be the highlight of their trip - active, safe, educational and fun! 202-842-BIKE. www.bikeandroll.com.

GRAY LINE DC / MARTZ GROUP have operated for over a century. We provide safe, courteous, and reli-able transportation service to our customers. We also provide Sightseeing Tour opportunities in and around Washington, DC. Our dedication and commitment to our customers has kept us moving strong for over 100 years. We look forward to working with your organi-zation, school, community, and family to make your trip to Washington, DC a won-derful experience. 301-674-6586. www.graylinedc.com.

ENTERTAINMENT & RECREATION

ALEXANDRIA'S ORIGINAL GHOST & GRAVEYARD TOUR

is a one-hour walking tour led by lantern light through the historic city of Alexandria, Virginia. Please contact Alexandria Colonial Tours at 201 King St., #302, Alexandria, VA 22314. Phone 703-519-1749. Visit us online at www.alexcolonialtours.com.

LASER TAG & FAMILY AMUSEMENT CENTER, 3447 Carlin Springs Rd., Falls Church, VA 22041. Food, fun, cheaper than a restaurant! Incredibly low group rates. Play laser tag, video games, and eat cheaper than the cost of most restaurants alone! Kids of all ages love our laser tag arena and video arcade. Located just 5 miles from Washington, DC. 703-578-6000. www.UltraLaserTag.com.

LAZY SUSAN DINNER THEATRE, Drawer Q, Woodbridge, VA 22194. The Lazy Susan Dinner Theatre is one of the oldest and most prestigious dinner theatres in the Washington, D.C. area. The Lazy Susan presents a scrumptious Pennsylvania-Dutch Buffet followed by a popular Broadway musical, mystery or comedy, in an informal atmosphere perfect for individual and group parties. 703-550-7384. lsdt@ix.netcom.com. www.lazysusan.com.

MADAME TUSSAUDS DC is a fully interactive attraction that features exhibits such as the Presidential Gallery, where one has a quick meeting of the past 43 US Presidents, and the "Behind the Scenes", where you learn the trade secrets of Madame Tussaud herself and her wax figures. And don't forget about the Tussauds' signature Glamour Room, which allows you to rub elbows with Hollywood's A-list. 888-929-4632. www.madame-tussauds.com.

TOBY'S THE DINNER THEATRE OF COLUMBIA,

5900 Symphony Woods Rd., Columbia, MD 21044. Located only 30 minutes from D.C., Toby's Dinner Theatre offers award-winning Broadway and original musicals with an exceptional buffet-style dinner. From our customer's first contact with our Group Sales staff to watching our servers transform into the glamorous, talented performers on stage, our commitment to your students' enjoyable Toby's experience is first and foremost. 410-730-8311/800-888-6297. www.tobysdinnertheatre.com.

THEME RESTAURANTS

BUCA DI BEPPO gets to the heart of fresh Italian cooking with family-style favorites like Chicken Parmigiana, Ravioli Pomodoro and housemade Lasagna. Dishes are served with generous portion sizes meant to be shared by everyone at the table. At Buca, groups of all sizes and ages step into Little Italy and enjoy a variety of group menus to satisfy everyone's palate and budget. 202-232-8466/866-941-BUCA(2822). www.Bucadibeppo.com.

HARD ROCK CAFE. Located at 999 E St NW, Hard Rock Cafe is conveniently located next to Fords Theater and the FBI building, and just a short walk from Metro Center, The White House, Capital Hill, and the Smithsonian Museums. Hard Rock Cafe is a perfect stop on your sight seeing adventure. Complete your tour of the city with an authentic rock-n-roll dining experience. Call 202-628-6583 for group bookings. www.hardrock.com/dc.

NEARBY ATTRACTIONS

BALTIMORE, MARYLAND (45 miles from D.C.) Where learning and fun is around every corner. (See Baltimore Featured City Page on pages 208-209.)

COLONIAL WILLIAMSBURG, VIRGINIA (115 miles from D.C.) America's largest living history experience! Beautifully restored colonial buildings, talented historical re-enactors, and countless museums and special demonstrations bring 18th Century America to life for visitors of all ages.

MEDIEVAL TIMES DINNER & TOURNAMENT (33 minutes from D.C.) once again suspends the guest between past and present with a heart-pounding show that tells a tale of devotion, courage, and love. The magical new production highlights the power and grace of our incredible horses and gallant Knights in combat, all against the backdrop of a sweeping new musical score. Join us for an unforgettable journey through time! For reservations, visit medievaltimes.com, or call 1-888-We-Joust.

MT. VERNON (25 miles from D.C.) For more info 703-780-2000. Mount Vernon was once home to George Washington. In addition to the mansion and gardens, visitors are welcome to explore a demonstration farm and gristmill Washington used in his innovative farming techniques. www.mountvernon.org. REGION: Fairfax County, Northern VA.

WILMINGTON HIGHLIGHTS

AMF PRICE LANES. If you need some fun, come bowling with us at Price Lanes. We can accommodate any group event, provide just the right food and beverages, and take care of any special needs. AMF staff will help you plan an unforgettably enjoyable event at a strikingly different place. We'll do all the work while you have all the fun! 302-998-8806. www.amf.com. (See main listing on page 39.)

CHRISTINA RIVER TAXI. A 90 minute cruise on a patoon boat, the Christina River. The Christina Riverboat Company also offers special tours and chartered services such as The History Tour, a one-hour narrated tour that highlights Wilmington's historical riverfront area. 302-530-5069. www.riverfrontwilm.com.

GREENBANK MILLS & PHILIPS FARM. Experience early 19th-century Delaware in a 300-year-old gristmill, textile mill and farm site with an eighteen foot waterwheel powered by nearby Red Clay Creek. 302-999-9001.

KALMAR NYCKEL FOUNDATION offers educational sails and a tour of the shipyard includes our working sail loft/museum, blacksmith shop, block and tackle demonstration and New Sweden Center Museum. Fort Christina Park is adjacent to our shipyard and can be included in a tour. 302-429-7447.

THE NEW CANDLELIGHT THEATRE is the perfect place to enjoy high quality performances with delicious cuisine in a fun atmosphere. Upcoming shows feature family favorites including "Oklahoma" and "Joseph and the Amazing Technicolor Dreamcoat." Check out our website for more shows and showtimes at www.newcandlelighttheatre.com or contact our box office at 302-475-2313. Group rates are available. (See main listing on page 43.)

WILMINGTON & WESTERN RAILROAD, 2201 Newport Gap Pike (Rt.41N), Wilmington, DE. Delaware's Museum in Motion! Wilmington & Western Railroad offers trips back in time where you can ride on vintage trains. Fun for all ages - Steam and diesel powered locomotives dating to the early 1900's. Imagine yourself riding on a real railroad with its ever-changing natural beauty and wildlife. 302-998-1930. www.wwrr.com. (See main listing on page 42.)

OTHER AREAS OF INTEREST:

BRANDYWINE ZOO. 302-571-7747 • DELAWARE ART MUSEUM. 302-571-9590 • DELAWARE CENTER FOR CONTEMPORARY ARTS. 302-656-6466 • DELAWARE MUSEUM OF NATURAL HISTORY. 302-658-9111 • HAGLEY MUSEUM & LIBRARY. 302-658-2400 • ROCKWOOD PARK. 302-761-4340 • WINTERTHUR. 302-888-4827.

HIGHLIGHTS OF CONNECTICUT LEARNING STANDARDS
http://www.state.ct.us/sde/dtl/curriculum/currkey3.htm

ARTS – Create, perform, and respond to all of the arts, including dance, music, theatre, and visual arts; appreciate the importance of the Arts in expressing experience; be prepared to apply art skills and understanding.

HISTORY – Gain a knowledge of history, civics and government, geography, and economics: Local, US, and World History; themes; US Constitution and Government; Citizenship; Political Systems; International Relations.

LANGUAGE ARTS – Reading, writing, listening, speaking, viewing, and acting; construct their own oral and written compositions and interpret the works of others.

PHYSICAL EDUCATION – Physical Activity; Responsible Behavior; Respect for Differences.

SCIENCE – Understanding Inquiry; Matter; Energy Transfer; Forces and Motion; Matter and Energy in Ecosystems; how organisms are structured for efficiency and survival; Heredity and Evolution; Changing Earth; Energy; Earth in the Solar System; Science and Technology in Society.

HIGHLIGHTS OF DELAWARE LEARNING STANDARDS
http://www.doe.k12.de.us/DPIServices/DOE_Standards.htm

ENGLISH – Use written and oral English for various purposes and audiences; construct and examine the meaning of texts through listening, reading, and viewing; access, organize, and evaluate information gained by listening, reading, and viewing; students will connect self to society and culture.

PHYSICAL EDUCATION - Enhancing life skills to support a healthy, active lifestyle; activities to help students explore how physical activities can provide enjoyment, fitness, social interactive and self-expression.

SCIENCE – Nature and Application of Science and Technology; Materials and their Properties; Energy; Earth in Space; Earth's Systems; Life Processes; Diversity and Continuity of Living Things; Ecology.

SOCIAL STUDIES – (CIVICS) Structure and purpose of government; constitutional democracy; (GEOGRAPHY) how humans respond to environment and an understanding of culture; (ECONOMICS) understand systems and how they change on a micro and macro level; examine patterns of international trade; (HISTORY) analyze historical phenomena; knowledge of events and phenomena in history.

VISUAL AND PERFORMING ARTS (DANCE, MUSIC, THEATER, VISUAL ARTS) – Create art; Understand the Arts in relation to diverse cultures, times, and places; Reflect upon, describe, analyze, interpret, and evaluate works.

HIGHLIGHTS OF NEW JERSEY LEARNING STANDARDS

http://www.state.nj.us/education/

HEALTH & SAFETY – Enhancing life skills to support a healthy, active lifestyle; all students will apply health and skill-related fitness concepts and skills for a healthy lifestyle.

LANGUAGE ARTS LITERACY – Students will write and speak in clear, varied, organized language for different audiences and purposes; listen actively to information from a variety of sources and access, view, evaluate, and respond to texts.

SCIENCE – Processes, Organisms, and Diversity; Matter; Natural laws of motion, forces, and energy; Structure, dynamics, and geophysical systems of Earth; Understanding of the universe; The environment as a system of interdependent components; The relationship between science and technology.

SOCIAL STUDIES – Utilize Historical Thinking, Problem Solving, and Research Skills to understand: Civics, World History, US and NJ History, Economics, Geography.

VISUAL & PERFORMING ARTS – Create and respond to dance, music, theater, and visual art; principles of dance, music, theater, and visual art; develop critique; understand the role of art to culture, history, and society.

HIGHLIGHTS OF NEW YORK LEARNING STANDARDS

http://www.emsc.nysed.gov/deputy/Documents/learnstandards.htm

THE ARTS – Creating, performing, and participating in Arts; use materials and resources; respond critically to works, connecting the work to others and to human endeavor and thought; understanding cultural contributions of the Arts.

HEALTH, PHYSICAL EDUCATION, FAMILY SCIENCES - Personal Health and Fitness; A Safe and Healthy Environment.

ENGLISH LANGUAGE ARTS- Listen, speak, read, and write for: Information and Understanding, Response and Expression, Analysis and Evaluation, and Social Interaction; use communication to understand people and their views.

MATHEMATICS, SCIENCE, AND TECHNOLOGY – SCIENCE: Analysis, Inquiry, Design, Setting, Environment, Development of Ideas; TECHNOLOGY: Access, generate, process, and transfer information; INTERCONNECTEDNESS: Understand relationships and themes from these disciplines and apply them here and elsewhere.

SOCIAL STUDIES – History of the US and NY, World History, Geography, Economics, Civics, Citizenship, and Government.

HIGHLIGHTS OF PENNSYLVANIA LEARNING STANDARDS

http://www.pde.state.pa.us/stateboard_ed/cwp/view.asp?a=3&Q=76716&stateboard_edNav=l

ARTS AND HUMANITIES – Provides an opportunity to observe, reflect, and participate in the arts of their culture and the cultures of others. Sequential study in the arts and humanities provides knowledge and analytical skills to evaluate and critique a media-saturated culture.

CIVICS , GEOGRAPHY, GOVERNMENT, HISTORY – Analysis; PA, US, and World History; Gov't; Citizenship; US in World Affairs; Geography; Physical Characteristics of Places; Human Characteristics of Places; People and Places; Economics; Markets and Governments; Work and Earnings.

ENVIRONMENTAL AND ECOLOGY – Watersheds and Wetlands; Resources; Environmental Health; Agriculture; Integrated Pest Management; Ecosystems and their Interactions; Threatened, Endangered, and Extinct Species; Humans and the Environment; Environmental Law.

HEALTH, SAFETY, AND PHYSICAL ED – Concepts of Health; Healthful Living; Safety; Physical Activity; Movement.

LANGUAGE ARTS ORAL AND VISUAL COMMUNICATIONS – Writing; Reading/Vocabulary; Inquiry/Research.

SCIENCE/ TECHNOLOGY – Unifying Themes; Inquiry and Design; Biological Sciences; Physical Science; Chemistry; Physics; Earth Sciences; Technology Education; Technological Devices Science; Technology and Human Endeavors.

ACTIVITIES THAT SUPPORT THE SCOUT BADGE PROGRAM

Provides the opportunity for scouts to explore the following activities earning awards for various scout badges.

BOY SCOUTS (6TH-12TH GRADE)-EAGLE RANK REQUIRED BADGES

CAMPING: Safety, planning, knowledge of equipment, implementation.

CITIZENSHIP: In the community, in the nation, in the world.

COMMUNICATIONS: Interpersonal, Leadership, Team Building.

EMERGENCY PREPAREDNESS OR LIFE SAVING

ENVIRONMENTAL SCIENCE: Air Pollution, Conservation, Ecology, Endangered Species, Land Pollution, Pollution Prevention, Resource Recovery, Water Pollution.

FAMILY LIFE: Importance of family life to individuals and society.

FIRST AID

PERSONAL FITNESS: Health, Nutrition. Comprehensive Exercise Program.

PERSONAL MANAGEMENT: Financial planning & Time Management.

SWIMMING OR HIKING OR CYCLING: Safety aspects and implementing.

CUB SCOUTS (1ST-5TH GRADE) & BOY SCOUTS (6TH-12TH GRADE)

Activities for other Merit Badges not required for Eagle Rank.

ART: Architecture, Art, Basketry, Photography, Pottery, Sculpture.

HEALTH: Cooking, Fire Safety, Wilderness Survival.

MULTI-MEDIA: Cinematography, Radio.

PERFORMING ARTS: Dance, Music, Theater.

PHYSICAL EDUCATION/RECREATION: Archery, Athletics, Backpacking, Canoeing, Climbing, Golf, Horsemanship, Motorboating, Orienteering, Rowing, Skating, Small-Boat Sailing, Snow Sports, Sports, Whitewater Rafting.

SCIENCE: Animal Science, Archaeology, Astronomy, Aviation, Bird Study, Chemistry, Computers, Electricity, Energy, Fish and Wildlife Management, Fishing, Forestry, Gardening, Genealogy, Geology, Insect Study, Mammal Study, Nature, Nuclear Science, Oceanography, Plant Science, Reptile and Amphibian Study, Space Exploration, Weather.

SOCIAL STUDIES: American Cultures, American Heritage, American Labor, Coin Collecting, Indian Lore, Law, Orienteering, Pioneering, Railroading.

TECHNOLOGY: Computers.

GIRL SCOUTS: Activity Categories for Badge Achievement.

ARTS: Architecture, Art, Arts & Crafts, Colors and Shapes, Origami, Folk Arts, Museum Discovery, Photography, Visual Arts.

HEALTH & SAFETY: First Aid, Fitness, Food & Nutrition, Health & Nutrition, My Body, Safety, Outdoor Cooking, Outdoor Survival, Pet Care, Women's Health.

LIFE SKILLS: Budgets-Money Management, Career Exploration, Conflict Resolution, Family Living, Fitness, Fashion, Your Heritage, Law and Order, Leadership, Travel to Explore Different Cultures or Places, Understanding Yourself and Others, Self-defense, Service Projects.

PERFORMING ARTS: Dance, Music, Theater.

PHYSICAL EDUCATION/RECREATION: Adventure Sports, Backpacking, Camping, Canoeing, Field Games & Sports, Hiking, Horseback Riding, Kayaking, Orienteering, Outdoor Adventurer, Rope Course, Skating, Sports and Games, Teamwork, Whitewater Rafting.

SCIENCE/ENVIRONMENTAL: Aerospace, Animals, Anthropology, Birds, Earth and Sky, Ecology, Environmental Study, Food Chain, Inventions, Maps, Math, Matter, Ocean, Plants, Rocks, Science, Shapes, Senses, Solar System, Space Exploration, Water, Weather, Wildlife, Wind.

SOCIAL STUDIES: Celebrating People, Historical Figures, Multicultural, My Community, My Heritage, Orienteering People of the World.

TECHNOLOGY: Computers.